PENGUIN BOOKS

BYZANTIUM
The Early Centuries

John Julius Norwich was born in 1929. He was educated at Upper Canada College, Toronto, at Eton, at the University of Strasbourg and, after a spell of National Service in the Navy, at New College, Oxford, where he took a degree in French and Russian. In 1952 he joined the Foreign Service and remained in it for twelve years, serving at the embassies in Belgrade and Beirut and with the British Delegation to the Disarmament Conference at Geneva. In 1964 he resigned from the service in order to write.

He has published two books on the medieval Norman Kingdom in Sicily, *The Normans in the South* and *The Kingdom in the Sun*, published in Penguin in one volume entitled *The Normans in Sicily*; two travel books, *Mount Athos* (with Reresby Sitwell) and *Sahara*; books on *The Architecture of Southern England* and *Glyndebourne*; and two anthologies of poetry and prose, *Christmas Crackers* and *More Christmas Crackers*. He is the author of *A History of Venice*, which was originally published in two volumes; and of *Byzantium: The Early Centuries*, *Byzantium: The Apogee* and *Byzantium: The Decline and Fall*, a three-volume history of the Byzantine Empire. Many of his books are published by Penguin. In addition he has written and presented some thirty historical documentaries for television and is a regular lecturer on Venice and numerous other subjects.

Lord Norwich is chairman of the Venice in Peril Fund, Co-chairman of the World Monuments Fund and a member of the Executive Committee of the National Trust. He is a fellow of the Royal Society of Literature, the Royal Geographical Society and the Society of Antiquaries, and a Commendatore of the Ordine al Merito della Repubblica Italiana. He was awarded a CVO in 1993.

JOHN JULIUS NORWICH

BYZANTIUM

The Early Centuries

PENGUIN BOOKS

PENGUIN BOOKS

Published by the Penguin Group
Penguin Books Ltd, 27 Wrights Lane, London W8 5TZ, England
Penguin Books USA Inc., 375 Hudson Street, New York, New York 10014, USA
Penguin Books Australia Ltd, Ringwood, Victoria, Australia
Penguin Books Canada Ltd, 10 Alcorn Avenue, Toronto, Ontario, Canada M4V 3B2
Penguin Books (NZ) Ltd, 182–190 Wairau Road, Auckland 10, New Zealand

Penguin Books Ltd, Registered Offices: Harmondsworth, Middlesex, England

First published by Viking 1988
Published in Penguin Books 1990
5 7 9 10 8 6

'Sailing to Byzantium' by W. B. Yeats is taken from *The Collected Poems of W. B. Yeats* and is
reproduced by kind permission of A. P. Watt Ltd, on behalf of Michael B. Yeats and
Macmillan London Ltd.
The translations of Procopius by B. H. Dewing, published in the Loeb Classical Library, are
reproduced by kind permission of Wm Heinemann Ltd and Harvard University Press
The translations by G. A. Williamson of Eusebius's *The History of the Church*,
© G. A. Williamson, 1965

Printed in England by Clays Ltd, St Ives plc
Filmset in Garamond

For Moll

Contents

List of Illustrations

Maps

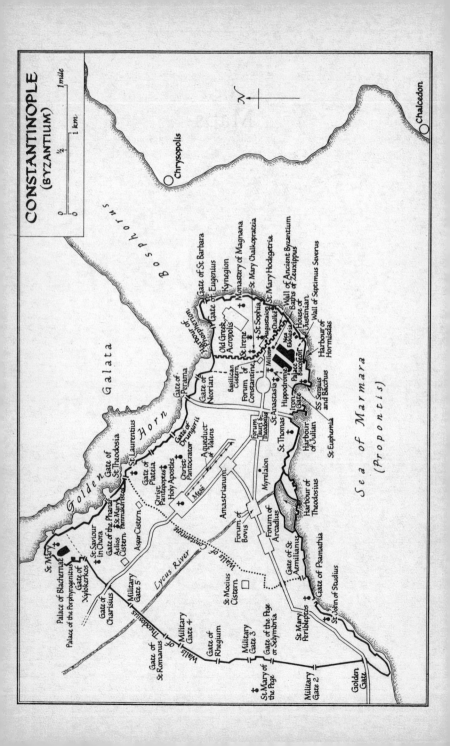

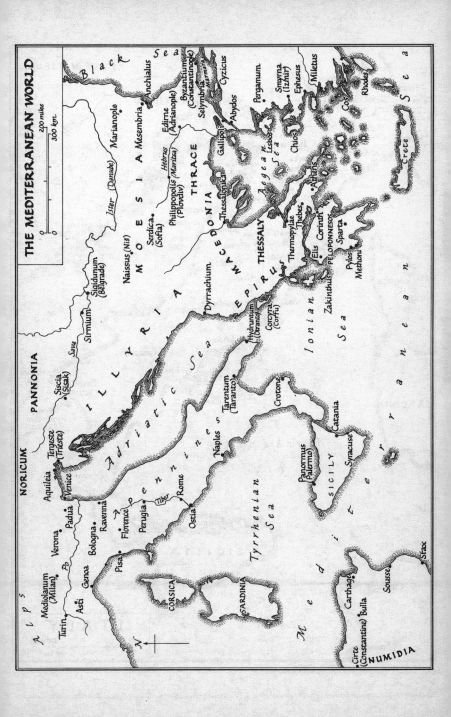

THE MEDITERRANEAN WORLD

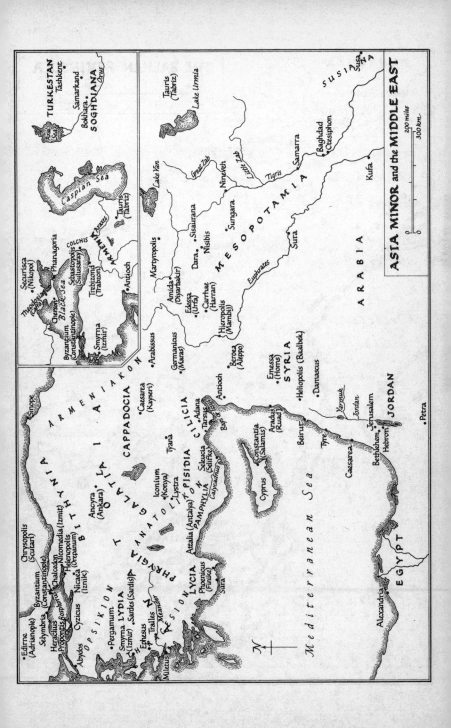

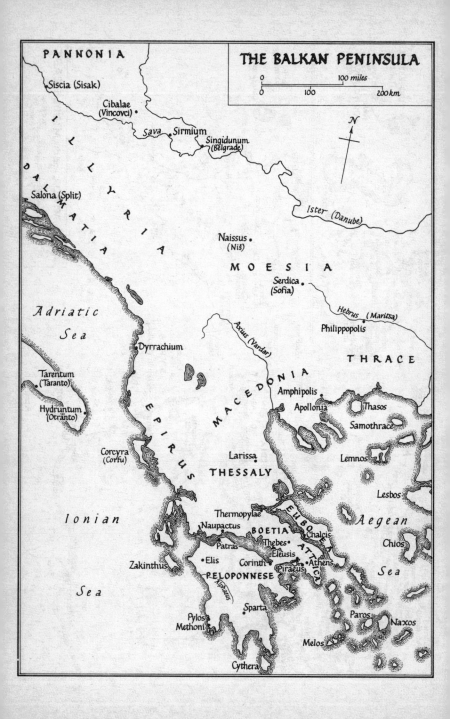

Family Trees

THE FAMILIES OF DIOCLETIAN, CONSTANTINE THE GREAT, VALENTINIAN AND THEODOSIUS

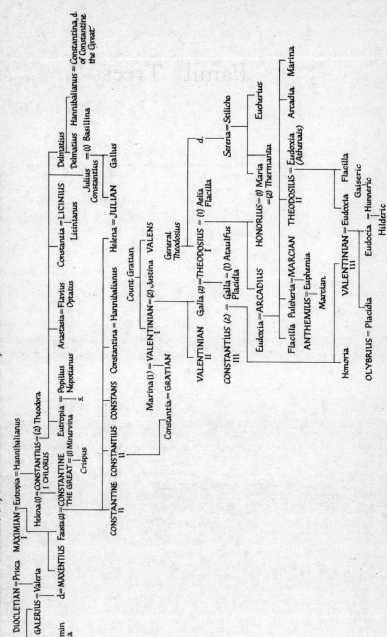

THE FAMILY OF LEO I

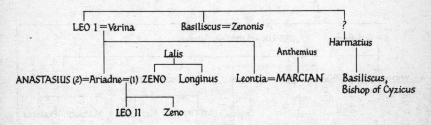

THE FAMILY OF LEO III

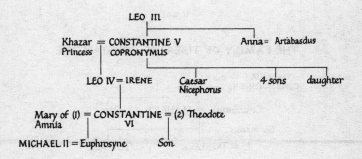

THE FAMILIES OF JUSTINIAN AND THEODORIC

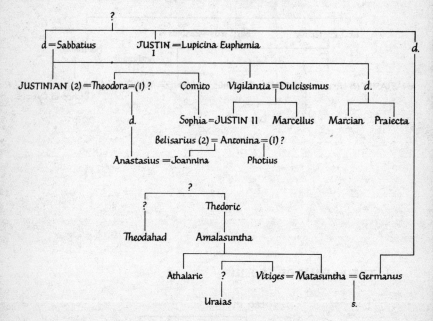

THE FAMILY OF TIBERIUS CONSTANTINE

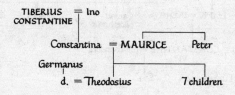

THE FAMILY OF HERACLIUS

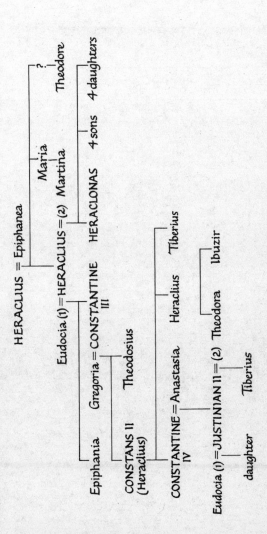

Acknowledgements

My heartfelt thanks are due to Mollie Philipps, for all her hard work on the illustrations; and to Kim Erkan for her invaluable help in Istanbul.

As so often in the past, I have once again to express my gratitude and admiration to the London Library, in which virtually every word of this book has been written; and to its Librarian Douglas Matthews, for having produced yet another superb index.

Introduction

Of that Byzantine Empire the universal verdict of history is that it constitutes, without a single exception, the most thoroughly base and despicable form that civilisation has yet assumed . . . There has been no other enduring civilisation so absolutely destitute of all the forms and elements of greatness . . . Its vices were the vices of men who had ceased to be brave without learning to be virtuous . . . Slaves, and willing slaves, in both their actions and their thoughts, immersed in sensuality and in the most frivolous pleasures, the people only emerged from their listlessness when some theological subtlety, or some chivalry in the chariot races, stimulated them to frantic riots . . . The history of the Empire is a monotonous story of the intrigues of priests, eunuchs and women, of poisonings, of conspiracies, of uniform ingratitude, of perpetual fratricides.

This somewhat startling diatribe is taken from W. E. H. Lecky's *History of European Morals*, published in 1869; and although to modern ears it is perhaps not quite so effective as the author meant it to be – his last sentence makes Byzantine history sound not so much monotonous as distinctly entertaining – the fact remains that, for the past 200 years and more, what used to be known as the Later Roman Empire has had an atrocious press. The long campaign of denigration seems to have been given its initial impetus in the eighteenth century by Edward Gibbon who, like all classically educated Englishmen and Englishwomen of his day, saw Byzantium as the betrayal of all that was best in ancient Greece and Rome; and it continued until well into the present century. After the First World War, under the influence of Robert Byron, David Talbot-Rice, Steven Runciman and their friends and followers, the pendulum began to swing; but it was only after the Second – when the ease, speed and relative comfort of travel in the Levant made Byzantine monuments at last generally accessible – that the Empire came into its own again and was at last recognized, in its own very different way, as a worthy successor to the two mighty civilizations which had gone before.

The trouble was, for most of us, that we knew so little about it. The old attitudes died hard. During my five years at one of England's oldest and finest public schools, Byzantium seems to have been the victim of a conspiracy of silence. I cannot honestly remember its being mentioned, far less studied; and so complete was my ignorance that I should have been hard put to define it in even general terms until I went to Oxford. Many people, I suspect, feel similarly vague today; and it is for them, above all, that this book has been written.

It does not tell the whole story. The Byzantine Empire, from its foundation by Constantine the Great on Monday 11 May 330 to its conquest by the Ottoman Sultan Mehmet II on Tuesday 29 May 1453, lasted for a total of 1,123 years and 18 days; and, as I soon discovered when writing a history of Venice a few years ago, that sort of span simply cannot be dealt with in one volume of manageable size. One or two historians have tried it, but the results never seem to me entirely satisfactory: either the reader is presented with so sketchy and disconnected an account that he loses his way, or else he is greeted by a remorseless fusillade of facts that sends him running for cover. I have preferred a more leisurely approach, and have consequently limited this first volume to what amounts, very roughly, to the first 500 years. The two opening chapters form a prologue, being concerned essentially with the early years of Constantine and his rise to power – a story that seems to me not just fascinating in itself, but also indispensable if we are to understand what follows; only in Chapter 3 do we come to the inauguration of Constantinople as the New Rome, the point at which the Roman Empire – though it never cast off its old title – can properly be called the Byzantine. The volume ends 470 years later with the coronation of Charlemagne as Roman Emperor of the West on Christmas Day, 800 –one of the most convenient dates in all history – and the appearance, for the first time, of a rival to the old imperial throne on the Bosphorus. A sequel will carry the saga on to the Crusades; and a third volume will bring it to its heroic – and almost unbearably tragic – end.

What, you may ask, ever induced me to take on so formidable an assignment? In fact the idea originated not with me at all but with my friend Bob Gottlieb, some time before he left my American publishers to edit the *New Yorker*; and though I remember feeling a little daunted by the magnitude of the task he suggested, I do not think there was any real hesitation. For over a quarter of a century already I had been captivated by the Byzantine world – ever since my first visit to Greece in 1954 and, in the following year, my posting to the British Embassy,

Belgrade; and three years subsequently spent in Beirut – when that enchanting city was still one of the happiest places in the world to live in – had only deepened my affection for the Eastern Mediterranean and all that it stood for. It was no coincidence, when I finally left the Foreign Service in 1964 to try to earn my living by my pen, that I turned for my first book – written jointly with Reresby Sitwell – to the one place which, more than any other, still breathes the very spirit of Byzantium: Mount Athos.

My most recent preoccupation has been with Venice, first a province and later an offshoot of the Empire, where St Mark's – designed, incidentally, on the model of Constantine's Church of the Holy Apostles – and the Cathedral of Torcello both contain Byzantine mosaics worthy to rank with those of Constantinople itself. And yet how astonishingly different the two cities are to write about! Throughout her history Venice, protected from *terra firma* by the still, shallow waters of the lagoon, radiated security; until her very end she was inviolate, and she knew it. Constantinople, on the other hand, lived under almost perpetual threat of attack. Siege followed siege; again and again the city was saved only by the heroism of the Emperor and his subjects. The inhabitants, too, could scarcely have been more dissimilar. The Venetians were cynics: hard-faced, commercially-minded men of the world. The Byzantines were mystics, for whom Christ, his Mother and the Saints were as real as members of their own families. Finally and most important of all, Venice was governed by faceless committees – elected groups of black-robed men, working in secret, their composition constantly changing, taking their decisions collectively, avoiding all individual prominence. Byzantium was an autocracy, ruled by an Emperor half-way to heaven, Equal to the Apostles, God's Vice-Gerent on Earth, who held the life of every one of his subjects in the hollow of his hand. Some of these Emperors were heroes, others were monsters; but they were never, never dull.

For that reason alone, this book has been a constant pleasure to write; but it is also, in its modest way, a tribute. Our civilization has never adequately acknowledged the debt it owes to the Empire of the East. Were it not for that great oriental bastion of Christendom, what chance would Europe have had against the armies of the King of Persia in the seventh century, or those of the Caliph of Baghdad in the eighth? What language would we be speaking today, and what god would we worship? In the cultural field, too, our indebtedness is great. After the barbarian invasions and the fall of the Emperor in Rome, the light of learning was almost extinguished in western Europe, apart from a few fitful monastic flickers; it was on the banks of the Bosphorus that it continued to blaze, and that the old classical heritage was preserved. Much of what we know of antiquity – especially of Greek and Latin literature and of Roman law – would have been lost for ever but for the scholars and scribes and copyists of Constantinople.

These tremendous services, however, have long since been taken for granted and forgotten. In our own day there remains to us only one continual reminder of the genius of the Byzantines: the splendour of their art. Never in the history of Christianity – or, one is tempted to add, of any other of the world's religions – has any school of artists contrived to infuse so deep a degree of spirituality into its work. Byzantine theologians used to insist that religious painters and mosaicists should seek to reflect the image of God. It was no small demand; but in the churches and monasteries of the Empire we see it, again and again, triumphantly accomplished.

Finally let me emphasize that this book makes no claim to academic scholarship. No professional Byzantinist perusing its pages will find anything that he does not know already – except, very likely, the occasional statement and opinion with which he will disagree. So be it. For periods as remote as that with which we are dealing the surviving records are often pitifully thin, and on those occasions when we have two chroniclers covering the same ground we are as likely as not to find them contradicting one another. The luckless historian can only weigh the probabilities and tell his story as best he can.

Nevertheless, though the backwaters of the river are sometimes murky, the main stream flows clear enough; and along that stream I have tried to steer as straight – and as accurate – a course as I can. There is still a long way to go before we reach the sea; but the journey will be, I trust, its own reward.

John Julius Norwich
London, December 1987

Once out of nature I shall never take
My bodily form from any natural thing,
But such a form as Grecian goldsmiths make
Of hammered gold and gold enamelling
To keep a drowsy Emperor awake;
Or set upon a golden bough to sing
To lords and ladies of Byzantium
Of what is past, or passing, or to come.

W. B. Yeats
'Sailing to Byzantium'

I

Constantine the Great

[to 323]

With such impiety pervading the human race, and the State threatened with destruction, what relief did God devise? ... I myself was the instrument he chose ... Thus, beginning at the remote Ocean of Britain, where the sun sinks beneath the horizon in obedience to the law of Nature, with God's help I banished and eliminated every form of evil then prevailing, in the hope that the human race, enlightened through me, might be recalled to a proper observance of God's holy laws.

Constantine the Great,
quoted by Eusebius, *De Vita Constantini*, II, 28

In the beginning was the word – surely one of the most magically resonant place-names in all history. Even had its Empire never existed, even had there been no W. B. Yeats to celebrate it, even had it remained what it was at the outset – a modest Greek settlement at the furthest extremity of the European continent, without pretensions or ambitions – Byzantium would surely have impressed itself upon our minds and memories by the music of its name alone, conjuring up those same visions that it evokes today: visions of gold and malachite and porphyry, of stately and solemn ceremonial, of brocades heavy with rubies and emeralds, of sumptuous mosaics dimly glowing through halls cloudy with incense. Historians used to maintain that the town was founded in 658 BC by a certain Byzas, leader of a group of colonists from the Greek city of Megara. They now inform us that Byzas may never have existed, and we can only pray that they are right. Magic is always best left unexplained.

Next, the site; and this too was supreme. Standing on the very threshold of Asia and occupying the easternmost tip of a broad, triangular promontory, its south side washed by the Propontis – which we nowadays call the Sea of Marmara – and its north-east by that broad, deep and navigable inlet, some five miles long, known since remotest antiquity as the Golden Horn, it had been moulded by nature at once into a magnificent harbour and a well-nigh impregnable stronghold, needing as it did major fortification only on its landward side. Even an attack from the sea was difficult enough, the Marmara itself being protected by two long and narrow straits – the Bosphorus to the east and the Hellespont (or Dardanelles) to the west. So perfectly suited, in fact, was the place for colonization that the inhabitants of Chalcedon, who had founded their own town seventeen years earlier on the opposite shore of the Bosphorus, became proverbial for their blindness: how otherwise, it was said, could they possibly have missed so infinitely preferable a site only a mile or two away?

Finally, the man: Constantine I, Emperor of Rome. No ruler in all history – not Alexander nor Alfred, not Charles nor Catherine, not Frederick nor even Gregory – has ever more fully merited his title of 'the Great'; for within the short space of some fifteen years he took two decisions, either of which alone would have changed the future of the civilized world. The first was to adopt Christianity – the subject, only a generation before, of official persecutions more brutal than any that it has suffered before or since – as the official religion of the Roman Empire. The second was to transfer the capital of that Empire from Rome to the new city which he was building on the site of old Byzantium and which was to be known, for the next sixteen centuries, by his name: the city of Constantine, Constantinople. Together, these two decisions and their consequences have given him a serious claim to be considered – excepting only Jesus Christ, the Buddha and the Prophet Mohammed – the most influential man in all history; and with him our story begins.

It is all too typical of our fragmentary knowledge of the later Roman Empire that although we can say with confidence that Constantine was born at Naissus in the Roman Province of Dacia – the present Yugoslav town of Niš – on 27 February, we cannot be certain of the year. Traditionally it is given as AD 274, but it could equally well have been a year or two on either side. His father Constantius – nicknamed 'Chlorus', the Pale – was, already at the time of his son's birth, one of the most brilliant and successful generals in the Empire; his mother Helena was not, as the twelfth-century historian Geoffrey of Monmouth would have us believe, the daughter of Coel, mythical founder of Colchester and the Old King Cole of the nursery rhyme, but a humble innkeeper's daughter from Bithynia. Some historians have questioned whether she and Constantius were ever actually married; others, pagan and therefore hostile to the family, have gone further still and suggested that as a girl she had been one of the supplementary amenities of her father's establishment, regularly available to his clients at a small extra charge. Only later in her life, when her son had acceded to the supreme power, did she become the most venerated woman in the Empire; only in 327, when she was already over seventy, did this passionately enthusiastic Christian convert make her celebrated pilgrimage to the Holy Land, there miraculously to unearth the True Cross and so gain an honoured place in the Calendar of Saints.

Whatever the year of his birth, Constantine can still have been little more than a child when his father became one of the four rulers of the Roman Empire. As early as 286 the Emperor Diocletian, having reached the conclusion that the Empire had grown too unwieldy, its enemies too widespread and its lines of communication too long to be properly governable by any single monarch, had raised an old comrade-in-arms named Maximian to share his throne. He himself, who had always taken more interest in his eastern dominions, had based himself at Nicomedia (the modern Izmit) on the Sea of Marmara, roughly equidistant from the Danube and the Euphrates; under his patronage it had grown in size and magnificence until it bore comparison with Antioch, Alexandria – even with Rome itself. But Rome, by Diocletian's day, had little to sustain it but the memory of past glories; its geographical position alone disqualified it from serving as an effective capital for the third-century Empire. When Maximian assumed the throne of the West, it was understood from the outset that he would be ruling principally from Mediolanum, more familiar to us as Milan.

Two Emperors were better than one; before long, however, Diocletian decided to split the imperial power still further by appointing two 'Caesars' – generals who, while remaining junior to himself and Maximian (to whom he had given the title of 'Augusti'), would also exercise supreme authority in their allotted territories and would ultimately inherit the supreme positions in their turn. One of these first Caesars, a rough, brutal professional soldier from Thrace named Galerius, was given charge of the Balkans; the other, to be based in Gaul but with special responsibility for the reimposition of Roman rule in rebellious Britain, was Constantius Chlorus.

The drawbacks of such an arrangement must have been obvious, even at the time. However much Diocletian might emphasize that the Empire still remained single and undivided, with a single law and structure of command, it was inevitable that he or his successors would sooner or later find themselves with four Empires instead of one, each of them at loggerheads with the rest. And this, as things turned out, is exactly what happened. For some years all went smoothly enough – years which the young Constantine spent at Diocletian's court, possibly in some degree a hostage to ensure his father's proper behaviour (for none of the four tetrarchs entirely trusted his colleagues) but also as a prominent member of the imperial entourage.

It was in this capacity that he accompanied the Emperor on his campaign to Egypt in 295–6, passing on his return journey through Caesarea in Palestine – where, we read, he made a lasting impression on a young Christian scholar named Eusebius. In later years this man was to become the local bishop and Constantine's first biographer: at this time, however, he was still a layman of about thirty, a friend and disciple of Pamphilus, the leading proponent of the Origenist theological school for which Caesarea was famous. As he later reported in his *Life of Constantine*, his hero

... commanded the admiration of all who beheld him by the indications he gave, even then, of imperial greatness. For no one could be compared with him in grace and beauty of form, nor in stature; while in physical strength he so far surpassed his contemporaries as to fill them with terror.[1]

Two years later, we find Constantine as his master's right-hand man in another campaign against the Persians; and since during those years he seems seldom to have left Diocletian's side, we must assume that he witnessed, in 303, the deliberate burning of the newly completed cathedral at Nicomedia – the dramatic inauguration of those famous Persecutions that were to rage, scarcely controlled, for the next eight years. But then, in 305, there occurred an event unparalleled in the history of the Roman Empire: the voluntary abdication of the Emperor. After twenty years on the imperial throne, Diocletian had had enough of power; he now withdrew from the world to live in relative obscurity in the vast palace that he had built for himself at Salona (the modern Split) on the Dalmatian coast – forcing an intensely unwilling Maximian to abdicate with him.[2]

The full – and diabolically complicated – sequence of events that

1 Eusebius, *De Vita Constantini*, I, 19.
2 Soon after his retirement, Diocletian received a message from the ever-restless Maximian, encouraging him to resume the purple. Gibbon tells us that 'he rejected the temptation with a smile of pity, calmly observing that, if he could show Maximian the cabbages which he had planted with his own hands at Salona, he should no longer be urged to relinquish the enjoyment of happiness for the pursuit of power'.

followed this unprecedented step need fortunately not detain us here; suffice it to say that Galerius and Constantius Chlorus – who had by now abandoned Helena to marry Maximian's adopted stepdaughter Theodora – were proclaimed Augusti as arranged, but that the appointment of their successors, the two new Caesars, was hotly disputed; and that Constantine, finding himself passed over and fearing for his life, fled at night from Galerius's court at Nicomedia – to avoid pursuit, hamstringing the post-horses behind him as he went – and joined his father at Boulogne. There he found that a Roman army under Constantius's command was preparing a new expedition to Britain, with the objective of driving the marauding Picts back across Hadrian's Wall. Father and son crossed the Channel together, and within a few weeks their operation had proved successful. Shortly afterwards, however, on 25 July 306, Constantius Chlorus died at York; and the breath had scarcely left his body before his friend and ally, the charmingly named King Crocus of the Alemanni who was commanding the auxiliary Frankish cavalry, acclaimed Constantine as Augustus in his father's stead. During the short summer campaign, the young man seems to have earned the genuine admiration and respect of the local legions, who immediately took up the cry. There and then they clasped the imperial purple toga around his shoulders, raised him on their shields and cheered him to the echo.

It was a notable triumph, and one which became greater still as the word spread through Gaul, province after province pledging the young general its loyalty and support. But Constantine still needed official recognition. One of his first actions, therefore, after his proclamation was to send to Galerius at Nicomedia, together with the official notification of his father's death, a portrait of himself with the attributes of Augustus of the West, and wearing the imperial wreath of bay. Lactantius tells us that Galerius's instinctive reaction when he received this portrait was to hurl it into the fire; only with difficulty were his advisers able to persuade him of the danger of setting himself up against an infinitely more popular rival. On one point, however, the Emperor remained firm: he refused point-blank to recognize the young rebel – for such, in fact, Constantine unquestionably was – as an Augustus. He was prepared, reluctantly, to acknowledge him as Caesar; but that was all.

For Constantine, it was enough – for the present. Perhaps he did not yet feel ready for the supreme power; at any rate he remained in Gaul and Britain for the next six years, governing those provinces on the whole wisely and well – though he could be capable, when roused, of cruelty and even brutality. (After a rebellion by certain Frankish tribes in 306, thousands were thrown to the wild beasts in the circus – to the point, wrote one contemporary, that the animals themselves became exhausted with so much slaughter.) On the other hand, he vastly improved the condition of slaves and the otherwise oppressed, while his reputation for sobriety and sexual rectitude stood out in dramatic contrast to that of most of his predecessors.

This rectitude did not, however, prevent him from putting aside his first wife, a certain Minervina, in 307 in order to make an infinitely more distinguished alliance – with Fausta, the daughter of the old Emperor Maximian. The latter had by now revoked his involuntary abdication of two years before, had resumed the purple in defiance of Galerius and had made common cause with his son Maxentius; together the two had won over not only the whole of Italy to their cause but, as far as could be ascertained, Spain and North Africa as well. Their position, however, was not yet secure. A concerted attack by Galerius – flinging in his armies from the Danube, quite possibly reinforced by the eastern legions – could still be dangerous for them; and if Constantine were simultaneously to march down against them from Gaul their future would be bleaker still. The marriage was therefore diplomatically advantageous to both sides: for Maximian and Maxentius it meant that they could probably count on Constantine's alliance if and when they needed it, while the latter for his part could now claim family links with two Emperors instead of one.

How long Constantine would have been content to rule only a relatively remote corner of an Empire that he was determined to make entirely his own, we cannot tell; for, in April 311, a few days after issuing an edict of toleration in favour of the Christians – and so putting an end, in theory at any rate, to the Great Persecution – Galerius, the senior Augustus, died at Sirmium (now Sremska Mitrovica) on the river Sava. Both Eusebius and his fellow-chronicler Lactantius dwell, with a morbid and most un-Christian delight, on the manner of his death:

Suddenly an abscess appeared in his privy parts, then a deep-seated fistular ulcer; these could not be cured and ate their way into the very midst of his entrails. Hence there sprang an innumerable multitude of worms, and a deadly stench was given off, since the entire bulk of his members had, through gluttony, even before the disease, been changed into an excessive quantity of soft fat, which then became putrid and presented an intolerable and most fearful sight to those that came near it. As for the physicians, some of them were wholly unable to endure the exceeding and unearthly stench, and were butchered; others, who could not be of any assistance, since the whole mass had swollen and reached a point where there was no hope of recovery, were put to death without mercy.[1]

The death of Galerius left three men sharing the supreme power: Valerius Licinianus, called Licinius, one of the late Emperor's old drinking companions whom he had elevated to be his fellow-Augustus three years before and who was now ruling in Illyria, Thrace and the Danube provinces; his nephew Maximin Daia, whom he had named Caesar in 305 and who now took over the eastern part of the Empire; and Constantine himself. But there was a fourth who, though not technically of imperial rank, had long felt himself to be unjustly deprived of his rightful throne: this was Galerius's son-in-law Maxentius. As the son of the old Emperor Maximian – who had met his end the previous year, by execution or enforced suicide, after an ill-judged attempt in Constantine's absence to raise the legions against him in southern Gaul – Maxentius had long hated his brilliant young brother-in-law, and, as we have seen, had spent the years since Constantine's accession steadily strengthening his own power-base around the Mediterranean. As early as 306, before he and his father had even established themselves in Italy, he had adopted the title of 'Prince of the Romans' and had had himself proclaimed by the Praetorian Guard in Rome; now, five years later, he was as powerful as any of his three rivals – powerful enough, indeed, to take his father's death as a pretext for openly declaring his hostility to Constantine, branding him a murderer and a rebel, and ordering his name to be removed from all inscriptions and commemorations throughout Italy.

War, clearly, was unavoidable; and immediately on receiving the news of Galerius's death Constantine began to make his preparations. Before marching against his adversary, however, he had to come to an agreement with Licinius, to whom the territories seized by Maxentius properly belonged. Fortunately for Constantine, Licinius could not lead an army himself to reclaim them, being already fully occupied in maintaining his position against Maximin Daia in the East; he therefore seems to have been only too happy for Constantine to undertake the reconquest of Italy on his behalf. The agreement was sealed by another betrothal – this time of Licinius himself to Constantine's half-sister Constantia.

His diplomatic ground prepared, Constantine set off in the autumn of 311 for Colmar, where he spent the winter making his plans and

1 Eusebius, *Historia Ecclesiastica*, VIII, 16.

preparing supplies for his army. Zosimus tells us that it consisted of 8,000 cavalry and some 90,000 infantry. It was probably only about a third of the total manpower available to him, but Gaul could not be left ungarrisoned. Anyway, he had a fair idea of Maxentius's strength and he believed that these numbers would suffice. To make doubly sure, he himself assumed the supreme command; and, in the early summer of 312, he marched.

The factual story of Constantine's Italian campaign and his overthrow of Maxentius can be quickly told. Crossing the Alps over the Mont-Cenis pass, he took Susa – the first town of any importance that lay on his route – by storm, refusing however to allow his soldiers their normal rights of plunder and pillage. They were, he told them, not conquerors but liberators. Outside Turin, the going was a good deal harder: Maxentius's army here included a number of units of *clibinarii*, horsemen who, together with their mounts, were heavily armed and armoured in a manner which was probably derived from the Persians and which, a thousand years later, was to be imitated and developed in medieval chivalry. But even they were obliged to yield as groups of Constantine's strongest men advanced upon them, swinging huge iron-bound clubs at shoulder height; and when they retreated in disorder to the city walls the citizens refused to open the gates to let them in. So Turin fell; then Milan; then – though only after heavy fighting – Brescia and Verona. Constantine continued his eastward drive as far as Aquileia, not far short of Trieste; only there did he turn, swinging back through Ravenna and Modena and southward towards Rome.

Throughout the long advance, Maxentius had remained in his capital – where, according to most of the Christian and even one or two of the pagan historians, he spent his time in ever more revolting occult practices: casting spells, calling up devils, even sacrificing unborn babies in his efforts to avoid his approaching fate. Such stories can be largely discounted; for all his faults, Maxentius had never lacked courage. Given his trusted Praetorian Prefect Ruricus Pompeianus and several excellent provincial generals (although, sadly for him, none of them proved as good as Constantine) his decision to stay in Rome had been, strategically, a perfectly sound one. But now, with Constantine's army approaching and Pompeianus killed in battle, he took personal command and marched out of the city with the last, and best, of his reserves.

The two armies met on 28 October 312 – the seventh anniversary of Maxentius's seizure of power – at Saxa Rubra, the 'red rocks' on the Via

Flaminia some seven or eight miles north-east of Rome, where the little
river Cremera flows into the Tiber;[1] and it was here, as later legend has
it, just before or perhaps even during the battle, that Constantine experienced his famous vision. As Eusebius describes it:

... a most marvellous sign appeared to him from heaven, the account of
which it might have been difficult to receive with credit, had it been related by
any other person. But since the victorious Emperor himself long afterwards
declared it to the writer of this history when he was honoured with his acquaintance and society, and confirmed his statement by an oath, who could hesitate to
accredit the relation, especially since the testimony of after-time has established
its truth? He said that at about midday, when the sun was beginning to decline,
he saw with his own eyes the trophy of a cross of light in the heavens, above
the sun, and bearing the inscription Conquer by This (*Hoc Vince*). At this sight
he himself was struck with amazement, and his whole army also.[2]

Inspired, it is said, by so unmistakable an indication of divine favour,
Constantine routed the army of Maxentius, driving it southward to where
the Tiber takes a sharp turn to the west and is crossed by the old Milvian
Bridge.[3] Next to this bridge – which was extremely narrow – Maxentius
had constructed another on pontoons, over which he could if necessary
make an orderly retreat and which could then be broken in the middle
to prevent pursuit. Over this his shattered army stampeded, the soldiers
now fleeing for their lives, Constantine's men hard on their heels. They
might still have escaped, had not the engineers in charge of the bridge
lost their heads and drawn the bolts too early. Suddenly the whole
structure collapsed, throwing hundreds of men into the fast-flowing
water. Those who had not yet crossed made blindly for the old stone
bridge, now their only chance of safety; but, as Maxentius had known, it
was too narrow. Many were crushed to death, others fell and were
trampled underfoot, still others were flung down by their own comrades
into the river below. Among the last was the usurper himself, whose
body was later found washed up on the bank. His severed head, stuck
on a lance, was carried aloft before Constantine as he entered Rome in
triumph the following day. Later it was sent on to North Africa as a
warning. Meanwhile the name of Maxentius was erased from all public
monuments, just as his conqueror's had been in the previous year.

*

1 The site is now known as Grotta Rossa.
2 *De Vita Constantini*, I, 28.
3 Originally built in 109 BC, the Ponte Milvio still stands, though it has been many times rebuilt
and restored – most recently by Pius IX in 1850 after Garibaldi had blown it up.

The Battle of the Milvian Bridge made Constantine absolute master of all Europe from the Atlantic to the Adriatic, from Hadrian's Wall to the Atlas. It also marked, if not his actual conversion to Christianity, at least the moment when he set himself up as a protector and active patron of his Christian subjects. Not only, during his two and a half months in Rome, did he generously subsidize from his private purse twenty-five already existing titular churches and establish several new ones; he also instructed his provincial governors to do likewise throughout his dominions. On his departure from the city he presented the newly elected Pope Melchiades with the old palace of the Laterani family on the Coelian Hill which the Empress Fausta – who had joined him soon after his arrival – had occupied during her stay. It was to remain a papal palace for another thousand years. Next to it he ordered the building, at his own expense, of the first of Rome's Constantinian basilicas, St John Lateran, still today the Cathedral Church of the city. Significantly, it was given an immense free-standing circular baptistery: there was to be a formidable increase in the rate of conversions during the years to come.[1]

To what extent, therefore, did the vision of the Cross that the Emperor is said to have experienced near the Milvian Bridge constitute not only one of the decisive turning-points of his life – comparable to that experienced by St Paul on the Road to Damascus – but also, in view of its consequences, a watershed of world history? The question is not an easy one to answer, and before we can even attempt to do so we must ask ourselves another: what actually happened? The earliest version of the story is that of our second principal source for the period, the Christian scholar and rhetorician Lactantius who, having somehow survived the persecutions, was at about this time appointed by Constantine to be tutor to his son Crispus. Whether or not he was already a member of the imperial entourage, Lactantius would have had plenty of opportunities shortly afterwards to question the Emperor directly about what took place. Writing probably within a year or two of the event, he records:

Constantine was directed in a dream to cause *the heavenly sign* to be delineated on the shields of his soldiers, and so to proceed to battle. He did as he had been commanded, and he marked on their shields the letter X, with a perpendicular line drawn through it and turned round at the top, thus ☧, being the cypher of Christ.[2]

---

1 Constantine's baptistery no longer stands. Its present octagonal successor dates from the time of Pope Sixtus III (432–40).
2 *De Mortibus Persecutorum*, Chap. xliv.

He says no more. We have no mention of a vision, only of a dream. There is not even any suggestion by this devout Christian apologist that the Saviour or the Cross ever appeared to the Emperor at all. As for 'the heavenly sign', it was simply a monogram of *chi* (X) and *rho* (P), the first two Greek letters in the name of Christ, that had long been a familiar symbol in Christian inscriptions.

Perhaps more significant still is the fact that Eusebius himself makes no reference to either a dream or a vision in the account of the battle which he gives in his *Ecclesiastical History* of about 325. It is only in his *Life of Constantine*, written many years later after the latter's death, that he produces the passage quoted above, following it up with a rather fuller version of Lactantius's story in which he tells how, on the night after the vision, Christ appeared to the Emperor in a dream and ordered him to have a standard made in the likeness of the sign that he had seen in the heavens, 'and to use it as a safeguard in all engagements with his enemies'. This, Eusebius tells us, Constantine did on the very next day. The result, which was known as the *labarum*, consisted of a cross fashioned from a gold-encrusted spear, surmounted by a wreath encircling the sacred monogram. When Eusebius saw it some years later a golden portrait of the Emperor and his children had been suspended, somewhat surprisingly, from the cross-bar.

What conclusions, then, are we to draw from all this? First, surely, that the vision of the Cross above the battlefield – that vision that we see endlessly depicted, on canvas and in fresco, in the churches and art galleries of the west – never occurred. Had it done so, it is unthinkable that there should not be a single reference to it in any of the contemporary histories until the *Life of Constantine*. The Emperor himself never seems to have spoken of it – except, apparently, to Eusebius – even on those occasions when he might have been expected to do so. Soon after his death, too, we find his son, Constantius II, being assured by Bishop Cyril of Jerusalem that the sight of a cross, recently traced in the sky by meteors, was a greater grace even than the True Cross found by his grandmother Helena in the Holy Land; could the Bishop possibly have omitted to mention Constantine's vision had he known of it? Finally there is Eusebius's specific statement that 'the whole army . . . witnessed the miracle'. If that were true, 98,000 men kept the secret remarkably well.

There can be little doubt, on the other hand, that at a certain moment shortly before the fateful battle the Emperor underwent some profound spiritual experience. Lactantius's bald account may well be substantially true; but experiences of this kind are not necessarily attended by such easily describable manifestations as dreams. There are indications that Constantine had been in a state of grave religious uncertainty since his execution of his father-in-law Maximian two years before, and was increasingly tending towards monotheism: after 310 his coins depict, in place of the old Roman deities, one god only – Helios or, as he was more generally known, *Sol Invictus*, the Unconquered Sun – of whom Constantine also claimed to have had a vision some years before, while fighting in Gaul. Yet this faith too – by now the most popular and widespread in the entire Empire – seems to have left him unsatisfied; Eusebius tells how, on his journey into Italy, knowing that he was shortly to fight the most important battle of his life – that on which his whole future career would depend – he prayed fervently for some form of divine revelation. No man, in short, was readier for conversion during that late summer of 312 than was Constantine; and it is hardly surprising that, up to a point at least, his prayers were answered.

If we accept this hypothesis Eusebius's story becomes a good deal easier to understand, revealing itself less as a deliberate falsehood than as a possibly unconscious exaggeration, and less the fault of the writer than that of the Emperor himself. Throughout his life, and particularly after the Milvian Bridge, Constantine cherished a strongly developed sense of divine mission. In later years this sense grew ever more pervading; what then could be more natural than that, looking back on the great events of his life as it neared its end, he should have allowed his memory to add a gentle gloss here and there? In his day the existence of miracles and heavenly portents was universally accepted; from the reflection that he could have had a vision and that, in the circumstances, he should have had a vision, it was but a short step to the persuasion that the vision had actually occurred. And Eusebius would have been the last person to cross-examine him.

One question, however, remains to be answered: how complete was Constantine's conversion? There is no doubt that from 312 onwards the Emperor saw himself as supreme guardian of the Christian Church, responsible for its prosperity and welfare; on the other hand his coins continued, at least until 324, to depict him as a companion of the Unconquered Sun and – more significant even than this – he still jibbed at the prospect of his own baptism, which he was to continue to postpone until he lay on his deathbed a quarter of a century later. This reluctance may to some extent have been due to political considerations; he was anxious not to alarm those of his subjects who still clung to the old gods. But he certainly did not hesitate to give mortal offence, during his stay in Rome, by refusing to take part in the traditional procession to the Capitol for the sacrifice to Jupiter.

The truth is probably rather more complicated: that while Constantine felt a genuine sympathy towards Christianity and genuinely believed the God of the Christians to have been responsible for his mystical experience (whatever that may have been) on the way to the Milvian Bridge, he was not yet ready to embrace the Christian religion *in toto*. While by now almost certainly accepting the concept of the *Summus Deus*, the Supreme God, he was perfectly ready to believe that this God might manifest himself in several different forms: as Apollo, or *Sol Invictus*, or Mithras (whose cult was still popular, especially in the army), or indeed the God of the Christians. Of all these manifestations he may have preferred the last, but as a universal ruler, feeling himself to be above all sects and hierarchies, he saw no reason not to keep his options open.

And the Roman Senate agreed with him. To celebrate his victory over Maxentius and his re-establishment of law, order and the imperial administration in the city, they erected in his honour the great triumphal arch that still stands a little to the south-west of the Colosseum. Much of its relief decoration is in fact reused, having previously served as part of various earlier monuments dedicated to Domitian, Trajan, Hadrian and Marcus Aurelius; Gibbon describes the whole structure as 'a melancholy proof of the decline of the arts, and a singular testimony of the meanest vanity'. The inscription, however, dates explicitly from the time of Constantine. In translation, it reads:

TO THE EMPEROR CAESAR FLAVIUS CONSTANTINE WHO BEING IN-
STINCT WITH DIVINITY AND BY THE GREATNESS OF HIS SPIRIT
AVENGED THE STATE IN A JUST WAR ON THE TYRANT AND ALL HIS
PARTY.

Instinctu divinitatis: the phrase is a curious one, and must have been deliber-ately chosen for its ambiguity. There is no mention of Christ, nor of the Cross; no indication, even, of the precise divinity referred to. Yet Constantine must certainly have approved the text before it was passed to the stone-carvers. It is only natural that he should have been treading warily, as doubtless were the senators who drafted the inscription in the first place; one suspects, none the less, that his approval was not unwil-lingly given, since he himself had as yet made no final commitment to any one god. *Instinctu divinitatis:* he could not have put it better himself.

*

Apart from the triumphal arch – and the colossal statue of the seated Emperor, seven times life-size, which was placed in the remodelled (and hastily renamed) Basilica of Maxentius and of which the terrifying, staring, nine-ton head survives in the Capitoline Museum – the Roman Senate showed to Constantine, during the last two months of 312, one further mark of favour. They proclaimed him Supreme Augustus. It was in this capacity that he left the city in early January 313 for Milan, where he had arranged to meet Licinius.

The Augusti had three principal issues to discuss. The first was the future of Italy. Theoretically it formed part of that area of the Empire which was subject to Licinius, but the latter had not raised a finger to assist Constantine in its recapture and cannot seriously have expected that his colleague would now freely hand it back to him. Next was the question of religious toleration and, in particular, the future status of the Christians. It was obvious that a single policy should prevail throughout the Empire; at the same time the elderly Licinius was unlikely to feel as well disposed towards Christianity as his fellow-Emperor, and some sort of understanding would have to be reached between them. Finally there came the problem created by the third living Augustus, Maximin Daia.

This odious young man – the exact date of his birth is unknown, but he seems still to have been in his early thirties – had started making trouble in 310 when, after five years as a Caesar, he had demanded the rank of Augustus. His uncle Galerius, sadly aware that with Constantine, Maximian and Maxentius all having claimed the title in the recent past it was in danger of becoming seriously devalued, had refused point-blank, offering him instead that of *Filius Augusti*; but Maximin Daia had angrily rejected this belittling alternative and had assumed the Augustan attributes of his own accord. On Galerius's death he had seized the Eastern Empire as far as the Hellespont, from which point of vantage he had made continual trouble for Licinius in Thrace until, in the winter of 311–12 on a barge in the middle of the Bosphorus, the two had patched up an uneasy truce. Moreover, he loathed Christianity. He had blatantly ignored his uncle's Edict of Toleration in 311 and was still wallowing in Christian blood – even on occasion sending his soldiers in pursuit of Christian refugees over the imperial borders into Armenia, whose King was consequently on the point of declaring war against him.

The talks between the two Emperors passed off amicably enough. Licinius seems to have accepted with a good grace that Constantine should keep the territories that he had conquered, and was duly married – according to what rite is unfortunately not recorded – to Constantia.

Where the Christians were concerned, the new brothers-in-law agreed the final text of a further edict, confirming that of Galerius and granting Christianity full legal recognition throughout the Empire. Before this could be promulgated, however, news reached Milan that brought the meeting to an abrupt and premature end: Maximin Daia had broken the truce of the previous winter, crossed the straits with an army – estimated by Lactantius at 70,000 – and seized the little town of Byzantium on the European shore. Licinius moved fast. Taking the small force that he had with him at Milan, summoning reinforcements to join him in Illyria and Thrace and picking up what further units he could along his route, he left immediately for the East. By late April we find him a few miles from Heraclea Propontis, another small settlement on the Marmara to which Maximin was laying siege; and on the last day of the month the two armies met at a spot known as the Serene Fields, some eighteen miles outside the town.

Outnumbered though he was, well past his own youth and with his men exhausted from the length and speed of their march, Licinius proved by far the more brilliant general of the two. Maximin's army was ignominiously routed, he himself fleeing from the field disguised as a slave. He finally made his way to Cilicia, where he died the following year – as disagreeably, Lactantius is happy to inform us, as his fellow-persecutors:

He swallowed poison ... which began to burn up everything within him, so that he was driven to distraction by the intolerable pain; and during a fit of frenzy, which lasted four days, he gathered handfuls of earth, and greedily devoured it. After various excruciating torments he dashed his forehead against the wall, and his eyes started out of their sockets ... In the end he acknowledged his own guilt and implored Christ to have mercy on him. Then, amidst groans like those of one burnt alive, did he breathe out his guilty soul in the most horrible kind of death.[1]

Licinius, meanwhile, had made his triumphal entry into the eastern capital, Nicomedia – where, somewhat belatedly on 13 June, he promulgated the edict on which he and Constantine had agreed at Milan:

When I, Constantine Augustus, and I, Licinius Augustus, had come under happy auspices to Milan, and conferred together on all matters that concerned the public advantage and welfare ... we resolved to make such decrees as should secure respect and reverence for the Deity; namely to grant both to the

1 Lactantius, *De Mortibus Persecutorum*, Chap. xlix.

Christians and to all others the right freely to follow whatever form of worship might please them, to the intent that whatsoever Divinity dwells in heaven might be favourable to us and to all those living under our authority.[1]

Here, once again, is a text that bears all the signs of cautious drafting. Still we find no mention of Jesus Christ, only of 'the Christians' as a sect; and – although they are the only group specifically named – it is made abundantly clear that 'all others' (the Manicheans, for example) are also included in what is, in effect, a general edict of toleration. As to the reference to 'whatsoever Divinity dwells in heaven' (*quo quicquid est divinitatis*), this phrase may have been insisted on by the pagan Licinius; but a comparison with the inscription on the triumphal arch suggests that it probably corresponded fairly closely with Constantine's own thinking. In one respect only does the ordinance discriminate in favour of the Christians: they alone are to have restored to them all their property – land, churches and chattels – confiscated during the Persecutions. But, it should be remembered, no other sect had suffered comparable losses.

The removal of Maximin Daia had the effect of polarizing the Empire. Once again there were only two Augusti, Constantine in the West and Licinius in the East – where he immediately instituted a reign of terror. Not only were all his predecessor's chief ministers executed; so too were numerous members of Maximin's family – which, in view of the various marriage alliances concluded among past Augusti and their Caesars, included the families of Diocletian and Galerius. Even the latter's widow Valeria, even his mother-in-law Prisca, Diocletian's widow whom Galerius had entrusted on his deathbed to Licinius's care, were shown no mercy; both were arrested in their homes at Thessalonica and put to the sword.

The reason for this blood-bath was not simply vengeance, nor yet vindictiveness; it was the conviction on the part of Licinius that there was room in the Empire for one ruling family only – the family of Constantine, of which he himself, since his marriage to Constantia, was a member. This conviction did not, however, bind him closer to his co-Augustus; indeed, the honeymoon inaugurated at Milan was to prove all too short. Within six months of the two Emperors' departure from the city, Licinius had entered into a conspiracy against Constantine – though

---

1 Lactantius, *De Mortibus Persecutorum*, Chap. xlviii.

fortunately it was brought to light before any harm was done. Soon afterwards, in the early summer of 314, he ordered the removal of all his colleague's statues and portraits from the town of Aemona – now Ljubljana – on the border of the Italian Province.

It was, in effect, a declaration of war. Constantine, who had returned to Gaul, immediately marched south-east with some 30,000 men into the Pannonian plain, to meet his adversary near Cibalae – the present Vinkovci – in the Sava Valley. The battle was joined before dawn on the morning of 8 October: Licinius fought with determination and courage but was finally obliged to yield, his retreating army being pursued by Constantine right across the Balkan peninsula to Byzantium. There at last the two Emperors came to an understanding: Licinius agreed to give up all his dominions in eastern Europe – they included Pannonia and the whole of what we now know as the Balkans – with the single exception of Thrace; in return, Constantine undertook to recognize his authority throughout Asia, Libya and Egypt.

The two Emperors were friends again; but they did not remain so for long. Indeed, the story of the next decade is one of a steady deterioration in the relations between them. In 317 Constantine named his two young sons – Crispus, the fourteen-year-old child of his marriage to his first wife Minervina, and another Constantine, the infant son of the Empress Fausta, who was hardly out of his cradle – as joint Caesars of the West; simultaneously, Licinius at Nicomedia conferred the same rank on his own natural son, Licinianus; but these moves were doubtless concerted in advance and do not necessarily reflect any particular rivalry. By the following year, however, Constantine had moved his court from Sirmium to Serdica, the modern Sofia – a curious choice of capital for a ruler whose domains extended to the Straits of Gibraltar and beyond, and one which was logically justifiable only on the assumption that it was from the Eastern Empire, rather than from the Gauls or the Franks or the Donatists in North Africa, that trouble was to be expected.

In fact, that trouble was to be largely of Constantine's making. His apologists do their best to lay the blame on Licinius for his duplicity and faithlessness as well as for his undeniably growing hostility to the Christian religion: from 320 or thereabouts he imposed a ban on all episcopal synods, expelled a large number of bishops and priests (though by no means all of them) and dismissed from his household staff all who would not sacrifice to the pagan gods. By now, however, it was becoming clear that Constantine was determined to put an end to Diocletian's disastrous division of the Empire and to rule it alone. From 320, in defiance of recent tradition, he did not even include an easterner as one of the two annually elected Consuls, naming instead himself and his younger son; in 321 both his sons were named.[1] That same year he began to gather together a huge war fleet, and to enlarge and deepen the harbour at Thessalonica in readiness for its reception.

Licinius also began to prepare for war, and for some time the two Augusti watched each other, waiting. In the autumn of 322, however, while repelling an attack by the Sarmatians – a nomadic barbarian tribe normally inhabiting the regions north of the lower Danube – Constantine, inadvertently or otherwise, led his army into Thrace. Licinius made a violent protest, claiming that this was a deliberate infringement of his territory for purposes of reconnaissance, and an obvious prelude to a full-scale invasion; he then advanced, with a force estimated at some 170,000, up to Adrianople – the modern Edirne. When Constantine marched, he would be ready to receive him.

It was in the last week of June 323 that the army of the West crossed the Thracian border; and on 3 July, on a broad, sloping plain just outside Adrianople, it found itself confronted by that of the East. Constantine's force was slightly the smaller of the two; but it was largely composed of hardened veterans, who had little difficulty in wearing down their comparatively inexperienced opponents. Once again Licinius fought with conspicuous courage, ordering a retreat only when some 34,000 of his men lay dead on the field. Then he withdrew to Byzantium, just as he had done nine years before. This time, however, he sought no terms; instead, he declared Constantine deposed, named his chief minister, one Marcus Martianus, as Augustus in his place, and settled down to withstand a siege.

Constantine for his part dug himself in – reflecting yet again, one is tempted to think, on the strategic position and superb natural defences of the little town – and waited patiently for his fleet. He had entrusted its command to his son Crispus, now a man of twenty, married and a father, with five years' campaigning experience already behind him; it consisted of some 200 thirty-oared war galleys backed up, we are told, by 2,000 transports. To defend the Hellespont, Licinius could boast a yet more

1 This dual consulate was one of the oldest and most venerable institutions of the Roman Republic, in which the Consuls were, during their year of office, the supreme civil and military magistrates of the State. By late imperial days the title had become purely honorary, with the two chosen Consuls at liberty, in Gibbon's memorable phrase, 'to enjoy the undisturbed contemplation of their own greatness'; each year, however, was known by the names of the Consuls appointed for it, and the office itself remained so elevated as to be held by only the very highest dignitaries – not infrequently the Emperors themselves: Constantine's own consulate in 320 was in fact his sixth.

numerous armada of some 350 vessels under his admiral, Abantus; in-
explicably, however, this man had decided to take his stand, not at the
Aegean end of the strait where his superior numbers could be put to
proper advantage, but at its north-eastern extremity where it widens into
the Sea of Marmara. When the invasion fleet arrived, it attacked at once.
The ensuing engagement lasted two full days, but at last Crispus's lighter,
faster and more manoeuvrable ships, having sunk 150 of the defenders,
smashed their way through and sailed on to Byzantium.

The moment he heard of their advance, Licinius slipped out of the
town and crossed the Bosphorus into Asia; but Constantine was ready.
Swiftly embarking his army in the newly arrived transports, he set off
immediately in pursuit, and on 18 September scored another major
victory at Chrysopolis (now Üsküdar or, more familiarly, Scutari).
Licinius hastened back to his capital at Nicomedia; great as his losses
had been, his spirit was not yet broken and he had every intention of
making a last stand. It was his wife who dissuaded him. If he surrendered
now, she pointed out, he might yet escape with his life. The next day she
herself went off to see her half-brother in his camp to plead with him on
her husband's behalf.

And Constantine granted her request. He summoned Licinius, greeted
him with every sign of cordiality and even invited him to dinner. Then
he sent him into exile at Thessalonica, under close surveillance but in a
degree of comfort appropriate to his rank. He showed similar mag-
nanimity to his own self-styled successor Martianus, whom he simply
banished to Cappadocia. Particularly in view of Licinius's conduct when
he himself had taken over the Eastern Empire, such clemency was remarkable indeed; alas, it did not last. A few months later, both men
were summarily put to death.

The reasons for the Emperor's sudden change of heart are unknown.
It is possible, as the Christian historian Socrates asserts – though he was
writing a century later – that Licinius had been up to his old tricks again
and was conspiring with the barbarian tribes (presumably the Sarmatians)
for Constantine's murder and his own return to power; possible, but
hardly likely. A far more probable solution to the problem can be found
in the words of a prayer which Constantine wrote himself at about this
time and circulated throughout the Empire in the form of an encyclical
letter. After a long opening section in which he describes and deplores
the previous Persecutions, 'my own desire is,' he continues, 'for the
general advantage of the world and all mankind, that Thy people should
enjoy a life of peace and undisturbed concord.'

It was true; after the war against Licinius and for the rest of his life we find him repeating these sentiments again and again and striving continually, at whatever cost, to avoid war or anything that might lead to it. By now, however, he can have had no doubts left in his mind that, if the Roman Empire were to remain at peace, it must continue to be united under a single head; and he must strongly have suspected that Licinius would never be content to remain for long in obscurity. The Empire, in short, was not – for all its vastness – big enough for both of them; and if the promise of peace required the elimination of the only two other claimants to the title of Augustus, it was surely cheap at the price.

2

The Adoption of the Faith

[323–6]

For my own part, I hold any sedition within the Church of God as formidable as any war or battle, and more difficult still to bring to an end. I am consequently more opposed to it than to anything else.

Constantine the Great, opening
the Council of Nicaea, AD 325

During the years of civil war, throughout which the holy *labarum* was invariably carried before him into battle and never failed – as he saw it – to bring him victory, Constantine turned more and more exclusively towards the God of the Christians. For some years, as we have seen, he had been legislating in their favour. Confiscated property was restored; the clergy were exempted from municipal obligations; episcopal courts were given the right to act as courts of appeal for civil cases. Other laws, too, suggest a degree of Christian inspiration, such as that of 319 prohibiting the murder of slaves, regardless of their offence; that of 320 forbidding prison authorities to maltreat those in their charge; or – most celebrated of all – the law of 7 March 321 proclaiming Sunday, 'the venerable day of the Sun', as a day of rest. (This might be thought to be a throwback to the worship of *Sol Invictus*; in fact, Sunday had been gradually replacing Saturday as the Christian sabbath since the days of St Paul, and had been already enjoined on the faithful by a church council held at Elvira in Spain fifteen years before.) But in none of this legislation even then, is the name of Christ himself mentioned or the Christian faith in any way professed.

Now at last, with the Empire safely reunited under his sole authority, Constantine could afford to come into the open. In the long prayer quoted at the end of the previous chapter he makes his persuasion clear:

Although mankind has fallen deeply, and has been seduced by manifold errors, yet hast Thou revealed a pure light in the person of Thy Son (lest the power of evil should utterly prevail) and hast thus given testimony to all men concerning Thyself.

On the other hand, there must be no coercion: pagans must be allowed to continue in the old faith if they choose to do so. The prayer goes on:

Let those, therefore, who are still blinded by error be made welcome to the same degree of peace and tranquillity which they have who believe ... Let no man molest another in this matter, but let everyone be free to follow the bias of his own mind ... For it is one thing voluntarily to undertake the struggle for immortality, another to compel others to do likewise from fear of punishment.

But, though paganism might be tolerated, there must be no heresy. If the Church were to stand henceforth as the spiritual arm of an indivisible Empire, how could it itself be divided? Unfortunately it was. For years Constantine had battled in vain against two schismatic groups, the Donatists in North Africa and the Meletians in Egypt. These fiercely intractable Christians refused to accept the authority of any bishop or priest who had defected from the Church during the Persecutions and returned to it later, thus denying the orthodox view that the moral worthiness of the minister – who, as St Augustine had pointed out, was only a surrogate for Christ – had no effect on the validity of the sacrament. (The Donatists indeed went even further, maintaining that all who communicated with the *traditores* were themselves infected, and that consequently, since there was but a single holy Church, it consisted of Donatists alone.) Now there had emerged a third faction – which, to judge by the number of adherents that it was collecting inside and outside the Church and the vociferousness with which it was upheld or denounced, threatened to sow more discord than the other two put together.

This group had formed itself around a certain Arius, presbyter of Alexandria, a man of immense learning and splendid physical presence who had been a disciple of the famous St Lucian of Antioch, martyred during the Persecutions. His message was simple enough: that Jesus Christ was not co-eternal and of one substance with God the Father, but had been created by Him at a specific time as his Instrument for the salvation of the world. Thus, although a perfect man, the Son must always be subordinate to the Father, his nature being human rather than divine. Here, in the eyes of Arius's archbishop, Alexander, was a dangerous doctrine indeed; and he took immediate measures to stamp it out. In 320 its propagator was arraigned before nearly a hundred bishops from Egypt, Libya and Tripolitania and excommunicated as a heretic.

The damage, however, was done: the teaching spread like wildfire.

Those were the days, it must be remembered, in which theological arguments were of passionate interest, not just to churchmen and scholars but to the whole Greek world. Broadsheets were distributed; rabble-rousing speeches were made in the market place; slogans were chalked on walls. Everyone had an opinion: you were either for Arius or against him. He himself, unlike most theologians, was a brilliant publicist; the better to disseminate his views, he had actually written several popular songs and jingles – for sailors, travellers, carpenters and other trades – which were sung and whistled in the streets.[1]

After his excommunication, however, he could not stay in Alexandria. Departing in haste, he made first for Caesarea where Eusebius, now Bishop, espoused his cause with enthusiasm; he then travelled on to Nicomedia itself, where he was warmly welcomed by Licinius and Constantia and where the Bishop – confusingly, another Eusebius – called a local synod which declared overwhelmingly in his favour. Another synod, this time of Syrian prelates drummed up by Eusebius of Caesarea, did likewise; whereupon Arius, his position immeasurably strengthened, returned to Egypt and demanded to be reinstated. Alexander refused, and serious rioting broke out.

By the autumn of 323, when Constantine assumed complete control of his Empire, what had started as a subtle point of theology had become a dangerous *cause célèbre*, not only in Egypt but throughout the Levant. Strong measures, it seemed, would have to be taken if the situation were not to deteriorate further, and the Emperor accordingly dispatched Bishop Hosius of Cordova – who for the past ten years had been his principal adviser on Christian affairs – to Egypt, with orders to settle the dispute in whatever way he saw fit, once and for all. Not surprisingly, the Bishop failed. The next year he tried again; this time his instructions were to deliver a letter from Constantine himself, addressed impartially to the two protagonists:

Constantine the Victor, Supreme Augustus, to Alexander and Arius:

Having enquired faithfully into the origin and foundation of your differences, I find their cause to be of a truly insignificant nature, and quite unworthy of such fierce contention . . . Now therefore must ye both exhibit an equal measure of forbearance, and accept the advice which your fellow-servant feels justly entitled to give.

What is this advice? It was wrong ever to propose such questions as these, or to reply to them when propounded. For points of discussion which are enjoined

1 'We do him too much honour when we hail him as the father of religious music in the Christian church' (*Dictionnaire de Théologie Catholique*, article on 'Arianism'). We certainly do.

by the authority of no law, but rather suggested by a contentious spirit which is in turn the consequence of misused leisure, should be confined to our own thoughts, and neither hastily produced in public assemblies nor ill-advisedly entrusted to the public ear. For how very few are those who are able either accurately to comprehend or adequately to explain matters so sublime and abstruse.[1]

Wise counsel indeed – which, had it only been heeded over the centuries, would have spared the world untold bitterness and bloodshed. It fell, however, on deaf ears, and resulted only in bringing both Arius and Alexander separately to Nicomedia to lay their respective cases before the Emperor.

It was now, towards the end of 324, that Constantine decided on the final solution to the problem. There would be no more synods of local bishops; instead, there would be a universal Council of the Church – a Council of such authority and distinction that both parties to the dispute would be bound to accept its rulings. The first proposal was that it should be held in Ancyra – the modern Ankara; but the venue was soon changed to Nicaea (Iznik). Not only was this city more accessible; it was also nearer to Nicomedia – a point of no little importance, for it soon became clear that the Emperor had every intention of participating himself.

Nicaea too boasted an imperial palace; and it was here that the great Council was held, between 20 May and 19 June 325. Despite the Emperor's hopes for a large attendance from the western churches, these were poorly represented: the controversy was of little interest to them. Apart from Bishop Hosius there were only the Bishops of Calabria and Carthage, two others respectively from Gaul and Illyria, and a couple of priests, sent from Rome – more as observers than anything else – by Pope Sylvester. From the East, on the other hand, the delegates arrived in force: 270 bishops at the lowest count but in fact probably 300 or more, many of them with impressive records of persecution and imprisonment for their faith. The proceedings were opened by Constantine in person.

When the whole assembly was seated with due dignity, a general silence prevailed pending the Emperor's arrival. First, three of his immediate family entered in order of rank, then came others heralding his own approach – not the soldiers or guards who normally attended him, but friends in the faith. And now, all rising at the signal that indicated the Emperor's entrance, at last he himself proceeded through the midst of the assembly like some heavenly Angel of God,

1 *De Vita Constantini*, II, 64–72.

clothed in a garment which glittered as though radiant with light, reflecting the glow of a purple robe and adorned with the brilliant splendour of gold and precious stones. When he had advanced to the upper end of the seats, he at first remained standing; and when a low chair of wrought gold had been set for him, he waited to sit down until the bishops had signalled to him to do so. After him the whole assembly did the same.[1]

It is plain from Constantine's letter to the two chief disputants that the doctrinal point at issue interested him not at all. If not altogether a westerner by birth, he was certainly one by upbringing: despite a naturally religious nature, his military cast of mind had little patience with theological niceties. He was, however, determined to put an end to the controversy. He therefore played a prominent part in the ensuing debate, arguing, encouraging, assuaging ruffled feelings, forever urging the importance of unity and the virtues of compromise, and even on occasion switching from Latin into halting Greek in his efforts to convince his hearers.

It was he, too, who proposed the insertion, into the draft statement of belief, of the key word that was to settle, at least temporarily, the fate of Arius and his doctrine. This was the word *homoousios* – meaning consubstantial, or 'of one substance', to describe the relation of the Son to the Father. Its inclusion in the draft was almost tantamount to a condemnation of Arianism, and it says much for Constantine's powers of persuasion – and, it must be suspected, of intimidation too – that he was able to secure its acceptance. Many of the bishops of Arian sympathies protested, as might have been expected; gradually, however, he won them round, pointing out to them that the word was of course to be interpreted only 'in its divine and mystical sense' – in other words, that it could mean precisely what they chose it to mean. By the time he had finished, nearly all the pro-Arians – including both Bishops Eusebius – had agreed, albeit reluctantly, to sign the final document; only seventeen maintained their opposition – a number that the threat of exile and possible excommunication subsequently reduced to two.[2] The Council had delivered its verdict: Arius, with his remaining adherents, was formally condemned, his writings placed under anathema and ordered to be burnt. He was also forbidden to return to Alexandria. His exile to

1 *De Vita Constantini*, III, 10.
2 According to later legend, a number of bishops with Arian sympathies inserted the letter i – the Greek *iota* – into the controversial word in the copy of the declaration that each was obliged to sign, so that it read *homoiousios*, meaning 'of like substance'. This would, however, have been taking a considerable risk and there is no evidence that it was actually done.

Illyricum, however, did not last long; thanks to persistent appeals by the Arian bishops, he was soon back in Nicomedia, where events were to prove that his stormy career was by no means over.

Having dealt satisfactorily, as it imagined, with the Arian question, the Council turned its attention to other matters, including the proper date for Easter. In most of the oriental churches this was still calculated according to the Jewish calendar, without regard for the day of the week; in Alexandria and the West, on the other hand, the feast was always fixed on a Sunday – that following the first full moon after the vernal equinox. At Nicaea, it was probably the Emperor's passionate hatred of the Jews that decided the issue: he himself made it clear, in the circular letter that he addressed to the various churches after the Council,[1] that the very thought of celebrating the Resurrection of Christ on the same day as the Passover filled him with horror. In any case the Council finally agreed that all Christendom should thenceforth adopt the western system, the correct date to be calculated each year at Alexandria and communicated to Rome for onward transmission to the churches.[2]

And so the first Ecumenical Council of the Christian Church was brought to its end, a month less a day after it began. For Constantine it had been a triumph. He had succeeded in getting every major issue settled in the way he had wished; still more important from his point of view, the voting had been almost unanimous. He had established not only a great confederacy of both the eastern and the western churches but also his own moral supremacy over it, binding Church and State together with bonds that were to remain unbroken for a thousand years. He had, in short, good reason to congratulate himself; and the bishops too, whom he pressed to stay on another few weeks in Bithynia so that they could attend his *vicennalia* – the celebration of his twenty years on the throne – with the magnificent banquet that he proposed to give in their honour. Eusebius of Caesarea – who, like his namesake of Nicomedia, had somehow come to terms with his conscience over the Arian question – was naturally present, and describes the occasion with rapture:

Not one of the bishops was absent from the imperial banquet, the circumstances of which were splendid beyond description. Detachments of the Emperor's personal guard and other troops surrounded the entrance to the palace with

---

1 *De Vita Constantini*, III, 18.

2 This decision was observed for twelve and a half centuries; it was only after the correction of the calendar by Pope Gregory XIII in 1582 that the Eastern and Western calendars got out of alignment once again.

drawn swords, and through the midst of them the men of God proceeded without fear into the innermost of the imperial apartments, in which some were the Emperor's own companions at table, while others reclined on couches arranged on either side. One might have thought that a picture of Christ's kingdom was thus foreshadowed, and that the scene was less like reality than a dream.[1]

When at last the bishops left, each carried with him a personal present, placed in his hands by the Emperor himself. They were, Eusebius tells us, deeply impressed by all that they had seen – just as Constantine had intended them to be.

Early in January 326, Constantine left for Rome. The Romans had been deeply offended by his decision to hold his *vicennalia* at Nicaea instead of in their city as tradition demanded; he had therefore agreed to repeat the celebration among them, as a means of smoothing their feelings and of showing them that they had not, after all, been entirely ignored. He was accompanied on the journey by several members of his family: his mother Helena, his wife the Empress Fausta, his half-sister Constantia, her stepson Licinianus and his own first-born, the Caesar Crispus. The party, however, was not a happy one, for relations among these individuals could hardly have been worse.

Helena, for a start, never forgot that Fausta was the daughter of the Emperor Maximian, the adoptive father of that Theodora who had stolen her husband Constantius Chlorus nearly forty years before; while Fausta for her part fiercely resented Constantine's recent elevation of his mother to the rank of Augusta – like herself – during the *vicennalia* celebrations of the previous year. For Constantia there was the memory of her husband Licinius, less than two years dead, murdered despite his brother-in-law's express undertaking to save his life; for her stepson, similar sentiments were made still more bitter by the reflection that his own hopes of power had been extinguished and that he was now obliged to stand by while his younger rival Crispus enjoyed those honours which should equally have been his. As for Crispus himself, for some time now he had been conscious of his father's growing jealousy – jealousy aroused by his splendid victory in the Hellespont (for which he had received scant recognition) and, even more, by his popularity with the army and citizenry, which by now comfortably exceeded the Emperor's own. In the past year, he had seen his command in Gaul taken from him and given to his stepbrother Constantine II – who was still little more than a child

1 *De Vita Constantini*, III, 15.

– and had been passed over for the 326 Consulate in favour of his still younger brother Constantius.

None of these reasons alone, however, could altogether account for the train of events that began, so far as we can make out, when the imperial party reached Serdica, or possibly Sirmium, some time in February. Suddenly and without warning, Crispus and Licinianus were arrested; a few days later, at Pola – the modern Pula – they were put to death. Shortly afterwards they were followed by another, still more august victim: the Empress Fausta herself, who met her fate in the *calidarium* of the bath-house – though whether by scalding, stabbing or suffocation by steam we shall never know.

What, we may ask, launched Constantine into this sudden frenzy of slaughter – which, according to his near-contemporary Eutropius, was subsequently extended to many of his friends as well? The existing evidence is far from clear. One possibility must be that Crispus, sensing the depth of his father's animosity and seriously concerned for his own future, deliberately plotted with Licinianus – who would have needed little encouragement to lend himself to such a conspiracy – for the Emperor's overthrow. The plot would have been discovered in time, and Constantine would have acted with his usual decisiveness. The later executions would have occurred as other members of his entourage were found to have been implicated.

Such a solution may be straightforward enough; but it fails to explain the fate of Fausta. Conceivably, she too might have been involved in an intrigue against her husband; after all, her father Maximian had also met his death at Constantine's hands. But that had been sixteen years before, and he had richly deserved it; besides, she had since borne her husband five children, a fact which suggests that she must have been at least in some measure reconciled to him. It seems, therefore, that we must look for another solution to the problem.

Unfortunately for Fausta's reputation, at least four ancient historians associate her in one way or another with the fate of her stepson. Aurelius Victor maintains that she encouraged Constantine to get rid of Crispus; Philostorgus agrees, adding that she deliberately fabricated slanders against the young Caesar, while herself having an affair with a man from the circus. Zosimus, however – writing admittedly in the following century – introduces a new element altogether. 'Crispus,' he writes, 'was suspected of having adulterous relations with his stepmother Fausta, and was therefore executed.'[1] One might well be inclined to ascribe this

1 *Historia*, II, 29.

manifestly improbable story to the chronicler's known hostility towards Constantine and his whole family, were it not for the fact that it is to some extent confirmed by another fifth-century writer, St Apollinaris Sidonius, Bishop of Auvergne, who writes gleefully of the scurrilous couplet said to have been posted up on the doors of the palace on the Palatine Hill when the imperial party arrived in Rome:

> Who would now want the golden age of Saturn?
> Ours is a diamond age – of Nero's pattern.[1]

If this theory is correct, there are three possibilities. The first is that Crispus and Fausta were indeed having an affair; why then, however, were they not executed at the same time? The second is that Crispus made proposals to Fausta, who angrily rejected them and informed his father; but if so, why was she executed at all? We are left with a third hypothesis: that Crispus had no designs of any kind on Fausta and was unjustly accused by her – perhaps, as Gibbon suggests, because *he* rejected *her* advances – and that Constantine, discovering the falseness of her allegations only after his son's death, ordered that she too must suffer a similar fate. According to Aurelius Victor, his informant on this occasion was his mother Helena, who would certainly not have been sorry to see her daughter-in-law receive her just deserts.

Constantine's second visit to Rome had not begun well. It continued, if anything, worse. News of the family upheavals had preceded him to the city, and had done nothing to diminish the sense of mistrust that he had long inspired there, particularly among the nobility. There were several reasons for this: as Romans, they had not forgiven him for holding his real *vicennalia* elsewhere, and were increasingly concerned by the reports reaching them of the splendid new city that was rapidly growing up by the Bosphorus; as Republicans – or at least inheritors of the republican tradition – they were scandalized at the sight of a ruler who appeared to be less a Roman *imperator* than an oriental potentate, robed in silk and damask and attended by a multitude of fawning courtiers; and as staunch upholders of the traditional religion, they deplored his desertion of the

---

1 *Saturni aurea saecla quis requirat?*
   Sunt haec gemmea, sed Neroniana.
                    Letters, V, 8.

The age of Saturn – commemorated annually in the Roman *saturnalia* – had been, according to legend, one of unbounded sexual licence; Nero was popularly believed to have enjoyed incestuous relations with his mother Agrippina. The implications could hardly have been clearer.

old gods and his adoption of the despised Christian faith, which they associated with the rabble of the streets and the lowest dregs of Roman society. They saw their Emperor, in short, as a traitor not only to his religion but also – what was to them very nearly as important – to his class. They had watched, powerless, as the walls of his great new basilica rose ever higher next to the old Lateran Palace; and on 3 January 326, only months before his arrival in the city, they had sat in sullen silence while his nominee, one Acilius Severus, formally took office as its first Christian Governor.

And now, after thirteen years, he was back in their midst. They received him with all due ceremony, but left him in little doubt of their true feelings; as for his own, he scarcely troubled to conceal them. He appeared dutifully at the *vicennalia* celebrations; as on his previous visit, however, he categorically refused to participate in the traditional Capitoline procession to the Temple of Jupiter – waiting, we are told, until the parade was already drawn up before announcing his decision. By any standards, this was dangerous behaviour, giving as it did quite unnecessary offence both to the Romans and to his own soldiers, the large majority of whom were still pagan. It says much for their loyalty, and for Constantine's own self-confidence, that he should have felt himself able to ride roughshod over their susceptibilities in this way; had, perhaps, his recent domestic tragedy left him slightly unbalanced? It is hard otherwise to account for what was certainly, even for him, an unusually truculent and overbearing mood.

But if the Emperor showed himself less tactful and diplomatic towards his Roman subjects than on his previous visit after the battle of the Milvian Bridge, he proved if anything still more assiduous in his determination to make Rome a Christian city. He endowed another great basilica, dedicated this time to St Paul, at the site of his tomb – and near that of his martyrdom – on the road to Ostia;[1] and another in honour of the Holy Apostles, on the Appian Way – personally carrying, we are told, the first twelve basketfuls of earth from the site, one for each of them.[2] His most important creation of all, however, was the basilica that

[1] The present church of S. Paolo fuori le Mura is, alas, a reconstruction, replacing the ancient basilica built by Constantine's successors which was virtually destroyed by fire in 1823. The much-restored mosaics on the triumphal arch – the gift of Galla Placidia – are still worth careful study, and the romanesque cloister is the finest in Rome; but of Constantine's own day nothing survives.

[2] Now known as S. Sebastiano, the present church is baroque through and through – though the catacombs beneath both it and its neighbour S. Callisto pre-date Constantine and are full of mystery and magic.

he commanded to be built above the traditional resting-place of St Peter on the Vatican Hill, close to Nero's Circus. This, so far as we can tell, must have been begun a year or two earlier, since it was consecrated on 18 November 326, within a few months of the Emperor's arrival.[1]

Constantine's frenetic building activity in Rome proves beyond all doubt that he saw the city as the chief shrine of the Christian faith, excepting only Jerusalem itself; and he was determined to do all he could to ensure that it would be architecturally and financially worthy of its dignity. Personally, on the other hand, he never liked it, or felt at home in it, or stayed in it a moment longer than he could help. His heart was in the East, and it was there that the body of his work was to be done. Soon after the consecration of his Vatican basilica he left the old imperial capital for the last time. There was another city, eight hundred and more miles away, where he was awaited with impatience by whole regiments of architects, builders and engineers.

He had business in Byzantium.

1 It is consequently difficult to accept the old tradition that Constantine marked out the ground plan of the basilica with his own hands, just as he had delineated the walls of Constantinople. As everybody knows, old St Peter's was demolished by Pope Julius II at the beginning of the sixteenth century; the present building was consecrated 1,300 years to the day after its predecessor, on 18 November 1626. Between 1940 and 1949, excavations in the *grotte Vaticane* revealed the remains of a monument that may actually mark the tomb of St Peter.

3
Constantinople

[326–37]

Constantinople dedicated: almost every other city stripped naked.

St Jerome

When Constantine first set eyes on Byzantium, the city was already nearly a thousand years old: whether or not we accept the story of its foundation by Byzas, there can be no doubt that a small settlement was flourishing on the site by about 600 BC, with its acropolis on the high ground where the church of St Sophia and the palace of Topkapi stand today. In AD 73 it had been incorporated into the Roman Empire by Vespasian; it was unfortunate that when, 120 years later, Septimius Severus was struggling for control of the Empire, the city ill-advisedly backed his rival and had to submit to a three-year siege, after which the victorious Severus sacked it without mercy, razing its tremendous ramparts – so beautifully built, it was said, that they seemed to be carved from a single piece of stone – to the ground. Before long, however, realizing the importance of its strategic position, the same Emperor decided on a complete recon-struction; and it was this Severan city that Constantine inherited.

His own decision to transform it yet again seems to have been taken towards the end of 324, some six months or so before the Council of Nicaea. Inevitably, when his new city of Constantinople became both the centre of the late Roman world and the most splendid metropolis known to mankind, stories were to grow up – encouraged, very probably, by Constantine himself – about the supernatural circumstances attending its foundation: how the Emperor had first decided to build his new capital on the plain of Troy, but how God had come to him by night and led him instead to Byzantium;[1] how, when he hesitated at Chalcedon, a flight of eagles had flown down from the mountains, picked up the builders' tools and materials and carried them in their talons to

1 Sozomen, *Ecclesiastical History*, II, 3.

the mouth of the Bosphorus; how, as William of Malmesbury tells us, Constantine dreamt of a wrinkled old woman who was suddenly transformed into a young and beautiful girl, and how a few nights later the dead Pope Sylvester appeared in another dream and explained that the woman was Byzantium herself, whom he was destined similarly to rejuvenate: and finally how he personally traced out the line of the walls with his spear – replying, when his companions showed astonishment at its length, with the words: 'I shall continue until he who walks ahead of me bids me stop.'[1] In fact, however, there would have been no call for such supernatural guidance; at that time the Emperor was merely planning a commemorative city on the model of Adrianople or Caesarea, bearing his name and serving, by its sheer magnificence, as a perpetual reminder of his greatness and glory to future generations. A fine city, to be sure; but nothing more.

What decided him to make it the capital of his Empire was, almost certainly, his second visit to Rome. His disillusionment with that city was now complete: its republican and pagan traditions could clearly have no place in the new Christian Empire that he was so carefully shaping. Intellectually and culturally, it was becoming calcified, growing more and more out of touch with the new and progressive thinking of the Hellenistic world. The Roman academies and libraries were no longer any match for those of Alexandria, Antioch or Pergamum. In the economic field, too, a similar trend was apparent. Not only in Rome but throughout much of the Italian peninsula, malaria was on the increase and populations were dwindling; during a century in which the financial problems facing the whole Empire frequently brought it to the verge of collapse, the incomparably greater economic resources of what was known as the *pars orientalis* constituted an attraction which no government could afford to ignore.

Strategically, the disadvantages of the old capital were more serious still, and had been for some time: none of Diocletian's tetrarchs, for example, had dreamt of living there. Already for the best part of a century, the principal dangers to imperial security had been concentrated along the eastern borders: the Sarmatians around the lower Danube, the Ostrogoths to the north of the Black Sea and – most menacing of all – the Persians, whose great Sassanian Empire by now extended from the former Roman provinces of Armenia and Mesopotamia as far as the Hindu Kush. Less than seventy years before, in AD 260, the Roman Emperor Valerian had actually been taken prisoner by the Persian King

1 The Constantinian walls actually followed a line a little over a mile inside the Theodosian walls that we know today. No trace of them survives above the ground.

Shapur I and had spent the rest of his life in captivity, suffering the ultimate indignity of being regularly used as the royal mounting-block. In 298, admittedly, Galerius had settled the score by gaining a decisive victory over King Narses, sealing it with a forty-year treaty of peace; but this treaty had only a dozen years more to run, and after its expiry a renewal of warfare was a virtual certainty. In such an event what possible part, it might be asked, could Rome be expected to play? The plain truth was that the focus of the Empire – indeed, of the whole civilized world – had shifted irrevocably to the East. Italy had become a backwater.

There were other, less material considerations too – among them a widespread belief that Rome's days were numbered. The Sibylline oracle had prophesied – in one of those appalling puns so beloved of the ancients – that the mighty *Roma* would one day be reduced to a *rhumē*, or mule-track, and many people feared that the end of the city would also bring about the end of the world. This idea had been developed in several literary works, among them the *Divine Institutes* of Lactantius – who, during his years as tutor to the Caesar Crispus, would have had countless chances of discussing it with the Emperor himself; and Constantine, who was even by the standards of his day an unusually superstitious man, may well have believed that by founding – in the name of Christ the Saviour – a 'New Rome' in which the spirit of the old would somehow be immanent, he might also be giving the entire world a new lease of life.

This superstitiousness was still more in evidence when the time came for the city's consecration. Only after agonizing discussions with his augurs and astrologers did the Emperor designate, as the most auspicious day for the ceremony, 4 November 328, 'in the first year of the 276th Olympiad, when the sun was in the constellation of the Archer and at the hour dominated by the Crab'. The rites then performed – in which we know that the pagan High Priest Praetextus and the neo-platonist philosopher Sopater both played an important part – were by no means exclusively Christian; the contemporary accounts leave us with a clear impression that Constantine was once again hedging his bets, seeking blessings from all possible sources in the hope of securing a blanket benediction for the city that was to bear his name. There is even a hint of the same attitude in those famous words quoted above, 'I shall continue until he who walks ahead of me bids me to stop.' Who, one is tempted to ask – and once again Gibbon's phrase is irresistible – who was 'this extraordinary conductor'? Constantine, so far as we know, never identified him – perhaps because he was not too sure himself.

*

The members of the imperial suite whose questions prompted so gnomic a reply can be forgiven their concern; for the walls that the Emperor so confidently traced – running some two and a half miles, in a sweeping convex arc, between points now approximately marked by the Orthodox Patriarchate on the Golden Horn and the Samatya Gate on the Marmara shore – enclosed an area well over five times more extensive than its predecessor. Clearly a city of such a size would take many years to create; the New Rome, like the Old, could not be built in a day. But Constantine had already decreed that the ceremony of formal dedication should coincide with his silver jubilee in the early summer of 330 – only a year and a half away – so construction work continued at a furious rate, concentrating above all at the eastern end of the peninsula, on and around the old acropolis.

The focal point here was the *Milion,* or First Milestone. It consisted of four triumphal arches forming a square and supporting a cupola, above which was set the most venerable Christian relic of all – the True Cross itself, sent back by the Empress Helena from Jerusalem a year or two before. From it all the distances in the Empire were measured; it was, in effect, the centre of the world. A little to the east of it, on a site occupied in former times by a shrine of Aphrodite, rose the first great Christian church of the new capital, dedicated not to any saint or martyr but to the Holy Peace of God, St Eirene. A few years later this church was to be joined – and somewhat overshadowed – by a larger and still more splendid neighbour, St Sophia, the Church of the Holy Wisdom; but for the time being it had no rival. A quarter of a mile or so away from it towards the Marmara stood Constantine's huge Hippodrome, in the central *spina* of which was erected one of the most ancient classical trophies in the city – the so-called 'Serpent Column' brought by Constantine from Delphi, where it had been erected in the Temple of Apollo by thirty-one Greek cities in gratitude for their victory over the Persians at the battle of Plataea in 479 BC.[1] Half-way along its eastern side, the imperial box gave direct access by a spiral staircase to that vast complex of reception halls, government offices, domestic apartments, baths, barracks and parade grounds that was the Palace.

Directly westward from the Milion ran a broad thoroughfare, already begun by Severus, known as the *Mesē*; and where this crossed the old Severan walls the Emperor laid out a magnificent new forum, oval in

1 The heads of the three intertwined bronze serpents are believed to have been chopped off by a drunken member of the Polish Embassy to the Sublime Porte in 1700; a part of one of them was recovered in 1847 and can be admired in the Archaeological Museum.

shape – it was probably inspired by the somewhat similar one at Gerasa (Jerash) in Arabia – and paved entirely in marble. At its centre stood a great hundred-foot column of porphyry, brought from Heliopolis (the City of the Sun) in Egypt, itself standing on a twenty-foot marble plinth. Within this plinth had been deposited a number of remarkable relics, including the hatchet with which Noah had built the ark, the baskets and remains of the loaves with which Christ had fed the multitude, St Mary Magdalen's jar of ointment and the figure of Athene brought back by Aeneas from Troy. On the summit stood a statue. The body was that of an Apollo by Phidias; but the head, which was surrounded by a metal halo with representations of the sun's beams radiating from it, was that of Constantine himself. The right hand carried a sceptre, while in the left was an orb in which had been placed a fragment of the True Cross.[1]

Once again, Christian and pagan elements are combined; but this time Apollo, *Sol Invictus* and Jesus Christ all seem subordinated to a new supreme being – the Emperor Constantine. We shall never know for certain, but the existing evidence surely points to the fact that by the last decade of the Emperor's life he was rapidly giving way to religious megalomania. From being God's chosen instrument it was but a short step to being God himself, that *summus deus* in whom all other Gods and other religions were subsumed.

Beyond the forum, there was as yet relatively little building: the Mesē turned north-west, and after running a mile or so through open fields split into two, the left-hand branch leading towards Thessalonica, the right-hand towards Adrianople. Around the Palace, the Church and the Hippodrome, however, tens of thousands of labourers and artisans worked day and night; and, thanks to the wholesale plunder by which the towns of Europe and Asia were deprived of their finest statues, trophies and works of art, it was already a fine and noble city – though not yet a very large one – that was dedicated, as Constantine had determined that it should be, in a special ceremony that marked the climax of his silver jubilee celebrations.

The festivities, which continued for forty days and nights, may well have included the first of those extraordinary annual exhibitions of

1 The Column of Constantine still stands – but only just. After an accident in 416 it was bound together with iron hoops (renewed by Sultan Mustafa III in 1701). In 1106 the Emperor's statue was blown down in a gale, and later in the same century the capital was replaced by Manuel Comnenus. The monument also sustained serious damage by fire on several occasions, which is why the English have usually known it as the Burnt Column; the Turks prefer to call it the Hooped Column (*Cemberlitaş*). By any name it is a pitiful sight today.

Emperor-worship which, in later years, regularly marked the birthday of the city. On these occasions virtually the whole populace would throng to the Hippodrome to watch a sumptuous procession, the centrepiece of which was another colossal statue of Constantine, this time fashioned of gilded wood and holding in its left hand a small representation of the *Tychē*, or genius of the city. This was solemnly carried in a triumphal car on a circuit of the theatre with an escort of soldiers in full ceremonial dress, each carrying a lighted taper. As it passed, all would bow; and when it arrived opposite the imperial box the Emperor himself would rise and make a deep obeisance.

Whether or not Constantine ever adored his own likeness in this manner is uncertain. From the few facts that have come down to us, the general impression is that the Christian element in the dedicatory celebrations was a good deal more in evidence than it had been for the consecration eighteen months before. At last, as the forty days reached their culmination, the Emperor attended High Mass in St Irene, while the pagan population prayed for his prosperity and that of the city in such temples as he had authorized for their use.[1] It is with this Mass, at which the city was formally dedicated to the God of the Christians, that the history of Constantinople really begins – and, with it, that of the Byzantine Empire.

The date was 11 May 330. It was, we are credibly informed, a Monday.

Only half a dozen years before, Byzantium had been just another small Greek town, with nothing other than its superb site to distinguish it from a thousand others across the length of Europe; now, reborn and renamed, it was the 'New Rome' – its official appellation (though never generally adopted) proudly carved on a stone pillar in the recently completed law courts. By now, moreover, Constantine had made it abundantly clear that this was to be no empty title. The old Rome, to be sure, was never actively made to suffer for its relegation to secondary status: its people kept all their ancient privileges, continuing to enjoy their free issue of bread and other commodities. Its trade, too, went on as before; the port of Ostia remained busy. But several of the old Roman senatorial families were already beginning to trickle away to Constantinople, lured by the promise of magnificent palaces on the Bosphorus

---

1 Constantine is known to have given authority for two of these, one dedicated to the *Tychē* and one, close by the Hippodrome, to the Dioscuri – Castor and Pollux, the Heavenly Twins; and there may well have been others, quite apart from several remaining from former times.

to say nothing of extensive estates in Thrace, Bithynia and Pontus; while a larger and infinitely more sumptuous Senate House had risen in the new capital to accommodate them in a second, Constantinopolitan Senate – the *clari* – which was to function in parallel to that of the *clarissimi* in Rome.

Meanwhile all the cities of the Empire were ransacked for works of art with which the growing city was to be adorned – preference being normally given to temple statues of the ancient gods, since by removing them from their traditional shrines and setting them up in public, unconsecrated places for aesthetic rather than religious purposes, Constantine could strike a telling blow at the old pagan faith. Among the most important appropriations were the Zeus from Dodona, the Athene from Lindos – though this may have been taken by Theodosius the Great half a century later – and the Apollo from Delphi; but these were accompanied by some thousands of other, lesser sculptures of unknown description and unrecorded provenance. The speed of the new city's transformation seemed to its inhabitants, native and immigrant alike, almost a miracle in itself[1] – the more so in that the Emperor was simultaneously engaged on another vast work of self-commemoration at Cirte in Numidia (which he had decided to call by his own name, Constantine) and a complete reconstruction, in honour of his mother, of the little town of Drepanum on the Asiatic shore of the Marmara which he had named, predictably, Helenopolis.

Meanwhile in 327 Helena herself, with all the zeal of a passionate convert, had set off at the age of seventy-two for the Holy Land, where Bishop Macarius of Jerusalem took her on a tour of the principal shrines and where, according to tradition, she found the Cross in a cistern beneath a temple to Aphrodite – distinguishing it from those of the two thieves by laying it on a dying woman, who was miraculously restored to health. Eusebius, curiously enough, while writing at some length about the Empress's journey and her benefactions to the various churches, fails to mention this momentous event; on the other hand we find Macarius's second successor, Bishop Cyril – who was himself, as a very young man, almost certainly in Jerusalem at the time – speaking of

---

1 'A particular description, composed about a century after its foundation, enumerates a capitol or school of learning, a circus, two theatres, eight public and one hundred and fifty-three private baths, fifty-two porticoes, five granaries, eight aqueducts or reservoirs of water, four spacious halls for the meetings of the senate or courts of justice, fourteen churches, fourteen palaces, and four thousand, three hundred and eighty-eight houses which, for their size or beauty, deserved to be distinguished from the multitude of plebeian habitations' (Gibbon, Chap. XVII).

it only a quarter of a century later as if it were common knowledge. Further corroboration is provided by a significant action of Constantine himself: soon after the Cross arrived in his new capital, he sent a piece of it to Rome, to be placed in the old Sessorian Palace which his mother had always occupied during her visits to the city and which he now ordered to be converted into a church. Still known as S. Croce in Gerusalemme, the building has been indissolubly associated with St Helena ever since.[1]

The Empress, Eusebius reports, having been granted by her son 'authority over the imperial treasury, to use and dispense monies according to her own will and discretion in every case', was taking full advantage of her prerogative. Thanks to her, endowments were provided for the Church of the Nativity at Bethlehem and that of the Ascension on the Mount of Olives, together with others at Mamre (the shrine near Hebron associated with Abraham), Tyre and Antioch; most important of all, however, was the Church of the Holy Sepulchre at Jerusalem, where Helena gave new impetus to the ambitious building programme which her son had initiated in 325 to mark the successful conclusion of the Council of Nicaea. As a result of this undertaking, the whole uneven surface of the rock which surrounded the Tomb was levelled to form a vast courtyard, with a portico along one side and colonnades around the other three. At one end was the Tomb itself, enclosed in a small circular aedicule known as the Anastasis; immediately to the east stood Constantine's new basilica, with two aisles along each side and a deep atrium running across its entire breadth. Its outer walls were of finely polished stone, while those of the interior were covered with revetments of polychrome marble, rising to a gilded and coffered roof.

Little of these splendid edifices remains today. Fires and earthquakes have taken their toll, and the passage of sixteen and a half centuries has done the rest. It must also be admitted that with only a limited quantity of first-class architects and craftsmen available at any given site, all too much of the imperial construction work was hasty and slipshod; walls were too thin, foundations too shallow. Yet the vision was there, and the energy, and the determination to preserve, perpetuate and adorn the great shrines of the Christian faith; and if few of these shrines nowadays possess a single stone recognizably dating from the time of Constantine,

1 The Chapel of St Helena in the crypt of this church is – with the communicating Chapel of St Gregory – part of the ancient Palace. According to legend it was once the Empress's bedroom; it is now thought more probably to have served as her private chapel.

there still remain a remarkable number whose very existence is due, in large measure, to him.

And, of course, to his mother. By now an old woman, she had for years enjoyed immense popularity across the Empire; and her zeal for the religion that she had so enthusiastically embraced had in its turn been responsible for untold quantities of conversions. Her journey to the Holy Places caught the imagination of all Christendom; and even if we may question her finding of the True Cross, we can deny neither the number nor the generosity of her benefactions to churches and monasteries, hospitals and orphanages, wherever she went. We do not know the length of her stay in the Levant, nor the circumstances of her death; there is no certain evidence that she ever returned to Constantinople, and she does not seem to have been present at any of the dedication ceremonies. It may well be, therefore, that she died, as one suspects she would have wished to die, while still in the Holy Land – the first recorded Christian pilgrim, and the founder of the pilgrim tradition that has continued from her day to our own.

Throughout the triumphal ceremonies by which Constantine inaugurated his new capital – and, as he believed, a new era for the Roman Empire – he was uncomfortably aware that, in one vital respect, he had failed. Despite the Council of Nicaea, despite all that he had done to bind together the Christian Church, it remained as divided as ever it had been. To some extent – though this he is unlikely to have admitted, even to himself – the fault was his own: personally uninterested in the nicer distinctions of theological doctrine and swayed above all by his determination to achieve unity within both Church and State, he vacillated constantly between opposing camps, allowing himself to be persuaded by whatever favourite happened to have his ear at any given moment. But the greater part of the blame lay with the Christian leaders themselves. Obviously, they believed that vital issues were at stake – issues for which, as many had already proved, they were ready to face exile and even martyrdom; none the less, by their eternal bickering and squabbling, by the hatred and bigotry, intolerance and malice that they showed to each other and by the readiness with which they stooped to every form of dishonesty to achieve their ends, they set a sad example to their flocks – an example which, moreover, countless generations of their successors have been all too ready to follow.

Archbishop Alexander died in 328, and was succeeded in his Alexandrian see by his former chaplain, Athanasius. The two had been to-

gether at the Council of Nicaea, where Athanasius had proved even
more skilled and quick-witted a dialectician than his master. In the years
to come, he was to show himself to be something more: the leading
churchman of his time, one of the towering figures in the whole history
of the Christian Church, and a canonized saint. (He was long erroneously
believed to have been the author of the Athanasian Creed, which still
bears his name.) Arius and his adherents were to have no more redoubtable adversary.

For the moment, however, their star was once again in the ascendant.
Even after Nicaea, Arius had never lost the support of the Emperor's
family – in particular that of his mother and his half-sister Constantia –
while the Asian bishops (as opposed to those of Europe and North
Africa) were also overwhelmingly pro-Arian in their sympathies and took
full advantage of their proximity to the imperial court to further their
cause. Already in 327 they had persuaded Constantine to recall Arius
from exile and to receive him in audience; the Emperor, impressed as
much by the brilliance and obvious sincerity of the man as by his assurance that he willingly accepted all the points of faith approved at Nicaea,
had gone so far as to write at least two personal letters to Archbishop
Alexander urging (though taking care not to command) that he should
be allowed to return to Egypt. He seems to have been genuinely surprised when the archbishop proved reluctant to comply – and was
probably still more so in the following year when Alexander's flock, by
their election of the firebrand Athanasius, showed themselves equally
obdurate.

Not that Athanasius, even on home ground, was universally popular;
firebrands seldom are. For internal political reasons unconnected with
the Arian controversy, the local Meletian Church under its own Bishop
John Arkaph was bent on his destruction, and over the next few years
unleashed against him, in quick succession, accusations of fraud, bribery
and even sacrilege. When all three charges failed to stick, they tried one
of murder, claiming that a Meletian bishop had been flogged to death
and dismembered at his instigation. According to one version of the
story, Athanasius was actually able to produce the missing bishop, all in
one piece, before the examining magistrate; in any event he had no
difficulty in establishing that his alleged victim was alive and well, and
the case collapsed. Arkaph and his followers now had one last try:
rape. They found a young woman whom they managed to bribe or
frighten into claiming that she had been violated by the archbishop – an
experience which, she added, was made the more regrettable by the fact

that she had vowed herself to perpetual virginity. Unfortunately, she failed to recognize her ravisher in court; and once again Athanasius was found to have no case to answer.

Whether Constantine was, as he maintained, genuinely troubled by these continuing accusations – groundless as they invariably proved to be – or whether he was simply falling ever more under the influence of the pro-Arians around him, he seems gradually to have come to the conclusion that Athanasius, rather than Arius, was now the chief impediment to that Church unity for which he strove. By this time, too, he was making plans for celebrating, in 335, the thirtieth year of his reign by the formal consecration of the rebuilt Church of the Holy Sepulchre in Jerusalem. Here he proposed to summon a vast convocation of bishops, drawn from every corner of the Empire; and he was determined that doctrinal harmony should prevail among them. He accordingly gave orders that the bishops on their way to Jerusalem should hold a synod at Tyre, in the presence of a high imperial official, in order – as he rather disarmingly put it – 'to free the Church from blasphemy and to lighten my cares'.

The synod was called for July. It was, as soon became clear, to be attended almost exclusively by bishops of the Arian persuasion, and consequently to be less a gathering of distinguished churchmen than a trial of Athanasius; and the archbishop seems to have realized as much. In the previous year, when a similar exercise had been proposed at Caesarea, he had categorically refused to attend and the idea had been abandoned; on this occasion, however, he resolved to face his enemies and duly presented himself before the tribunal. He was soon to regret his decision. All the old charges were now revived, and new ones introduced; hosts of new witnesses were called, each one apparently prepared to swear black and blue that the archbishop had broken every commandment and committed every crime in the statute book. He himself fought back with characteristic vigour, not hesitating to meet his accusers with their own weapons; and the synod soon degenerated into a general uproar of lie and counter-lie, of calumny and curse, insult and invective. Finally a commission of inquiry was appointed, consisting of six of Athanasius's most implacable opponents, with orders to proceed forthwith to Egypt, there to gather further evidence. At this point the archbishop, believing – probably rightly – that his life was in danger, slipped away to Constantinople. He was deposed in his absence, after which the synod broke up and its members continued their journey to Jerusalem.

Once arrived in the capital, Athanasius went straight to the Palace,

but was refused an audience; and we have it on Constantine's own authority that, one day when he was riding into the city, the archbishop
suddenly appeared in his path and flung himself in front of his horse.
'He and his companions looked so weighed down by their troubles,'
wrote the Emperor, 'that I felt an ineffable pity as I realized that this
was Athanasius, the holy sight of whom had once been enough to draw
the Gentiles themselves to the worship of the God of All.' The whole
episode, we can assume, had been expertly stage-managed by Athanasius;
but despite its promising beginning it did not succeed. Six bishops,
including the two Eusebii, hastened to Constantinople at the Emperor's
bidding, with a new and dangerously damaging allegation: that the
archbishop was even now planning to call all the workers at the port of
Alexandria out on strike. If he were not immediately reinstated,
they would refuse to load the transports with the grain on which
Constantinople depended for its survival, and the capital would be
starved into submission. In vain did Athanasius deny the charges; where
his beloved city was concerned, Constantine was deaf to the voice of
reason. In a rage, he banished the still protesting archbishop to
Augusta Treverorum – the modern Trier – ,and then turned back to
the interrupted task of getting Arius reaccepted in Alexandria.

Now, however, it was the Emperor's turn to fail. Every attempt by
Arius to return brought new outbreaks of rioting in the city – led by the
great St Anthony himself, aged eighty-six, who had left his desert her-
mitage to champion the cause of orthodoxy and who now wrote several
personal letters to the Emperor on behalf of Athanasius. Although these
were written in Coptic – Anthony spoke no Greek – they seem to have
had some effect, inducing Constantine, probably some time in 336, to
summon Arius back to Constantinople for a further investigation of his
beliefs. It was during this last inquiry – so Athanasius later wrote, with
considerable *Schadenfreude*, to his Egyptian flock – and while the pro-
Arian bishops were trying to persuade the Patriarch of Constantinople
to allow him to attend Mass on the following day (a Sunday), that

Arius, made bold by the protection of his followers, engaged in light-hearted
and foolish conversation, until he was suddenly compelled by a call of nature to
retire; and immediately, as it is written,[1] 'falling headlong, he burst asunder in
the midst and gave up the ghost' . . .

This story, to be sure, comes from the pen of Arius's arch-enemy; but

1 Acts, I, 18.

73

although there are – predictably – several different versions of exactly what occurred,[1] the unattractive circumstances of his demise are too well attested by contemporary writers to be open to serious question. Inevitably, it was interpreted by those who hated him as divine retribution: the archbishop's biblical reference is to the somewhat similar fate which befell Judas Iscariot. It did not, however, put an end to the controversy – nor even to the exile of Athanasius, which lasted until after Constantine's own death in 337. Only on 23 November of that year did he finally return to Alexandria, starting up as he did so yet another period of factional strife in that unhappy diocese. Constantine's dream of spiritual harmony throughout Christendom was not to be achieved in his lifetime; indeed, we are still awaiting it today.

One would like to hear more about the *tricennalia* celebrations in Jerusalem. Eusebius writes with wonderment of the numbers of the assembled bishops, and of the distant lands from which they had come: they even included, he tells us, 'a holy prelate from Persia, deeply versed in the sacred oracles'. All, he goes on, were received by the Imperial Notary and entertained with feasts and banquets, while there were also lavish distributions of food, clothing and money to the poor of the city. Most of his account, however, is devoted to the endless series of sermons and dissertations that were pronounced, and in particular to an interminable one of his own which he was to repeat, in the presence of the Emperor, on his return to Constantinople. Of the dedication of the Church of the Holy Sepulchre itself he tells us nothing at all.

Still less do we know how the *tricennalia* were marked in Rome. The Christians, we read, celebrated them by transferring the presumed remains of St Peter and St Paul from the catacombs of St Sebastian to the two splendid new basilicas that Constantine had built near the sites of their respective martyrdoms. But those who had remained faithful to the old religion, who despised the Emperor as an apostate and his new city as an upstart, who believed Rome to be the eternal capital of the Empire and the world, unchallengeable and unchangeable – in what way did they observe Constantine's anniversary? Did they invite him to par-

1 Socrates Scholasticus, for example, records that Arius was taken short while 'parading proudly through the midst of the city, attracting the notice of all the people', just as he was passing through the Forum of Constantine. Socrates is admittedly writing in the first half of the following century, but he inspires confidence when he writes that 'the scene of the catastrophe is still shown at Constantinople . . . behind the shambles in the colonnade: and, in the way that people still point to it as they pass by, the memory of this extraordinary way of death is perpetually preserved.'

ticipate, as they had ten years before? Were they offended, or relieved, by his non-appearance? We cannot tell. As for the Emperor himself, it is doubtful whether he spared the matter a moment's thought.

His place at such a time was his new capital, where the celebrations – in contrast to those that had marked the city's consecration and dedication – were exclusively Christian. (Between 331 and 334 he had issued a series of decrees effectively closing down all pagan temples in the Empire.) In the course of these festivities, however, he took the opportunity of announcing the promotion of his two nephews – the sons of his half-brother Delmatius – to key positions in the State. The elder of the boys, named after his father, was proclaimed Caesar; the younger, Hannibalianus, was appointed King of Pontus and given the hand of his first cousin, the Emperor's daughter Constantina, in marriage. With the additional title of King of Kings – shamelessly appropriated from the Persians – he was then sent off with his bride to rule in Pontus, that wild, mountainous region that extends back from the rainswept southern shore of the Black Sea.

The elevation of these two youths brought the number of reigning Caesars effectively to five, Constantine's three sons by Fausta having already been raised to similar rank – the youngest, Constans, only two years previously, at the age of ten. It has been suggested that by multiplying their number the Emperor was deliberately attempting to reduce the Caesars' prestige: with advancing age he was becoming ever more convinced of a special divine dispensation that singled him out from his fellow-men, even those of his own family. The Caesars enjoyed vice-regal powers in the various provinces of the Empire to which he had appointed them, but such glory as might attach to their station must be seen, he was determined, only as a reflection of his own. Never at any time in his life did he consider appointing a second Augustus, as Diocletian had intended.

But his very reluctance to delegate authority in the capital imposed on Constantine a workload of almost Herculean proportions; and early in 337 he seems to have suspected that he was ill. He had spent the winter in Asia Minor mobilizing his army – for the young King Shapur II of Persia was making no secret of his territorial ambitions and it was now plain to everyone that war could not be long in coming – during which he had shown all the energy, stamina and endurance that had long made him a legend among his men. Then, shortly before Easter, he returned to Constantinople – there to put the finishing touches to the great Church of the Holy Apostles which he had begun a few years before on the high spur of land which forms the city's fourth hill.[1] Perhaps he already suspected that he had been stricken, for it was at this time that he gave orders for his tomb to be prepared in the church; but only after Easter was past did his health begin seriously – and obviously – to fail. The baths of the capital having proved useless, he moved on to those at Helenopolis, the city that he had rebuilt in honour of his mother; and it was there, so Eusebius tells us, that, 'kneeling on the pavement of the church itself, he for the first time received the imposition of hands in prayer'[2] – becoming, in short, a catechumen. Then he started back to the capital, but when he reached the suburbs of Nicomedia found that he could go no further; nor could the momentous step that he had so long considered be any further delayed. Summoning the local bishops, he addressed them:

The long-awaited time has finally come, when I have hoped and prayed to obtain the salvation of God ... Now I too may have the blessing of that seal which confers immortality, the seal of salvation itself. I had thought to receive it in the waters of the Jordan ... but it pleases God, who knows what is best for us, that I should receive it here. So be it, then, and without delay; and should it be the will of Him who is Lord of life and death that my existence here should be prolonged ... I shall prescribe for myself henceforth a way of life that befits his service.

And so at last Constantine the Great, for years a self-styled bishop of the Christian Church, was baptised by Bishop Eusebius of Nicomedia; and when it was done, 'he arrayed himself in imperial vestments white and radiant as light, and lay himself down on a couch of the purest white, refusing ever to clothe himself in purple again'.

Why – the question has been asked all through history – why did Constantine delay his baptism until he was on his deathbed? The most obvious answer – and the most likely – is Gibbon's:

The sacrament of baptism was supposed to contain a full and absolute expiation of sin; and the soul was instantly restored to its original purity, and entitled to the promise of eternal salvation. Among the proselytes of Christianity, there were many who judged it imprudent to precipitate a salutary rite, which could not be repeated; to throw away an inestimable privilege, which could never be recovered.

---

1 As additional evidence for the claims of Constantinople to be the successor to Rome, it too was held to be built on seven hills – though to identify them all needs a good deal more credulity and imagination than is required for their Roman counterparts.

2 *De Vita Constantini*, IV, 60–71.

There was indeed nothing unusual, in those early days of Christianity, in deferring baptism until the last possible moment; forty-three years later, we shall find the devout Theodosius the Great doing much the same. And Constantine himself seems to corroborate this explanation in the last sentence of his speech – though whether Eusebius has reported the words which his hero actually spoke, rather than those which the good bishop felt he ought to have spoken, is another open question. A more recent historian[1] has suggested that the Emperor's first sentence may be the more revealing: if he had had to wait so long for something he wanted so much, it could only be because that thing had heretofore been denied him. This interpretation is certainly possible, but seems somehow less likely. Constantine had been guilty of many sins – the murder of his wife and son for a start – but these would have been washed away by his baptism; and although his appearance, especially at formal functions, might have provoked an occasional shudder among the more traditionally minded of his subjects,[2] there is no contemporary evidence to suggest that his private life in his seventh decade was such as to debar him from the Church. (Later stories of a growing *penchant* for homosexuality are almost certainly without foundation.) In any case, few churchmen would have jeopardized their careers by refusing their Emperor an earlier request for baptism had he made one.

After a reign of thirty-one years – the longest of any Roman Emperor since Augustus – Constantine died at noon on Whit Sunday, 22 May 337. His body was placed in a golden coffin draped in purple and brought to Constantinople, where it lay in state on a high platform in the main hall of the Palace, surrounded by candles set in tall golden candlesticks and presenting, so Eusebius assures us, 'a marvellous spectacle such as no mortal had exhibited on earth since the world itself began'. And there it seems to have remained, not for a few days only but for some three and a half months, during which time the court ceremonial was carried on in Constantine's name precisely as if his death had never occurred. No one was yet sure which of the five young Caesars was to

1 John Holland Smith, *Constantine the Great*.

2 'The Asiatic pomp which had been adopted by the pride of Diocletian assumed an air of softness and effeminacy in the person of Constantine. He is represented with false hair of various colours, laboriously arranged by the skilful artists of the times; a diadem of new and more expensive fashion; a profusion of gems and pearls, of collars and bracelets; and a variegated flowing robe of silk, most curiously embroidered with flowers of gold. In such apparel,' sniffs Gibbon, 'scarcely to be excused by the youth and folly of Elagabalus, we are at a loss to discover the wisdom of an aged monarch and the simplicity of a Roman veteran.'

assume the vacant throne, and the uncertainties of an openly acknowledged interregnum were not to be risked unnecessarily.

Where the succession was concerned, the army was the first to make
its wishes known. Although the title of Augustus continued, in theory at
least, to be elective, the soldiers everywhere proclaimed that they would
accept no one but Constantine's sons, reigning jointly. With Crispus
dead, that left the three sons born to Fausta: the Caesar in Gaul Constantine II, the Caesar in the East Constantius, and the Caesar in Italy
Constans;[1] and of these it was naturally Constantius, now a young man
of twenty, who hastened to the capital after his father's death and
presided over his funeral.

This was an extraordinary occasion, as Constantine had intended that
it should be. The burial itself he had personally planned down to the last
detail, and in view of his known love of ceremonial and parade it seems
more than likely that the preliminaries were also carried out according to
his instructions. The funeral procession was led by Constantius, with
detachments of soldiers in full battle array; then came the body itself in
its golden coffin, surrounded by companies of spearmen and heavy-
armed infantry. Vast crowds followed behind. From the Great Palace it
wound its way round the north-eastern end of the Hippodrome to the
Milion, and thence along the Mesē to a point some quarter of a mile
short of the Constantinian walls, where it turned off to the right to the
newly-completed church of the Holy Apostles. 'This building,' Eusebius
tells us,

[Constantine] had carried to a vast height and brilliantly decorated by encasing
it from the foundations to the roof with marble slabs of various colours. The
inner roof he had formed of finely fretted work, overlaying it throughout with
gold. The external covering . . . was of brass rather than tiles; and this too was
splendidly and profusely adorned with gold, reflecting the rays of the sun with a
brilliancy that dazzled those that beheld it, even from a distance. And the dome
was entirely surrounded with delicately carved tracery, wrought in brass and
gold.

But that was only the beginning:

He had in fact chosen this spot in the prospect of his own death, anticipating
with extraordinary fervour of faith that his body would share their title with the

---

1 The distressing lack of imagination shown by Constantine in the naming of his children has
caused much confusion among past historians, to say nothing of their readers. The latter can take
comfort in the knowledge that it lasts for a single generation only – which, in a history such as this,
is soon over.

Apostles themselves and that he should then become, even after death, the object with them of the devotions which should be here performed in their honour. He accordingly caused twelve sarcophagi to be set up in this church, like sacred pillars, in honour and memory of the number of the Apostles, in the centre of which was placed his own, having six of theirs on either side of it.

For the last few years of his life Constantine had regularly used the title *Isapostolos*, 'Equal of the Apostles'; now at his death he gave, as it were, physical substance to that claim. From the moment that the idea first took shape in his mind, his agents had been scouring the Eastern Mediterranean for alleged relics of the Twelve to place in their respective sarcophagi; and his choice of his own position in the midst of his peers, with six of them on each hand, strongly suggests that he saw himself as yet greater than they – a symbol, perhaps of the Saviour in person: God's Vice-Gerent on earth.

It was, indeed, a fine resting-place; but Constantine was not to occupy it for long. In his capital, as in so many cities of the Empire, he had tried to build too much, too quickly. There was in consequence a chronic shortage of skilled workmen, and a general tendency to skimp on such things as foundations, wall thicknesses and buttressing. The Church of the Holy Apostles, for all its outward magnificence, was at bottom jerry-built. Within a quarter of a century of its completion, the state of the fabric began giving cause for alarm. Before long the great golden dome was in imminent danger of collapse, and the unpopular Patriarch Macedonius gave orders for the Emperor's body to be removed to safety in the nearby Church of St Acacius the Martyr. Unfortunately, there were many in the city to whom such a step was nothing short of sacrilege, and many others who gratefully seized any weapon with which to attack the Patriarch; serious rioting broke out, in the course of which – according to Socrates – several people were killed, and 'the courtyard [of the church] was covered with gore, and the well also which was in it overflowed with blood, which ran into the adjacent portico and thence even into the very street'.

The Church of the Holy Apostles did not, in the event, collapse as the Patriarch had feared it would; it stood – if somewhat unsteadily – for two centuries until, in 550, it was completely rebuilt by Justinian. Of those twelve apostolic sarcophagi, and the great tomb of the Emperor among them, not a trace remains.

4
Julian the Apostate

[337–63]

O thou mother of Gods and of men, who sharest the throne of the great Zeus
... O life-giving Goddess, who art the wisdom and the providence and the
creator of our very souls ... Grant to all men happiness, and that highest
happiness of all which is the knowledge of the Gods; and grant to the Roman
people that they may cleanse themselves of the stain of impiety ...

Julian, *Hymn to Cybele,*
Mother of the Gods

Young Constantius had behaved impeccably during those first few weeks
in Constantinople after the Emperor's death, and had favourably impressed many of the leading citizens by his comportment during the
funeral. Once his father had been laid safely away in his huge apostolic
tomb, however, and he and his two brothers had jointly received, on 9
September, their acclamation as Augusti, he abruptly shed the mild-
mannered mask that he had worn until that moment. A rumour was
deliberately put about to the effect that, after Constantine's death, a
scrap of parchment had been found clenched in his fist – accusing his
two half-brothers, Julius Constantius and Delmatius, of having poisoned
him and calling on his three sons to take their revenge.

The story seems improbable, to say the least; but it was vouched for
by the Bishop of Nicomedia and accepted unhesitatingly by the army in
Constantinople. Its effect was horrendous. Julius Constantius was
pursued to his palace and butchered on the spot with his eldest son; so
too was Delmatius, together with both his sons, the Caesars Delmatius
and Hannibalianus, King of Pontus. Soon afterwards Constantine's two
brothers-in-law – his close friends Flavius Optatus and Popilius Nepotianus, who had been respectively married to his half-sisters Anastasia
and Eutropia – met similar fates; both were senators and former Consuls.
Finally the blow fell on Ablavius, the Praetorian Prefect, whose daughter
Olympias was betrothed to the new Emperor's younger brother Con-

stans. Apart from three little boys – the two sons of Julius Constantius and the single offspring of Nepotianus and Eutropia, who were presumably spared because of their age – the three reigning Augusti, when they met in the early summer of 338 at Viminacium on the Danube to divide up their huge patrimony between them, were the only male members of the imperial family still alive.

The demarcation – of such vital importance for the peace and stability of the Empire – proved straightforward enough, the brothers continuing to control, with a few adjustments, the same regions in which they had previously ruled as Caesars. To Constantius went the old County of the East, including the whole of Asia Minor and Egypt. This gave him responsibility for the always delicate relations with Christian Armenia, as well as for the conduct of the war with Persia which was now beginning in earnest. His elder brother, Constantine II, was to remain in charge of Gaul, Britain and Spain, while to the younger brother, Constans – though he was still only fifteen – went the largest area of all: Africa, Italy, the Danube, Macedonia and Thrace. This distribution theoretically gave Constans authority over the capital itself; but as neither he nor Constantius was to spend any time there during the coming year, and as in 339 Constans was voluntarily to surrender the city to his brother in return for his support against Constantine II, the point proved of little significance.

It was perhaps inevitable, given their characters and upbringing, that the three Augusti should sooner or later start quarrelling among themselves; one feels, none the less, that with a measure of self-control they might have preserved the peace for a little longer than they in fact managed to do. The initial blame seems to have been Constantine's. The eldest of the three – born early in 317, he had been appointed Caesar when only a month old – he found it impossible to look on his co-Emperors as equals and was forever trying in one way or another to assert his authority over them. It was Constans's refusal to submit to his will that led Constantine, in 340, to invade Italy from Gaul in an attempt to bring his refractory young brother to heel. But the latter, for all his tender years, was too clever for him, and ambushed him with his army just outside Aquileia. Constantine was struck down and killed, and his body thrown into the river Alsa. From that time onward there were two Augusti only, and Constans, aged just seventeen, held supreme power in the West.[1]

Unfortunately, the character of Constans was no better than that of

---

[1] Constans was to visit Britain in 343, the last legitimate Roman Emperor ever to do so.

his surviving brother. Sextus Aurelius Victor, the Roman Governor of Pannonia whose *History of the Caesars* is one of the principal sources for the period, describes him as 'a minister of unspeakable depravity and a leader in avarice and contempt for his soldiers'; he certainly neglected the all-important legions along the Rhine and Upper Danube whose duty it was to secure the Empire's eastern frontier against the unremitting pressure from the barbarian tribes, preferring to take his pleasures with certain of his blond German prisoners, as dissolute and debauched as himself. By 350 the army was on the brink of revolt, and matters came to a head when, on 18 January of that year, one of his chief ministers gave a banquet at Augustodunum – the modern Autun – while Constans was away on a hunting expedition. Suddenly in the course of the festivities, a pagan officer of British extraction named Magnentius donned the imperial purple and was acclaimed Emperor by his assembled fellow-guests. On hearing the news Constans took flight, but was quickly captured and put to death.

The usurper did not last long. Constantius, realizing that the revolt in the West was potentially more serious even than the Persian menace, marched against him with a large army, pausing only to appoint his young cousin Gallus – one of the three survivors of the massacre of 337 – Caesar of the East, and to marry him off to his sister Constantina, widow of the less fortunate Hannibalianus. In September 351 Magnentius was soundly defeated at Mursa – now Sisak, in Croatia – and two years later, having failed to regain his following or to rebuild his scattered forces, decided his position was hopeless and fell on his sword. The Emperor, however, still felt threatened. Late in 354, suspecting – almost certainly wrongly – that Gallus was plotting his overthrow, he had the young Caesar beheaded, thereby widowing the luckless Constantina for the second time.

Constantius was now the undisputed sole ruler of the Roman Empire. His defeat of Magnentius, however, did not mean the end of his problems in Gaul. The German confederations beyond the Rhine, emboldened by the neglect of the frontier by Constans and the ensuing rebellion, were making themselves increasingly troublesome. Among his own army, too, several other minor conspiracies had been brought to light. On the other hand the Persian War was by no means over, and he could not stay in the West indefinitely. Much as he would have preferred to keep the power in his own hands, by the autumn of 355 he had at last come to accept the fact that he would have to appoint another Caesar.

On the assumption that any new Caesar was to be chosen from within the Emperor's immediate family, there was only one possible candidate. A philosopher and a scholar, he had no military or even administrative experience; but he was intelligent, serious-minded and a hard worker, and his loyalty had never been in question. Messengers were accordingly dispatched post-haste to Athens to fetch him: the Emperor's twenty-three-year-old cousin Flavius Claudius Julianus, better known to posterity as Julian the Apostate.

The child, as everybody knows, is father to the man; and since, for the past sixteen centuries, historians have been trying to explain Julian's curious and complex character in terms of his early life, it may be worth our while to trace those formative years, very briefly, here. His father, Julius Constantius, was the younger of the two sons born to the Emperor Constantius Chlorus by his second wife Theodora – a branch of the imperial family that had been obliged to keep an extremely low profile after the succession of Constantine and his elevation of Theodora's predecessor and sworn enemy, Helena, to Augustan rank. Julius Constantius had thus spent the greater part of the first forty-odd years of his life in what was effectively a comfortable but unproductive exile when, soon after Helena's death, Constantine had invited him, with his second wife and his young family, to take up residence in his new capital; and it was in Constantinople that his third son Julian was born, in May or June of the year 332. The baby's mother, Basilina, a Greek from Asia Minor, died a few weeks later; and the little boy, together with his two considerably older stepbrothers and a stepsister, was brought up by a succession of nurses and tutors under his father's benevolent, if somewhat distant, supervision. Then, when he was still only five, Julius Constantius was murdered – the first victim of that family blood-bath that followed the accession of his nephew to the throne.

It was a day that Julian never forgot. Whether he actually witnessed the murder of his father and stepbrother is not recorded; nor do we know – though we can easily guess – how near he himself came to sharing their fate. But the experience left a permanent scar, and although a child of his age could hardly have understood why it occurred or who was responsible, the truth soon became apparent as he grew up. And, as it did so, his early respect for his cousin turned to an undying hatred.

To Constantius, on the other hand, young Julian was no more than a minor irritation. The only real problem was what to do with him. The Emperor sent him first to Nicomedia where, with Bishop Eusebius as his tutor, he could be assured of a conscientious, if somewhat narrow, Christian upbringing; then, when Julian was eleven, he and his brother Gallus found themselves effectively exiled to Macellum, the ancient palace of the Kings of Cappadocia. There they remained for six years, with only books for company; not until 349 were they allowed to return to the capital. Gallus was called to the imperial court; Julian, however, by now formidably well read in both classical and Christian literature, obtained permission to apply himself to serious study.

The next six years were the happiest in his life – spent wandering across the Greek world from one philosophical school to another, sitting at the feet of the greatest thinkers, scholars and rhetoricians of the day; reading, arguing, discussing, disputing. First he was in Constantinople; from there he returned to Nicomedia, but not to old Eusebius. The name that attracted him now – significantly enough – was that of Libanius, a celebrated philosopher who had firmly rejected Christianity and all it stood for and remained a proud and self-confessed pagan. By this time the direction of Julian's own sympathies may have been suspected: when one of his former Christian teachers forced him to swear a solemn oath that he would not attend Libanius's lectures, he had them taken down and copied at his own expense. After some time at Nicomedia he passed on to Pergamum, thence to Ephesus and finally to Athens. It seems to have been while he was at Ephesus that he made his decision to renounce Christianity for ever and to transfer his allegiance to the pagan gods of antiquity; but the process was a gradual one, to which it is impossible to ascribe a precise date. In any case he had no choice, in his exposed position, but to keep his new faith a secret; it was to be another ten years before he was able to avow it openly.

Julian arrived at Athens in the early summer of 355. He had not been there long before he caught the eye of a fellow-student. 'It seemed to me,' wrote St Gregory Nazianzen later,

... that there was no evidence of a sound character in that oddly disjointed neck, those hunched and twitching shoulders, that wild, darting eye, that swaying walk, that haughty way of breathing down that prominent nose, those ridiculous facial expressions, that nervous and uncontrolled laughter, that ever-nodding head and that halting speech.[1]

As one of the Empire's leading Christian theologians, Gregory was admittedly *parti pris*; the portrait he paints is hardly an attractive one. And yet, despite its obvious exaggerations, it still has a somehow authen-

1 St Gregory Nazianzen, *Orations*, V, 23.

tic ring, and it is at least partly corroborated by other descriptions that
have come down to us. Julian was obviously not a handsome man.
Burly and stocky, he did indeed hold his head at a curious angle; he had
fine, dark eyes under straight brows, but their effect was spoiled by the
overlarge mouth and sagging lower lip. In manner – not surprisingly in
one who had grown up without a single friend of his own age – he was
awkward, uncertain and quite painfully shy: not the sort of material, in
short, of which Emperors are made. But then he had no ambitions in that
direction. He asked no more than to be allowed to remain at Athens,
with his teachers and his books; and, when the call came to present
himself before Constantius at Milan, he himself tells us how he prayed
to Athena to bring him death rather than allow him to set forth on so
fateful a journey.

But his prayers went unanswered; the Emperor's command could not
be disobeyed. On Julian's arrival at Milan the situation proved to be just
as he had feared. After an agonizing wait of several days, he was duly
received by Constantius – the two had met only once before, some seven
or eight years previously at Macellum – and informed that he was
henceforth a Caesar. His hair was trimmed short, his scholar's beard
shaved, his ungainly body squeezed into a tight-fitting military uniform;
and on 6 November he received his formal acclamation from the assembled
troops. As he acknowledged their doubtless somewhat perfunctory
cheers, he – and they – could hardly have failed to remember the unfortunate Gallus, acclaimed in similar fashion not five years before and
already twelve months in his grave. The Emperor's words, as he presented the new Caesar to the legions, were nothing if not affectionate; but
Julian knew that, if he were to avoid the fate of his half-brother, he
would have to tread warily indeed; and the interminable panegyric which
he composed at this time in praise of Constantius leaves us in no doubt
that he intended to do so.

There has long been a tradition – initiated, in fact, by Julian himself – to
the effect that when he was sent into Gaul as Caesar in the late autumn
of 355 it was as little more than a figurehead: that, as Libanius was later
to put it in his funeral oration, 'he had authority to do nothing save to
wear the uniform'. There were even suggestions that he was being deliberately sent by Constantius to almost certain death. All this was, of
course, nonsense. The Emperor could boast a formidable record of family
murders already; had he seriously wished to eliminate Julian – who, as a
wandering scholar, had presented no conceivable threat to his security –

he would have found a far quicker and surer way of doing so. (And he would hardly have given Julian the hand of his sister Helena in marriage, as he also did at this time.) Besides, the need for a Caesar in the West was genuine and undeniable. The truth seems to be that Julian, on assuming what he had expected to be the unfettered command of the army in Gaul, was piqued to discover that both the Praetorian Prefect and the *magister equitum* – the civil and military commanders respectively – were directly responsible to Constantius himself. Here, he believed, was a deliberate attempt on the part of the Emperor to diminish his authority. The thought that he was not yet twenty-four and totally without experience in the field does not seem to have struck him.

But he learned fast. It was he, rather than his cautious generals, who led the whirlwind campaign in the summer of 356 that took his army from Vienne to Autun, Troyes and Rheims and thence to Metz, through the Vosges to Coblenz and finally to Cologne – which had been taken by the Franks ten months before and which he now recaptured for the Empire. The following year saw a still greater triumph near Strasbourg, in which 13,000 legionaries smashed a Frankish enemy of 30,000 or more, leaving some 6,000 dead on the field at a cost of just 247 of their own men. The next two years brought still further victories. By the end of the decade the imperial rule had been re-established for the whole length of the frontier, with Julian himself now settled in Paris and, finally, in undisputed control.

In the East, on the other hand – to which Constantius, after a brief visit to Rome, had long since returned – the situation was a good deal less happy. In 359 the Emperor had received a letter from the Persian King:

Shapur, King of Kings, brother of the Sun and Moon, sends salutation . . .

Your own authors are witness that the entire territory within the river Strymon[1] and the borders of Macedon was once held by my forefathers; were I to require you to restore all this, it would not ill become me . . . but because I take delight in moderation I shall be content to receive Mesopotamia and Armenia, which was fraudulently extorted from my grandfather . . .

I give you warning that if my ambassador returns empty-handed I shall take the field against you, with all my armies, as soon as the winter is past.

Constantius had no intention of surrendering any of the disputed territory to King Shapur. He was, however, fully aware that he now faced the greatest challenge of his reign, and in January 360 sent a tribune

1 The modern Struma.

to Paris demanding huge reinforcements for the army of the East: four auxiliary units formed of members of Gallic or Frankish tribes loyal to the Empire were to leave at once for Mesopotamia, while all other units were to make available 300 men each. By Caesar and soldiery alike, the imperial command was received with horror. Julian was faced with the prospect of losing, at a single stroke, well over half his army; he had moreover promised the Gallic detachments that they would never be sent to the East. They for their part knew that, if they allowed themselves to be marched away, they would be unlikely ever again to see their wives and families. These would be left destitute behind them, an easy prey for the barbarian bands who, finding the frontier almost unguarded, would once again come swarming into imperial territory.

We shall never know for certain just what took place in Paris during those fateful spring days. According to Julian's own account – in a letter which he wrote to the people of Athens late in the following year – he was determined that the Emperor's orders should be obeyed, however unwelcome they might be to him personally. He summoned all the units in question to Paris, told them the news and exhorted them to accept the inevitable, emphasizing the unprecedented opportunities and rich rewards that awaited them when victory was theirs and, in a further effort to reconcile them to their fate, promising that their families would be transported with them to the East at public expense. But the legionaries, their anger now further inflamed by the anonymous pamphlets that were being circulated from hand to hand, vilifying Constantius and declaring him unworthy of imperial office, would have none of it. By evening, Julian saw that he was faced no longer with disaffection but with open mutiny. Yet even then – he called upon all the gods to witness – he had no idea what was in his soldiers' minds. Were they planning to proclaim him as their Augustus, or to tear him to pieces?

Just about sunset, when Julian had retired to an upper chamber of the palace for some much-needed rest, a trembling chamberlain came to report that the army was marching on the palace. 'Then,' wrote Julian,

peering through a window, I prayed to Zeus. And as the shouting grew louder and the tumult spread to the palace itself I entreated the god to give me a sign; and he did so, bidding me cede to the will of the army and make no opposition against it. Yet even then I did not yield without reluctance but resisted as long as I could, refusing to accept either the acclamation or the diadem. But since I alone could not control so many, and since moreover the gods, whose will it was, sapped my resolution, somewhere about the third hour some soldier or other gave me the collar;[1] and I put it on my head and returned to the palace – lamenting, as the gods knew, in my heart.

Does Julian, perhaps, protest a little too much? There is no evidence that he conspired against Constantius, nor that he would ever have wavered in his loyalty if that fateful order for reinforcements had not ultimately made loyalty impossible. But his four and a half years in Gaul had taught him courage and confidence and had given him, for the first time, political ambitions. By now, too, he seems to have believed himself divinely appointed to restore the old religion to the Empire; and it seems unlikely to say the least that, once he had received – or thought he had received – the sign from Zeus, he should have continued to show much reluctance to accept the diadem.

The only difficulty was that no diadem existed. Ammianus Marcellinus – a member of the imperial bodyguard, who was almost certainly in Paris at the time and was probably an eye-witness of much of what took place – writes that the soldiers first proposed to crown Julian with his wife's necklace; when he objected that female adornments would be unsuitable for such a purpose they suggested the frontlet of a horse, but once again he demurred. At last one of the standard-bearers tore the great gold chain from his neck – an emblem of his office – and placed it on Julian's head.

The challenge, unwilling or not, had been flung down. The die was cast. There could be no going back.

Julian was in no hurry to march to the East. The distance involved was immense, and he was far from certain of the loyalties of the many imperial garrisons stationed along the road. If they were to maintain their allegiance to Constantius, he might well find his way blocked – and, quite possibly, his retreat as well. He preferred to bide his time, to send ambassadors to his cousin informing him of what had occurred and suggesting some kind of accommodation between them.

The envoys found Constantius at Caesarea (now Kaiseri) in Cappadocia – ironically enough, on that very estate of Macellum where he had kept the adolescent Julian six years a prisoner. On receiving the messsage he flew into so furious a rage that they at first feared for their lives. For the moment, tied down as he was in the East, all he could do openly was to send Julian a stern warning; in secret, however, he began encouraging the barbarian tribes to renew their offensive along the

1 See below.

Rhine. That way he might at least tie his rival down and prevent him from any eastward advance. In the short term this plan proved moderately successful, and for much of the remainder of the year Julian found himself fully occupied on the frontier. Then in late October he moved south to Vienne, where on 6 November he celebrated the fifth anniversary of his inauguration as Caesar – wearing, Ammianus tells us, 'a splendid diadem inlaid with precious stones, though when first entering on his power he had worn but a paltry-looking crown like that of a president of the public games'.

The coming of spring saw more trouble on the Rhine, put down only after a somewhat discreditable episode in which the chieftain of the Alemanni was invited to dinner by the local Roman commander and – almost certainly on Julian's orders – arrested as soon as he crossed his host's threshold. But by then it had become clear that negotiations between the two Emperors were getting nowhere and that Constantius, taking advantage of a lull in the Persian campaign, was preparing an all-out offensive against his cousin. Julian, we read, was still profoundly uncertain about how best to react: whether to meet him half-way, securing as best he could the allegiance of the troops stationed along the Danube, or whether to wait for him in Gaul, on his own home ground, where he could be sure of his troops. Once again he prayed to the gods for a sign; and once again, we are told, it was vouchsafed to him. Pausing only to make a ritual sacrifice of a bull to Bellona, goddess of war, he assembled his army at Vienne and set out for the East.

Now the Rhine could not be left entirely undefended; moreover, if the whole story about the refusal of the Gallic troops to leave their homeland were not a complete fabrication, there must have been several units reluctant to follow their Emperor on this new expedition. Julian thus had only some 23,000 fighting men on whom to rely – pitifully few in comparison with the number that Constantius could be expected to hurl against him. To conceal this disparity and to make his strength appear greater than it actually was, he therefore broke up his army into three. Ten thousand were to cross the Alps into North Italy and make their way through modern Croatia; a similar number were simultaneously to march through Raetia and Noricum, an area roughly corresponding to Switzerland and the Tyrol. Finally, a select group of 3,000 under Julian himself were to head through the southern part of the Black Forest to the upper Danube in the neighbourhood of Ulm, there to embark on river boats and sail downstream. All three columns were to meet at Sirmium on the river Sava, some twenty miles to the west of Belgrade.

Not surprisingly, Julian's detachment arrived first; the impatient Emperor decided against waiting and pressed on to the south, pausing only when he reached Naissus, where he had decided to pass the winter and consolidate. He had been there only three or four weeks when messengers arrived from the capital: Constantius was dead. He, Julian, had already been acclaimed Emperor by the massed armies of the East. The struggle for power was over, almost before it had begun.

Constantius, the messengers reported, had been at Hierapolis (the modern Mambij, in northern Syria) when he had – most unwillingly – taken the decision to march against his rival. He had retraced his steps as far as Antioch, and had just set out on the 700 miles to Constantinople when he had come upon a headless corpse by the roadside, which he immediately took for an evil omen. By the time he reached Tarsus he was stricken by a low fever, but he refused to stop and dragged himself on a mile or two to the little village of Mopsucrenae. There it became clear that he could go no further; and there, on 3 November 361, he died. Until that last illness he had always enjoyed perfect health. He was forty-four years old.

To Julian, this was yet another proof that the gods were working on his behalf. Neither then nor later, however, did he show any sign of relief or jubilation. He hastened on to Constantinople, in order to be present when the body of his predecessor reached the capital. On the day of its arrival he himself, dressed in the deep mourning that he had ordered for the whole city, was on the quayside to supervise the unloading of the coffin. Later he led the funeral procession to the Church of the Holy Apostles, weeping unashamedly – and, as far as we can tell, genuinely – as his father's murderer and his own life-long enemy was laid to rest. Only after the ceremony was over did he assume the attributes of Empire.

And he never entered a Christian church again.

Within days of Julian's accession to the imperial throne, it was plain to all in Constantinople that the new regime was going to provide a marked contrast to the old. A military tribunal was established at Chalcedon across the Bosphorus to try certain of Constantius's chief ministers and advisers whom the new Emperor suspected of having abused their powers. Some were acquitted, others let off with periods of banishment or forced residence; but several were condemned to death – including two, the sinisterly named Paul the Chain and his collaborator Apodemius, joint chiefs of Constantius's detested intelligence network, who were sentenced to be buried alive. More deserving of sympathy was Ursulus, who had served Julian with distinction in Gaul as his minister of finance and who, though subsequently transferred to the East, had never shown him the slightest disloyalty. Some years before, however, at the siege of Amida in Upper Mesopotamia, he had unwisely cast aspersions on the Empire's military efficiency; and the eastern generals had never forgiven him. Julian had taken care not to be a member of the tribunal himself; as Emperor, however, he could easily have intervened to save his old friend. It was a disappointment to many of his admirers that he did not do so.

In the Palace itself, the new broom was even more dramatically apparent. Ever since the days of Diocletian, the Emperor had been growing more and more of a being apart, separated from his subjects by a court increasingly rigid with ceremonial, approachable only by his senior ministers – in the intervals between their successive prostrations – and surrounded by whole regiments of domestics whose numbers increased with every passing year. As Libanius was later to claim in his funeral oration on Julian:

There were a thousand cooks, as many barbers, and even more butlers. There were swarms of lackeys, the eunuchs were more in number than flies around the flocks in spring, and a multitude of drones of every sort and kind. There was one refuge for such idle gluttons, to have the name and title of being one of the Emperor's household, and in very quick time a piece of gold would ensure their enrolment.[1]

The purge that followed Julian's arrival was swift and thorough. Literally thousands of chamberlains and major-domos, of grooms and barbers and bodyguards, were summarily dismissed without compensation, until the Emperor was left with only the skeleton staff required to meet his own needs – those of a single man (for his wife Helena was by now dead), ascetic and celibate, to whom food and drink were of little interest and creature comforts of none.

Similarly radical reforms were made in the government and administration – usually in the direction of the old republican traditions. There was, for example, a significant increase in the power of the Senate, which Julian henceforth made a point of attending regularly and in person, travelling there on foot as a sign of respect. The taxation system was tightened up and rationalized; so too were the imperial communications, and in particular the *cursus publicus*, which ensured the proper provision of horses, mules and oxen for the transport of government servants

1 Oration XVIII, 130.

travelling on duty and for the carriage of official freight. Once famous for its efficiency, this organization had been allowed by Constantius to fall into the hands of unscrupulous agents whose animals were often so overworked and undernourished that, so Libanius tells us, 'most of them dropped down dead as soon as they were unhitched – or even before, while they were still in the traces'.[1]

But these measures were of the kind that any strong ruler might enforce on succeeding a weak and corrupt regime. Where Julian stands alone among all the Emperors of Byzantium is in his convinced and dedicated paganism. During his years as Caesar, he had been obliged to pay lip-service to the Christian faith: as late as April 361 we find him attending Easter mass at Vienne. But his inner rejection of that faith had long been an open secret, and from the moment that the news was brought to him at Naissus of Constantius's death he made no more pretence. It was as a professed pagan that he attended his predecessor's funeral in the Church of the Holy Apostles, and as a pagan that he settled down, after much divine consultation, to frame the laws which, he was convinced, would ultimately eliminate Christianity and re-establish the worship of the ancient gods throughout the Roman Empire.

There would, he believed, be no need for persecution. Persecution meant martyrs, and martyrs always seemed to have a tonic effect on the Christian Church. The first thing to do was to repeal the decrees by which pagan temples had been closed, their property confiscated and their sacrifices declared illegal. Then, in the ensuing atmosphere of complete religious toleration, an amnesty would be proclaimed for all those orthodox Christian churchmen whom the pro-Arian government of Constantius had sent into exile. Orthodox and Arian would soon be at each other's throats again, of that he was sure – for, as Ammianus notes, 'he had found by experience that no wild beasts are so hostile to men as are Christian sects in general to one another'.[2] After that it would be only a question of time before the Christians saw the error of their ways and embraced once again the old faith that they should never have left.

Such reasoning, over-simplified though it may be, must seem to modern minds quite impossibly naïve. Julian was, however, that unique combination – a Roman Emperor, a Greek philosopher and a mystic. As an Emperor, he knew that his Empire was sick. It no longer functioned as it had in the golden age of the Antonines two centuries before. The army had lost much of its old invincibility and was now, more often

1 Oration XVIII, 143.
2 Ammianus Marcellinus, XXII, v, 4.

than not, barely able to keep the peace along the frontier. The government was inefficient, plagued by pluralism and corruption. The old Roman virtues of reason and duty, honour and integrity were gone. The Emperors themselves, his immediate predecessors, had been sensualists and sybarites, living in an unreal world of fantasy and self-indulgence; still capable, perhaps, of leading their forces into battle when absolutely necessary but happier by far to recline in their palaces, surrounded by their women and their eunuchs.

All this, clearly, was the result of moral degradation. As a philosopher, however, Julian was not prepared to leave it at that. He was determined to discover the cause of the decline; and, because he was a deeply religious man living in an age in which men instinctively sought spiritual solutions to worldly problems, he concluded that this all-important question could be answered in a single word: Christianity. Here, as he saw it, was a faith that rode roughshod over the old virtues, emphasizing instead such effete, feminine qualities as gentleness, meekness and the turning of the other cheek. Worse still, it preached the disastrous creed of free and easy absolution. In a curious little composition entitled *The Caesars*, composed for the Saturnalia of December 362, Julian makes his views clear enough – picturing Jesus (who has taken up his abode with Incontinence) 'crying aloud to all comers: "Let every seducer, every murderer, every man guilty of sacrilege, every scoundrel, come unto me without fear. For with this water will I wash him and straightway make him clean. And though he should be guilty of those same sins a second time, let him but smite his breast and beat his head and I will make him clean again."'

In a word, Christianity had emasculated the Empire, robbing it of its strength and its manhood and substituting a moral fecklessness whose effects were everywhere apparent. Comparisons with other places and periods are always dangerous; yet to say that Julian looked on the Christians of the fourth century in something of the same light as a conservative of the old school might have looked on the hippies and Flower Power people in the 1960s might not be too wide of the mark.

Conservatives of the old school, however, are not normally mystics. Julian was. Dearly as he loved philosophical and theological debate, his approach to religion was always emotional rather than intellectual. Seldom during his short reign did he miss an opportunity of publicizing his views – shocking many of his subjects, pagan as well as Christian, by descending to the market place to give public lectures and firing off long, impassioned treatises and tracts in refutation of those contemporary thinkers whom he thought wrong-headed. When he took up his pen, he worked furiously, frenziedly and at almost unbelievable speed. The 17,000 words of his *Hymn to Cybele* were, he tells us, written in a single night. Unfortunately, it reads like it. Julian's style is diffuse, undisciplined and oddly self-indulgent – all those faults that he most deplored and that were most conspicuously absent from his daily life: a style that might have found favour among some of the woollier of the neo-platonists whom he admired, but that would have cut little ice with Socrates or Aristotle. No matter. He wrote, as he earnestly believed, under divine guidance. The gods were always with him, inspiring his tongue, directing his pen, for ever ready with a sign of encouragement or warning to lead him in the path of righteousness and truth. Never, one suspects, never for a single second, did he bethink himself that he might be wrong, or that the old religion might not, after all, prevail.

It appeared, on the other hand, in no great hurry to do so. In the summer of 362 Julian transferred his capital to Antioch, in preparation for the Persian expedition that he was preparing for the following year; and as he marched through the heartland of Asia Minor – covering the 700 miles in something under six weeks – he was concerned to note that the Christian communities, having overcome their initial fears that the Emperor might institute a new wave of persecutions, had settled down as before and were showing no sign whatever of tearing each other to bits; nor were the pagans – who represented an almost infinite variety of beliefs, from the primitive animism of the peasantry to the arcane mysteries evolved by the neo-platonist intellectuals – noticeably stronger or more cohesive than in Constantine's day. (The overwhelming majority of them probably practised no religion at all, or did so more out of respect for tradition than any real spiritual conviction.) In vain did Julian journey from temple to temple, personally officiating at one sacrifice after another until he was nicknamed 'the butcher' by his subjects. In vain did he try to impose upon his fellow-pagans an organized priesthood with its own hierarchy on the Christian model, urging them to establish hospitals and orphanages, even monasteries and convents, in order, as it were, to beat the Christians at their own game. The prevailing apathy was unshakeable. Ruefully, Julian himself told the local citizens the story of his visit to the great festival of Apollo, held annually at Daphne, the rich residential suburb of Antioch:

I hurried there from the temple of Zeus Kasios, believing that at Daphne if anywhere I should enjoy the sight of your wealth and public spirit. And, like a man seeing visions in a dream, I pictured to myself what a procession it would be – the beasts for the sacrifice, the libations, the choruses in honour of the god, the incense, and the youth of your city gathered about the sacred precinct, their souls dressed in reverence and they themselves clothed in white raiment. But when I entered the shrine I found neither incense, nor barley-cake, nor a single beast for sacrifice ... And when I enquired what sacrifice the city proposed to offer to celebrate the annual festival of the god, the priest answered: 'I have brought from my own house a goose as an offering, but the city has so far made no preparations.'[1]

If the pagans could not be galvanized into life, there was no alternative but to increase the pressure on the Christians; and on 17 June 362 Julian published an edict which, innocuous though it appeared at first sight, struck a body-blow at the Christian faith. For any schoolteacher, it declared, the first and most important requirement was an irreproachable moral character. In consequence, no teacher would henceforth be permitted to follow his calling without first obtaining the approval of his local city council and, through that, of the Emperor himself. In an explanatory circular Julian made it clear that in his view no Christian who professed to teach the classical authors – who in those days occupied virtually all the school curriculum – could possibly be of the required moral standard, since he would be teaching subjects in which he did not himself believe. He must consequently abjure either his livelihood or his faith.

This edict has been denounced by Christian writers down the ages as the most heinous of Julian's crimes against the Church. Even in his own day, the pagan Ammianus Marcellinus considered that it 'deserved to be buried in eternal silence'. Its effects, moreover, were felt far beyond the academic world. Christian demonstrations were held in protest, and there were riots when, on discovering that the temple of Apollo at Daphne had been defiled by the burial within its precincts of a Christian martyr (ironically enough, at the command of Julian's own brother Gallus), the Emperor ordered its exhumation and removal. On this latter occasion, several of the demonstrators were arrested. They were later released, though only after at least one of them had been put to the torture; but on 26 October the whole temple was burnt to the ground. Julian retaliated by closing down the Great Church of Antioch, confiscating all its gold plate.

Tension was now rising fast. Further incidents followed and, as the situation began to escalate, more than one hot-blooded young Christian

1 *Misopogon*, 361–2.

courted – and achieved – martyrdom. There were, to be sure, no out-and-out persecutions of the kind that had been seen under Decius or Diocletian; but Julian – whose emotional stability was a good deal more uncertain than either of theirs – would have been fully capable of instituting such persecutions had he thought them necessary. It was a blessed day indeed for the Christians when, on 5 March 363, he set off for the East at the head of some 90,000 men, never to return alive.

There was nothing new about the war with Persia. The two vast Empires had been fighting along their common frontier – with occasional deep inroads into each other's territories – for the best part of two and a half centuries. In 298 Galerius's victory over King Narses had theoretically ensured forty years of peace; but in 363 Narses's second successor, Shapur II, had decided to take his revenge. Shapur was at the time fifty-four years old, and had occupied the Persian throne for the same period – technically, indeed, a little longer, since he is perhaps the only monarch in all history to have been crowned *in utero*. The quotation from Gibbon is irresistible:

The wife of Hormouz remained pregnant at the time of her husband's death, and the uncertainty of the sex, as well as of the event, excited the ambitious hopes of the princes of the house of Sassan. The apprehensions of civil war were at length removed by the positive assurance of the Magi that the widow of Hormouz had conceived, and would safely produce a son. Obedient to the voice of superstition, the Persians prepared, without delay, the ceremony of his coronation. A royal bed, on which the queen lay in state, was exhibited in the midst of the palace; the diadem was placed on the spot which might be supposed to conceal the future heir of Artaxerxes, and the prostrate satraps adored the majesty of their invisible and insensible sovereign.

It had been fortunate for Constantius that for much of the 350s, when he had been busy in Gaul with the revolt of Magnentius and its aftermath, Shapur too had been occupied elsewhere. For the rest of his reign, however, both before and after that period, the Persian King had caused him almost constant anxiety. The climax came in 359 when, after a prolonged siege, Shapur captured the key fortress of Amida – the present Turkish city of Diyarbekir, which controlled both the headwaters of the Tigris and the approaches to Asia Minor from the East – and went on from there to build up a dangerously strong position in Upper Mesopotamia. By now, therefore, a major Roman offensive was essential if the situation were not to get seriously out of hand; and Julian – conscious as he was of following in the footsteps of Pompey, Trajan and Septimius Severus and even, there is reason to suspect, believing that he might be the reincarnation of Alexander the Great himself – was impatient to achieve similar glory.

His road ran first of all due east, by way of Beroea – the modern Aleppo – where he slaughtered a white bull on the acropolis as a tribute to Zeus. At Hieropolis he wheeled slightly to the north, crossing the Euphrates and the present Syrian-Turkish frontier – possibly to perform a further sacrifice at the great temple of the Moon at Carrhae, now Harran. From here he followed the flow of the rivers: first the Belikh as far as Raqqa and then the Euphrates itself to the point, just south of Baghdad, where it comes to within some thirty miles of the Tigris and where the army was able to take one of the several minor waterways linking the two. Thus, after a few minor sieges and skirmishes but no real difficulties, Julian found himself on the west bank of the Tigris, gazing up at the walls of Ctesiphon,[1] the Persian capital.

On the opposite shore, however, occupying the land between those walls and the river, was a Persian army, already drawn up and ready for battle; and the Roman generals were concerned to note that it numbered, besides the normal cavalry, a quantity of elephants – always a powerful weapon, not just because their men had no experience of dealing with them but because their smell terrified the horses to the point of panic. None the less, Julian gave the order to advance across the river. The first attempt to land on the further bank was repulsed; but the second, with the whole weight of the army behind it, succeeded and battle was joined. It ended – to the surprise of many on both sides – in an overwhelming victory for Roman arms. According to Ammianus, who was there and who took part in the fighting, 2,500 Persians were killed at the cost of a mere seventy Roman lives.

The date was 29 May; already by the next day, however, suddenly and without warning, the situation had changed. Doubt and uncertainty spread over the Roman camp. Within the space of a week, the siege of Ctesiphon was abandoned – almost before it had begun – and the army was thinking only of retreat. What had happened? There was much talk among Julian's apologists about Persian skulduggery, and it may well have been a trick of some kind that led him to order the burning of his considerable river fleet – though how much good this would have been to him on his return journey upstream is open to question. But the most

1 Now a most spectacular ruin, some twenty miles south-east of Baghdad.

97

likely explanation – and that given by Ammianus, who should know – is that the Emperor had at last been brought face to face with military realities: that Ctesiphon was virtually impregnable, and that Shapur's main army – larger by far than that which had just been defeated – was rapidly approaching. And there was another problem too: despite the recent victory, morale in the Roman army was dangerously low. Food was short, the Persians having pursued a scorched-earth policy for miles around; the rivers were all in flood, with the result that the men were floundering from one quagmire to the next; the heat was murderous; and the flies, Ammianus tells us, were so thick that they blotted out the light of the sun. Julian, he goes on, was still in favour of advancing further into Persian territory; but his generals refused. Even had they themselves been willing, they knew that they could never have persuaded their men to follow. On 16 June the retreat began.

Continually, remorselessly harried by the Persian cavalry, the army trudged back to the north-west along the left bank of the Tigris. Then, on 26 June, when it had reached a point a short distance downstream from Samarra, it suddenly came under heavy attack. Once again the dreaded elephants were brought into action, once again the air was thick with spears and arrows. Without pausing to strap on his breastplate, Julian plunged into the thick of the fray, shouting encouragement to his men as he fought in their midst; and just as the tide of battle was turning and the Persians were beginning to retreat, a flying spear struck him in the side. Trying to pull it out, he succeeded only in severing the sinews of his right hand; meanwhile, those nearest him lifted him from the ground where he had fallen and carried him to his tent. The spear was extracted from deep in his liver, but the damage was done. He died just before midnight.[1]

Julian was thirty-one at the time of his death, and had occupied the imperial throne for just nineteen and a half months. As an Emperor he was a failure. He was responsible for virtually no lasting legislation, he wasted his time and energy on a hopelessly quixotic attempt to revive an ill-defined and moribund religion, to the detriment of that which was to give the Empire its binding force for a thousand years to come; he made

1 According to legend, Julian scooped up a handful of the blood that was flowing from his wound and murmured the words *Vicisti Galilaee!* – 'Thou has conquered, Galilean!' He is said to have been killed by St Mercurius, one of the Christian army officers whom he had had executed, but whom the Virgin had temporarily resurrected for the purpose – a fact subsequently proved by his contemporary St Basil who, commanded in a dream to visit the martyr's tomb, there found the blood-stained lance.

himself thoroughly unpopular with his subjects, Christian and pagan alike, who hated his puritanism and his ceaseless sermonizing; and he came near to destroying the entire imperial army – as well as himself – in a campaign which, however brilliantly organized on the ground, ended in near catastrophe through want of clear-sighted forward planning and properly focused objectives.

And yet, of all the eighty-eight Emperors of Byzantium, it is Julian who, more than any other – not excepting the great Constantine himself – has caught the imagination of posterity, from Gregory Nazianzen in the fourth century to Gore Vidal in the twentieth. He has been depicted by medieval writers as a devil, a serpent, even as Antichrist; by those of the Renaissance as a tragic hero; by those of the eighteenth century as the archetypal philosopher-prince, the apostle of reason and enlightenment; and by the Romantics in their favourite guise of outsider and rebel – noble, courageous, but ultimately defeated. It is arguable that this last interpretation – even when, as has several times occurred, Julian's life is embellished with the love interest which in history it had so conspicuously lacked – comes nearest the truth.

The real tragedy of Julian lies not in his misguided policies or in his early death, but in the hairsbreadth by which he failed to achieve the greatness which he in so many ways deserved. Few monarchs have possessed his most outstanding qualities in such abundance: his intelligence, the depth of his education and culture; his energy and tireless industry; the courage and inspiring leadership that he invariably showed in battle; the utter integrity and incorruptibility of his public and private life; his apparent immunity to physical temptation of whatever kind; his astonishing ability to sublimate himself in the service of his Empire and, above all, of his gods. Sadly, however, he also possessed two faults, which together made any lasting achievement impossible. The first was his religious fanaticism, which warped his judgement and robbed him of that instinctive sense of priorities which is essential to any successful ruler; the second was a certain lack of sharpness and definition in his thinking. The latter trait, which is all too evident in his literary effusions and which was ultimately to sabotage the Persian expedition, may well derive from the former: Julian could on occasion be curiously indecisive. Again and again we find him asking the gods for guidance, when he should have been taking decisions for himself. On the other hand this very weakness gave him, once he had resolved upon his actions, a quite extraordinary self-confidence; and even when it was plain to all that a disastrous mistake had been made, his courage never deserted him.

Perhaps, had he lived, Julian would have overcome both these faults and proved himself one of the greatest of all the Roman Emperors. But he did not live. He died, in the most characteristic way he could have died, bravely but unnecessarily, leaving the world with nothing but the ineffaceable memory of a marvellous, misguided young visionary who attempted to change the world and failed, his talents and high qualities betrayed, his promise unfulfilled.

5
The Empire at Bay

[363-95]

He who has tasted of the Fountain of living water, what else can he desire? What kingdoms? What powers? What riches? Perceiving how miserable even in this world is the condition of kings, how mutable the imperial state, how short the span of this life, what slavery sovereigns themselves endure, seeing that they live not according to their own will but by the will of others.

St Ambrose, *Epistles*, xxix, 18

Finding itself on Julian's death not only without an Emperor but also – still more important at so critical a moment – without a leader, the Roman army assembled *en masse* early the following morning to nominate his successor. Their first choice was Sallustius Secundus, the Praetorian Prefect of the East, but he declined absolutely, pleading age and infirmity. Then what seems to have been a relatively small group of soldiers started shouting the name of Jovian, the commander of the imperial guard. Jovian was thirty-two, a bluff, genial soldier, popular with his men; he was also, perhaps significantly, a Christian – a persuasion which in no way diminished his well-known *penchant* for wine and women. But he was in no sense distinguished, and certainly not of imperial calibre. Why therefore he should have been proposed remains a mystery; and more surprising still is the fact that the cry should then have been taken up by the entire Roman army – so surprising, indeed, that Ammianus Marcellinus (who was, once again, almost certainly an eye-witness) maintains that the whole thing was a mistake and that most of those present understood the cry to be not '*Jovianus!*' but '*Julianus!*' and concluded that their former Emperor had unexpectedly recovered and resumed his rank and title. It was only when the tall, prematurely stooping figure of Jovian was paraded before them that 'they realized what had happened, and gave themselves up to tears and lamentations'.

And so, under a new and deeply uninspiring leader, the sad and weary retreat continued along the east bank of the Tigris, still under constant harassment from the Persians, who had been informed by a deserter of Julian's death and hoped to take advantage of any consequent confusion. Within a few days, however, it was noted that they were avoiding pitched battles; and at the beginning of July, after the Roman army had succeeded in making a forced crossing of the river despite all that he could do to prevent it, Shapur decided to offer terms. These were humiliating in the extreme, but Jovian accepted them. The resulting treaty provided for thirty years of peace, together with the restitution to Persia of five frontier provinces conquered by Diocletian and of eighteen important fortresses – including the two key strongholds of Nisibis (Nusaybin) and Singara (Sinjar). Further, the Romans bound themselves not to assist King Arsaces of Armenia against Persian attack – a promise tantamount to renouncing all their claims over that country.

Jovian had made a disastrous beginning to his reign. 'We should have fought ten battles,' explodes Ammianus, 'rather than give up a single one of those fortresses'; and there must have been many in the army who enthusiastically agreed with him. He goes on to suggest that, since the negotiations had taken place only a hundred miles from Roman territory, the army could easily have fought its way to safety without this wholesale capitulation, and that Jovian was interested only in getting home as soon as possible, in order to consolidate his hold upon the throne. Whether this charge is justified or not – and it is only fair to point out in his defence that a hundred miles through desert terrain is a long way for an army under constant attack and already running dangerously short of food – one could argue that Jovian, in return for all that he had conceded, might at least have been entitled to ask the Persian King for provisions enough to see his men safely back into imperial territory; but his requests, if they were ever made, were refused. During the next section of the march, which led the army westward from the Tigris through Hatra to Nisibis, they had to pass through seventy miles of merciless desert, during which they were forced to kill all their camels and pack-mules; even then, they barely survived. When they finally reached Nisibis, the Emperor refused to enter a city which he had just surrendered, preferring to pitch his camp outside the walls; and the following day, on the arrival of a representative of Shapur to hoist the Persian standard, he ordered a mass evacuation of the populace, so that not a single citizen should be left to receive the conquerors. In vain the inhabitants begged to be allowed to remain, and to defend their city on their own account; Jovian would not break his bond. Ammianus paints an affecting picture of the scene:

The whole city was a place of mourning and lamentation, and in every quarter nothing was heard but one universal wail, matrons tearing their hair when about to be driven from the homes in which they had been born and brought up, the mother who had lost her children, or the wife the husband, about to be torn from the place rendered sacred by their shades, clinging to their doorposts, embracing their thresholds and pouring forth floods of tears.

Every road was crowded, with everyone straggling away as best they could. Many, too, loaded themselves with as much of their property as they thought that they could carry, while leaving behind them abundant and costly furniture, which they could not remove for want of beasts of burden.

At Nisibis Julian's embalmed body – which had been carried by the soldiers all the way from the place where he fell – was entrusted to his old friend and remote kinsman Procopius – whom some said that he had secretly appointed to succeed him – for burial at Tarsus, where he had intended to establish his court after his victorious return. As for Jovian, he led the army on to Antioch, the holy *labarum* being borne once again before it as in the days of Constantine and his sons. On his arrival there he immediately issued an edict of general religious toleration, restoring full rights and privileges to the Christians throughout the Empire. That his own sympathies lay with the orthodox Nicene faith, rather than with the Arians formerly favoured by Constantius, was made abundantly clear by the deep reverence which he showed to old Athanasius of Alexandria – now restored to the see from which Julian had removed him – who had travelled at once to Antioch to congratulate the new Emperor on his accession. Doubtless encouraged by the assurances of the splendid old patriarch that his re-establishment of the true faith would be rewarded by a long and peaceful reign, Jovian left Antioch in mid-October, moving with his army in easy stages through Anatolia. He was acclaimed with obvious enthusiasm in all the towns (largely Christian) through which he passed; only at Ancyra – the modern Ankara – where on 1 January 364 he assumed the Consulship with his infant son Varronianus, did the deafening howls of the latter during the ceremony of induction lead the more credulous of those present, despite Athanasius's predications, to fear an evil omen.

As well they might have. A few days later, on 16 February 364 – by which time he had progressed as far as the little town of Dadastana, about half-way between Ancyra and Nicaea – he was found dead in his bedroom. 'By some,' writes Gibbon, his death 'was ascribed to the consequences of an indigestion, occasioned either by the quantity of the wine or the quality of the mushrooms which he had swallowed in the evening.

According to others, he was suffocated in his sleep by the vapour of charcoal, which extracted from the walls of the apartment the unwholesome moisture of the fresh plaster.' Surprisingly enough, foul play was not suspected.

The choice of Jovian as Emperor had marked the restitution of Christianity as the official religion of the Roman Empire, but it had also signalled something else: the end of a dynasty which had dominated it for more than half a century. The male line of Constantius Chlorus was now extinct; the diadem was once again a prize open to all. And there could be no clearer indication of this changed state of affairs than the virtual unanimity with which the army, some ten days after Jovian's death, acclaimed Valentinian as his successor. At first sight the new Emperor might have seemed still more unfitted to the purple. Uncouth of manner, almost illiterate and possessed of a furious and quite uncontrollable temper, he was the son of a Pannonian rope-maker who had himself risen from the ranks to positions of high authority in both Africa and Britain. Like his father before him, Valentinian made no attempt to conceal his peasant origins; but at forty-two he still boasted a magnificent physique and a commanding – some said forbidding – presence. He was a devout Christian and a superb soldier, though capable of unspeakable cruelty when the mood took him. When, after his acclamation, he was pressed to nominate a co-Augustus, he refused to be hurried: only after the army finally reached Constantinople on 28 March did he name – to the general dismay – his younger brother Valens.

It was a curious choice. Valens was an Arian and, in appearance, little short of grotesque – bandy-legged and pot-bellied, with a ferocious squint into the bargain. Seven years younger than his brother, he possessed none of his courage or toughness and very little of his ability, equalling him only in his reputation for brutality. He was, however, precisely what Valentinian wanted: a faithful lieutenant who freely acknowledged his brother's superiority and could be trusted to provoke no difficulties or quarrels. Valens, the Emperor rather surprisingly announced, would be responsible for the East while he, Valentinian, would rule the West from his capital at Milan.

Would he, one wonders, have reversed the two roles had he foreseen the crisis that his brother would have to face within a year of installing himself in Constantinople? Early in the spring of 365, a few days after he had left for Syria – where, in defiance of the treaty signed less than two years before, trouble was again brewing along the Persian frontier –

Valens was recalled with the news that Procopius, that distant cousin of the Emperor Julian who had been responsible for his burial arrangements, had raised the standard of revolt. Playing on the old loyalties to the house of Constantine – to which he claimed, rather unconvincingly, to belong – Procopius had quickly gained the support of the army in the capital; Thrace and Bithynia soon followed. Valens, panic-stricken, fled to Ancyra, his despair growing still deeper when he heard that no help could be expected from his brother, already fully extended with the barbarian tribes in Gaul. 'Procopius,' Valentinian had characteristically remarked as he turned down the appeal for assistance, 'is enemy only to my brother and myself; the Alemanni are the foes of the whole Roman world.'

Fortunately for the two emperors, however, the rebel soon over-reached himself, antagonizing several influential men who, having previously declared themselves in his favour, now transferred their support to Valens. Their example led to further widespread defections, and by the end of May the revolt was at an end. Procopius himself was captured at Philippopolis in Thrace – now Plovdiv – and decapitated, his severed head being dispatched as a trophy to Valentinian in Gaul. Meanwhile Valens instituted a programme of appalling retribution on all those whose loyalties had even briefly wavered, ordering throughout the affected provinces tortures and executions, burnings and banishments on such a scale as to earn for himself a degree of fear and hatred among his subjects that not even a twenty-five per cent reduction of taxes in the following year was altogether able to remove.

For the next decade we find the two Emperors almost constantly caught up in their respective struggles: Valens engaged first with the Gothic tribes along the Danubian frontier, building forts and establishing garrisons over its entire length, and then in 371 setting out on his long-delayed journey to the East, where Shapur had taken King Arsaces prisoner, driven him to suicide and reduced Armenia to the status of a Persian satellite; Valentinian dealing with the repeated incursions of the barbarians into Gaul and, after 367, faced with a serious upheaval in Britain, the result of invasions by the Picts and Scots. Being himself pinned down in Europe, he entrusted this latter crisis to a certain Theodosius, one of his finest generals, who moved in with spectacular success and left the island in 370 happier and more peaceful than it had been for a generation or more. Only three years later still could the Emperor leave Gaul in safety; almost immediately, however, new troubles broke out – this time with a normally quiet and law-abiding tribe, the Quadi, who lived just across the Danube from his own Pannonian homeland. Resenting the way in which imperial forts had been built on what they held to be their side of the river, and believing, moreover, that the Romans had been responsible for the recent murder of their King, they had invaded imperial territory in protest and laid waste a certain amount of land along the frontier. They had then sent an embassy to Valentinian, explaining why they had thus taken the law into their own hands and claiming that the real aggressors were the Romans themselves.

On the face of it, the Quadi seem to have had a case; but to Valentinian this was unpardonable presumption, an insult to Rome. The anger welled up within him as he listened, his normally rubicund face turning a deeper and deeper purple until he suddenly fell forward in a fit of apoplexy and died, at Bregetio in Valeria, on 17 November 375. In his eleven-year reign he had worked, as few Emperors had ever worked, for the good of the Empire and, above all, the integrity of its frontiers. As an orthodox Christian, he had shown tolerance for those who did not share his own strongly-held Nicene faith; he had, for example, refused to replace such Arian bishops as he found still in possession of their sees. As a ruler he had set up schools and medical services, and had dispensed justice with a fair, impartial hand; and if his punishments were often severe – even cruel – at least they were visited on the guilty and not the innocent. None the less, his harshness and austerity had won him little love from his subjects; and few of them were heartbroken to see him go.

Already as early as 367, after a serious illness during which he had worried greatly about the succession, Valentinian had persuaded his troops to recognize his seven-year-old son Gratian as his co-Augustus. As he lay on his deathbed, however, knowing that Gratian was far away at Trier and Valens a good deal further still at Antioch, he sent for his son by his second marriage, also called Valentinian and still only four, and had him proclaimed co-Emperor with his stepbrother. On his death, therefore, the Empire theoretically had three rulers to carry on the government; a malformed, middle-aged sadist utterly devoid of wisdom or judgement, a delightful boy of sixteen and a child scarcely out of its cradle. On those three the future of the Empire now depended, and at one of the most critical moments of its history; for only a year after Valentinian's death it found itself confronting a new wave of invaders, infinitely more formidable than any it had so far encountered: the Huns.

Nowadays we tend to think of all these barbarian tribes that swarmed southward and westward into Europe during the fourth and fifth centuries as being very much the same, but we are wrong: by the time of which we are speaking the Goths were a relatively civilized people, the majority of them Arian Christians. Although the western branch, the Visigoths, was still ruled by local chieftains, the Ostrogoths of the east had already evolved into a united and prosperous kingdom. The Huns, on the other hand, were savages – a vast, undisciplined, heathen horde, Mongolian in origin, who had swept down from the Central Asian steppe, destroying and laying waste everything in their path. In 376 they flung themselves on the Goths with unprecedented fury. King Ermanaric, after several courageous stands against them, finally took his own life; his successor was killed a short time later in yet another hopeless battle. The Ostrogoths' resistance was now at an end; and although one venerable old Visigothic chieftain, Athanaric, did his best to rally his people and withdrew, undefeated, to the mountains of Transylvania, the greater number sought permission from Valens to settle within the Empire, on the plains of Thrace.

Their request was granted, the Emperor giving express orders to his local representatives to provide the refugees with food and shelter while they established themselves in their new homes. Alas, his instructions were ignored: the local authorities, led by Lupicinus, Count of Thrace, saw in the new arrivals only opportunities for exploitation and extortion, robbing them of virtually everything that they possessed and reducing them to the brink of starvation. By the summer of 377 the settlers, now desperate, were driven to active resistance. Advancing *en masse* to Marcianople – the capital of the imperial province of Lower Moesia, some twenty miles inland from the modern port of Varna, in Bulgaria – they demanded to see Lupicinus, who refused to receive them. A day or two later he emerged with an army, intending to teach them a lesson; in fact he was soundly defeated, narrowly escaping with his life. Within days, all the Goths of Thrace were up in arms, to be joined by the Visigoths and even the Huns in a full-scale barbarian attack on the Roman Empire.

The war raged throughout the winter, despite the arrival of heavy reinforcements from both the eastern and the western Emperors. At last, in the spring of 378, Valens headed in person for the Balkans, encouraged by a promise from Gratian to come quickly to his aid. Having defeated a sizeable Gothic force on the Maritsa river to the north-west of Adrianople, he was advancing towards Philippopolis on his way to meet his nephew when news of an attempt to cut him off from his capital forced him to retire. Back again in Adrianople, he received word from Gratian asking him to delay any major confrontation until reinforcements could be sent; but these were still many miles away and the Gothic army, according to the most reliable information, was a small one – only some 10,000 men in all. His general, Sebastian, favoured an immediate attack, and Valens allowed himself to be persuaded. It was the greatest mistake of his life – and also the last. The battle that followed, fought on 9 August 378, was a *débâcle*. The Emperor was killed by an arrow, Sebastian and his second-in-command Trajan fell at his side, and two-thirds of the Roman army perished with them.

Everything now depended on Gratian, still only nineteen. Despite a magnificent victory that he had gained the previous February over yet another barbarian tribe, the Lentienses, at Argentaria in Alsace, he himself could not yet leave the West; instead, he turned to Theodosius, the son of that other Theodosius who had scored such signal successes in Britain ten years before. Sadly, in 376, the father had been disgraced and executed by Valens as the result of some court intrigue, since when his son had retired to the family estates in Spanish Galicia; now, however, he willingly responded to the Emperor's call, and within a few months had proved himself a leader of such distinction that, in January 379, Gratian raised him to be his co-Augustus. Establishing his headquarters at Thessalonica, he devoted the next two years to restoring order in Thrace and confidence among the Goths, vast numbers of whom were recruited into the legions.

None of this, to be sure, was achieved without sacrifice: the Goths were granted complete autonomy, exemption from taxation and an exceptionally high rate of pay for their military services, either as treaty-bound allies (*foederati*) or directly subordinate to the Emperor. This in turn meant increased financial burdens, and proportionately higher taxes for those ordinary citizens who were not exempt. It also led to continued resentment against the barbarians as a whole, and fears that the Germanic element in the army was now becoming dangerously strong. If, on the other hand, this was the price of retaining the Eastern Empire, Theodosius was happy enough to pay it. By the summer of 380, thanks to his quiet, patient diplomacy, the Goths were happily settled in their new homes and Thrace was once again at peace; on 24 November he made his formal entry into Constantinople, and on 11 January 381 welcomed old Athanaric to the capital, receiving him outside the walls and personally escorting him to his place of residence. The excitements of the

splendid city and the lavishness of the entertainment he received obviously proved too much for the old man, who died a fortnight later; but
he was given a sumptuous funeral, the Emperor himself accompanying
his body to the grave. Such consideration for their former leader deeply
gratified the Goths, disposing them still further towards a lasting reconciliation; the Romans, too, welcomed the new accord. 'Now that the
wounds of strife are healed,' declared the court orator Themistius,
'Rome's most courageous enemies will become her truest and most loyal
friends.'

Gratian's elevation of Theodosius to the supreme power was perhaps
the most lasting benefit that he conferred on the Empire. And yet, ironically, that very year – 383 – that saw the conclusion of the final peace
treaty with the Goths also witnessed the Emperor's downfall. Few had
ever shown greater promise. In the course of his short life, his piety and
purity of heart had never left him. As a fervent Nicene Christian, he had
been the first Emperor to refuse the title and insignia of *Pontifex
Maximus*; in Rome, he had swept away the altar and statue of Victory
that Julian had restored to the Senate House, and had expropriated the
immense wealth of the Temple of Vesta and its chosen virgins for the
benefit of the imperial treasury. But he had other interests besides religion. His tutor, Ausonius, proudly described him as possessing a *mens
aurea*, a golden mind: he was remarkably well read and, if reports are
true, a very passable poet. He was also a superb athlete and a magnificent
horseman, while his skill as a hunter was – according once again to
Ausonius – almost supernatural: he could kill a lion with a single arrow.
Finally, he remained all his life an inspired leader in the field. But, at the
age of twenty-four, he was already growing lazy. The pleasures of the
chase and the excitements of the amphitheatre were taking up more and
more of his time. More dangerous still, he no longer attempted to conceal
the predilection he felt for the barbarian element in the army (and particularly for his own personal guard of tall, blond Alani) whom he openly
favoured at the expense – and to the increasing resentment – of their
Roman colleagues. Matters came to a head when one of the imperial
generals serving in Britain, Magnus Clemens Maximus, was suddenly
acclaimed Augustus by his men; a few days later he landed in Gaul,
where his army met Gratian's just outside Paris. After some inconclusive
skirmishing the Emperor would probably have won the day had not his
Moorish cavalry suddenly and unexpectedly defected to Maximus. He

fled, but was taken prisoner soon afterwards at Lyons and there, on 25 August, was murdered while attending a banquet – under a promise of safe conduct – with his captors.

In Constantinople, Theodosius received the news with horror. For the moment, however, he was powerless. The Persian King Ardashir II – who had succeeded his brother Shapur four years before – had just been deposed in favour of his nephew Shapur III, an unknown quantity who needed watching; meanwhile the Huns were still causing trouble along the northern frontier. This was no time to embark on a long punitive expedition against Maximus. Reluctantly, Emperor acknowledged usurper – as did most of the provinces of the West.

Except Italy. Thither Gratian's co-Emperor Valentinian II, now twelve years old, hastily moved his court from Sirmium, and there in Milan he maintained, somewhat precariously, his authority – ruling largely through his Sicilian mother,[1] the redoubtable Justina, and under the guidance of the still more formidable Bishop Ambrose, who actually travelled to Trier in the winter of 383–4 in an attempt to reach an understanding with Maximus. The young Emperor's life cannot have been made happier by the machinations of his fanatically Arian mother, who feared the bishop's growing influence over her son and was forever intriguing against him; but Ambrose – who does not hesitate to compare her in his writings with Jezebel and Herodias – gave as good as he got, and out-manoeuvred her every time. His only failure was in his attempts to wean the boy from his mother's heretical persuasion; only after Justina's death was he eventually to persuade Valentinian to accept the Nicene faith, and by then it was too late: Maximus had been given the excuse he needed.

In 387 the pretender crossed the Alps into Italy, ostensibly to deliver the Empire from the taint of heresy. Justina and Valentinian fled, first to Aquileia and thence to Thessalonica, where Theodosius was able to join them. The past year had not been easy for the Emperor of the East. In January he had had to contend with serious disturbances at Antioch, where the populace had rioted in protest against a special tax laid upon the city in connection with his forthcoming *decennalia*, wrecked the public baths and smashed the statues of himself and his family. The local authorities had over-reacted, and the resulting massacre – graphically described, with its consequences, by St John Chrysostom, who was there – had

---

1 Zosimus (iv, 19, 43) claims that Justina had been the wife of the usurper Magnentius before her marriage to Valentinian: possible, but hardly likely.

included many women and children among its victims. It was Easter before order was restored by the Emperor's emissaries, and one of the proudest cities of Asia received the imperial pardon by which it regained its former rights and privileges. Then there had been the usual difficulties with the Persians. The new King had formally notified him of his accession by means of an embassy laden with magnificent presents – including, incidentally, elephants – but in subsequent diplomatic negotiations had showed that he could strike just as hard a bargain as his father. From the partition of Armenia that finally resulted in 387, the Empire emerged with only one-fifth of the country under its control, four-fifths having been appropriated by Shapur.

But peace, at least, had been assured. The long-planned expedition against Maximus was finally a possibility. Theodosius spent the winter at Thessalonica with Valentinian and Justina – now his mother-in-law, since his recent marriage *en secondes noces* to her daughter Galla[1] – actively preparing for war. Only in June 388 was he ready, with Valentinian, to march; but once started he moved fast, pressing up through the mountain passes of Macedonia and Bosnia (successfully foiling a plot to assassinate him on the way) and eventually meeting Maximus at Siscia – the modern Sisak – on the Sava. Despite the fatigue of their long march, his troops plunged, fully armed, into the river, swam to the opposite bank and put the rebels to flight. One or two more battles followed, but thenceforth the campaign was largely a matter of pursuit until Maximus was finally driven to surrender at Aquileia. Brought before Theodosius, he confessed to him that he had claimed to have his approval when he usurped the throne; and for a moment it looked as if the Emperor was about to spare the life of his old colleague. But the soldiers dragged their prisoner away before he could do so. They knew Theodosius's reputation for clemency, and preferred to take no chances.

Appointing the Frankish general Arbogast as *Comes* – and thus effective Governor – of Gaul, Theodosius and Valentinian spent the winter in Milan and in the following year moved on with the former's four-year-old son Honorius to Rome where, on 13 June 389, they made their solemn entry into the city. The senior Emperor's energetic efforts to weaken the hold of paganism cannot have endeared him to the local members of the old regime; but his easy approachability and charm of

---

1 Zosimus believes (iv, 44) that Theodosius was at first reluctant to take arms against Maximus, and agreed to do so only after Justina, knowing of his recent widowhood and his extreme susceptibility to attractive women, sent Galla to plead with him. The Emperor, he suggests, was not only persuaded but besotted: and Galla's efforts resulted not only in war but in marriage.

manner won him a personal popularity such as no predecessor of his had enjoyed for a century or more. The two Augusti then returned to Milan, remaining there all through the following year – the year of that famous confrontation between Theodosius and Ambrose for which both of them, perhaps unfairly, are best remembered.

The incident that set the two on a collision course was one at which neither was personally present: the murder, at Thessalonica, of the captain of the imperial garrison. For some years already, resentment had been building up among the citizens over the billeting of troops: Roman soldiers, they pointed out, had been bad enough in the past, but these new barbarian ones were a good deal worse. Flash-point was reached when the captain – himself a Goth, by the name of Botheric – ignoring all their protests, imprisoned the city's most popular charioteer on charges of gross immorality. Suddenly and, it seemed, spontaneously, the mob attacked the garrison headquarters, smashed their way into the building and cut down Botheric where he stood. When the incident was reported to Theodosius in Milan, he flew into an ungovernable rage. In vain Ambrose pleaded with him not to take vengeance on the many for the crimes of a few; he ordered the troops in the city to show it no mercy, and to reassert their authority in whatever way they saw fit. A short while afterwards he repented and countermanded the order, but too late. It had already been received, and the soldiers were only too eager to obey. They deliberately waited until the people were all gathered in the Hippodrome for the games; then, at a given signal, they fell on them with unbridled brutality. Seven thousand were dead by nightfall.

Reports of the massacre at Thessalonica spread rapidly through the Empire – losing, we may be sure, nothing in the telling. The disturbances at Antioch three years before had been insignificant in comparison. On that occasion, in any case, the responsibility had rested with the local authorities; this time the guilt fell on the Emperor himself – an Emperor, moreover, who had always enjoyed a reputation for humanity and justice. A crime on such a scale could not be overlooked; certainly, Ambrose was not the man to overlook it.

At this time, it must be remembered, Ambrose was the most influential churchman in Christendom – more so by far than the Pope in Rome, by reason not only of the greater importance of Milan as a political capital but also of his own background. Member of one of the most ancient Christian families of the Roman aristocracy, son of a Praetorian Prefect of Gaul and himself formerly a *consularis*, or governor, of Liguria and Aemilia, he had never intended to enter the priesthood; but on the death in 374 of the previous bishop, the Arian Auxentius, an acrimonious dispute had arisen between the orthodox and Arian factions in the city over which he, as governor, was obliged to arbitrate. Only when it finally emerged that he alone possessed sufficient prestige to make him equally acceptable to both parties did he reluctantly allow his name to go forward. In a single week he was successively a layman, catechumen, priest and bishop.

Once enthroned, Ambrose had started as he intended to go on, distributing his entire personal fortune among the poor and adopting an extreme asceticism in his private life. Since first hearing of the murder of Botheric he had done everything in his power to urge Theodosius towards moderation; when he saw that he had failed, he withdrew from the city rather than meet the Emperor and then wrote him a letter in his own hand, telling him that, despite his continuing high regard, he must regretfully withhold communion from him until he should perform public penance for his crime.

And Theodosius submitted – less, we may be sure, for reasons of political expediency than for those of genuine remorse. His handling of the affair had been not only unworthy of him; it had also been uncharacteristic. Almost certainly, he had allowed himself to be persuaded by his military entourage. At all events it seems to have been an immense relief to his spirit when, bare-headed and dressed in sackcloth, he presented himself in the cathedral of Milan to acknowledge his misdeeds and humbly beg forgiveness. But it was also something more. It was a turning-point in the history of Christendom – the first time that a minister of the Gospel had had the courage to assert the rights of the spiritual power over the temporal, and the first time that a Christian prince had publicly submitted to judgement, condemnation and punishment by an authority which he recognized as higher than his own.

Early in 391 the two Emperors left Milan – Theodosius to return to Constantinople, Valentinian to accept the transference of power in Gaul, where Arbogast the Frank had been ruling as *Comes* in his absence. On his arrival at Vienne, however, it soon became clear to him that Arbogast had no intention of handing over the reins as he was morally obliged to do. Instead, he was governing just as he always had, ignoring the Emperor completely and not even making a show of consulting him on important issues. Determined to assert his authority, Valentinian one day handed the Frank a written order, demanding his immediate resignation. Arbogast looked at it for a moment and then, slowly and contemptuously, tore it to pieces. At that moment war between the two was declared; and a few days later, on 15 May 392, the young Emperor, now just twenty-one, was found dead in his apartment. Much trouble was taken to suggest that his death was the result of suicide, and indeed foul play was never conclusively proved: Valentinian may well have taken his own life in the despairing knowledge that if he did not do so, someone else unquestionably would. Neither was murder hinted at by Ambrose in his subsequent funeral oration – unless some inference can be drawn from the bishop's assurances to the sorrowing princesses that their brother's soul had been carried up instantly to heaven, a reward not in theory accorded to those who had died by their own hand.[1]

Arbogast – a non-Roman and, incidentally, a pagan – knew that he could not assume the diadem himself; but he was perfectly content with the role of kingmaker. He therefore named his henchman Eugenius, a middle-aged Christian grammarian who had formerly served as head of the imperial chancery, as the new Augustus. Eugenius is unlikely to have had much appetite for the honour, but he was in no position to refuse. Ambassadors were dispatched to Theodosius, informing him of his brother-in-law's unfortunate demise and notifying him of the unanimous acclamation of Eugenius as his successor. But Theodosius would have none of it. The right of designating his fellow-Emperor belonged to him, and to him alone. Nine years before, receiving a similar embassy on behalf of Maximus, he had been forced to temporize (though he had dealt with Maximus later, all the same); this time he felt stronger, knowing that for the moment at any rate both his northern and eastern frontiers were secure. He sent an evasive reply and began to make his preparations.

All through the year 393 those preparations continued, while Arbogast succeeded, despite the vehement opposition of Ambrose, in having his protégé acclaimed in Italy also. For his principal support he relied on the pagan old guard in Rome and the other ancient cities; though they knew Eugenius to be a Christian, they were happy to welcome an Emperor who proclaimed universal toleration and who willingly permitted the re-erection of the ancient altars. By the middle of the year, Rome was undergoing a full-scale pagan revival. The sky above the newly restored temples was cloudy with the smoke of sacrifice, while in their dark recesses aged augurs peered anxiously into the entrails of the still-steaming victims. Garlanded processions once more threaded their way through the streets; matrons and maidens were terrorized as of old

1 Ambrose, *De Obitu Valentiniani; Opera*, Vol. vii.

by the frenzied devotees of the Floralia, Lupercalia and Saturnalia. Thus, when in the early summer of 394 Theodosius marched for the second time against an upstart pretender, he was aware that he was fighting not just for legitimacy but also for his faith. He was well equipped to do so since, apart from the Roman legionaries, his army contained some 20,000 Goths – many of them serving under their own chieftains, among whom there was included a brilliant young leader named Alaric. As second-in-command he had appointed a Vandal, Stilicho, who had recently married his niece Serena. But however sanguine he may have felt over the outcome of the campaign, his heart was heavy within him: on the eve of his departure his beloved second wife, Galla, had died, probably in childbirth. She had been the love of his life, and the few years they had spent together had been idyllically happy. Fortunately, they already had one child of their own, a daughter, whom they had called Galla Placidia and on whom he doted; we shall hear more of her as the story goes on.

The army of Arbogast and Eugenius was roughly similar in strength when it set out from Lombardy in late July. Eugenius in particular was troubled; for Ambrose, who had pointedly absented himself from Milan during the pseudo-Emperor's stay, had openly condemned him as a betrayer of his faith, ordering the local clergy to refuse communion to him and all his Christian followers. As they rode out of the city, Arbogast vowed that on his victorious return he would stable his horses in the basilica; and it may have been as much as a gesture of defiance as anything else that the army carried before it as it marched not the holy *labarum* of the Christian Emperor but a crude representation of Hercules Invictus.

The two forces met on 5 September a little north of Trieste, on the little tributary of the Isonzo known then as the Frigidus but now as the Wipbach or Vipacco. The first day ended in near-disaster, with the slaughter of at least half the Goths and the disorderly withdrawal of the remainder of the army; but the following morning began somewhat more auspiciously, with the arrival of a sizeable detachment whom Arbogast had sent to cut off the Emperor's retreat but who now declared themselves prepared, for a price, to transfer their loyalties. The battle was rejoined with a new optimism; and further confirmation of divine benevolence was afforded when a violent tempest blew up from the east, accompanied by winds of hurricane force. Theodosius and his men had these winds behind them; the soldiers of Arbogast and Eugenius, on the other hand, found themselves blinded by clouds of dust and battered with such violence that they could barely stand upright; the throwing of spears, even the loosing of arrows, was out of the question. The gods, it seemed, were against them after all. Exhausted and demoralized, they soon surrendered. Eugenius was beheaded as he grovelled at the Emperor's feet; Arbogast escaped, but after a few days' wandering in the hills found the old Roman solution for his troubles and fell on his sword.

The triumphant Theodosius passed on to Milan, where his first action was to pardon all the surviving adherents of Eugenius. He then turned his mind to the question of the succession. Valentinian having died unmarried and childless, the obvious course was to divide the Empire between his own two sons, giving to the elder, Arcadius, the East and to the younger, Honorius, the West. Both were at the time in Constantinople, but instructions were sent to Honorius to come at once to Milan. By the time the imperial envoys delivered their message, winter had set in; and it was mid-January before the ten-year-old prince – escorted by his cousin Serena, the wife of Stilicho – could make his way through the snows to Milan. Once there, he was horrified to find that his father had fallen seriously ill. Theodosius's joy at seeing his son acted on him briefly like a tonic: he was actually able to attend the start of the games in the Hippodrome which he had ordered in celebration of the boy's safe arrival. Half-way through, however, he suddenly collapsed; and the following night – that of 17 January 395 – he died in his fiftieth year. For forty days his embalmed body lay in state on its purple-covered bier in the atrium of the Palace; on 25 February it was brought to the Cathedral, where High Mass was sung and Bishop Ambrose delivered his funeral oration – the text of which still survives. Only then did the cortège set off, under heavy escort, on the long homeward journey to Constantinople.

The reign of Theodosius had been, on the face of it, unspectacular. He had made no major conquests, had instigated no radical or far-reaching reforms. In all the years that he had wielded the supreme power, he had never impressed his Empire – as Julian had done in a fraction of the time – with the stamp of a huge and dominating personality. On the contrary, he had been quiet, cautious almost to a fault, and totally without flamboyance. Readers of this brief account of his career may well find themselves wondering, not so much whether he deserved the title of 'the Great' as how he ever came to acquire it in the first place. If so, however, they may also like to ask themselves another question: what would have been the fate of the Empire if, at that critical moment in its history after the battle of Adrianople, young Gratian had not called him from his Spanish estates and put the future of the East into his hands?

Such questions, of course, can never be satisfactorily answered. It is conceivable that some other leader might have emerged, possessed of that same remarkable combination of generalship and diplomacy required to transform the Goths, in little more than two years, from an implacable enemy into a peaceful, even valuable, community within the Empire. But it is unlikely – and unlikelier still that he could have achieved his result with the same smoothness and sureness of touch. Had such a figure failed to appear, the probability is that the whole Empire of the East would have been lost, swallowed up in a revived Gothic kingdom, with effects on world history that defy speculation. At best, the Goths would have become to the East what the Alemanni had long been – and what they themselves were soon to become – to the West: a perpetual threat to imperial security, a steady drain on manpower and a brake on progress, forever holding down the Emperor and his army when their presence was required elsewhere.

Here, surely, was Theodosius's most important single legacy to the Empire. But it was not the only one. So far in these pages we have seen him only when on campaign, or visiting Milan or Rome; it is easy to forget that, of the sixteen years of his reign, well over half were spent in Constantinople, working tirelessly in the twin causes of good government and religious orthodoxy. In his civil legislation he showed, again and again, a consideration for the humblest of his subjects that was rare indeed among rulers of the fourth century. What other prince would have decreed that any criminal, sentenced to execution, imprisonment or exile, must first be allowed thirty days' grace to put his affairs in order? Or that a specified part of his worldly goods must go to his children, upon whom their father's crimes must on no account be visited? Or that no farmer should be obliged to sell his produce to the State at a price lower than he would receive on the open market?

Where religious matters were concerned, Theodosius's interest had showed itself as early as February 380, only thirteen months after his elevation, while he was still based at Thessalonica. We know that he fell seriously ill at that time and, in the belief that he was dying, had himself baptised. It may well have been this that prompted him, even before his complete recovery, to issue on the last day of the month an edict proclaiming that only those who professed the consubstantiality of the Trinity (in other words the Nicene Creed) could be considered *Catholic*

Christians – a designation that appears here for the first time. 'All others,' the edict continues, 'we pronounce to be mad and foolish, and we order that they shall bear the ignominious name of heretics, and shall not presume to bestow on their conventicles the title of churches: these are to be visited first by the divine vengeance, and secondly by the stroke of our own authority, which we have received in accordance with the will of heaven.' Further confirmation was given in the following year by the first Council of Constantinople, at which some 150 bishops from Thrace, Egypt and Asia Minor, meeting in the Church of St Irene, formally condemned the Arian heresy and its related sects – decreeing, *inter alia*, that the see of Constantinople should thenceforth come second in honour and dignity only to that of Rome itself. At this time, too, the Arians were expressly forbidden to congregate in cities, while all church buildings were ordered to be returned immediately to the orthodox faith. As for the pagans, they also found the Emperor's attitude hardening against them. In 385 he strengthened the existing legislation against sacrifices; in 391 he forbade all non-Christian ceremonies in Rome and Egypt; and in 392 he outlawed every form of pagan worship, public and private, throughout the Empire.

This steadily increasing religious intolerance has not, over the years, enhanced Theodosius's reputation. But we must remember that he was fighting, every moment of his reign, to keep the Empire strong and united against the barbarian menace; and that in those anxious times, when religion was as constant a preoccupation in men's lives as politics might be today, it could prove a uniquely powerful force for unification or division. And even Theodosius never attempted to change his subjects' convictions: never were they required to recant, or to abjure their faith. Nor did he ever sink to persecution. His chief fault was that ferocious temper of his – a temper that he tried, but all too frequently failed, to govern, and that led him time and again to words and actions which he later bitterly regretted; but once the fit was past, he was always quick to apologize, to remit or reduce punishments hastily ordered or even, when the occasion demanded, to do public penance.

Had he earned his title? Not, perhaps, in the way that Constantine had done or as Justinian was to do. But, if not ultimately great himself, he had surely come very close to greatness; and had he reigned as long as they did his achievements might well have equalled theirs. He might even have saved the Western Empire. One thing only is certain: it would be nearly a century and a half before the Romans would look upon his like again.

6

The Fall of Rome

[395–410]

A dreadful rumour reaches us from the West. Rome is occupied: her citizens ransom their lives for gold; but no sooner are they stripped of their possessions than they are again besieged and, having already lost their goods, they must now lose their lives as well. My voice is choked with sobs as I dictate these words. The city that has conquered the universe is now herself conquered . . . She dies of hunger before dying by the sword – scarcely do any men survive to be led off into captivity. The fury of the starving fastens on to nourishment unspeakable; they tear each other to pieces, the mother not sparing even the infant at her own breast . . .

St Jerome, Letter cxxvii, 12

Theodosius the Great was the last Emperor to rule over a united Roman Empire before the final collapse of the West. From the moment of his death the Western Empire embarks on its inexorable eighty-year decline, the prey of the Germanic and other tribes that progressively tighten their grip upon it until the day when the ironically named young Romulus Augustulus makes his final submission to a barbarian king. The states that rise from its ashes, amalgams of Teuton and Latin, of conquerors and conquered, have little to do with the old order: their laws, languages and institutions are shaped by new influences from the north and east. The gravitational pull that once held them together is no longer there; they move off centrifugally, each in its own direction. But the Empire of the East, in contrast with that of the West, survives. For various reasons – not least the hopeless mediocrity of its fifth-century rulers – its development is slow at first; gradually, however, it gains momentum, acquiring as it does so an individual, oriental personality of its own. Latin gives way more and more to Greek, the world of the intellect to that of the spirit; yet the classical tradition remains unbroken. The Byzantine Empire is less the inheritor than the continuation of the ancient world. That world itself, however, has passed away; and, for more than one recent historian, it is on the fateful night of 17 January 395 that the Middle Ages begin.

When Theodosius died his elder son, Arcadius, was not yet eighteen; Honorius, as we have already seen, was ten. The care of both he therefore entrusted to his nephew-by-marriage Stilicho, the most trustworthy of the surviving male members of his family. Stilicho's star was now rising fast. Of his early life we know little, except that he was the son of a Vandal chieftain who had fought loyally but with no outstanding distinction under Valens, and that he had been a member of the diplomatic mission to Persia that had negotiated the treaty with Shapur III. It was then, presumably, that he attracted the attention of Theodosius, for a few months later we find him married to Serena – the Emperor's niece, adopted daughter and particular favourite: the only one, it was rumoured, who could calm him in those terrible rages when no one else dared approach.

The poet Claudian, whose admiration for Stilicho borders on idolatry, tells us that the tall, good-looking young Vandal with the prematurely grizzled hair possessed so powerful a presence that people instinctively made way for him in the street; despite this advantage, however, and despite his new imperial connections, he does not seem to have attracted the notice of contemporary historians until the battle of the Frigidus. It was in recognition of the courage which he showed during that encounter that he was appointed *magister militum* in Italy. In this capacity, though technically responsible for the well-being of both the young Emperors, Stilicho's principal charge was Honorius, now Emperor of the West; Arcadius, far away in Constantinople, fell under less desirable influences – the strongest and most pernicious of which was that of the Praetorian Prefect Rufinus.

It was almost certainly Rufinus who, five years before at Milan, had incited Theodosius to order the Thessalonica massacre. Originally a lawyer from Aquitaine, he too was outstandingly handsome; unlike Stilicho, however, he had reached his present exalted position, while still in his early middle age, less through any military or diplomatic ability than through a combination of high intelligence and a totally unscrupulous eye to the main chance. His greed and avarice were renowned throughout Constantinople, as was his corruption; not surprisingly, therefore, he had become possessed of immense and steadily increasing wealth. Above all he was ambitious, and his ambitions were centred on a single object: the imperial throne.

Even to an energetic and self-willed young Emperor, such a man as

Rufinus would have been dangerous enough; Arcadius, alas, was neither. Small, dark and swarthy, slow in both speech and movement, with heavy-lidded eyes that always seemed about to close in sleep, he was in fact even stupider than he looked; and his character was as weak as his intellect. People meeting him for the first time found it hard to believe that he was his father's son. One thing only prevented him from being a mindless puppet in Rufinus's hands: the influence of the so-called Superintendent of the Sacred Bedchamber (*Praepositus Sacri Cubiculi*[1]), an elderly eunuch named Eutropius. Physically, with his egg-bald head and wrinkled yellow face, Eutropius was even less prepossessing than his master; nor would his past life, which included outstandingly successful careers first as a catamite and subsequently as a procurer, normally have been considered ideal recommendations for a trusted position in the Imperial Household. But, like Rufinus – whom he naturally detested – he was intelligent, unscrupulous and ambitious; he too wished to control the Emperor; and to that end he was determined to thwart his enemy in every way he could.

Rufinus, he knew, planned to marry his daughter to Arcadius. Once he had become a member of the imperial family it would be but a short step to the throne itself, and Eutropius's own chances of survival would be slim. The eunuch's only hope was to find a rival candidate for the Emperor's affections; and, in default of progeny of his own, he picked on a young Frankish girl of startling beauty who, after a sophisticated upbringing in Constantinople, had exchanged her outlandish barbarian name for a more harmonious Greek one and was now known as Eudoxia. Taking advantage of Rufinus's brief absence in Antioch to supervise the execution of a distinguished official, he introduced her into the Palace and, with a skill born of long practice, quickly aroused the Emperor's interest. By the time the Praetorian Prefect returned to the capital, Arcadius and Eudoxia were betrothed. It was typical, however, of the devious character of Eutropius that he allowed no public announcement to be made of the bride's identity; and Zosimus relates with glee the colourful if somewhat improbable tale of how, on the wedding morning, an imposing procession of court officials wound its way through the streets to fetch her. Eager to catch a glimpse of their future Empress, an

---

1 'The wardrobe of the sovereign, the gold plate, the arrangement of the Imperial meal, the spreading of the sacred couch, the government of the corps of brilliantly attired pages, the posting of the thirty *silentiarii* who, in helmet and cuirass, standing before the second veil, guarded the slumbers of the sovereign, these were the momentous responsibilities which required the undivided attention of a Cabinet Minister of the Roman Empire' (T. Hodgkin, *Italy and her Invaders,* Book I, Chap. 3).

expectant crowd had gathered outside the house of Rufinus; and great was their astonishment when the cortège marched straight past it, stopping instead at the far more modest residence of Eudoxia – who shortly afterwards appeared in full nuptial array, to be borne in state to the Palace and her waiting bridegroom.

At just about the time of the wedding – it took place on 27 April 395 – the Goths within the Empire rose again in revolt. By this time they had adopted as their leader the twenty-five-year-old Alaric, who had noted that the vast majority of the Eastern troops that had accompanied Theodosius to the West were still in Milan, and that the Eastern Empire was consequently almost defenceless. The opportunity was too good to miss: pretending fury at the appointment of Stilicho in preference to himself as *magister militum* after the battle of the Frigidus, in a matter of weeks he and his followers spread havoc through Moesia and Thrace, advancing to within a short distance of the walls of Constantinople itself. Here he turned back – probably bribed by Rufinus, who, disguised as a Goth, is known to have paid several visits to his camp and whose neighbouring estates remained suspiciously undevastated – and headed west again towards Macedonia and Thessaly. But although the citizens of the capital breathed again, it had been an uncomfortable moment; and Arcadius sent an urgent message to Stilicho in Milan, ordering him to bring back the eastern army with all possible speed.

Stilicho started as soon as he could, having further strengthened the eastern army with several crack contingents from the West; but instead of leading them directly back to Constantinople he marched straight down to confront Alaric in Thessaly. There he found to his irritation that the Goths had withdrawn inside a fortified stockade; and he was still trying to persuade them to come out and fight when he received another order from the Emperor. The army was to come at once to the capital; he himself however was to advance no further, but must return to the West where he belonged. The order probably came as a blow to Stilicho, who already had ambitions where the Eastern Empire was concerned; but he did as he was bid. The eastern army he placed under the command of a Gothic captain named Gainas and dispatched to Constantinople; then, taking the western elements with him, he set off for home.

After the departure of the imperial army, Alaric and his followers were once again free to continue their advance unimpeded. Southward they marched through Thessaly, passing without obstruction through the historic defile of Thermopylae and emerging into Boeotia and Attica. Few towns or villages on their path escaped their attentions; the port of Piraeus was completely destroyed, and the same fate would surely have befallen Athens itself had its walls been less formidable. Zosimus tells us that Alaric's courage failed him only when he was vouchsafed a vision of the goddess Athena in full armour standing upon the ramparts while Achilles, scowling horribly, patrolled the battlements; however this may be, he was certainly regaled at a sumptuous banquet by the commander of the garrison and persuaded to come to terms. Pausing only to set fire to the great temple of Demeter at Eleusis, he and his army crossed the isthmus of Corinth into the Peloponnese, ravaging the Argolid and descending southward to sack Sparta and the rich cities of the central plain. Then, in the spring of 396, they struck to the west, meeting the sea somewhere near Pylos and swinging north again up the coast into Elis. But here a surprise awaited them: Stilicho was back, together with a new army brought by sea from Italy. Suddenly, at Pholoe on the river Alphaeus – not far from Olympia – the Goths found themselves surrounded. At last, it seemed, the *magister militum* had them at his mercy. But now there occurred one of those inexplicable twists of which early history is so maddeningly full, especially when contemporary records are poor or in short supply. Just as Stilicho was on the point of victory, and about to give the Goths their *coup de grâce*, he deliberately allowed them to escape.

Why? Zosimus's claim that he was 'wasting his time with harlots and buffoons' is patently ridiculous, while Claudian's suggestion that he had received orders from Arcadius, who had come to a secret agreement with Alaric, is scarcely borne out by the facts: had such a contract existed, the Goths would hardly have continued across the Gulf of Corinth and north as far as the mountains of Epirus, pillaging and plundering as they went. Only in the following year did they finally conclude a peace treaty with the Empire. By its terms, Alaric was invested with the title of *magister militum per Illyricum* – a curious reward for the havoc he had caused. Obviously, he had struck some bargain at Pholoe; but it must have been with Stilicho, not with Arcadius. Later in the chapter we shall have to speculate – though that is all we can do – on the nature of this bargain; but for the moment we must wait, and let the story unfold.

And what, it may be asked, of the great army of the East, so hastily summoned home by the Emperor Arcadius? Its newly appointed commander, Gainas, led it as instructed along the Via Egnatia[1] to Constantinople, halting in the Campus Martius just outside the Golden Gate, where by tradition Emperors came out to welcome their returning armies. Here on 27 November Arcadius duly appeared, accompanied by Rufinus, who – and at this point we may raise our eyebrows a little – was expecting to be made co-Emperor on that very day, and was consequently even more proud and arrogant than usual. After the review, however, he seemed to relax somewhat and began mingling with the troops, insidiously soliciting their support for his forthcoming elevation. At first he did not notice that they were slowly closing in around him; when he did so it was already too late. Suddenly, a sword flashed. Others followed, and a moment later Rufinus fell dead to the ground. His body was swiftly hacked to pieces, and his magnificent head carried on a pike through the streets. One group of soldiers, with a particularly nasty sense of the macabre, even struck off his right hand at the wrist and carried it from house to house, crying, 'Give to the insatiable!' as they pulled the tendons to make the fingers jerk open and shut.

According to Claudian one of the assassins shouted, as he struck, that he was acting on behalf of Stilicho; but there is no other evidence to suggest that the murder had been instigated by the *magister militum* of the West. It may equally well have originated with Eutropius, or with Gainas and his soldiers on their way to the capital, or with any combination of the three. In fact, whoever was responsible, the death of Rufinus had little effect on the conduct of affairs. Now that Eutropius alone had the Emperor's ear, corruption, peculation and the open buying and selling of offices became more widespread than ever. 'One man,' laments Claudian,

gives his country seat for the government of Asia; another uses his wife's jewels for the purchase of Syria; yet a third buys Bithynia, and buys it too dear, by the sacrifice of the home of his fathers. In the public antechamber of Eutropius there hangs a tariff, showing the prices of the various provinces ... The eunuch seeks to wipe out his personal ignominy in the general disgrace and, as he has sold himself, now desires to sell everything else.[2]

In 399 Eutropius managed to get himself nominated Consul – a step which almost certainly hastened his downfall. Although the title had long been purely honorary, it remained the highest distinction that the

---

1 The imperial highway which ran from the Adriatic across the Balkan peninsula and Thrace to Constantinople.

2 *In Eutropium*, i, 199–207. 'But,' warns Professor Bury, 'we must make great allowance for the general prejudice existing against a person with Eutropius' physical disabilities.'

Empire could bestow, one which the Emperors themselves were proud
to bear – usually more than once – during their reigns; when it was given
outside the imperial family it had been invariably reserved for Romans
of high birth and with long records of distinguished service behind
them. To see it now assumed by an erstwhile slave and emasculated male
prostitute was more than the free-born Roman population of Constantinople could stand. Ironically, matters were brought to a head not by
the Senate or the Roman aristocracy but by a Goth – that same Gainas
whom Stilicho had entrusted with the army of the East and whose
soldiers had cut down Rufinus four years before. On his arrival in the
capital his appointment as *magister militum per orientem* had been confirmed; thus, when in the spring of 399 a new revolt broke out among
the Gothic settlers in Phrygia, Gainas was – despite his own Gothic
origins – one of the two generals sent out to crush it. On his arrival,
however, he secretly changed sides; and in the ensuing battle he and the
rebels swiftly destroyed the Roman elements in the army and were left
masters of the field. Still posing as a loyal servant of the Emperor, he
then sent a message to Arcadius informing him that the insurgents were
too numerous to be put down by force and that it would be necessary to
come to terms with them; fortunately they were making only a few most
reasonable demands which, he recommended, should be accepted without
further ado. The first of these proved to be the surrender of Eutropius.
Arcadius hesitated; he needed his old chamberlain and relied on him.
But now another powerful voice was heard – that of the Empress
Eudoxia herself.

Eudoxia is the first of that long line of Byzantine Empresses, beautiful,
worldly and ambitious, whose names were to become bywords for luxury
and sensuality. Widely rumoured to entertain whole strings of lovers –
one of whom, a nobleman whom we know only as John, was probably
to be the father of her son Theodosius – she was said to flaunt her
depravity, together with her court ladies, by wearing a fringe combed
down low over the forehead, the recognized trademark of a courtesan.
She owed her position entirely to Eutropius; foolishly, however, he had
reminded her of the fact once too often, and she was furthermore deeply
jealous of his influence over her husband. In the four years since their
marriage, relations between herself and Arcadius had deteriorated to the
point where they no longer made any secret of their mutual loathing.

And so, reluctantly, the Emperor gave the order; and Eutropius fled
in terror to seek asylum in the Church of St Sophia, flinging himself at
the feet of the bishop, St John Chrysostom – who, he whimperingly

pointed out, also owed his elevation to him alone. This lugubrious cleric, who had been lured by a trick to the capital in the previous year and had never wanted the see in the first place, had no more affection for his self-styled benefactor than did Eudoxia; but he could not deny the right of sanctuary. When the soldiers arrived soon afterwards to demand the surrender of the fugitive, he stood implacably before them and turned them away, while the trembling eunuch cowered beneath the high altar.

Eutropius was safe in St Sophia; unfortunately, as he well knew, he was also trapped there. On the following day – a Sunday – after a cold and uncomfortable night, he had to suffer the additional humiliation of listening to a blistering sermon of the kind that had earned the preacher his name,[1] pronounced in the presence of a vast congregation but addressed to him alone, on the text: 'Vanity of vanities, all is vanity'.[2] It was probably this homily – which must have shrivelled him up more than ever – that persuaded Eutropius to surrender himself at last, on condition that his life should be spared. He was exiled to Cyprus, but at the insistence of Gainas was shortly afterwards brought back and – on the transparently specious grounds that his physical immunity was assured only in Constantinople – tried at Chalcedon, where he was condemned and executed.

Gainas had won; but he was not long to enjoy his victory. Early in the year 400 he returned to the capital, where he tried to set up a power base as Rufinus and Eutropius had done before him; but hostile groups within the city prevented his ever acquiring a similar degree of authority, and a secret attempt to capture the imperial palace – presumably with the object of murdering its occupants and seizing the throne for himself – was foiled almost before it started. In the absence of adequate contemporary information it is impossible to establish the full story; some time towards the end of the summer, however, after six months of increasing unrest, Gainas suddenly ordered his army of Goths to prepare for departure. Suspecting that some fresh coup was being planned, the anxious populace gathered in the streets; and so highly charged was the atmosphere that fighting broke out between them and the departing barbarians. Most of the latter had already left the city; but the remainder, heavily outnumbered, fell easy victims to the anti-Gothic feeling that had been building up for years. The gates were shut to prevent their escape, and 7,000 were dead by morning – many having been burnt alive in their church near the imperial palace, in which they had taken sanctuary.

1 *Chrysostom*, literally 'the golden-mouthed'.
2 St John Chrysostom, *Homily to Eutropius*; *Oeuvres*, Vol. I, p. 353.

Gainas himself, with what was left of his army, wandered rather hopelessly through Thrace before attempting to cross the Hellespont into Asia, where he sustained still heavier losses at the hands of a loyalist army that awaited him on the other side. He then struggled northward again towards the Danube, eventually falling captive to the Hunnish King Uldin, who cut off his head and sent it as a present to Arcadius. Yet another adventurer, seeking to turn the growing confusion in the Empire to his own advantage, had paid the price of his temerity.

The fourth century had been a fateful one indeed for the Roman Empire. It had seen the birth of a new capital on the Bosphorus – a capital which, although not yet the sole focus of a united political state, was steadily growing in size and importance while the world of the Western Mediterranean subsided into increasing anarchy; and it had seen the adoption of Christianity as the official religion of the Emperor and his subjects. It ended, however, on a note of bathos: in the West with silence and inertia in the face of the barbarian menace, in the East with a whimper – the only possible description for the reactions of the most feckless Emperor yet to occupy the throne of Constantinople as he watched successive strong men meet their variously violent deaths, while his own vicious and domineering wife insulted and humiliated him in public, holding him up to ridicule as a fool, an incompetent and a cuckold. The new century, on the other hand, began with a bang. In the early summer of 401, Alaric the Goth invaded Italy.

The greatest of all the Gothic leaders – and the only one whose name was to reverberate down the halls of history – Alaric effortlessly dominates the early years of the fifth century. When it opened, he was still only some thirty years old, having been chief of the Visigoths since the age of twenty-five. In this capacity he had left friends and enemies alike in no doubt of his mettle, speading terror from the walls of Constantinople to the southern Peloponnese; but, by the obvious readiness with which he had accepted the title of *magister militum* when it had been offered him, he had also shown something else: that he was not fundamentally hostile to the Roman Empire. The truth, indeed, was quite the contrary: Alaric fought not to overthrow the Empire, but to establish a permanent home for his people within it, in such a way that they might enjoy their own local autonomy while he, as their chieftain, would be granted high imperial rank. If only the Western Emperor and the Roman Senate could have understood this simple fact, they might still have averted the final catastrophe. By their lack of comprehension they made it inevitable.

To any intelligent observer, the only surprising thing about Alaric's invasion was that he had delayed it so long. It was, after all, four years since he had withdrawn with his army into Illyricum, and he was obviously not going to remain there for ever. In those four years the Empire might have been expected to take some measures to avert the coming onslaught; it was typical of Honorius – whose only interest at this time seems to have been the raising of poultry – that nothing of any kind had been done. Thus, as news of the invasion spread, blind panic spread with it. Claudian lists a whole succession of portents and prophecies, prodigious hailstorms, an eclipse of the moon and even a comet, ending with the appearance of two wolves which suddenly started up under the Emperor's horse while he was reviewing his cavalry and whose stomachs were subsequently found to contain human hands. Slowly and, it seemed, irresistibly, the huge Gothic host lumbered down the valley of the Isonzo, their wives and families trailing behind: as so often with the barbarian invaders, this was not just an army but an entire nation on the march. Not pausing to besiege either Aquileia or Ravenna, the two greatest cities of north-east Italy (Venice was still only a cluster of desolate sandbanks in the lagoon) they headed west towards Milan, the young Emperor fleeing before them to Asti in Piedmont; and it was just a few miles from that city that they found the Roman army awaiting them, the familiar figure of Stilicho at its head.

The battle was fought just outside Pollentia – now the little village of Pollenzo, but in imperial days an important manufacturing city – on Easter Sunday, 402. Of its outcome the chroniclers of the time give widely differing reports. It seems to have been the worst kind of battle: protracted, bloody and ultimately indecisive. At any rate the Goths advanced no further but retired once more to the East. On their way, Alaric made a surprise attack on Verona where, if Claudian is to be believed, he sustained an indisputable defeat at the hands of Stilicho. Once again, however, the Vandal captain allowed him to withdraw beyond the frontiers of Illyricum, his army still basically intact.

Stilicho had now had Alaric twice at his mercy – possibly three times, if we include that curious moment in Thessaly in 395 – only to let him go again; and the moment has now come to examine his motives rather more closely. From the start, his attitude towards the Gothic leader seems to have been strangely ambiguous. Professor Bury, in his *History of the Later Roman Empire*, first voices his suspicions when Stilicho tarries in Milan with the army of the East after the battle of the Frigidus; perhaps, he suggests, he had advance warning of Alaric's revolt and deliberately held back so that his own intervention might be even more essential at a later stage. Next comes the incident of the Thessalian stockade: does that, one wonders, ring altogether true? Was Alaric really so reluctant to fight? Or was Stilicho reluctant to weaken him? Oddest of all is the Goths' escape at Pholoe: Should we perhaps link this with Stilicho's known ambition to seize Illyricum and the Balkan peninsula from the Eastern and to attach it to the Western Empire – possibly under the dominion of his son Eucherius as co-Emperor – and deduce that Alaric may have agreed, in return for his freedom, to become his accomplice in the scheme? The hypothesis certainly seems plausible enough in view of subsequent events. We know too that Stilicho had growing dynastic ambitions; indeed, he was already the Emperor's father-in-law, having married his daughter Maria to Honorius in 398.[1] Whatever the truth may be, it seems clear that he saw the Goths as being potentially useful allies in any future action against the Eastern Empire, and he had no desire either to break their strength completely or to sacrifice all of their goodwill.

At this time, however, Stilicho was still concealing his long-term plans; it was another five years before he came out into the open. Meanwhile relations between East and West had steadily deteriorated, largely owing to the character and the tribulations of the Bishop of Constantinople, St John Chrysostom. This saintly but insufferable prelate, by his scorching castigations of the Empress and her way of life, had made himself dangerously unpopular at court; and in 403 his long and impassioned dispute with Theophilus, Bishop of Alexandria, gave Eudoxia the excuse for which she had been waiting: Chrysostom was deposed and exiled to Bithynia. But however many enemies he may have had in high places, he enjoyed considerable support among the people: riots broke out, followed by furious fighting in the streets between the local citizenry and the people of Alexandria who had come to Constantinople to support their bishop. That night, moreover, there was an earthquake – which so frightened the superstitious Empress (it was rumoured that she had a miscarriage on the spot) that the exiled prelate was recalled and reinstated.

John had won the first round; and if only he had agreed to moderate his tone a little all might have been well. Alas, he did nothing of the kind. Only a few weeks later he made a vigorous protest when a silver statue of Eudoxia – who had had herself proclaimed Augusta three

---

1 The marriage evoked 500 lines of peculiarly flatulent verse from Claudian, the Epithalamium ending with an affecting picture of an infant son sitting on his parents' knees. Maria is said, however, to have lived and died a virgin.

years before – was erected in the Augusteum, just outside St Sophia: the noise of the inauguration ceremony, he claimed, interrupted his services. Thereafter the breach between bishop and imperial family was complete, Eudoxia refusing to allow her husband any communication at all with the leading ecclesiastic of the Empire. Early the following spring, in the course of another synod summoned to decide upon the dispute with Alexandria, Chrysostom was again condemned; a recent sermon of his, containing the passage, 'Again Herodias rages . . . again she demands the head of John on a platter,' may not have helped his case. On this occasion, doubtless remembering the events of the previous year, Arcadius contented himself with debarring the bishop from his church; but matters came to a head at Easter when two thousand catechumens awaiting baptism gathered in the Baths of Constantine instead. What began as a service rapidly degenerated into a demonstration; the soldiers were called in to restore order; and the baptismal water, we are told, ran red with blood. On 24 June the recalcitrant bishop was exiled for the second time; once again, disaster overtook Constantinople. That same evening St Sophia was destroyed by fire – arson was suspected but never proved – the flames being blown by a strong north wind on to the Senate House nearby. By next morning the two buildings were charred and blackened shells, and the city's most important collection of antique statuary was lost. Less than four months later, on 6 October, there came the final, unmistakable sign of divine displeasure: the Empress had another miscarriage, which on this occasion proved fatal.

Shortly before his departure, Chrysostom had appealed to Pope Innocent I in Rome, protesting against his unjust sentence and demanding a formal trial at which to confront his accusers. The Pope summoned a synod of Latin bishops, which unanimously declared the previous synod invalid and, through Innocent and Honorius, called on Arcadius to restore Chrysostom to his see; a general assembly of Greek and Latin bishops, they suggested, could then meet in Thessalonica and settle the question once and for all. Meanwhile Honorius had addressed a stern letter to his brother, deploring the various disturbances which his mishandling of the affair had brought upon the capital and chiding him for the indecent haste with which the sentence of exile had been implemented without papal approval. To this letter a deeply offended Arcadius sent no reply, and there was a pause while the parties considered their next moves. At last, in 406, a delegation was sent jointly by Honorius and Innocent to Constantinople. Including as it did no less than four senior bishops, it could not be ignored; but once again

Arcadius made his attitude plain enough. The envoys were not even permitted to enter the city. Instead, they were clapped into a Thracian castle, where they were interrogated and their letters snatched from them; only then, insulted and humiliated, were they allowed to return to Italy.

Thus, when St John Chrysostom died in a remote region of Pontus – possibly as a result of ill-treatment by his guards – in September 407, he left the Roman Empire profoundly split; and Stilicho decided that the time had come to put his long-cherished designs on Illyricum into effect. Alaric, he knew, was standing by to help him, awaiting only the signal to march. His first step was to order a blockade on the Eastern Empire, closing all Italian ports to Arcadius's ships. It was, in effect, a declaration of war; but Stilicho was still in Ravenna preparing the army for the coming campaign when a messenger arrived from Honorius, who was then in Rome, with news that stopped him in his tracks. Alaric, it appeared, was dead. Meanwhile the Roman Governor of Britain, Constantinus, had declared himself Augustus, crossed to Gaul and raised the standard of revolt. Clearly, Illyricum would have to wait a little longer; there was more urgent business to attend to. Leaving the army at Ravenna, Stilicho hastened to confer with Honorius in Rome.

On his arrival, he found that the first half of the message had been based on a false rumour. Alaric was alive and well in Illyricum, but greatly displeased that the enterprise which he and Stilicho had planned together was still further postponed. His preparations, he pointed out, had cost him much time and considerable expense, for which he expected compensation: 4,000 pounds of gold, to be paid at once. The members of the Roman Senate, to whom this demand was addressed, were predictably horrified; but Stilicho realized that the sum must be found and, taking full advantage of his special prestige as the Emperor's father-in-law, finally succeeded in persuading them. Only one senator had the courage to protest. 'This is not a peace,' he cried; 'it is a commitment to slavery.' But even he seems to have regretted his words, for it is recorded that as soon as the session broke up he sought refuge from Stilicho's wrath in a Christian church.

Early in May 408, the Emperor Arcadius died aged thirty-one, leaving the throne to his seven-year-old son, named Theodosius after his grandfather. For Stilicho, there could hardly have been better news. If he played his cards right, he would now be able to achieve everything he wanted in the East without bloodshed or even expense; there would certainly be no need for Alaric and his Goths, who would be left free to deal with the usurper Constantinus in Gaul. He easily dissuaded Honorius from his intention of going in person to Constantinople, pointing out that the arrival of a Western Emperor in the capital of the East would create more problems than it could possibly solve; far better that he should remain at Ravenna, where he had permanently established his court after the battle of Pollentia six years before. As *magister militum*, he himself would have no difficulty in arranging everything satisfactorily on his son-in-law's behalf.

But, for the second time in two years, his plans came to nothing. Perhaps his personal ambition was growing a little too obvious; many Christians, certainly, had been shocked by the speed with which, on the death of his daughter the Empress Maria earlier that year, he had induced Honorius to marry her younger sister Thermantia almost before the body was cold. Perhaps, too, he had incurred more disapproval than he knew by insisting on the huge payment to Alaric. Or possibly the old jealousies were slowly coming to the surface again: he was, after all, not a Roman but a Vandal, and Vandals were expected to know their place. Moreover the unrelenting severity of his discipline had caused serious dissatisfaction in the army: twice in the past year, at Bologna and again at Pavia, there had been minor mutinies. In short, he had become dangerously unpopular. At the court of Ravenna, the hostility to him was most marked in a certain minister named Olympius; and it was he, while travelling through Italy with Honorius in Stilicho's absence, who had managed to persuade the Emperor that his father-in-law was plotting treason against him.

We do not know the precise nature of the accusations, nor can we tell whether or not they had any foundation. The one certain fact of the story is that Stilicho was arraigned, accused, tried, found guilty and, at Ravenna on 23 August 408, put to death. His son Eucherius fled to Rome, where he managed to prolong his life by a few months; his sister Thermantia was removed from the imperial palace – still, it was said, as virginal as Maria had been before her – and sent back to her mother Serena. Serena herself was spared, but some months later was strangled by order of the Roman Senate on a charge of impiety. (Years before, visiting Rome in the company of her uncle Theodosius, she had entered the Temple of Rhea, Mother of the Gods, snatched a necklace from the statue of the goddess and mockingly put it round her own neck. The incident had never been forgotten.) [1]

1 'We may observe,' snorts Gibbon, 'the bad taste of the age, in dressing their statues with such awkward finery.'

With the execution of Stilicho, all the pent-up hatred of Roman for barbarian suddenly found its release. In garrison after garrison throughout the Empire, the Roman legionaries sprang to arms and fell upon the Gothic, Hunnish or Vandal auxiliaries, sparing neither them nor their families. The massacres were terrible; so, however, were the consequences. Those barbarians who escaped death formed themselves into bands for their own safety, wandered through the countryside looting and pillaging, and finally found their way to Alaric, swelling his army by some 30,000. Previously loyal to the Empire, they had now become its implacable enemies, determined not to rest until they had taken vengeance on the murderers of their brothers, wives and children. For much of the tribulation that the Romans were to suffer in the next two years, they had only themselves and their countrymen to blame.

They also found, at one of the most critical moments in their history, that they lacked a commander. Whatever dark designs Stilicho may have harboured against the Eastern Empire, he had always remained a faithful servant of the West; had he been anything else, he would have had no difficulty in eliminating the idiotic Honorius years before. In such an event, his close connections with the imperial house would probably have outweighed the disadvantage of his barbarian origin and enabled him to assume the purple; even had they not, he could surely have arranged for a successor both capable and trustworthy. As it was – unless we are to accept as true the accusations of Olympius (described by Zosimus as one who, 'behind an outward appearance of deep Christian piety, concealed the most consummate villainy') – his loyalty never wavered. Stilicho was one of those barbarians who believed in the Empire; and for all his severity and occasional deviousness, he was a fine leader of men. Only when he had gone did the Romans realize just how irreplaceable he was.

Alaric too believed in the Empire – in his fashion. But he did not believe in Honorius. Still less did he trust the Roman Senate who, having reluctantly agreed to pay him the compensation he had asked, now tried to fob him off with only part of it. To do so, as they should have seen, was tantamount to an open invitation to invade; yet even now they made no attempt to mobilize the army – which had been stood down after Stilicho's death – or to strengthen their defences. So Alaric invaded; and in September 408 he found himself before the walls of Rome, his huge army of Goths drawn up behind him. Now at last the Romans began to understand the sheer magnitude of the catastrophe that they had brought upon themselves. They had never really believed that what they still persisted in seeing as an undisciplined horde of skin-clad savages could constitute a serious danger to the greatest city of the civilized world; even now there were those who maintained that the Goths lacked the patience and endurance required for successful siege warfare, and that within a few days they would turn their attention somewhere else.

A few days, however, were all that were needed for Alaric to establish a stranglehold. Every road, every bridge, every footpath, every inch of the walls was kept under constant watch, while patrols along the Tiber ensured that no provisions or supplies could be smuggled in by water. Inside the city, strict rationing was introduced. Soon the daily ration was cut to a half, soon afterwards to a third. By now, several cases of cannibalism had been reported. Daily, as winter approached, the weather grew colder, and before long the combination of cold and undernourishment brought the inevitable disease. Still the watch-towers were manned to the north-east, in the hope that an army of relief might appear from Ravenna to save the city in the nick of time; but gradually it became clear that there was no such relief to be expected: Honorius was not lifting a finger to save the old capital.

As Christmas approached, the defenders knew that they could hold out no longer. Ambassadors were dispatched to Alaric, and a ransom was agreed: 5,000 pounds of gold, 30,000 of silver, 4,000 silken tunics, 3,000 hides dyed scarlet and 3,000 pounds of pepper. The first two items involved the stripping of statues and their adornments from churches and pagan temples alike, and the melting down of countless works of art. This time, however, there were no renegations, no half-measures; the Romans had learnt their lesson, and the ransom was paid in full.

But the future remained uncertain, and Alaric still wanted a home for his people. Returning northward from Rome he stopped at Rimini, where he met the Praetorian Prefect, Jovius, with some new proposals. Honorius would make available the provinces of Venetia, Dalmatia and Noricum[1] which, while remaining part of the Empire, would be allotted to the Goths as their permanent home, and would also grant them annual subsidies of money and corn to enable Alaric to keep them under arms; in return, Alaric would agree to a solemn military alliance, under the terms of which he would be the effective defender and champion of

---

1 Noricum roughly consisted of eastern Austria south of the Danube, plus the present Yugoslav Republic of Slovenia. The total area covered by the three provinces demanded by Alaric amounts to some 30,000 square miles, enclosed by a line drawn through Passau, Vienna, Dubrovnik and Venice.

Rome and the Empire against any enemy whatever. To many a Roman, the offer seemed not unreasonable; Jovius himself certainly did not reject it out of hand, forwarding it to the Emperor only with the suggestion that Alaric might be prepared to moderate his demands if he were offered the title of *magister utriusque militiae* –'master of both militias', i.e. cavalry and infantry – that Stilicho had borne before him.

Honorius, however, would have none of it. The grant of lands he refused point-blank; as for the title, he had no intention (he replied to Jovius) 'that such an honour should ever be held by Alaric, or by any of his race'. It was, so far as we know, the first time he had shown a trace of spirit, or of anything resembling a will of his own; but he could hardly have chosen a more inopportune moment to do so. His army was demoralized and rudderless; it would not stand the faintest chance against Alaric when the Goths renewed their attack, as sooner or later they inevitably must. The Eastern Empire to which he had appealed for help could in no way be relied upon, being in a state of turmoil after the succession to the throne of a child of seven; to the west, Gaul, Britain and Spain were in the hands of a usurper against whom a single half-hearted expedition had ended in failure and who could at any moment march into Italy. If he did so, Alaric and his Goths might well prove an invaluable bulwark.

Thus Honorius, effectively defenceless, insisted on defiance; while Alaric, who could have crushed him with hardly an effort, still strove for peace. Jovius's mistake – and we can only hope it was a mistake – of reading the Emperor's letter aloud to the Goth did not improve the latter's temper; so anxious was he to reach an agreement, however, that a few weeks later he sent a delegation of bishops to Ravenna to use their influence with Honorius, while substantially reducing his own requirements. He would forget Venetia and Dalmatia; all that he now asked for his people was Noricum on the Danube – a province already so devastated by barbarian invasions as to be practically worthless – and enough of a subsidy to allow him to feed his men.

In the circumstances, the generosity of these terms was astonishing; besides, the Emperor can hardly have been unaware of the consequences of another rejection. And yet, once again, he set his face against any compact with the Goths. Alaric's patience was finally exhausted. For the second time in twelve months, he marched on Rome and immediately set up a blockade; on this occasion, however, he changed his tactics. His purpose, he told the Romans, was not to put their city to fire and the sword but simply to overthrow Honorius, now the single obstacle to peace in Italy. If they agreed, they must declare their Emperor deposed and elect a more reasonable successor; he, for his part, would lift the siege forthwith.

The Roman Senate, meeting in emergency session, did not take long to decide. No one could contemplate the prospect of another siege, with all the horrors that it brought in its train. Besides, it was pointed out, Honorius had shown no concern for his people, either now or in the previous year; so long as he personally was safe behind the dikes and ditches of Ravenna, he seemed oblivious to the fate of anyone else. He had, in short, forfeited their allegiance. They wanted no more of him. So the gates were opened, and Alaric entered Rome in peace; Honorius was declared deposed, and it was agreed that he should be succeeded as Augustus by the Prefect of the City, an Ionian Greek named Priscus Attalus.

It was not, on the face of it, a bad choice. Attalus was an intelligent man of pronounced artistic tastes, himself a Christian but acceptable to the pagans on account of his tolerant views and his love of antique literature and culture. Fortunately, too, he had been baptised by an Arian Gothic bishop and thus enjoyed the support of all the Christian Goths, Arians to a man. Appointing Alaric his *magister militum*, he at once prepared to march on Ravenna; but, before he could leave, there was one major problem to be settled. Africa, the small but vital province (roughly corresponding to what is now Northern Tunisia) on which Rome was entirely dependent for its corn, was then governed by Heraclian, the officer who had been responsible for the execution of Stilicho and who was expected to remain loyal to Honorius. For Alaric, there was only one solution: the immediate dispatch to Carthage, the capital, of an army which would depose Heraclian and ensure continued supplies. Attalus, on the other hand, preferring a more diplomatic approach, sent over a young man named Constans with instructions to take over the province peaceably in his name. This done, he set off with his *magister militum* for Ravenna.

With the news of events in Rome and the imminent approach of his enemies, Honorius had finally abandoned his sang-froid and had entered a state bordering on panic. He sent messages to Attalus, agreeing to his rule in Rome on condition that he himself might continue as Augustus in Ravenna; meanwhile he ordered ships to be made ready at the neighbouring port of Classis, to take him and his entourage to safety in Constantinople. Just as they were about to sail, however, there arrived at the same port six Byzantine legions – some 40,000 men, if Zosimus is to be believed – sent in the name of young Theodosius II, who had received his uncle's appeal and had responded at once. The appearance of reinforcements on such a scale restored the Emperor's courage. He would, he declared, hold out in Ravenna, at least until he heard the news from Africa: if Heraclian had stood firm, all might not yet be lost.

Nor was it; a few days later there came a report that was all Honorius could have wished: Heraclian had dealt with the unfortunate Constans just as effectively, and in much the same manner, as he had dealt with Stilicho less than two years before. To Alaric, this was a serious blow. It meant, first of all, that he could no longer hope to oust the Emperor from Ravenna; more worrying still, perhaps, it pointed to a serious lack of political acumen on the part of Attalus. Again he pressed for the forcible removal of the African governor, but Attalus was stubborn: as Augustus, he maintained, he could not send an army of Goths against a Roman province. And the Senate agreed with him. Something, on the other hand, would have to be done, and quickly: Heraclian had already cut off the grain supply and famine was again beginning to threaten. One day, it was said, when Attalus was attending the Circus, the cry was heard from the topmost tiers: *'Pretium pone carni humanae!'* – 'Put a price on human flesh!'

Alaric had had enough. In the early summer of 410 he summoned Attalus to Rimini and, in a broad open space just outside the walls, publicly stripped him of the diadem and the purple. Then, after one more unsuccessful attempt to reach an agreement with Honorius, he marched back to Rome and besieged it for the third time. Maddeningly, we know little of the details: Zosimus, that most irritating of chroniclers, gives up at this critical moment, and such other sources as have been preserved are pitifully sketchy. But, with food already short, the city did not hold out for long. Some time towards the end of August, the Goths burst in by the Salarian Gate in the northern wall, just at the foot of the Pincian Hill.

After the capture, there were the traditional three days of pillage; but this early sack of Rome seems to have been a good deal less savage than the school history-books would have us believe – quite restrained, in fact, when compared with the havoc wrought by the Normans in 1084 or the armies of Charles V in 1527. Alaric himself, devout Christian that he was, had given orders that no churches or religious buildings were to be touched, and that the right of asylum was everywhere to be respected. Yet a sack, however decorously conducted, remains a sack; the Goths were far from being saints and, despite occasional exaggerations, there is probably all too much truth in the pages that Gibbon devotes to the atrocities committed: the splendid edifices consumed by the flames, the multitudes of innocents slain, of matrons ravished and of virgins deflowered.[1]

When the three days were over, Alaric moved on to the south, intending to sail his army over to Africa, deal once and for all with Heraclian and deliver Italy from famine. But he had got no further than Cosenza when he was attacked by a sudden violent fever, and within a few days he was dead. He was still only forty. His followers carried his body to the river Busento, which they dammed and temporarily deflected from its usual channel. There, in the stream's dry bed, they buried their leader; then they broke the dam, and the waters came surging back and covered him.

1 *The Decline and Fall of the Roman Empire*, Chap. XXXI.

7

Of Heresies and Huns

[410–53]

If you ask a man for change, he will give you a piece of philosophy concerning the Begotten and the Unbegotten; if you enquire the price of a loaf, he replies: 'The Father is greater and the Son inferior'; or if you ask whether the bath is ready, the answer you receive is that the Son was made out of nothing.

St Gregory of Nyssa

It is one of the clichés of Constantinople that it should, ideally, be approached from the sea. Only then, we are told, can the uniqueness of its geographical position be properly appreciated, to say nothing of that famous skyline of dome and minaret which has symbolized, for as long as any of us can remember, the Mysterious East. With this opinion we cannot easily disagree; but, for those of us on whom Byzantium will always cast a more powerful spell than Islam, there is another approach every bit as satisfying and very nearly as spectacular. No one, surely, whose first arrival has been by road from Edirne, can ever forget that first astonishing sight of the Land Walls, looming up from the surrounding plain, their huge russet-striped towers splintered and occasionally shattered, magnificent witnesses to the bludgeonings – by attacking armies and, more recently, by Turkish traffic – that they have endured for nearly sixteen centuries. Running just over four miles from the Marmara to the upper reaches of the Golden Horn – and thus enclosing a far greater area than those earlier fortifications traced by Constantine – they totally close off the city by land; only once, after more than a thousand years, were they ever breached – a breach that was to spell the end of the Byzantine Empire.

But that was over 500 years ago; they are still standing today, and still known as the Theodosian Walls after Theodosius II, in whose reign they were first built. And yet, although this tremendous construction remains the only achievement of his forty-two-year reign for which the name of Theodosius is generally remembered, the sad truth is that he can take little of the credit. Those walls – a single line of them, rather than the triple fortification that we see today – were begun in 413, when the Emperor was still a boy of twelve; they were conceived and carried to their completion not by him but by his Praetorian Prefect Anthemius, who for the first six years of his reign was his guardian and the effective Regent of the East.

Anthemius was the first highly-placed layman at Constantinople since the days of Theodosius the Great to combine ability with high principle. Apart from the Walls, he was also responsible for a new peace treaty with Persia; for a much strengthened Danube fleet after a damaging but ultimately unsuccessful invasion by the Hun King Uldin; for improvements in the corn supply from Alexandria; and for the restoration of good relations with the Western Empire after the death of Arcadius. But he did not last long. After 414 he disappears from view, to be succeeded as the power behind the throne by the Emperor's own sister, the princess Pulcheria; and with this faintly awesome figure there is inaugurated a period of thirty-six years – the remainder of her brother's reign – during which virtually all the effective influence in the state was concentrated in female hands.

Pulcheria had been born only two years before Theodosius; she was thus still barely fifteen when she was proclaimed Augusta and took over the reins of government. By now it must have been generally apparent that her brother would be no improvement on Arcadius: he was weak, vacillating and easily led. She herself, by contrast, was strong and determined, with a love of power for its own sake; but she was also excessively, extravagantly pious, taking a particular pleasure in the rebuilding of the ruined St Sophia. Under her influence, her two younger sisters Arcadia and Marina developed similar inclinations: the prevailing mood in the imperial palace, it was said, was more that of a cloister than a court, thronged from morning till night with priests and monks while the princesses, all three of whom had vowed themselves to perpetual virginity, stitched away at their altar-cloths and chasubles to the sound of hymns, psalmodies and muttered prayers. It was all a far cry, people somewhat wistfully observed, from what it had been in Eudoxia's day.

How far Theodosius allowed himself to be drawn into his sister's devotions is a matter for conjecture. Born in the purple[1] and proclaimed co-Augustus at his birth, he had in fact granted his first petition

---

1 *Porphyrogenitus*, or born in the purple, was a title used exclusively of a prince who was born after his father had become Emperor – theoretically at least, in the Purple Chamber of the Great Palace.

(addressed to him by Porphyrius, Bishop of Gaza, and requesting the destruction of all pagan temples in his diocese) immediately after his baptism, when he was still only a few days old;[1] and from his earliest childhood he had been obliged to live in that stultifying seclusion from his fellows that was considered appropriate for God's Vice-Gerent on Earth. Despite his upbringing, however, and his hereditary defects of character, he seems to have possessed considerable charm: 'he was much loved,' writes Socrates the Church historian, 'by Senate and people alike.' And he was certainly far from stupid. Religion in the fifth century was too much a part of everyday life not to have interested him in some degree, but his tastes lay more in the direction of secular learning and culture: in the classical authors both Latin and Greek, in mathematics and the natural sciences, and above all in the art of illustrating and illuminating manuscripts, where his skill soon earned him the sobriquet of *kalligraphos*, the calligrapher. His interests, however, were not exclusively intellectual and artistic. He had a passion for hunting, and there is evidence – though not, it must be admitted, contemporary – to suggest that it was he who introduced to Constantinople the Persian game of *tsukan*, which we know today as polo. Immersed as he was in these pursuits, he had no objection to leaving affairs of state to his sister, long after he had reached the age when he should have taken them over himself. Only in 420, when he was nineteen and his thoughts began to turn to other channels, did he send for Pulcheria on a matter of state importance. It was time, he told her, that she found him a wife.

Now it happened – these are admittedly the facts as given by later historians, but who are we to contradict them? – that at about this time there presented herself at the Palace a young Greek girl of startling beauty named Athenais. She was the daughter of a certain Leontius, a professor at the university of Athens, and she had come to enlist the Emperor's support against her two brothers, who had refused to share her father's estate with her after his death and had thus condemned her to penury. According to one version of the story, Leontius had deliberately cut her off with a hundred gold pieces since, as he wrote in his will, 'she will

1 The Bishop's deacon, Marcus, tells how he and his master stood outside the church and, when the baptismal procession emerged, shouted the words, 'We petition Your Piety', and held out the document. 'And he who carried the child . . . halted, and commanded silence, and having unrolled a part he read it . . . and placed his hand under the head of the child and cried out: "His Majesty has ordered the requests contained in the petition to be ratified."' Later, at the Palace, 'the Emperor ordered the paper to be read, and said: "The request is hard, but to refuse is harder, since it is the first mandate of our son"' (quoted by Bury (op. cit.), from the *Abhandlungen* of the Berlin Academy, 1879).

have her good luck, which is better than that of any other woman'. If so, he was right. Pulcheria, who saw her first, was immensely impressed – not only by her beauty but by the exquisite Greek in which she framed her appeal. She took her straight to Theodosius, who at once fell passionately in love. The potential difficulty of the girl's paganism was quickly overcome: after a few weeks' instruction by Bishop Atticus she was baptized into the Christian faith, marking the occasion by a change of name from Athenais to Eudocia. Her new sister-in-law, it need hardly be said, stood as her godmother. On 7 June 421, she and Theodosius were married.

Into the well-nigh insufferable atmosphere of the imperial palace, Athenais[1] arrived like a fresh spring breeze. She too was genuinely religious – in the circumstances she could hardly have been anything else – but her Christianity was somehow lightened by her pagan background. Her father had steeped her from childhood in the Hellenistic tradition, and she knew the Greek poets and philosophers even better than the Bible and the patristic writings; in short, there was a whole extra dimension to her mind compared to those of the three dismal princesses, and she cheered up the court wonderfully. Her star rose still higher when, the year after her marriage, she presented her husband with a baby daughter – to whom, in a gesture towards his mother's memory as inappropriate as it was confusing, he gave the name Eudoxia. It was perhaps in gratitude for his first-born child that, in 423, he raised his wife to the rank of Augusta.

Nothing, one would have thought, could be more natural; but her sister-in-law did not take it well. Pulcheria had always seen Athenais as her creation. She had found her, introduced her to Theodosius, organized her conversion, sponsored her at her baptism and educated her in the ways of the court. The girl was her protégée, beholden to her for all she possessed and all she had become. Now, suddenly, she was of equal rank. She was more beautiful, more sought-after, better educated and infinitely better liked. She was also far closer to her husband, and exerted a far greater influence over him than his sister could ever hope to do. As Pulcheria's jealousy grew, she began to find the Empress frivolous, irreverent and – which was probably true – increasingly disrespectful of herself. And so she determined, sooner or later and in any way she could, to cut her down to size.

1 From this point on she should properly be known as Eudocia; but since both her mother-in-law and daughter were called Eudoxia – the two names seem often to have been interchangeable – the possibilities of confusion will be appreciably lessened if we allow her, for the purpose of this narrative, to keep her pagan name. It is a much prettier name anyway.

That same summer the imperial couple received at the Palace the Empire's third Augusta: Galla Placidia, daughter of Theodosius the Great – and granddaughter, through her mother, of the elder Valentinian – who arrived in Constantinople with her two small children. Though still only in her early thirties, Placidia could already look back on an extraordinary life. Finding her half-brother Honorius's court in Ravenna intolerable, she had taken up residence in Rome, where she had survived all three of Alaric's sieges; after the third, however, she had been taken by the Goths as a hostage and kept by them in captivity for four years until, in 414, Honorius was finally induced to consent to her marriage with Ataulfus, Alaric's brother-in-law and successor. There had been a sumptuous wedding at Narbonne, and the two had finally established their court at Barcelona; but Ataulfus had died after little more than a year and Placidia had returned to Ravenna – where, in 417, reluctantly but at her brother's insistence, she took his closest adviser, a dark, swarthy Illyrian named Constantius, as her second husband.

Despite his unprepossessing appearance – his expression, we are told, was permanently sulky, his eyes darting suspiciously to right and left – and his execrable horsemanship, Constantius had enjoyed a distinguished military career, culminating in the defeat of the usurper Constantinus at Arles in 411;[1] and he seems to have genuinely loved Placidia, whose hand he had sought even before her first marriage. Two children, Honoria and Valentinian, were born to them in swift succession, and in 421 Constantius was raised to be co-Emperor with Honorius, Placidia herself being named Augusta. The news was received with dismay at the court of Theodosius, who refused to recognize the new elevations or to erect the traditional statues when they arrived from Ravenna; but fortunately this dissension did not last long, since Constantius – who detested his new position and had almost immediately gone into a decline – died in his turn, after a reign of barely six months.

So Placidia entered her second widowhood at the court of Ravenna, which soon proved even less congenial to her than before. Honorius, whose mind had never been altogether stable, was now becoming progressively more unbalanced. First he displayed embarrassing signs of falling in love with his half-sister, covering her with slobbering kisses in

1 He had guaranteed Constantinus's life in return for his surrender, and had sent him and his son Julian back under close escort to Ravenna; but at the twentieth milestone from the city the two prisoners were intercepted and executed on the Emperor's orders. The contemporary historian Olympiodorus claims that their impaled heads were subsequently exposed outside the gates of Carthage – a curious choice of city, which he does not attempt to explain.

public; then, finding that his affection was not reciprocated, he became by turns suspicious, jealous and at last openly hostile. Soon this hostility began to manifest itself not just in the Emperor personally but in his entourage as well, and even among his guards; and it was when the latter began attacking her own retainers in the streets of Ravenna that Placidia decided that she could stand no more and early in 423 sought refuge with her nephew in Constantinople, taking her children with her.

The two families seem to have got on cordially enough together, even agreeing on the marriage of little Valentinian – he was then four – with the baby Eudoxia when the two children should be of somewhat riper years; and there is no telling how long Placidia and her family might have remained on the Bosphorus had she not, towards the end of that summer, received news that must have caused both her and her hosts considerable relief: on 26 August Honorius had died of dropsy, in his fortieth year. Unfortunately this report was immediately followed by another: the empty throne had been seized by a certain Johannes, erstwhile holder of the not very illustrious office of *primicerius notariorum*, Chief of the Notaries.

Theodosius – urged on, we may be sure, by Pulcheria and perhaps even by Athenais – acted swiftly. He had no intention of seeing the Empire of the West, ailing as it might be, snatched away by a relatively unimportant member of the Civil Service. There and then he confirmed Placidia in the rank of Augusta, invested Valentinian with the title of Caesar and gave orders for the immediate preparation of an army to escort them back to Italy and restore them to their rightful thrones.

The expedition set forth the following year – the Emperor himself accompanying it as far as Thessalonica – and proved triumphantly successful. In those times, the surroundings of Ravenna were very different from what they are today. Over the past 1,500 years the sea has receded several miles; where we now see low-lying meadows and grassland there was once an island-studded lagoon on the Venetian pattern. Ravenna consequently enjoyed the reputation of being virtually impregnable – which was precisely why the terrified Honorius had established his court there after the battle of Pollentia nearly a quarter of a century before, but which had not prevented him from setting up additional defences along the numerous dikes and causeways that led to the city. These the Byzantines wisely ignored; instead, they somehow contrived to ford part of the lagoon itself – Socrates claims that they were guided by an angel disguised as a shepherd – thereby taking the defenders by surprise and capturing Ravenna, early in 425, with scarcely a casualty.

Johannes, after just eighteen months on the throne, was taken prisoner and brought in chains to Aquileia, where Placidia and her children were waiting. There in the Hippodrome his right hand was cut off, after which he was led around the city on a donkey, the people mocking him as he passed, and finally put to death. Meanwhile the victorious soldiery were allowed a three-day sack of Ravenna – to punish the inhabitants, so it was said, for having supported a usurper – and Valentinian, now six, was carried off to Rome for his coronation.

In Constantinople, Athenais's Hellenism was now making itself felt far beyond the confines of the imperial palace. For many years already the Latin element in the capital had been gradually giving way to the Greek, but its progress had been considerably faster under her influence – and under that of her protégé Cyrus of Panopolis, who served for many years as Praetorian Prefect of the city. A poet, philosopher and art-lover, and a Greek through and through – he was the first Prefect to publish his decrees in the Greek language – Cyrus added immeasurably to the architectural splendour of Constantinople, erecting more public buildings than anyone since the Founder himself. He was also instrumental, together with the Emperor and Empress, in transforming the relatively modest educational establishment instituted by Constantine into a large and distinguished university. The idea behind the latter enterprise was to provide a Christian counterpart to the essentially pagan university of Athens, which had so far successfully resisted various attempts to close it down; but the constitution of the new foundation made it clear that, if a pagan university was Greek, a Christian one did not necessarily have to be Latin: though both the Greek and Latin schools were allotted a staff of ten grammarians, the Greek school could boast five rhetors while the Latin school had to make do with only three.

A by-product, as it were, of the university was the compilation of what was known as the Theodosian Codex. Begun in 429, it was entrusted to a commission of nine scholars and was in essence a collection of all the legislation enacted in both East and West since the days of Constantine. Many of the laws had been annulled, others amended and not a few were found to be mutually contradictory; such indeed was the confusion that the first commission found itself unable to continue, and it was nine years before a second, reconstituted group managed to complete the task. The Codex was finally to be promulgated on 15 February 438, jointly by the Eastern and Western Emperors in what was obviously intended to emphasize the unity of the Empire, following as it did only a few months after the long-planned marriage of Valentinian and the fifteen-year-old Eudoxia.

That unity, however, was a good deal more apparent than real. The imperial law, as it had evolved up to that moment in both East and West, was now at last on a firm foundation; but almost immediately the two halves of the Empire began to diverge once again, the new edicts and enactments of the one being seldom if ever passed on to the other. Constantinople and Ravenna might remain friendly, but their separate ways were in fact leading them further and further apart.

By now, too, another rift had appeared within the framework of Byzantine life – a rift whose significance can be fully realized only if we first understand the extraordinary intensity with which religious thought permeated every level of Eastern Christian society. Already at the end of the preceding century, St Gregory of Nyssa had written the words quoted at the head of this chapter; and that essentially Greek passion for theological speculation that he describes had been, if anything, intensified since his day by such charismatic figures as St John Chrysostom and Bishop Theophilus of Alexandria – whose quarrels, as we have already seen, could easily stir up sufficient public feeling to cause demonstrations, riots and even fighting in the streets. And of all the issues most likely to cause serious dissent and to inflame tempers to flash-point and beyond, the most contentious concerned the relation of Jesus Christ to God the Father.

This impossible and – to most of us – obviously unanswerable question had lain at the root of the Arian heresy, which had bedevilled both Eastern and Western Christendom for a hundred years and more; it had been condemned in 325 at Nicaea, but had smouldered on in one form or another throughout the fourth century, sometimes affecting even the Emperors themselves. Constantius, for example, had favoured a compromise, according to which the Son was not of the same (*homoousion*) but of like (*homoiousion*) substance with the Father;[1] Valens, on the other hand, had been an out-and-out Arian. At the Council of Constantinople in 381, the impeccably orthodox Theodosius the Great had confirmed the findings of Nicaea and had promulgated several subsequent edicts designed to enforce what he called Catholicism on his subjects; but they had failed. The issue, though it should have been settled time and time again, had obstinately refused to lie down.

Now, in the reign of Theodosius's grandson and namesake, it assumed

1 An idea that had occurred to several delegates to the Council of Nicaea. See page 55n.

146

a new form – a polarization this time, with two opposing schools of
thought, one on each side of Nicaean orthodoxy. The first of these
schools to cause concern was that of a certain Nestorius, who in 427 had
been appointed Bishop of Constantinople and was consequently in a
particularly strong position to advance his theories. An impassioned
fanatic who, after only five days on the episcopal throne, had burnt
down a neighbouring church on hearing that it had been used for
clandestine services by Arians, Nestorius preached that Christ was not,
as the Nicaeans believed, a single person – both God and Man – but
that he possessed two distinct persons, one human and the other divine.
'I cannot speak of God,' he wrote, 'as being two or three months old';
in other words, he refused to attribute the frailties inseparable from
human life to a member of the Trinity. It followed – and this corollary
soon assumed overriding importance in the popular mind – that the
Virgin Mary could not be described as the *Theotokos*, the Mother of
God, since such a description would suggest that the divine nature was
born of woman. She was, Nestorius claimed, the Mother of Christ, and
no more.

Thanks in large measure to the power of the bishop's oratory, his
teachings rapidly gained ground in the capital and in the major cities of
the East. They found a worthy opponent, however, in Cyril, nephew of
Bishop Theophilus and his successor in the see of Alexandria, who was
determined to carry on the quarrel which had begun with his uncle and
St John Chrysostom – less, probably, for doctrinal reasons than because
of personal jealousy and his own long-cherished ambition to establish
the primacy of the ancient Alexandrian see over that of upstart Constantinople. As the dispute between the two protagonists and their followers grew ever more bitter the Emperor, who always tended to believe
those who were nearest him and was consequently a convinced Nestorian, decided in 430 to summon another Council of the Church that
would pronounce unequivocally in favour of his bishop. In doing so,
however, he seriously underestimated the Alexandrians. Cyril fought
with every weapon he possessed – including his knowledge of the rivalry
that existed between the two Augustae. Athenais, he was well aware,
was a Nestorian like her husband; it would be so much the easier to
attract Pulcheria to his own side. Before long Theodosius got wind of
his machinations and taxed him with them, but it was of no avail; the
damage had been done.

The Council met on 22 June 431 in the Church of the Theotokos – a
significant dedication – at Ephesus; and Cyril, who had beggared his

own diocese to find sufficient funds for the bribing of civil servants and ecclesiastics as necessary, carried all before him. With no apparent difficulty he assumed the presidency of the Council, and then summoned Nestorius to appear before it to answer the charges of heresy levelled against him. Not surprisingly, Nestorius demurred. He had travelled to Ephesus, he pointed out, as a delegate, not as a defendant; he would present himself at the church only when all the bishops who had signified that they would attend the Council had in fact arrived. But Cyril was not disposed to wait. He read out the correspondence that had passed between them – suitably edited, one suspects – after which the entire assembly cried anathema on the unfortunate Nestorius, who was thereupon dismissed from his episcopate and from all priestly communion. The number of delegates present by that time was 198; but when Nestorius later commented that 'the Council was Cyril', he was surely not so very far wrong. He retired into private life; his troubles, however, were not yet over. In 435 the Emperor – who had by this time totally renounced Nestorianism – banished him, first to Petra in Arabia and later to a distant oasis in Libya or Upper Egypt, where he died.[1]

Many years before – perhaps even while Galla Placidia and her children were still at Constantinople – Athenais had vowed that, if her daughter did in fact marry Valentinian and become Empress of the West, she herself would make a pilgrimage to Jerusalem in thanksgiving. The marriage duly took place in the summer of 437; and in the following year she set out for the Holy Land. Her journey, however, first took her to Antioch, where her pagan upbringing stood her in better stead than her more recently adopted faith. Though the population of Antioch was by now predominantly Christian the city remained, more than any other in Asia Minor, infused with the old Hellenistic spirit; and the Empress's familiarity with the literary and cultural traditions of antiquity, combined with the purity and perfection of her Greek, made a far deeper impression than ever it had in Constantinople. The climax came with a magnificent ceremony in the local Senate House, in the course of which she delivered a brilliant extempore speech in praise of the city and its history, ending with a quotation from the *Odyssey*:

1 Despite his disgrace, Nestorius was to have a more lasting influence than he knew. Some of his followers wandered eastward to Persia and Mesopotamia, where they later founded a separate Nestorian Church. After periods of considerable prosperity, they eventually fled from Mongol oppression under Tamburlaine and sought refuge in the mountains of Kurdistan, where a small number of them survived into modern times.

ὑμετέρης γενέης τε καὶ αἵματος εὔχομαι εἶναι.
I claim proud kinship with your race and blood.[1]

Jerusalem, Roman but never Greek, was very different. There may
well have been a few old men and women still alive whose fathers had
remembered the visit of the Empress Helena, 111 years before; and
Athenais clearly modelled herself on her predecessor. She remained in
the city a whole year, visiting all the Holy Places as a humble pilgrim,
attending the consecrations of churches, instituting new charities,
opening convents and hospices. When at last she returned to Constantinople she brought with her the usual profusion of relics – in which,
we are told, the Bishop of Jerusalem plied a profitable trade – including
the bones of St Stephen and the chains with which St Peter had been
fettered when imprisoned by King Herod.[2] Her husband welcomed her
warmly, and for a time all went on as before. But not, alas, for long.

What precisely it was that caused Athenais's downfall we shall never
know for sure; but the sixth-century historian John Malalas tells a story
which, improbable as it sounds, is curious enough to be worth repeating
here. One day, he relates, as the Emperor was on his way to church, a
poor man handed him a Phrygian apple of prodigious size. So huge was
this apple, and so impressed was Theodosius at the sight of it, that he
ordered the man to be given 150 *nomismata* and immediately sent it to
Athenais. She, however, did not eat it herself but had it taken instead to
Paulinus, Master of the Offices, who was confined by an injured foot to
his house; and Paulinus, not knowing how the Empress had obtained it,
dispatched it to the Palace as a gift from himself to Theodosius. The
Emperor received it with some surprise. At last, thoroughly mystified
and not a little suspicious, he summoned his wife and, concealing the
apple, asked her what she had done with it.

Poor Athenais – had she only given a truthful answer, all might yet
have been well; but at this critical moment she lost her head. 'I ate it,'
she replied. White with rage, her husband produced the fatal fruit. By
lying, he told her, she had revealed the truth of her relations with
Paulinus, who would be executed at once. But now Athenais struck

---

1 Such a claim seldom fails to touch the hearts of its audience. We may compare General Eisenhower,
addressing the crowd after receiving the Freedom of the City of London in 1945: 'I've got just as
much right to be down there hollering as you have – I'm a Londoner too'; or President Kennedy's
'*Ich bin ein Berliner*' in 1963.

2 One of these she sent on to her daughter Eudoxia, who immediately built the Roman church now
known as S. Pietro in Vincoli to receive them. There they were subsequently joined by similar chains
said to have tethered the saint during his later captivity in Rome.

back. To execute him, she claimed, would be tantamount to an open accusation of adultery, which she absolutely denied. After such an insult she could in any case no longer remain under her husband's roof; she accordingly sought his permission to return to Jerusalem, where she proposed to end her days.

It has been suggested, by Professor Bury among others,[1] that the apple was in ancient times a symbol of chastity, and that this strange story may consequently be allegorical, signifying that Athenais had indeed surrendered her virtue to Paulinus. It may be so, and perhaps she had; but such an interpretation certainly does not accord with her character as we know it. The Master of the Offices was by all accounts a highly honourable man, the closest friend of her husband since the two had played together as children. Athenais, too, he had known since before her marriage, which he had actively encouraged and at which he acted as *paranymphos*, or best man. On her deathbed, some twenty years later, the Empress swore once again that she was innocent; and if there is still any doubt, she must surely be given the benefit of it. A final point in her favour is that Paulinus was executed in 440, whereas she does not seem to have left for Jerusalem till some three years later – a long time to remain in a city in which she believed herself dishonoured.

It looks, therefore, as if we shall have to consign the story of the Phrygian apple to legend and conclude that, in all probability, the fate of Paulinus – who was in fact first exiled to Caesarea in Cappadocia, being assassinated on the Emperor's orders a short while later – had no connection with the Empress's resolve to leave the capital for ever. A far likelier explanation is to be found in the relentless machinations of Pulcheria, who must have been infuriated by the vastly increased reputation for holiness acquired by her sister-in-law as a result of her visit to Jerusalem and who doubtless intrigued against her with still greater determination than before. But, whatever the reason, it seems clear that Athenais did somehow fall from her husband's favour – she could never otherwise have left him as she did – and that even her departure did not altogether save her from his vindictiveness; for within a few months of her arrival in Jerusalem a certain Saturninus, Count of the Imperial Bodyguard, followed her there and killed the two leading members of her entourage, one a priest and the other a deacon, whom she had brought with her from Constantinople. She took her revenge by having Saturninus murdered in his turn and (perhaps subconsciously) by her enthusiastic adoption of the monophysite heresy[2] – until, in her last

1 Op cit., Vol. I, p. 133, fn.
2 See p. 155.

years, Pope Leo the Great himself finally succeeded in persuading her back into the orthodox fold. She lived on till 460, sad, lonely and embittered, a pathetic shadow of the brilliant, talented girl who had swept the young Emperor off his feet and, fifteen years later, had so dazzled the citizens of Antioch. When at last she died, she was buried in the Church of St Stephen which she had founded – in Constantinople long forgotten and even in Jerusalem, one suspects, feared rather than loved.

We have now followed – sketchily but, in a book primarily concerned with the Byzantine Empire, sufficiently – the career of the young Western Emperor Valentinian III from his childhood in Ravenna and Constantinople to his coronation in Rome and, twelve years later, his marriage to the Princess Eudoxia. He had proved a weak and ineffectual figure, utterly dominated by his formidable mother Placidia, who had continued to govern in his name long after he had reached manhood – indeed, until her own death in 450;[1] and he need no longer detain us here. As for his sister Honoria, she would not have gained so much as a mention in this book were it not for a single circumstance; but that circumstance must ensure for her at least a footnote in any account of her time. In the whole of history there can, after all, have been few princesses of any age or condition who would, of their own free will, have offered themselves in marriage to Attila the Hun.

Any self-respecting historian must try as best he can to tell his story in his own words. He may permit himself the occasional direct quotation from primary sources, if they add colour or flavour to his narrative; but he should, on the whole, steer clear of secondary ones, unless there are compelling reasons to the contrary. Such a moment now arises: for the Princess Honoria has provided Edward Gibbon with the inspiration for one of his most brilliant and characteristic paragraphs, which it would be unfair to the reader not to quote in full:

The sister of Valentinian was educated in the palace of Ravenna, and as her marriage might be productive of some danger to the state, she was raised, by the title of *Augusta*, above the hopes of the most presumptuous subject. But the

---

1 Her Mausoleum at Ravenna is the outstanding monument of the age. Of the three marble sarcophagi that stand beneath the glorious mosaics, that on the left contains all that remains of Constantius, her second husband, and their son Valentinian III; that on the right holds what there is of Honorius; while the central sarcophagus – the largest of all – is that of the Empress herself. In it her body is said to have sat, enthroned in robes of state, for eleven centuries, visible through a small peep-hole at the back; but in 1577, so the story goes, some children thrust a lighted taper through the hole. There was a sudden flash, and within seconds everything – throne, robes and Empress – was a heap of ashes.

fair Honoria had no sooner attained the sixteenth year of her age than she detested the importunate greatness which must for ever exclude her from the comforts of honourable love; in the midst of vain and unsatisfactory pomp Honoria sighed, yielded to the impulse of nature, and threw herself into the arms of her chamberlain Eugenius. Her guilt and shame (such is the absurd language of imperious man) were soon betrayed by the appearances of pregnancy: but the disgrace of the royal family was published to the world by the imprudence of the Empress Placidia, who dismissed her daughter, after a strict and shameful confinement, to a remote exile at Constantinople. The unhappy princess passed twelve or fourteen years in the irksome society of the sisters of Theodosius and their chosen virgins, to whose *crown* Honoria could no longer aspire, and whose monastic assiduity of prayer, fasting and vigils she reluctantly imitated. Her impatience of long and hopeless celibacy urged her to embrace a strange and desperate resolution. The name of Attila was familiar and formidable at Constantinople, and his frequent embassies entertained a perpetual intercourse between his camp and the imperial palace. In the pursuit of love, or rather of revenge, the daughter of Placidia sacrificed every duty and every prejudice, and offered to deliver her person into the arms of a barbarian of whose language she was ignorant, whose figure was scarcely human, and whose religion and manners she abhorred. By the ministry of a faithful eunuch she transmitted to Attila a ring, the pledge of her affection, and earnestly conjured him to claim her as a lawful spouse to whom he had been secretly betrothed. These indecent advances were received, however, with coldness and disdain; and the king of the Huns continued to multiply the number of his wives till his love was awakened by the more forcible passions of ambition and avarice.

Attila, jointly with his brother Bleda, had succeeded to the throne of the Huns in 434. Since 376, when it had first smashed its way into Europe from the steppes of Central Asia, this most savage of all the barbarian tribes had caused the Empire surprisingly little trouble. Neither an invasion – possibly prompted by Rufinus – of Armenia and Cappadocia in 395 nor a brief incursion into Bulgaria by King Uldin thirteen years later had produced any lasting results, and to increase his sense of security still further Theodosius had started, in about 430, to pay an annual subsidy – some might have called it a tribute – of 350 pounds of gold, the further to encourage his neighbours to keep the peace.

With the appearance of Attila, however – 'the scourge of God' as he was called – this relatively uneventful coexistence was to change. After over half a century's contact with the Romans, his people had become perhaps one degree less bestial than at their first arrival; but the vast majority still lived and slept in the open, disdaining all agriculture and even cooked foods – though they would often soften raw meat by putting it between their thighs and their horses' flanks as they rode. For clothing they favoured tunics made, rather surprisingly, from the skins of field-mice, crudely stitched together; these they wore continuously, without ever removing them, until they dropped off of their own accord. And, as they had always done, they still practically lived on their horses, eating, trading, holding their councils, even sleeping in the saddle. Attila himself was typical of his race: short, swarthy and snub-nosed, with tiny beady eyes set in a head too big for his body and a thin, straggling beard. He was not a great ruler, nor even a particularly able general; but so overmastering were the ambition and avarice with which Gibbon credits him – to say nothing of his pride, in both his person and his race, and his lust for power – that within the space of a few years he made himself feared throughout the length and breadth of Europe: more feared, perhaps, than any other single man – with the possible exception of Napoleon – before or since.

The details of his early campaigns are largely unrecorded; but within seven years of his succession he had built up a vast barbaric dominion of his own, stretching from the Balkans to the Caucasus and beyond. His first attacks on the Eastern Empire began in 441, and for the next six years there was sporadic fighting in Pannonia and along the Danube; but it was not until 447 that he gave Theodosius and his ministers serious cause for alarm. By this time his brother Bleda had died – no contemporary evidence exists to support later allegations that Attila had had him murdered – and he was in sole command of a people estimated at several thousand. His army now advanced in two directions at once: southward into Thessaly as far as Thermopylae, and eastward to Constantinople. The Theodosian Walls had, it seemed, been built just in time: the Huns had not the patience, the skill nor the discipline required for protracted siege warfare and soon turned away in search of more accessible plunder. But they inflicted a crushing defeat on the Byzantine army at Gallipoli, withdrawing only after the Emperor had agreed to treble the annual amount of Hun-money payable – as well as to hand over vast sums of past arrears which Attila claimed (probably rightly) that he had never received.

From this time forward, embassies passed almost constantly between Attila's camp and the court of Theodosius. If the majority came from the Hunnish side this was because Attila, seeing one after another of his ambassadors return from Constantinople weighed down with rich presents, had discovered a most effective means of benefiting those whom he wished to help at no cost to himself. He believed that the Emperor was now terrified of him, and he was right: what little spirit Theodosius had once possessed had long since evaporated. His only policy now was one of craven appeasement, for which he was perfectly ready not only to exhaust his own treasury but to bleed his subjects white into the bargain. Had Athenais, or even Pulcheria, remained at his side, one is tempted to believe that they might have persuaded him to take a firmer line; but the former was far away in Jerusalem, and the latter had long since lost her brother's ear. The most powerful influence at the court was now that of a eunuch named Chrysaphus; and it was he who in 448 managed to suborn one of Attila's envoys, Edeco, and to involve him, in return for a rich reward, in a plot to assassinate the King of the Huns.

In pursuance of this conspiracy, a more than usually distinguished Byzantine embassy set out later in the same year. It was led by a senior officer of noble lineage (a point to which Attila always attached great significance) named Maximin and his friend Priscus – to neither of whom it was revealed that certain members of their retinue had secret orders from Chrysaphus to murder Attila in the course of their mission. In the event, this hardly mattered. The plot was at once confessed to Attila by Edeco – whose role from the outset may have been that of an *agent provocateur* – and was dealt with by its intended victim with remarkable adroitness. Meanwhile the embassy, after a few initial embarrassments, was finally received with every show of cordiality by Attila himself.

Its significance to posterity, however, lies not in its more sinister aspect nor yet in its achievements – which were in any case minimal – but in the long and almost unbelievably detailed account of it left by Priscus. Thanks to him we have an unforgettable picture of the Hunnish court, as well as of its King – feasting, carousing, dispensing justice, entertaining the Roman emissaries with his tribesmen, moving alternately between towering, terrifying rages and quieter moods in which he shows his guests courtesy and even glimmerings of charm. They were surprised, too, by the simplicity of his tastes during the banquet that he gave in their honour:

While for the other barbarians and for us there were lavishly prepared dishes served on silver platters, for Attila there was only meat on a wooden plate . . . Gold and silver goblets were handed to the men at the feast, whereas his cup was of wood. His clothing was plain, and differed not at all from that of the rest, except that it was clean. Neither the sword that hung at his side nor the fastenings of his barbarian boots nor his horse's bridle was adorned, like those of the other Scythians, with gold or precious stones or anything else of value.[1]

[1] Trans. R. C. Blockley.

Priscus leaves us with the unmistakable impression that Attila, for all his brutishness, was in fact a remarkably astute diplomatist; and there is no telling how much longer he would have continued to drain away the wealth of the Eastern Empire had not Theodosius been killed, on 28 July 450, by a fall from his horse while hunting. He and Athenais had produced no male heir, but the problem of the succession was solved by Pulcheria. Despite her vow of virginity, she was able to contract a nominal marriage to Marcian, a Thracian senator and ex-soldier, whom she promptly named Augustus and placed, with herself, on the throne – giving out (whether truthfully or not it is hard to say) that he had been nominated by Theodosius on his death-bed.

One of the first acts of the new Emperor was to refuse the King of the Huns his annual tribute. It was a courageous step to take, though possibly not quite so courageous as it seemed: Marcian was almost certainly aware that Attila was at that moment preparing a vast operation against the Western Empire, and doubtless gambled on his unwillingness to delay this by a punitive expedition to the East. Nevertheless, a gamble it was; and there must have been rejoicing in Constantinople when the news arrived that the Hunnish army had started upon its march into Italy and Gaul.

But rejoicing, by its very essence, does not last long. All too soon the exhilaration dies, the problems of daily life reassert themselves. So, as the danger from the Huns began to fade, Marcian found himself obliged to turn his attention to a new threat, internal rather than external, spiritual rather than material, but none the less insistent for that: the ever-deepening split in Byzantine society occasioned by the monophysite heresy.

It was rooted in the same old enigma: the precise relation of the Father and the Son within the Trinity. The story of the Nestorians has already been told, with its grim moral concerning the fate awaiting those who upheld the principle of the two distinct persons in Christ, the human and the divine. That error had been dealt with forcibly enough at Ephesus in 431; since then, however, the pendulum had swung to the opposite extreme, and in 448 an elderly archimandrite named Eutyches was accused of disseminating the equally subversive doctrine that the Incarnate Christ possessed but a single nature, and that that nature was divine. Found guilty, condemned and degraded, Eutyches at once appealed to Pope Leo I (the Great), to the Emperor Theodosius and to the monks of Constantinople; and in doing so he unleashed a storm of scarcely imaginable ferocity. For three years the Church was in uproar, with councils summoned and discredited, bishops unseated and restored; with intrigues and conspiracies, violence and vituperation, curses and anathemas thundering between Rome and Constantinople, Ephesus and Alexandria. At last, in October 451, the fourth Ecumenical Council[1] was held in the Church of St Euphemia at Chalcedon to put an end to the chaos. Numbering as it did some five to six hundred bishops, whose views ranged across the whole breadth of the Christological spectrum, it is astonishing that this Council should have reached any decisions at all; in fact, it achieved everything it set out to do and more.[2] Eutyches, who had been rehabilitated and reinstated in 449, was once again condemned; and a new statement of faith was drawn up, known as the Chalcedonian Definition, according to which the doctrines of Nestorius and Eutyches were alike repudiated. Christ was established as the possessor of one person with two natures, united 'unconfusedly, unchangeably, indivisibly and inseparably': perfect God and perfect man.

But, successful as the Council of Chalcedon unquestionably was in the short term, it laid up a greater store of future trouble than it knew. Monophysitism, as soon became apparent, was by no means dead. In the years to come, both in Egypt and Syria – the latter once a stronghold of the Nestorians – bishop after bishop was openly to reject the findings of the Council; and when these provinces began their struggle for independence from Byzantine rule, the Single Nature of Christ was to be their rallying-cry.[3] With the West also, the seeds of discord were sown – notably in one of the thirty decrees which the delegates went on to promulgate when their main business was over. This decree, known as Canon Twenty-Eight, bestowed on the Bishop of Constantinople the title of Patriarch and reiterated the Theodosian ruling of 381 which had accorded him a pride of place in the Christian hierarchy second only to the Pope of Rome. So much the papal representatives present were

1 The three previous Councils had been those of Nicaea in 325, Constantinople in 381 and Ephesus in 431.

2 According to an 'Anonymous Englishman' writing in 1190, the two opposing camps, orthodox and monophysite, decided to resolve the dispute by placing their two respective formulas in the coffin of St Euphemia – a local virgin martyred in 303 – and leaving the decision to her. When they opened the coffin a week later they found the orthodox formula on her heart and the monophysite under her feet. There was no further argument.

3 The monophysite doctrine still survives today among the Copts and Abyssinians, the Jacobites of Syria and the Armenians.

prepared to allow; what they could not accept was the clear implication that the Pope's supremacy would henceforth be purely titular, and that in every other respect there would be complete equality between the sees of Rome and Constantinople. The eastern provinces in particular – those of Thrace, Pontus and Asia – would be responsible to the Patriarch alone, by whom their metropolitans would in future be ordained. From this moment was born the ecclesiastical rivalry between the Old Rome and the New which was to grow increasingly bitter over the centuries until, just 600 years later, it was to erupt into schism.

John Malalas – a sixth-century Syrian-Byzantine chronicler whose anecdotes, however apocryphal, are the very essence of the *ben trovato* – records that the King of the Huns sent envoys, shortly before the death of Theodosius II, to both the Eastern and the Western Emperors, bearing the message: 'Attila, thy master and mine, bids thee prepare a palace for his reception.' Despite the lack of contemporary evidence, there is nothing inherently improbable about this story: Attila had designs on both halves of the Roman Empire, and loved nothing more than to strike terror into the hearts of his enemies. Until now, he had directed his energies principally against the East; but developments among the various barbarian tribes in the Western provinces had recently provided several excellent pretexts for his intervention there. Still more fortunate, from his point of view, was the opportunity unexpectedly afforded by the luckless Princess Honoria, to whose imperial brother he could now forward the ring she had sent him, together with a demand couched in his usual peremptory style: that Valentinian should restore to her forthwith that part of his Empire which was her due, and of which he had so unjustly deprived her.

The details of Attila's western campaigns need not concern us here; none the less, it should never be forgotten that, in the summer of 451 and again in 452, the whole fate of western civilization hung in the balance. Had the Hunnish army not been halted in these two successive campaigns, had its leader toppled Valentinian from his throne and set up his own capital in Ravenna or Rome, there is little doubt that both Gaul and Italy would have been reduced to spiritual and cultural deserts, just as surely and just as completely as the Balkan peninsula was reduced by the Ottoman Turks a thousand years later. In 451 Attila crossed the Rhine, devastated the great frontier city of Metz with several other important garrison towns, and penetrated as far as the walls of Orleans. Before he could take the city, however, he was forced to turn back: an imperial army under the Roman general Aetius – the effective ruler of Gaul – was advancing from the east, strengthened by detachments of Visigoths and Burgundians, Bretons and Franks, all united for the first time against their common enemy; and though the ensuing battle, known sometimes by the name of the Catalaunian and sometimes by that of the Mauriac or Mauritian Plain,[1] was indecisive insofar as both sides sustained immense losses and neither was left master of the field, it had the effect of halting the Huns' advance. On the following morning Attila gave the signal for retreat and departed for his Hungarian heartland, there to rest and consolidate until spring should bring new ardour to his men.

Early in 452 he launched his army upon Italy. The opening of the new campaign was hardly encouraging: Aquileia held out for three months against the Hunnish onslaught, and Attila was on the point of giving up the siege when, Jordanes tells us, he saw a flight of storks heading away from the city with their young. Crediting them with a degree of foresight which in our own day is more usually accorded to rats, he pointed them out to his troops as a sure sign that the city was doomed. Thus encouraged, the Huns flung themselves with renewed vigour into the attack; and soon afterwards, the ninth greatest metropolis in the Roman Empire was an empty shell. Concordia, Altino and Padua followed in quick succession. Vicenza and Verona, Brescia and Bergamo would have suffered likewise had they not immediately opened their gates at the conqueror's approach – as would Pavia and Milan, where Attila triumphantly set up his court in the imperial palace. These last cities were not put to the torch like those of the Veneto; they were, however, mercilessly sacked, and many of their leading citizens taken into captivity.

This time the King of the Huns was carrying all before him. Aetius, who had assumed command in Italy, had no friendly barbarian tribes on whom to call, as he had had in Gaul the previous year. The imperial army alone stood no chance against the advancing multitude and there was, it seemed, nothing to prevent Attila from marching on Rome – the consequences of which would have been infinitely more terrible than anything ever contemplated by the relatively civilized, Christian, Alaric. And yet, at the very point of departure for his advance down the

---

1 The old chroniclers differ as to the site of the battle as well as its name. Hodgkin, after a careful analysis of all available evidence, plumps for Méry-sur-Seine, some twenty miles north-west of Troyes; if he is right – which he probably is – the actual fighting is most likely to have taken place in the broad, flat plain immediately to the south, between Méry and Estissac.

peninsula, he suddenly halted; and historians have been speculating ever since as to precisely why he did so.

Traditionally, the credit has always been given to Pope Leo the Great who, accompanied by two imperial dignitaries of the highest rank, travelled from Rome to meet Attila on the banks of the Mincio – probably near Peschiera, where the river issues from Lake Garda – and somehow persuaded him to advance no further; but the pagan Hun would not have obeyed the Pope out of mere respect for his office, and the question remains: what inducements was he offered in return? A substantial tribute is the likeliest answer – together, perhaps, with the hand of Honoria and an appropriate dowry. But there is another possibility: Attila, like all his race, was incorrigibly superstitious, and the Pope may well have reminded him of how Alaric had died almost immediately after the sack of Rome, pointing out that a similar fate was known to befall every invader who raised his hand against the holy city. The Huns themselves may also have been partly responsible for persuading their leader to retire: we have evidence to suggest that, after their devastation of all the surrounding countryside, they were beginning to suffer from a serious shortage of food, and that disease had broken out within their ranks. A final consideration was that troops were beginning to arrive from Constantinople, sent by Marcian to swell the imperial forces. A march on Rome, it began to appear, might not prove quite so straightforward as had first been thought.

For some, or all, of these reasons – just which we shall never know, primary sources for the period being in lamentably short supply – Attila made the decision to turn back. A year later, during the night following his marriage to yet another of his already countless wives, his exertions brought on a sudden haemorrhage; and, as his life-blood flowed away, all Europe breathed again. While the funeral feast was in progress, a specially selected group of captives prepared his body for the grave, encasing it in three coffins – one of gold, one of silver and one of iron. Then, when it had been lowered into the earth and covered over, first with rich spoils of war and then with earth until the ground was level above it, all those involved in the burial ceremonies were put to death, so that the great King's last resting-place might remain for ever secret and inviolate.

And so it has done, to this day.

8

The Fall of the West

[455–93]

Hesperium Romanae gentis imperium ... cum hoc Augustulo periit ... Gothorum dehinc regibus Romam tenentibus.

The western Empire of the Roman people ... perished with that little Augustus ... the Gothic Kings occupying Rome thereafter.

Count Marcellinus

Some time in the middle of March 455 – it must have been on or about the Ides – the Emperor Valentinian III, who had deserted Ravenna to take up residence in Rome, rode out of the city to the Campus Martius, there to do a little archery practice and to watch the athletes exercising in the spring sunshine. Suddenly, as he paused by some laurel bushes, two soldiers of barbarian origin stepped out from behind them and ran him through with their swords – none of his court or bodyguard lifting, so far as we can gather, a finger in his defence. To a considerable extent, Valentinian could be said to have brought it on himself. Only a few months before, he had personally killed in very much the same way his *magister militum* Aetius, who had effectively ruled the West for the past thirty years, for no better reason than that the latter had planned to marry off his son to one of the Emperor's daughters; and the murdered man's friends and supporters had there and then determined on revenge.

Valentinian left no son; and the choice of the army fell on an elderly senator, Petronius Maximus, generally believed to have been the grandson of the usurper Maximus who had been crushed by Theodosius the Great. As a young man he had had an outstanding career, having been Consul for the first time at the age of thirty-eight and Praetorian Prefect of Italy six years later; but he was now well past his prime, and if – as was popularly rumoured – he had bribed his way to power, he soon had cause to regret it: almost at once, he found the cares of Empire in the fast-disintegrating West too much for him. He showed, too, a deplorable lack of both political judgement and human sensitivity, first by refusing to punish the murderers of his predecessor and accepting them instead into the circle of his personal friends,[1] and secondly by insisting on immediately taking the widowed Empress Eudoxia as his wife. Eudoxia – now thirty-seven and, like her mother, one of the most beautiful women of her day – was still in deep mourning for her husband whom, despite his innumerable infidelities, she had genuinely loved; and she was horrified at the prospect of a marriage, against her will, to a tired old man nearly twice her age. Knowing that an appeal to Constantinople would have little chance of being answered, she therefore decided on a course of action similar to that chosen by her despairing sister-in-law Honoria a few years earlier: she invoked the assistance of a barbarian King.

So, at least, runs the traditional story. It does not, however, sound particularly convincing, and one of the only two chroniclers to report it – John of Antioch – describes it as hearsay. A less romantic but, alas, more probable version claims that Eudoxia proved well able to look after herself and indignantly rejected the new Emperor's advances. In such an event she would have had no reason to appeal to King Gaiseric; and indeed the latter's subsequent invasion of Italy requires no ex- planation of this kind. Neither Alaric nor Attila had bothered to find pretexts for aggression: the reputation of Rome provided motive enough for any barbarian chieftain out for plunder. But the point hardly matters. Whatever the reason, the city was once again under threat – and this time from the last of the three formidable peoples that, during the fifth century, devastated so much of Europe: the Vandals.

By comparison with the Goths and the Huns, the Vandals had little direct impact on the Byzantine Empire; they will not, in consequence, occupy much space in this book. Suffice it to say here that they were a Germanic tribe, in creed fanatically Arian, who had fled westward from the Huns at the end of the previous century and, after invading and laying waste a large area of Gaul, had settled in Spain in 409. There they had remained until 428, when the newly crowned King Gaiseric led his entire people – probably some 160,000 men, women and children – across the sea to the North African coast. (Already, it will be noted, the Vandals possessed a fleet – the only barbarians to do so.) A treaty concluded with Valentinian by which the Vandal state was acknowledged as part of

---

[1] According to Procopius (*History of the Wars*, III, iv) it was Maximus himself who had been responsible for Valentinian's murder, the Emperor having violated his wife shortly before. But Procopius (who was born in about 500) is, at least in the opinion of Gibbon, 'a fabulous writer for events which precede his own memory'.

the Empire proved short-lived; in 439 Gaiseric tore it up and declared an independent autocracy – similarly, a step that no other barbarian ruler had ever taken. Some time later he added Sicily to his dominions. By now, having established his capital at Carthage, he was the undisputed master of the whole western Mediterranean.

Thus, whether or not he ever received an appeal from Eudoxia, he would have been able and willing to answer one; and Valentinian had been less than three months in his grave when the Vandal fleet put to sea. In Rome, the reaction to the news was one of panic. The Emperor, cowering in his palace, issued a proclamation – not, as might have been expected, calling upon all able-bodied men to rally to the defence of the Empire, but announcing that anyone who wished to leave was free to do so. He need not have bothered. Already the terrified Romans were sending their wives and daughters away to safety, and the roads to the north and east were choked with carts as the more well-to-do families – and indeed all those with objects of value that they wished to preserve from Vandal clutches – poured out of the city.

Such spirit as was shown was directed less against the invaders than against Petronius Maximus himself. He too had resolved upon flight; but his subjects, who held him responsible for all their woes, were determined that he should not escape. On 31 May, with the Vandal fleet already approaching the Italian coast, the palace guard mutinied, fell upon their hopeless master, killed him, dismembered the body and flung the pieces into the Tiber. He had reigned for just seventy days; and three days after his death King Gaiseric stepped ashore at Ostia. For the fourth time in less than half a century, a barbarian army stood at the gates of Rome.

Had it not been for Pope Leo, who had turned back Attila on the banks of the Mincio three years before, it would have been the fifth; and now once again the Pope set out for the barbarian camp to plead on behalf of his city. This time he was on far weaker ground: Gaiseric was already on the threshold of his objective, his men were healthy and well-fed, and he had no advancing army in his rear. On the other hand, though an Arian, he was at least a Christian – and as such might be expected to show some respect for the papal dignity. Leo's mission was not entirely successful – that would have been too much to hope – but neither was it a total failure. The Vandal refused to be thwarted of his plunder; he promised, however, that there would be no killing, no torturing to discover the location of hidden treasure and no destruction of buildings, public or private. It may, perhaps, have been cold comfort; but it was better than nothing.

And so the gates were opened, and the barbarian horde passed into an unresisting city. For fourteen relentless days they quietly and systematically stripped it of its wealth: the gold and silver ornaments from the churches, the statues from the palaces, the sacred vessels from the Jewish synagogue, even the gilded copper roof – or half of it – from the Temple of Jupiter Capitolinus. Everything was carted to Ostia, loaded into the waiting ships and taken off for the enrichment of Carthage. Their work done, Gaiseric and his men departed in good order, forcing Eudoxia and her two daughters to accompany them[1] and leaving a desecrated and humiliated city behind. True to their word, however, they had left the people and the buildings unharmed. They had behaved like brigands, certainly; but not, on this occasion, like Vandals.

Less than two years after the death of Valentinian, in late January or early February 457, the Eastern Emperor Marcian followed him to the grave; and with Marcian the male Theodosian line – of which, through his marriage to Pulcheria, he must be counted an honorary member – came to an end. Such moments of dynastic exhaustion were always dangerous for the Roman Empire. Theoretically, the Augustus was still chosen by the army; if the diadem had long appeared to be almost hereditary, this was only because so many Emperors had followed the practice of nominating their sons and having them formally recognized during their own lifetimes. Marcian, without male issue, had nominated no one. Pulcheria would doubtless have saved the situation as before had she been alive; but she had died – a few months after Attila – in 453.[2] Her two younger sisters (who had in any case never involved themselves in affairs of state) had both predeceased her. The throne, in short, seemed emptier than it had since the death of Julian; and the people of Constantinople looked to the army to fill it – or, more precisely, to its chief: the *magister militum per orientem*, Aspar.

Aspar had first distinguished himself as long ago as 424, when he had been a member of the expedition to Ravenna which had deposed Johannes and placed young Valentinian on the throne. Eight years later, in 432, he had commanded the army sent out by Theodosius to North Africa to

---

1 Eudoxia was to remain seven years at Carthage. Only in 462, after repeated requests by Leo, was she permitted to return to Constantinople with her daughter Placidia – wife of the Roman senator (and later, briefly, Emperor) Olybrius. The other sister, Eudocia, Gaiseric had married off to his son Huneric.

2 She left all her immense wealth to the poor – a bequest which Marcian, to his eternal credit, faithfully carried out.

reinforce the local legions and, it was hoped, turn the tide against the Vandal invasion; despite his failure, his reputation for leadership and personal courage had remained undiminished. Since then he had served as Consul, and his sons had been Consuls in their turn; he now bore the title 'First of the Patricians', and would in fact almost certainly have succeeded Theodosius instead of Marcian – who, when he had first arrived in Constantinople, penniless, from Thrace, had joined Aspar's domestic staff and remained a member of it for nearly twenty years – but for two things: he was an Alan – a member of that formerly nomadic, pastoral Germanic clan that in 370 had been driven by the Huns from its homeland beyond the Black Sea – and, like nearly all the Christian barbarians, an Arian.

There could, in consequence, be no question of Aspar's own succession. Like the Frankish general Arbogast, however – whose position in the West had been strikingly similar sixty-four years before – he was quite content to be a kingmaker. Significantly, his choice fell on another of his underlings – the steward of his own household, an orthodox Christian from the province of Dacia named Leo. The legions obediently acclaimed their new Emperor and raised him on their shields according to tradition; but now, for the first time, a second ceremony was instituted. On 7 February 457, in the course of a solemn mass in the Church of the Holy Wisdom, Leo was formally crowned by Patriarch Anatolius – a clear reflection of the increased import-ance of the Patriarchate since the Council of Chalcedon and at the same time a sign that the old order was beginning to change: away from the venerable military traditions on which the Empire had been founded and towards that religious, mystical concept of sovereignty which was to grow ever more insistent as the centuries went by.

Leo had little formal education; he possessed, on the other hand, a full measure of good sound common sense and – equally important – a mind of his own; if Aspar had thought that he was placing a puppet on the throne of Byzantium, he soon found himself mistaken. A furi-ous dispute between the two broke out within weeks of Leo's acces-sion – probably over his refusal to appoint one of Aspar's sons to a position of high emolument – and was further exacerbated by the Emperor's determination to clip the wings of the dangerously power-ful Germanic element in the State, of which Aspar was the outstanding representative. In pursuance of this policy, he resolved to purge the army of Germans and to reconstruct it around a nucleus of Isaurians, a tough mountain folk hailing from a wild region of the Taurus south of Iconium and Lystra, around the basin of the Calycadnus river. Aspar, equally determined to preserve the status quo, fought back; and the rivalry between Emperor and general soon became the principal leitmotiv of Leo's reign.

It was perhaps inevitable that this rivalry should produce two distinct factions within the government. On the Emperor's side the leading influence was that of an Isaurian chieftain whose original name, Tarasicodissa Rousoumbladeotes, he very sensibly changed, before marrying Leo's daughter Ariadne, to Zeno. But Aspar too had adherents within the Palace, the chief among whom was Basiliscus, the brother of the Emperor's wife Verina. The two could scarcely have been more different. Aspar was a barbarian of little or no culture, who spent his leisure hours, wrote Priscus, 'with actors and jugglers and all stage amusements'; as a convinced Arian, he came near to denying the godhead of Christ; as a leader of men, he was the finest general of his time. Basiliscus, by contrast, was a Hellenized, well-educated Roman; a fanatical monophysite, for whom Christ was divine rather than human; something of a joke in Constantinople by reason of his consuming desire for the imperial diadem, which he made no attempt to conceal; and, as would soon be proved, a man totally unfitted for any sort of command. Despite their differences, however, they were flung together by their common hatred for the Isaurians; and when the Emperor decided in 468 to launch a massive naval expedition against King Gaiseric and his Vandals, he was persuaded by his wife and Aspar to put Basiliscus at its head.

To many a Roman, this expedition seemed long overdue. Thirteen years had passed since Gaiseric's sack of Rome, during which time the Empire had not stirred against him. The West, to be sure, was so near the point of collapse as to be no longer capable of avenging the insult; but the apathy of the East was harder to defend. Certain apologists for Marcian had attempted to excuse his inertia by claiming that in his youth, while a member of Aspar's ill-fated campaign of 432 against the Vandals, he had been captured, taken with a group of fellow-prisoners to the palace at Carthage, and there forced to wait for several hours in the courtyard with no protection from the broiling sun. Soon he had laid down to sleep; and Gaiseric, looking down from a window, had been astonished to see a huge eagle hovering above him, shading him with its wings. It was, he immediately understood, a sign from heaven; the young man clearly had a great future in store. Summoning him to his presence, he offered to release him on the spot in return for a promise that, whatever his destiny, he would never again take up arms against the Vandal Kingdom. Marcian had agreed, and had kept his word for the rest of his life.

It was a good story; but it is unlikely to have been widely believed.

Marcian had been a straightforward, down-to-earth character, not at all the sort to whom miracles occur. He had, on the other hand, inaugurated a blessed period – which Leo was to continue after his death – of peace, prosperity and good government, after eighteen years of which there could be no justification for leaving the Vandals still unpunished. Besides, he had another, even better reason for intervention: Gaiseric, a fanatical Arian, had initiated a savage persecution of the orthodox Christians. A number of churches and monasteries had been burnt to ashes, and many venerable ecclesiastics, if not actually put to death, had been dispossessed, driven from their homes, and even occasionally tortured. Leo's long-awaited announcement of his proposed expedition was therefore greeted with relief and satisfaction, and preparations began. They were conceived on a colossal scale: over a thousand ships, we are told, were collected from all over the eastern Mediterranean, and a hundred thousand men. If these figures are correct, the combined naval and military force should have been more than enough to wipe the Vandals off the face of Africa, and under virtually any other commander would certainly have done so.

Not, however, under Basiliscus. According to Procopius – our only source for the campaign[1] – it began promisingly enough, with two highly successful subsidiary expeditions in which Marcellinus, Lord of Dalmatia, drove the Vandals from Sardinia while a Byzantine general named Heraclius landed in Tripolitania with a small force and advanced on Carthage from the south-east. Basiliscus had meanwhile landed at a place called Mercurion near Cape Bon; but instead of marching directly on the Vandal capital and taking the enemy by surprise, he settled down there and showed no inclination to go further. This gave Gaiseric precisely the opportunity he needed. He sent envoys to Mercurion to say that he would do all that the Emperor required of him, and asking only for five days' grace, during which he would make the necessary arrangements. Basiliscus, already congratulating himself on a bloodless victory, was only too ready to agree.

It was the greatest mistake of his life. Gaiseric spent the five days preparing his war fleet, together with a number of empty hulks to be used as fire-boats. The wind then turned, exactly as he had foreseen; and on the fifth day his ships sailed before a fresh following breeze into

1 *History of the Wars*, III, vi. Despite Gibbon's strictures (p. 161n.), Procopius is probably quite reliable here. The true facts would have been well known in his day; and he had, moreover, been a member of the expedition against Carthage of 533, in which Belisarius succeeded where Basiliscus had failed.

Mercurion, towing the hulks behind them. Just as they entered the harbour, the sailors lit the fuses, releasing the blazing hulks to bear down into the centre of the densely packed Byzantine fleet. Basiliscus and his men were powerless to stop them or to quench the flames, which spread almost instantaneously from one vessel to the next. 'And,' writes Procopius,

as the fire advanced, the Roman fleet was naturally thrown into confusion, and the noise of the wind and the crackling flames was mingled with the cries of the soldiers and sailors as they shouted commands to one another, using long poles to push off the fire-boats and each others' ships ... And now the Vandals too were among them, ramming and sinking their vessels, taking prisoner such of the soldiers as attempted to escape and seizing their arms for plunder.

Within a few hours it was all over. The wretched Basiliscus, who had taken flight at an early stage of the battle, returned to Constantinople, where the mood of anger, disappointment and humiliation was such that he was obliged to seek refuge in St Sophia. Only after impassioned entreaties by his sister the Empress did Leo agree to spare his life.

It was fortunate for Leo that the blame for the North African *débâcle* fell so squarely on the head of its leader. If anyone else was held responsible it was Aspar, who was suspected in some quarters of having secretly sided with his fellow-Arian Gaiseric and bribed Basiliscus to betray his trust. This rumour was almost certainly baseless; it was, however, a reflection of Aspar's extreme unpopularity, which was in no way diminished two years later when he persuaded – or, more likely, intimidated – the Emperor into agreeing to the betrothal of his younger daughter, the Princess Leontia, to his own second son Patricius, and proclaiming the latter Caesar. Just what pressure he was able to bring to bear on Leo to do this we can only guess; but given the Emperor's strict orthodoxy and his repugnance to the prospect of an Arian successor it must have been considerable.

In other fields as well, the activities of Aspar and his sons were causing concern. Already in 469 they had tried to assassinate Zeno and very nearly succeeded; and towards the end of 471 the elder son, Ardabur, was found to be involved in dark intrigues with the Isaurian faction in an attempt to win it over to his father's side. For Leo, this was the last straw. One morning in the imperial palace his guards suddenly drew their swords and cut down both Aspar and Ardabur; Patricius was badly wounded, but is thought eventually to have recovered.

It was presumably these murders which led the contemporary historian Malchus to give Leo the nickname *Makelles*, the Butcher; he also shows his dislike by describing him as 'a repository of every vice' and castigating him for his rapaciousness and avarice. Yet even Malchus has to admit that Leo was generally accounted the most fortunate, or most successful – *eutuchesteros* – of all the Emperors that had preceded him, and there can be little doubt that he was, though perhaps not loved, at least respected by the vast majority of his subjects. If he hardly deserved his title of 'the Great' – bestowed on him, apparently, for his religious orthodoxy rather than for any outstanding strength of character or brilliance of statesmanship – he was on the whole a just and merciful ruler; and when he died on 3 February 474 he had, by the standards of the time, remarkably little blood on his hands.

Five months previously, Leo had nominated his successor: not, as everyone had expected, his son-in-law Zeno but the latter's seven-year-old son, called Leo like his grandfather. Whether the Emperor's decision was taken out of personal animosity towards Zeno, whether he felt that the Isaurians were not of imperial calibre or whether he simply wished the diadem to pass to his own flesh and blood we cannot tell; in the event, however, the question proved academic – Ariadne having instructed her son, when his father came to him to make his formal obeisance in the Hippodrome, to crown him co-Emperor on the spot. It was as well that she did. Nine months later young Leo was dead.

One of Zeno's first acts on his succession was to put an end to the Vandal War. As his peace-maker he appointed a distinguished senator, Severus, raising him to the rank of Patrician as a sign of the importance that he attached to the mission; and he could not have made a better choice. Severus impressed Gaiseric by refusing to accept any presents for himself; far better than any gift, he said, would be the release of the Roman captives. The Vandal King immediately freed all those who were in bondage to himself and his family and gave Severus permission to redeem as many more as he could.[1] Peace was signed before the end of the year; never again were the Vandals to cause the Empire concern.

It was an auspicious start; but already the storm-clouds were gathering. By now the Isaurians had made themselves thoroughly unpopular. Unlike the Germanic tribesmen they were subjects of the Empire, and could not therefore technically be called barbarians; in their behaviour, however,

---

1 Much of the necessary ransom money was personally raised by Severus on his return, from the sale of the magnificent robes and gold and silver vessels by which he had impressed the Vandal court with the majesty of Byzantium.

they had proved a good deal more objectionable than the Germans had ever been. The preferential treatment that they had received from Leo had gone to their heads: they were arrogant and noisy, with a regrettable propensity for violence. Inevitably, much of the hostility that they aroused now became focused on their most distinguished representative, the Emperor himself – who also had to face the implacable hatred of two powerful enemies within his own household: Verina the Empress Mother, and her brother Basiliscus.

The objectives of these two were not identical: Basiliscus, who had been understandably maintaining a low profile since the Carthaginian expedition eight years before, had emerged from his retirement on Leo's death still determined to secure the diadem for himself; the Empress, on the other hand, wanted it for her recently acquired lover Patricius, Master of the Offices at the palace.[1] Both, however, were united in their primary object – to get rid of Zeno; and with the aid of an Isaurian general, Illus – who had suddenly turned, for reasons unexplained, against his imperial benefactor – they managed to recruit a number of powerful adherents to their cause. In November 475, as the Emperor was presiding over the games in the Hippodrome, he received an urgent message from his mother-in-law: army, Senate and people were united against him, he must flee the city at once. The thought of resistance, or that Verina's words might have been largely bluff, never seems to have occurred to him. That very night he slipped away from Constantinople with his wife and mother, to seek refuge among the mountains of his native Isauria.

With Zeno out of the way, and the cause of Patricius espoused only by Verina, Basiliscus was proclaimed Emperor – remarkable testimony to the power of human ambition. He began by ordering – or at any rate permitting – a widespread slaughter of Isaurians in the capital; but if the purpose of thus eliminating the enemy faction was to strengthen his own hold on the throne, it failed. Basiliscus did not last long. He lost the sympathy of his sister by having her lover assassinated; he antagonized his subjects by vicious taxation; and he incurred the lasting enmity of the Church, first by his openly-expressed monophysite opinions and then by his ham-fisted attempts to impose them throughout the Empire. In these he was encouraged by the former monophysite Bishop of Alexandria, the aptly named Timothy the Weasel, who had been expelled from his see after the Council of Chalcedon and whom Basiliscus now saw fit to restore. At the insistence of this poisonous cleric, he not only abrogated the decrees of Chalcedon but even tried to abolish the

1 And no relation, it need hardly be said, to the son of Aspar.

Patriarchate of Constantinople, causing Patriarch Acacius to drape the high altar of St Sophia in black and to put all his priests into mourning; meanwhile Daniel, the famous stylite of the city,[1] actually descended from his pillar for the first time in fifteen years, haranguing the people and terrifying Basiliscus into the withdrawal of his edict. The heavens, too, showed themselves against the usurper: there could be no other explanation for the appalling fire of 476 which, beginning in the bazaar of the bronze-smiths, spread to the *Basilike*, the public library founded by Julian which was said to contain 120,000 books – including the intestine of a serpent, 120 feet long, on which were inscribed the entire *Iliad* and *Odyssey* in golden characters. Another tragic loss was the Palace of Lausus with its celebrated collection of antique sculpture, including the Hera of Samos, the Athena of Lindos and the Aphrodite of Cnidus. After all this it came as no great surprise when Illus, disgusted with the ruler whom he had helped to put on the throne, turned his coat again, joined Zeno in his mountain retreat and began to plan his restoration.

The person most directly responsible for the downfall of Basiliscus was, however, neither Zeno nor Illus but his own nephew Harmatius. This ridiculous young man, well-known throughout Constantinople as a dandy and a fop, was promoted by his uncle – despite the flagrant affair that he was carrying on with Basiliscus's own wife, his aunt Zenonis – to the rank of *magister militum*, an appointment which so delighted him that he took to parading around the Hippodrome dressed as Achilles. Sent with an army against Zeno and Illus, he was invited by them to negotiate and was easily persuaded – by the promise of the Praetorian Prefecture for himself and the rank of Caesar for his son – to declare himself in their favour. Thus, in July 477, Zeno returned to his capital unopposed. The would-be Augustus – who had, for the second time, sought sanctuary in St Sophia – was prevailed upon to surrender, on the undertaking that his blood would not be shed; and the real Emperor, true to his word, exiled him with his family to the wilds of Cappadocia where, the following winter, cold and hunger did for the lot of them.

After twenty months of exile, Zeno could at last turn his mind again to affairs of state. There had been several developments during his ab-

---

1 Daniel the Stylite had visited St Simeon on his column near Antioch, and on Simeon's death had determined to follow his example. After some time on a fairly modest pillar he moved to a magnificent double column erected for him by the Emperor Leo himself, crossing straight from one to the other on a makeshift bridge of planks. He died on 11 December 493, having remained aloft for a total of thirty-three years and three months. The author of his life claims that on this, his only venture down to ground level, he managed to persuade Basiliscus of the error of his ways and obtained from him a formal recantation in St Sophia; but this sounds suspiciously like wishful thinking.

sence that demanded his attention – among them, the final collapse of the Roman Empire of the West.

For seventeen years after the deaths of Aetius and Valentinian, the West had been dominated by the Suevian Count Ricimer,[1] yet another of those barbarian kingmakers so characteristic of the time. He had brought on to the scene a succession of no less than five puppet Emperors. One of these, Avitus, he had forced to abdicate (but allowed to become Bishop of Piacenza) and two, Marjorian and Anthemius, he had had murdered. Two only had kept their thrones: Libius Severus and Olybrius, the latter having died of dropsy in October 472, two months after Ricimer himself. After a four-month interregnum Ricimer's son and would-be successor Gundobad had raised up yet another nonentity, Glycerius; but in Constantinople Leo I had refused to approve him, appointing instead the husband of his wife's niece, one Julius Nepos. Landing in Italy early in 474, Nepos overthrew his rival with scarcely a struggle and was shortly afterwards proclaimed at Rome. Perhaps, men thought, the age of chaos was over. Ricimer was dead, Gundobad and Glycerius discredited; Julius Nepos had the blessing of the Emperor in Constantinople – by this time Zeno had succeeded Leo, but his policy towards the West was unchanged – and might well, with help from the East, re-establish Roman supremacy over the barbarian adventurers.

But such hopes were all too quickly dashed. In August 475 Orestes, commander-in-chief of the army, rose in revolt against the new Emperor. He had had a curious career. Born in Pannonia, he had found his way while still a young man to the court of Attila, where he had been employed by the King of the Huns as his personal secretary and had played an important part in frustrating the murder plot connected with the embassy of Priscus. After Attila's death he had entered the imperial service, and had headed the household troops under the short-lived Emperor Anthemius; next, on Nepos's accession and his own promotion to the supreme command, he had been ordered to Gaul, there to arrange for the transfer of Auvergne, which had been ceded by the Senate to the Visigothic King Euric. Instead of obeying, however, Orestes took up arms against his sovereign and, with his army behind him, marched on Rome.

In these circumstances, Julius Nepos had no alternative but flight,

1 The Suevians were one of the several Germanic tribes that had been forced to flee their homeland – for them, the valley of the Elbe – before the advancing Huns. The majority had by this time settled in Spain and Portugal.

first to Ravenna and then, as Orestes continued in his pursuit, across the
Adriatic to Salona – where, presumably, he must have had a somewhat
embarrassing encounter with his predecessor Glycerius and where, before
that fateful year was over, he was to receive the news that Zeno, his co-
Emperor, had almost simultaneously been obliged to seek refuge from
his enemies. No help, clearly, was to be expected from the East. Nepos
resigned himself to the inevitable and settled down to wait.

Orestes, meanwhile, had returned to Rome, where on 31 October he
had proclaimed as Emperor his son Romulus, nicknamed – though
perhaps only later – with the contemptuous diminutive Augustulus. The
date of his birth is unknown, but he was still little more than a child and
his father clearly intended to keep the reins of power firmly in his own
hands. So, for the best part of a year, he did; but then the army turned
against him, just as he had turned it against Julius Nepos. For a century
or more it had been composed largely of barbarian mercenaries; and
since the death of Attila the fellow-tribesmen of those mercenaries had
been pouring across the imperial frontiers, unchecked and uncontrolled,
in ever-increasing numbers. They now sought in their turn what barbarians within the Empire had always sought, and what many of them
had found – a country of their own to dwell in; and they demanded of
Orestes one-third of the land of Italy, with every Roman land-owner
making over that proportion of his estate to a Germanic immigrant.

The proposal was perhaps less outrageous than it sounds; in 418
Constantius III had willingly transferred two-thirds of south-western
Gaul to the Visigoths. That donation, however, had been the voluntary
grant of a remote corner of the Empire to protect the rest of the continent; this, by contrast, was a demand at sword-point for its very
heartland. Orestes must have believed that it would be open to nego-
tiation; indignantly, he refused. But he had misjudged the temper of his
men. Their answer was immediate mutiny, under the leadership of
Orestes's own standard-bearer, a Scyrian named Odoacer.[1] On 23 August
476 he was raised upon the soldiers' shields, and the fight was on. Orestes
fled first to Ticinum (the modern Pavia) where he took refuge with its
saintly bishop Epiphanius. A few days later, after Odoacer had stormed
and sacked the city, he slipped away to Placentia (Piacenza). This time
there was no escape. The mutineers caught up with him and killed him.

Few observers at that moment would have given much for the life

---

1 Or Odovacar. He was the son of Edeco, who may or may not have been the same as that envoy of
Attila who makes a brief appearance in Chapter 7. The Scyrians were another Germanic tribe, of
minimal importance in this story.

of poor Romulus Augustulus, lonely and frightened in the palace of Ravenna. But when Odoacer reached the city and summoned the miserable boy into his presence, his heart was softened. Romulus was very young, very pathetic and, by all accounts, quite outstandingly good-looking. Instead of putting him to the sword, the barbarian simply ordered him to abdicate, provided him with a generous pension and sent him off to live in peaceful obscurity with relatives in Campania. Then, as soon as he heard that Zeno had been reinstated – for he had never recognized Basiliscus – he sent ambassadors to Constantinople, to inform him of the new dispensation and to hand over the imperial insignia of the West as a sign that he, Odoacer, made no claim to sovereignty for himself. All he asked was the title of Patrician, in which rank he proposed to take over the administration of Italy in the Emperor's name.

The abdication of Romulus Augustulus on 4 September 476 is generally accepted as marking the end of the Roman Empire in the West. Historians, however, have gone to considerable lengths to persuade us that this is not so. The Empire, they point out, was one and indivisible; whether it was ruled at any given moment by a single Augustus, or two, or even three or four, was purely a matter of administrative convenience. Besides, they continue, Odoacer was always at pains to emphasize the Emperor's continued sovereignty over Italy. Here was simply a return to the days when the Empire had been governed by a sole ruler, just as it had been by Constantius II, and later by Julian.

All this is perfectly true; and it is also undeniable that most people in Italy at the time, watching the young ex-Emperor settle himself into his comfortable Campanian villa, would have been astounded to learn that they were living through one of the great watersheds of European history. For nearly a century now they had grown used to seeing barbarian generals at the seat of power. There had been Arbogast the Frank, then Stilicho the Vandal, then Aetius – who, though a Roman, was almost certainly of Germanic origin on his father's side – then Ricimer the Suevian. Was the Scyrian Odoacer, they might have asked, so very different from these?

The answer is that he was – though for one reason only. He had refused to accept a Western Emperor. In the past those Emperors may have been little more than puppets; nevertheless they bore the title of Augustus, and as such they were both a symbol and a constant reminder of the imperial authority. Without them, that authority was soon forgotten. Odoacer had requested the rank of Patrician; but the title that he preferred to use was *Rex*. In less than sixty years, Italy would be so far lost as to need a full-scale reconquest by Justinian. It would be two and a quarter centuries before another Emperor appeared in the West; when he did, his capital would be in Germany rather than in Italy, and he would be a rival rather than a colleague – not a Roman but a Frank.

Odoacer's decision was to have a second, equally important effect. The absence of any imperial representative in Italy created a political vacuum in the old capital. Instinctively, men looked for another father figure, someone possessed of a degree of prestige and offering a prospect of continuity far beyond the dreams of the most optimistic of barbarian adventurers. And so they raised up the Bishop of Rome, already the Primate of Christendom, investing him with temporal authority as well as spiritual and surrounding him with much of the pomp and semi-mystical ceremonial formerly reserved for the Emperors. The age of the medieval Papacy had begun.

The Emperor Zeno was, in all probability, no more perceptive in his appraisal of recent events in the West than the vast majority of his subjects. Apart from anything else, he had no intention of accepting the dethronement of his own nominated co-Augustus, Julius Nepos. Soon after his return to Constantinople he received a letter from Nepos in Dalmatia, congratulating him on the end of his exile and asking his help in effecting a similar restoration for himself. This appeal almost certainly coloured Zeno's reception shortly afterwards of the ambassadors from Odoacer. Nepos, he pointed out to them, was the Western Emperor. It was therefore to him, if their master wished to be made a Patrician, that his request should be directed. This, unquestionably, was the proper answer in the circumstances; but its effect must have been somewhat spoilt by the missive which Zeno had prepared for the envoys to pass on to Odoacer, in which the latter was already addressed as Patrician. A secretarial slip, or subtle diplomacy? We shall never know.

In any case, at that moment internal affairs seemed a good deal more pressing. The elimination of Basiliscus had done little to restore harmony within the State. Zeno's early suspicions focused on Harmatius, whose arrogance and narcissism had reached the point where there were fears for his sanity. To obtain the Praetorian Prefecture for himself and the rank of Caesar for his son he had unhesitatingly betrayed both his uncle and his mistress; what chance was there that he would remain loyal to his Emperor, particularly after the young Caesar had grown to manhood? The chroniclers all emphasize the struggle that Zeno had with his conscience, but its conclusion was foregone: Harmatius must be removed. A willing assassin was found among his many enemies, and the deed was soon accomplished. To the dead man's son – called, like his great-uncle, Basiliscus – the Emperor was more merciful: he was merely deprived of his rank and title and forced into the Church. A few years later we find him serving as *lector* in the chapel of the imperial palace at Blachernae, and he was to end his life as Bishop of Cyzicus. One suspects, somehow, that he may have welcomed his release from imperial responsibilities; if so, one can hardly blame him.

As the years passed, Zeno must often have wished that he could be relieved of them himself. In 479, only two years after his resumption of power, he had to face another insurrection – this time instigated by Marcian, grandson of his imperial namesake, son of the Western Emperor Anthemius and husband of Leontia, younger daughter of Leo the Great. (Her engagement to Patricius had naturally been broken off after the fall of Aspar.) His revolt was perhaps to some extent the consequence of the treatment of his mother-in-law Verina, who had recently been imprisoned for her part in a plot to assassinate Illus; he himself justified it, however, on the grounds that his wife, having been born in the purple, was of higher rank than her elder sister Ariadne, Zeno's wife, who had been born during the previous reign. Marcian and his adherents stormed the Palace, and would probably have succeeded in overthrowing the Emperor for the second time but for the swift intervention of Illus, who brought a detachment of Isaurian troops across the Bosphorus at dead of night and took the rebels by surprise. Their leader was sent in his turn into monastic exile, to Cappadocian Caesarea; he escaped, and attempted another coup, but that also failed. Even now – perhaps on account of his imperial blood – Zeno showed clemency: Marcian was ordained a presbyter, his wife Leontia entered the convent of the *Akoimētai*,[1] and the two are heard of no more.

Marcian's two insurrections, dangerous and symptomatic of the general disaffection as they undoubtedly were, had been quickly put down. More serious, and far more prolonged, was that which broke out in 483, the central figure of which was Illus himself. He acted, it must be said, under considerable provocation. Already six years before, soon after Zeno's return to power, one of the imperial slaves had been found lying

1 The *Akoimētai*, or 'sleepless ones', had been founded around 400 by a certain abbot Alexander. Their rule stipulated absolute poverty, no manual labour and the routine (which gave them their name) of perpetual prayer and adoration by means of alternating choirs. They quickly grew powerful and – thanks to their habit of openly voicing their disapproval of imperial behaviour – unpopular with the government. Nestorius had evicted them from Constantinople, but they had soon reestablished both male and female communities on the Asiatic shore of the Bosphorus.

in wait for him, drawn sword in hand. No one had directly accused the Emperor, who had at once surrendered the slave to his intended victim for summary punishment; but suspicions had inevitably been aroused. Then, in 478, the Palace guards had discovered another would-be assassin, this time an Alan, who later confessed that he had been acting under the instructions of the Prefect Epinicus and the Empress Verina. Realizing that his life would be in danger if he were to remain in Constantinople, Illus pleaded the recent death of his brother and retired for a while to his Isaurian homeland. In September 479, however, an earthquake severely weakened the city walls and Zeno, fearing that the Goths might seize the opportunity to attack, recalled him to the capital, actually riding out as far as Chalcedon to receive him; but the general refused point-blank to enter the city until Verina was surrendered into his charge. Zeno had no love for his mother-in-law and was only too happy to comply; the Dowager Empress was first sent off to Tarsus where she was forced to take the veil, and then immured in an Isaurian fortress.

After that, the atmosphere lightened for a time and Illus was appointed Master of the Offices, normally a sign of high favour; but one day in 482, as he was mounting the staircase to his box at the Hippodrome, he was attacked without warning by a member of the imperial Life Guard. His armour-bearer managed to deflect the blow; but the blade, while missing his head, sliced off his right ear, obliging him to wear a skull-cap for the rest of his days. This time the instigator of the crime was harder to deal with: it proved to be no less a figure than the Empress Ariadne herself, taking her revenge on Illus for his treatment of her mother – and, perhaps, of her sister as well.

What happened next is unclear: indeed, the whole story of Illus's revolt depends on such fragmentary – and occasionally self-contradictory – evidence that we are all too often thrown back on speculation and guesswork. The Master of the Offices seems to have prudently retired once again to Anatolia. Almost immediately after his departure, however, a revolt broke out in Syria, where a certain Leontius was staging a last-ditch attempt to restore the old pagan religion; and messengers sped after Illus, with orders to take command of the eastern armies and restore imperial rule. He, probably grateful for this opportunity to prove himself once again in the eyes of his sovereign, hurried at once to Syria; only on his arrival did he discover the local commander to be none other than the Emperor's incompetent and profligate brother Longinus, who deeply resented what he considered to be a usurpation of his own authority. A violent quarrel ensued, as a result of which Illus had Longinus arrested and imprisoned.

It was by any account a high-handed action to take against so powerful and influential a rival; but the Emperor's reaction, when the news was brought to Constantinople, was still more ill-judged. Issuing a command for the immediate release of his brother, he denounced Illus as a public enemy and ordered the confiscation and sale of all his property. In doing so, he virtually drove him into the opposing camp. Illus now made common cause with the rebel, and the two of them together released the old Empress Verina; she was only too pleased to crown Leontius at Tarsus and accompany him to Antioch, where on 27 June 484 he established a rival court.

He and Illus seem to have been content for the time to remain where they were; they certainly made no effort to march on Constantinople. This gave Zeno plenty of time to find new allies – among them a young barbarian named Theodoric, prince of the Ostrogoths, who had been a persistent thorn in Byzantine flesh for the past decade but who now agreed to lead an army of his subjects in the Emperor's name against the rebels. Thus the latter were soon expelled from Antioch and driven back into the Isaurian heartland, their leaders finally taking refuge in a castle known as Papirius. Here Verina died, lamented by no one; and here, after a four-year siege – during which Illus, always a scholar and intellectual, is said to have passed the time in philosophical study with his friend, the Egyptian sophist and neo-platonist Pamprepius – he and Leontius were betrayed by his sister-in-law, who in 488 gained admission to the castle by a trick (probably a non-existent promise of pardon) and then opened the gates to the besiegers. After so long a resistance, the defenders could expect no mercy: their heads were cut off and sent to Constantinople. The rebellion was at an end.

Theodoric the Ostrogoth, who had been partly responsible for the retreat of Illus and his friends to their Isaurian redoubt, did not take part in the ensuing siege. He had more important occupations elsewhere. Born around 454, the son of the Ostrogothic chieftain Theodemir, he had spent ten years of his boyhood as a hostage in Constantinople; and though he may have gained little intellectually from the experience – all his life he is said to have signed his name by stencilling it through a perforated gold plate – he had acquired an instinctive understanding of the Byzantines and their ways which served him in good stead when, on the death of his father in 471, he succeeded him as paramount leader of the Eastern Goths. He was not the only one: another Theodoric, son of Triarius and surnamed Strabo (the Squinter) was to set himself up in determined opposition to him. But the story of the kaleidoscopically changing relations between the two, and between the pair of them together and the Emperor in Constantinople, is too long and complex for our story. In any case the son of Triarius died in 481, leaving his namesake in undisputed control.

The main purpose of Theodoric's early life, as of so many barbarian leaders before him, was to find and to secure a permanent home for his people. To this end he spent the better part of twenty years fighting, sometimes for and sometimes against the Empire, arguing, bargaining, cajoling and threatening by turns. He helped Zeno in both the principal rebellions of his reign, that of Basiliscus and that of Illus; he became successively Patrician, *magister militum* and, in 484, even Consul; on the other hand we find him furiously devastating Macedonia in 479, laying waste Thessaly in 482 and, in 487, marching on Constantinople itself. This constant vacillation between friendship and hostility was, in the long term, unprofitable to both parties; and both Zeno and Theodoric must have heaved a deep sigh of relief when a decision was taken that was to affect the whole future of Europe, both East and West – although neither may have suspected it at the time. Which of the two rulers deserves the credit for the idea we shall never know. Jordanes, doubtless quoting from Theodoric's chief minister Cassiodorus, attributes it to the Ostrogoth; Procopius, with equal conviction, maintains that it originally came from the Emperor. All we can say for certain is that, some time in 487 or early 488, it was agreed between them that Theodoric should lead his entire people into Italy, overthrow Odoacer and rule the land as an Ostrogothic Kingdom under imperial sovereignty.

The advantages of this scheme were obvious to both parties: for Theodoric, there was the promised fulfilment of his life's dream – a rich and fertile land for himself and his people; for Zeno, the prospect of ridding himself of the Goths once and for all. The two men must have taken leave of each other without a pang of regret, and early in 488 the great exodus took place: men, women and children, with their horses and pack-animals, their cattle and sheep, lumbering slowly across the plains of central Europe in search of greener and more peaceful pastures.

These, however, were not to be won without a fierce struggle. For five years Odoacer fought back, in 490 coming near to destroying his enemy by besieging him in Pavia; only in the nick of time was Theodoric saved by the arrival of Visigothic reinforcements. A few months later he turned the tables, blockading Odoacer in his turn within the walls of Ravenna and holding him there until February 493, when the local bishop arranged an armistice. By this time, however, thanks in large measure to the assistance of the Church, which gave its full support to Theodoric – although he was, like Odoacer, an Arian – the conquest of Italy was virtually complete; and it must have come as a surprise to many when the conqueror agreed to what appeared to be remarkably generous terms: that Italy should be ruled by him and Odoacer jointly, with both of them sharing the palace of Ravenna.

The reason for this apparent generosity soon became clear: Theodoric had not the faintest intention of keeping his agreement, and had merely determined to lull his rival into a false sense of security. On 15 March, only ten days after his formal entry into Ravenna, he invited Odoacer, his brother, his son and his chief officers to a banquet in his wing of the palace. As the Scyrian took his place in the seat of honour, Theodoric stepped forward and, with one tremendous stroke of his sword, clove through the body of Odoacer from collar-bone to thigh. The force of the blow and its effect surprised even him: 'The wretch cannot have had a bone in his body,' he is said to have laughed.

The members of Odoacer's suite were quickly dealt with by the surrounding guards, while his brother was shot down by arrows as he tried to escape through the palace gardens. His wife, Sunigilda, was thrown into prison, where she later died of hunger; his son, Thelane, whom he had surrendered to Theodoric as a hostage, was first sent off to Gaul but was subsequently executed in his turn on the King's orders. The Scyrian line, in short, was wiped out; and Theodoric the Ostrogoth, his ambition at last achieved, laid aside the skins and furs that were the traditional clothing of his race, robed himself – as Odoacer had never done – in the imperial purple, and settled down to rule in Italy. Despite all the pomp and ceremonial of his court, however, he did not forget his agreement with Zeno. While reigning as King of the Ostrogoths he remained, as far as the Empire was concerned, a Patrician and *magister militum* but no more, a vassal who owed allegiance to the Emperor just as did the meanest of his subjects. The laws which he passed were known as *edicta*, rather than the *leges* which were the imperial prerogative; and though his coins carried his own monogram, the only portrait they bore was that of the Emperor. Theodoric himself, it need hardly be said, had no objection to this arrangement. The Roman citizens in Italy – who outnumbered the Goths many times over – were a good deal happier to be ruled by an imperial viceroy than by someone whom they would otherwise have looked upon as a foreign oppressor. To antagonize them was the last thing he would have wished; he allowed them to live just as they always had with all their estates intact, excepting only that they were debarred from military service. The civil service, by contrast, was their exclusive preserve.

Theodoric's reign began with perfidy and bloodshed; its close was also clouded, by the imprisonment and brutal execution (by slow garrotting) in 524 of the philosopher Boethius,[1] which left an indelible stain on his memory – though it is only fair to add that he afterwards repented, and bitterly regretted his action till the day of his death. With these exceptions, the thirty-three years that he occupied the throne were prosperous and peaceful; and the extraordinary mausoleum which he built – and which still stands in the north-eastern suburbs of Ravenna – perfectly symbolizes, in its half-classical, half-barbaric architectural strength,[2] a colossus who himself bestrode two civilizations and lost no opportunity to promote and increase the harmony between his people and the citizens of Rome. No other Germanic ruler, setting up his throne on the ruins of the Western Empire, possessed a fraction of his statesmanship and political vision; and when he died, on 30 August 526, Italy lost the greatest of her early medieval rulers, unequalled until the days of Charlemagne.

1 The only offence of Boethius was to have energetically defended his friend, the ex-Consul Albinus, who had been wrongly accused of treason. This led him and his father-in-law Symmachus to be similarly charged. While he was in prison he wrote *The Consolations of Philosophy*, a work which enjoyed immense popularity in succeeding centuries and was translated into Anglo-Saxon by Alfred the Great.

2 The erection of the gigantic 200-ton monolith which forms its roof ranks among the most astonishing engineering feats of the Middle Ages.

9
The Rise of Justinian

[493-532]

Ruling as we do over our Empire, which God has entrusted to us, by His divine authority, we know both the triumphs of war and the adornments of peace; we bear up the framework of the State; and we so lift up our hearts in contemplation of the support given to us by the Lord Omnipotent that we put not our trust in our own arms, nor in those of our soldiers, nor in our leaders in war, nor in our own skill; rather do we rest our hopes in the providence of the Supreme Trinity, from whence proceeded the elements of the whole universe and their disposition throughout the world.

Justinian, in his
Introduction to the *Digest*

In the spring of 491, while Theodoric the Ostrogoth was busy blockading Odoacer the Scyrian in Ravenna, the Emperor Zeno died in Constantinople. The last three years of his reign had been the best, at least where the security of the state was concerned: the insurrection of Illus and his friends was over and its ringleaders eliminated; yet more important, the Empire – or, at least, that part of it still controlled from the capital – was, since the departure of Theodoric, finally free of the Goths. The only major problem that Zeno had failed to solve was the religious one: despite the decisions of Chalcedon, the monophysite heresy continued to gain ground – especially in the eastern provinces, which were becoming dangerously disaffected as a result. An attempt, made in 482 by the Emperor together with Patriarch Acacius, to heal the breach by means of a circular letter known as the *Henoticon*, had proved spectacularly unsuccessful. It had sought to paper over the differences by affirming that Christ was both God and man, while avoiding the delicate word 'nature' altogether; and, like all such compromises, it had aroused the implacable hostility of both sides. Most outraged of all were Pope Simplicius in Rome and his successor Felix III, whose anger was still further increased by the appointment to the Patriarchate of Alexandria, with the blessing of both Zeno and Acacius, of one Paul the Stammerer, a cleric whose utterances, when comprehensible at all, were violently monophysite in character. At a synod held in Rome in 484, Pope Felix had gone so far as to excommunicate the Patriarch of Constantinople[1] – a sentence which, in default of any orthodox ecclesiastic courageous enough to pronounce it, had been transcribed on to a piece of parchment and pinned to the back of Acacius's cope during a service in St Sophia, when he was not looking, whereat the Patriarch, discovering it a few moments later, instantly excommunicated him back, thereby not only placing the see of Constantinople on the same hierarchical level as that of Rome but simultaneously confirming an open schism between the two churches that was to last for the next thirty-five years.

By the end of the decade the Emperor was obviously declining, both physically and mentally. His son, also called Zeno, had fallen into bad company at an early age and had died soon afterwards, worn out, it was said, by homosexual excesses and venereal disease. His expected successor was therefore his reprobate brother Longinus, whose star had steadily risen as that of his enemy Illus had declined and who by 490 – when he was appointed Consul for the second time – was in effective control of the State. Zeno, however, became obsessed by the prophecy of a well-known soothsayer, who had foretold that his place would be taken not by Longinus but by 'one who had served as silentiary'. Now the silentiaries were a corps of picked officials who made up the Emperor's personal entourage. Their name derived from their special duty of watching outside his private apartments and ensuring that his rest was not disturbed; in fact, however, they were considerably more distinguished than this particular function implies. Men of high culture and education, they ranked with senators and were employed on various important and confidential services, including the writing of court history. Their number was fixed at thirty, but to Zeno's senile mind the prophecy could refer to only one: a former member of the corps named Pelagius, now an eminent statesman and Patrician. The unfortunate man was given no opportunity to prepare his defence. His property was confiscated without ceremony; he himself was arrested and, shortly afterwards, strangled.

Pelagius had been popular and universally respected; Zeno was neither. In his youth he had been renowned as an athlete – the *Anonymus*

---

1 Something of an irony, since Felix was – as far as we can tell – the first Pope to have formally announced his election to the Emperor.

Valesii rather surprisingly attributes his fleetness of foot to the fact that he was born without kneecaps – but in all other fields he had been a failure. Even if he was not altogether to blame for the almost constant insurrections during his reign, these were inevitably seen as a reflection of his lack of ability; and the loss of the Western Empire put another indelible – if largely undeserved – stain on his reputation. By his senseless murder of Pelagius, Zeno sacrificed what little of his subjects' affection he had ever enjoyed; and there were few lamentations when, on 9 April 491, he died of a fit of epilepsy. The crowds are said to have greeted the appearance of the widowed Ariadne with the cry, 'Give the Empire an *orthodox* Emperor! Give the Empire a *Roman* Emperor!' Their meaning was clear: no more heretics on the one hand and no more Isaurians on the other. Longinus was passed over, and the soothsayer's prediction was proved correct: the choice fell on another former silentiary, Flavius Anastasius – owing in large measure to the influence of Ariadne, who married him some six weeks later. A native of Dyrrachium[1] and now in his early sixties, he had one blue eye and one black one – a peculiarity which, we are told, in no way detracted from his outstandingly handsome appearance, nor from his reputation for uprightness and integrity. 'Reign, Anastasius!' the people shouted when, on 11 April, he first appeared before them in the imperial purple. 'Reign as you have lived!'

Anastasius did so; and if his subjects found life under their new Emperor during the first years of his reign more irksome than they had expected, they had only themselves to blame. He was intelligent and highly cultivated, given neither to those outbursts of cruelty nor to those sudden fits of ungovernable rage that had characterized so many of his predecessors. His chief defect was an almost pathological parsimoniousness – a failing which, combined as it was with a strong puritanical streak, made Constantinople a duller place to live in than its inhabitants could ever remember. Contests with wild beasts were forbidden throughout the Empire; and such was the general tightening-up of public morals that the citizens were no longer permitted to hold nocturnal feasts, on the grounds that they led to unbridled licentiousness – which, it must be said, they very often did. Meanwhile the Emperor launched a simultaneous campaign against unnecessary public expenditure, with the result that at the end of his twenty-seven-year reign he left the imperial treasury richer by 320,000 pounds of gold than it had been on his

1 Later known as Durazzo and now the Albanian port of Durrës, Dyrrachium marked the western end of the Via Egnatia.

accession[1] – an achievement all the more remarkable in that he is also known to have abolished the so-called *chrysargyron*, a tax on receipts which fell particularly heavily on the poor and was among the most unpopular of all the imperial levies.

In his religious policy, Anastasius was somewhat less successful. A man of devout Christian piety even by the standards of the time, he had been in the habit during the previous reign of holding regular theological seminars in St Sophia and preaching in churches throughout the capital, despite the fact that as a layman he was technically unlicensed to do so; he had even at one moment been put on a short list of three candidates for the vacant bishopric of Antioch. Later, however, he had gradually moved towards monophysitism, to the point where Patriarch Euphemius was obliged to bar him from the pulpits and, after his accession, to refuse him coronation until he had signed a written declaration of orthodoxy.

Anastasius signed without hesitation. He was the least cynical of men, and it seems certain that up to that time he believed, rightly or wrongly, that he stood firmly in the Chalcedonian camp. But there were others less convinced, who were quick to ascribe his action to an eye for the main chance and a readiness to sacrifice his principles on the altar of political expediency. Such men could be trusted, too, to exaggerate any signs he might have given of monophysite tendencies, seeing in them a perfect weapon to be used against him. They represented essentially the Isaurian faction, and were led by Zeno's disaffected brother Longinus, who had never forgiven Anastasius for occupying a throne which he believed to be rightfully his. Before long he had gathered around him an unsavoury mob of troublemakers and hooligans, largely but by no means exclusively Isaurian; and the outbreaks of street fighting that ensued led to fires in which several more of the city's finest buildings, including much of the Hippodrome, were destroyed or damaged.

The Emperor fought back. In 492 Longinus himself was arrested and exiled to Alexandria, where he was forced to enter the priesthood; but strife in the city continued and soon escalated into full-scale civil war. The following year saw still more serious disturbances, during which the imperial statues were toppled over and dragged through the streets; only with great difficulty was order restored, after which an edict was published banishing all Isaurians from the capital including Lalis, the old mother of Zeno, and the rest of his family, all of whose property – even

1 It is never really possible to calculate the precise modern equivalents of such sums; but this figure, given by Procopius (*Anecdota*, xix, 7) compares interestingly with the 130,000 pounds which he mentions as the cost of Leo I's ill-fated African expedition in 468.

his former robes of state – was confiscated and sold. Now at last the capital was quiet; but in Anatolia the war continued for three more years. Only in 496 did peace finally return.

But the Isaurians, insufferable as they were, cannot take all the blame for the continuing unrest in Constantinople. Another major contributory cause was the division of the populace into two rival factions, the Blues and the Greens. Their names came originally from the Hippodrome, where they referred to the colours worn by the two principal teams of charioteers;[1] but the factions themselves had long since left the narrow confines of the arena. Their leaders were by now appointed by the government, who also entrusted them with important public responsibilities, including guard duties and the maintenance of the defensive walls. Thus, not only in the capital but in all the main cities of the Empire, they existed as two independent semi-political parties which combined on occasion to form a local militia. Their political affiliations naturally varied according to local conditions and the issues of the day; at this period, however, the Blues tended to be the party of the big land-owners and the old Graeco-Roman aristocracy, while the Greens represented trade, industry and the civil service. Many members of this last group came from the eastern provinces, where heresy was more widespread; thus the Blues had gradually come to be associated with religious orthodoxy, the Greens with monophysitism. But these were loose associations only, with exceptions on both sides, while the populace as a whole gave its adherence, indiscriminately though enthusiastically, to one faction or the other. Anastasius himself at first tried to maintain impartiality, and in 493 was actually pelted with stones by a group of Greens after refusing to release certain of their number who had been arrested after an affray; soon, however, his economic policies – which favoured the manufacturing industries – and his instinctive if only semi-conscious tendency towards the monophysites drew him to the Greens, of whom he was finally to become an open adherent.

Hostility between the two demes (as they were called) increased steadily as his reign continued, and the riots of 493 were seen to have been only the beginning of a new wave of internecine strife in the capital. Still worse troubles occurred in 501 during the festival of the Brytae, when the Greens attacked the Blues in the Hippodrome; among those killed was the Emperor's own illegitimate son. (It was because of this that the

1 Originally there had been four teams, but by this time the Reds and the Whites had been assimilated into the other two.

celebration was banned the following year.) Worst of all, however, were the disturbances of 511, for which Anastasius himself was very largely to blame, and which came dangerously near to toppling his throne. With advancing age – he was now in his eighties – his monophysite sympathies had become more and more pronounced and were now plain for all to see. Patriarch Euphemius was no longer in a position to protest: he had been accused – with what justice we cannot tell – of having given secret support to the Isaurians, and had been banished to a distant region of Anatolia. His successor Macedonius was the gentlest and mildest-mannered of men, but he too was beginning to find dealings with his sovereign impossible.

By now the monophysites had found themselves a war-cry. After the so-called *trisagion* – the words 'Holy God, Holy and Mighty, Holy and Immortal' which occur as a constant refrain in the Byzantine liturgy – they added the phrase 'who was crucified for us', seeing this as the most emphatic statement that could be made of their belief that it was not the man Jesus but God Almighty himself who met his death upon the Cross. In the atmosphere of Anastasius's Constantinople these were fighting words, and tempers ran high when the news spread through the city that they had been heard in the Chapel of the Archangel, which stood within the walls of the imperial palace. But worse was to come: on the Sunday following they were heard again, defiantly shouted during the morning mass in St Sophia itself. The orthodox congregation shouted back, louder still; fighting broke out; and the service ended in uproar.

At the subsequent inquiry, the examining magistrates – possibly acting on the Emperor's instructions – laid the blame not on the monophysite intruders but squarely on the shoulders of the harmless old Patriarch Macedonius. For the people of Constantinople, the vast majority of whom staunchly supported the decrees of Chalcedon, this transparently unfair attack on their beloved Patriarch was the last straw. They marched threateningly on the Palace, and there is no telling what might have ensued had not Macedonius responded to Anastasius's terrified appeal and hurried to his side. Some sort of reconciliation was hastily patched up, and the crowd dispersed.

It was a narrow escape, and should have been a salutary lesson; but the Emperor was now too old to change his ways. Macedonius – to whom he probably owed his life – was quietly exiled like his predecessor, and on 4 November 512 the fateful clause 'who was crucified for us' once again echoed through the great basilica. On this occasion the violence was far worse; by the time order had been restored the floor was covered in the blood of the dead and the wounded. A similar incident the next day at the Church of St Theodore resulted in further casualties; but on the 6th the orthodox mob was ready. At a huge rally in the Hippodrome they called death and destruction on all heretics, then poured out into the city to make good their words. Again the imperial statues were hurled to the ground and smashed; among the many houses burned to the ground were those of the Praetorian Prefect and the Emperor's nephew Pompeius. The rioting continued for another two full days; then at last Anastasius acted. Presenting himself in the Circus before some 20,000 of his furious subjects, he slowly removed his diadem and laid aside the imperial purple. He was ready there and then, he told them, to lay down the burden of the Empire; all that was necessary was that they should name his successor. Alternatively, if they preferred, he would continue in office, giving them his word that he would never again give them cause for dissatisfaction. The tall, white-haired figure was still handsome, the voice firm and persuasive. Gradually, the clamour ceased; once more, the situation had been saved.

There were plenty of other threats to the peace during the long reign of Anastasius. A three-year war with Persia resulted in the loss of several important strongholds along the eastern frontier, while repeated invasions by the Bulgars into Thrace obliged him to build a defensive wall across the thirty-odd miles from Selymbria (now Silivri) on the Marmara across to the Black Sea. Most dangerous of all was an insurrection led by a military adventurer of Gothic origins named Vitalian, who gained much popular support by claiming to be a champion of orthodoxy against a monophysite Emperor and who on three occasions advanced with his army to the very walls of Constantinople. None of these threats, however, had important long-term effects. It has seemed worth describing the religious riots in considerably greater detail than any of these simply to emphasize once again that aspect of daily life in the Byzantine Empire which it is hardest for the twentieth century to comprehend: the passionate involvement shown by all classes of society in what appear to most of us today to be impossibly abstruse niceties of theological doctrine. That such points should preoccupy deeply devout and scholarly men like Anastasius need occasion no particular surprise; that a plebeian mob should be inflamed to fury not by political slogans but by such questions as the relation of the Father to the Son or the Procession of the Holy Ghost puts a greater strain on our understanding, but is true none the less.

Some time towards the end of his reign, old Anastasius was consumed with curiosity to know which of his three nephews would succeed him on his death. Superstitious as always, he invited all three of them to dine with him in the Palace, and had three couches prepared on which they could afterwards take their rest. Under the pillow of one of these he slipped a small piece of parchment, on which he had inscribed the single word R E G N U M; whichever nephew chose that particular couch would, he believed, in due course assume the throne. Alas, a sad surprise awaited him: two of the young men, whose affection for each other seems to have gone somewhat beyond family feeling, chose to share the same couch; that which Anastasius had secretly marked remained unrumpled. From that moment he had no doubt that the next Emperor would come from outside his own line; but he still longed to know who it would be. After fervent prayers for a sign, it was revealed to him that his successor would be the man who first entered his bed-chamber the next day. Now the Emperor's first visitor was normally his personal chamberlain; that particular morning, however, it chanced to be Justin, Commander of the Excubitors, come to report the carrying-out of certain imperial orders. Anastasius bowed his head. It was, he knew, the will of God.

So runs the legend; and we may well imagine the old man reflecting, not perhaps for the first time, that the Almighty moves in a mysterious way. Justin was a Thracian peasant, now aged about sixty-six, uneducated and illiterate. Like Theodoric, he is said to have possessed a stencil – though of wood rather than gold – into which was cut the word LEGI, 'I have read it'; since only he had the right to use purple ink, his actual signature was unnecessary. Even then, according to Procopius,[1] the Emperor's hand had to be firmly guided across the page. The same source tells us how he and his two brothers had walked to Constantinople from their home at Bederiana – a village some sixty miles south of Naissus (Niš in present-day Yugoslavia) – 'with their cloaks slung over their shoulders . . . and when they reached the city they had nothing more than the cooked biscuit that they had brought with them from home'. His wife, Lupicina, had even humbler origins; she was a slave, and had already been the concubine of the man from whom Justin had bought her.

Despite, therefore, his signal service during the war in Isauria and his undoubted military capabilities, the new ruler was scarcely of imperial calibre. Procopius even goes so far as to compare him to a donkey, 'inclined to follow the man who pulls the rein, wagging his ears steadily the while'; but this is surely an exaggeration. Justin had, after all, risen from being a simple soldier to *Comes Excubitorum*, commander of one of

1 For this and the following references, see *Secret History*, vi–viii.

the crack palace regiments. He certainly seems to have possessed plenty of self-confidence and ambition, and not a little peasant cunning. According to another report, when Anastasius finally expired, at the age of eighty-seven, on the night of 9 July 518, the chief eunuch Amantius had his own candidate for the purple and confided his plans to Justin, supplying him with a considerable quantity of gold with which to bribe the soldiers. Justin, however, kept the money for himself and alerted his men to stand by their arms. The next morning, as the people poured into the Hippodrome and the Senate debated the succession behind closed doors, fighting broke out. The Excubitors were brought in to restore order, and of their own accord began to call for their *Comes* as the next Emperor. He first refused; but when the Senate, taking as usual the line of least resistance, joined their voice to that of the soldiers, he allowed himself to be persuaded.

A report that the regiment then formed a protective screen around its commander, drawing back to reveal him in full imperial regalia, suggests that despite appearances to the contrary Justin was not entirely unprepared for his elevation; even so, one may still wonder how it came about that so rough and unsophisticated a man should have obtained the support he did. First of all, he was uncompromisingly orthodox, standing four-square against the Anastasian party with its monophysite leanings and openly championing the Blues against the by now highly unpopular Greens. Second, he was well-liked and respected by the army and could be trusted to deal firmly with any renewed attempts at insurrection by Vitalian, who was still at liberty in Thrace. But his greatest advantage was his nephew, the real power behind his throne, the *éminence grise* who guided him more infallibly than any of those secretaries who steered his faltering pen across the wooden stencil. It was this nephew who, quite probably, engineered his uncle's elevation to the purple; it was he who dealt with Vitalian in typically Byzantine fashion, inviting him to Constantinople, lulling his suspicions by awarding him the Consulate and the rank of *magister militum* and then having him quietly assassinated; it was he who carried through the reconciliation with the Papacy after a thirty-five-year schism; and it was he who celebrated his own Consulship in 521 with the most lavish games and public spectacles in the Hippodrome that Constantinople had ever seen. No less than twenty lions, thirty panthers and an unspecified number of other exotic beasts were fought and killed – so much for Anastasius's reforms – in the vast circus; the equivalent of 3,700 pounds of gold was spent on decorations, stage machinery and largesse to the people; and the chariot races were of such superlative quality and aroused such excitement that the final contest had to be cancelled for fear of serious public disturbances. The contrast with the austere, penny-pinching days of the previous reign was dramatic, the message clear: the Empire stood on the threshold of a new and glorious age – an age in which, under a once-more benevolent God represented by a noble and dazzling Emperor, it would regain its lost territories and recapture its past greatness.

But the symbol of that age, and the identity of that Emperor, was not Justin; it was his nephew Justinian.

Justinian was born in 482, in a little village called Tauresina, not far from the birthplace of his uncle. His first language, like Justin's, was almost certainly Thracian, which was to become extinct a few hundred years later; but that whole region of the Balkan peninsula had long been thoroughly Romanized and the boy was probably bilingual in Latin at an early age. We do not know how or when he came to Constantinople. It was almost certainly at Justin's behest, when he was still a child: he was later known as a man of wide education and culture, of a kind that he could not possibly have acquired anywhere outside the capital. His schooling completed, his uncle must have arranged a military commission for him; for we find him as an officer in the *Scholae*, one of the palace regiments, at the time of Anastasius's death. By now, too, it seems that Justin had formally adopted him as a son, on which occasion he had abandoned his original name of Petrus Sabbatius and had assumed, as a mark of gratitude and respect to his benefactor, the name by which he is known to history.

But all this is little more than speculation. It is only from 518 onwards that we have firm historical evidence for Justinian's extraordinary career. One of his uncle's first actions on assuming the purple was to raise him to the rank of Patrician and appoint him Count of the Domestics, a position which gave him access to the innermost circles of power; and it was from this moment, that his effective domination began. Even if Justin did not owe his elevation to his nephew, he immediately showed himself willing to be guided by him in all things, and for the rest of his life thereafter – apart from a few months in 524–5 when Justinian was gravely ill – was content to be his mouthpiece and his puppet.

To Justinian, then, belongs the credit for what was incontestably the most important achievement of his uncle's reign: the healing of the breach with Rome, which had begun with the pinning of the sentence of excommunication on to the robes of Patriarch Acacius in 484. That breach was, in his eyes, an affront to the essential unity that lay at the heart of his entire political philosophy: as there was one God, so there must be one Empire, and one Church. Justin had not been on the throne a month before he wrote (at his nephew's dictation) to Pope Hormisdas, informing him of his accession – an honour, he somewhat disingenuously added, which he had been most unwilling to accept. The Pope replied, equally cordially; further exchanges followed; and on 25 March 519 a papal embassy arrived at Constantinople, having been met at the tenth milestone by a reception committee headed by Justinian himself. Two days later, in St Sophia, Patriarch John declared the Churches of the Old Rome and the New to be one and indivisible, and solemnly read a sentence of anathema on a whole string of heretics, including Timothy the Weasel, Paul the Stammerer and his own predecessor Acacius, 'formerly Bishop of Constantinople, who made himself accomplice and follower of these heretics, together with all who persevered in their fellowship and communion'. Finally the names of Zeno and Anastasius, together with those of the Patriarchs Euphemius and Macedonius – who had never veered from the orthodox path and had indeed suffered exile for their beliefs – were ceremonially struck from the diptychs.[1] The schism was at an end. The cost, from the Byzantine point of view, had been an almost unconditional surrender, involving the sacrifice of two innocent reputations; but to Justinian it was a small enough price to pay for a reunited Church.

Only a year or two after this – the date is uncertain, but it must have been soon after 520 – there came the second great turning-point in Justinian's life: his meeting with his future Empress. Theodora was not, to put it mildly, an ideal match. Her father had been a bear-keeper employed by the Greens at the Hippodrome, her mother some kind of circus performer, probably an acrobat; and these antecedents alone were more than enough to debar her from polite society. But they were not all. While still a child she had joined her elder sister on the stage, playing in low knockabout comedy, farce and burlesque. Already attractive and vivacious, she was also an inspired mimic; thus she soon acquired an enthusiastic following and before long had graduated to being Constantinople's most notorious courtesan – though we may doubt whether, even in her most abandoned moments, she altogether deserved the description of her by Procopius, surely one of the most outspoken pieces

1 These carried the lists of the orthodox faithful whose names were regularly remembered by the early Church during the celebration of the Eucharist.

of vilification ever directed against a queen or empress in all history:

Now for a time Theodora was still too immature to sleep with a man or to have intercourse like a woman, but she acted as might a male prostitute to satisfy those dregs of humanity, slaves though they were, who followed their master to the theatre and there took the opportunity to indulge in such bestial practices; and she remained some considerable time in a brothel, given over to such unnatural traffic of the body . . . But as soon as she reached maturity she joined the women of the stage and became a harlot, of the kind that our ancestors used to call 'the infantry' . . . The wench had not an ounce of modesty, nor did any man ever see her embarrassed: on the contrary, she unhesitatingly complied with the most shameless demands . . . and she would throw off her clothes and expose to all comers those parts, both in front and behind, which should rightly remain hidden from men's eyes.

Never was any woman so completely abandoned to pleasure. Many a time she would attend a banquet with ten young men or more, all with a passion for fornication and at the peak of their powers, and would lie with all her companions the whole night long; and when she had reduced them all to exhaustion she would go to their attendants – sometimes as many as thirty of them – and copulate with each in turn; and even then she could not satisfy her lust.

And although she made use of three apertures in her body, she was wont to complain that Nature had not provided her with larger openings in her nipples, so that she might have contrived another form of intercourse there. And though she became repeatedly pregnant, yet by various devices she was almost always able to induce an immediate abortion.

Often in the theatre, too, in full view of all the people . . . she would spread herself out and lie on her back on the ground. And certain slaves whose special task it was would sprinkle grains of barley over her private parts; and geese trained for the purpose would pick them off one by one with their beaks and swallow them. And when she rose again to her feet, so far from blushing she actually seemed to take pride in this performance.[1]

So it goes on, the sanctimonious old hypocrite clearly relishing every word he writes. Clearly too, his account is to be taken with more than a pinch of salt. Procopius loathed both Theodora and her husband, and this is not the only passage in his scurrilous *Secret History* in which he sets out to destroy the reputation of one or the other. There is no suggestion that he ever witnessed Theodora in action; thus his authority can only be the gossip of the market place, and that, we may be sure, lost nothing in the telling. All the same, such billowing black smoke must presumably issue from some sort of a fire; and there can be little doubt that Theodora was, as our grandparents might have put it, no better

1 *Secret History*, ix, 10-22.

St John Chrysostom.
A ninth-century mosaic from the north tympanum in St Sophia

The Virgin and Child flanked by Justinian and Constantine.
A tenth-century mosaic from a vestibule lunette in St Sophia

The interior of St Sophia

The Church of St Eirene, Istanbul
The interior of the Church of St Eirene

The head of an Emperor, possibly Arcadius

Theodosius I presents the victor's wreath, from the base of an obelisk in the Hippodrome, Istanbul

St Sophia, the south arcade

The interior of the Church of SS Sergius and Bacchus, Istanbul

The Third Ecumenical Council at Ephesus, AD 431. A
sixteenth-century fresco in the Church of St Sozomen,
Galata, Cyprus

The remains of the Church of the Virgin Mary, Ephesus

Theodosius the Great or
Valentinian I – a late fourth-
century bronze statue outside the
Church of S. Sepolcro, Barletta

The Theodosian Walls

A sixth-century mosaic from the
Imperial Palace, Constantinople

Justinian's basilican cistern: a
nineteenth-century engraving

A diptych of the Emperor Anastasius

Coins bearing the heads of Constantine the Great, Constantius II,
Galla Placidia, Julian the Apostate and the Empress Irene

The sixth-century apse of S. Apollinare in Classe, Ravenna

The Barberini Ivory; probably the Emperor Anastasius, known to have received an embassy from India in 496 (see lower panel). The right-hand panel (which presumably portrayed another warrior bearing a statuette of victory) is missing

The Aqueduct of Valens, Istanbul
◁ The Emperor Justinian and his court
◁ The Empress Theodora and her retinue.
Sixth-century mosaics from the Church of S. Vitale, Ravenna

St Sophia: a Byzantine capital

Classis, the port of Ravenna – from a sixth-century mosaic in S. Apollinare Nuovo, Ravenna

The Church of St John of Studium, Istanbul

than she should have been. Whether she was more depraved than others of her sort is open to question.

In any case she soon began to look around for better things, and so became the mistress of a moderately distinguished civil servant, whom she accompanied to North Africa. Once there, the two had a violent quarrel. Theodora was dismissed and, still according to Procopius, worked her passage home in the only way she knew. At some stage on her return journey, however, she found herself in Alexandria; and it has been suggested that while there she came into contact with the leading churchmen of the city – something which would go a long way towards explaining the pronounced monophysite tendencies which she was to display in later life. She may even have undergone some sort of religious experience, for she certainly seems to have been a changed woman by the time she returned to Constantinople.

One characteristic that remained constant, however, was her strong attachment to the Blue party and her hatred for the Greens. The story is told of how, after her father's death when she was six years old, her mother at once remarried in the hopes that her new husband would succeed to his predecessor's job as the Greens' bear-keeper. But she was disappointed: the post had been given to another applicant. Threatened with destitution, she appeared one day in the Circus, her three little girls accompanying her with garlands in their hair, and appealed to the assembled populace. The Greens, who might have been thought to have some moral obligation to the widow of their old employee, ignored her; but the Blues – more probably out of a desire to show their rivals in a bad light than from any genuine sympathy – took pity on her and found employment for her husband. From that moment on, Theodora's loyalties were fixed; for the rest of her life she never wavered.

Justinian too favoured the Blues, and before his succession spent much time and energy in securing their support. It was probably while doing so that he first met Theodora. She was by now in her middle thirties, as beautiful and intelligent as ever, and with all the wisdom and maturity that had been so noticeably absent in earlier years. He was at once captivated and, within a short time, enslaved. He made her his mistress and fathered a child who died in infancy, but this was not enough: despite her background, he was determined that she should be his wife. Inevitably, there were obstacles. One was a law which specifically forbade the marriage of senators and others of high rank to actresses; another, far more serious, was the implacable opposition of the Empress. On her husband's accession she had abandoned the name of Lupicina in favour of the nobler – if less original – Euphemia; but she was still essentially the peasant she had always been and, having finally found in her immediate entourage someone of still baser extraction than herself, she was determined to do her down in any way she could. While Euphemia lived the marriage was impossible, even for Justinian; but in 524, fortunately for him, she died. The old Emperor made no difficulties; he never attempted to stand against his nephew. Within weeks he had given his approval to a law permitting retired actresses on whom high dignity had been conferred to marry anyone they liked. The way was now clear, and in 525 the Patriarch in St Sophia declared Justinian and Theodora man and wife. Only two years later, on 4 April 527, they were crowned co-Emperor and Empress, and when on 1 August old Justin finally succumbed to the cancer from which he had long been suffering, they found themselves the sole and supreme rulers of the Byzantine Empire.

The plural is important. Theodora was to be no Empress Consort, spending her life quietly with her attendant ladies in the *gynaeceum* and appearing with her husband only at the most solemn ceremonies. At Justinian's insistence, she was to reign at his side, taking decisions and acting upon them in his name, giving him the benefit of her counsel in all the highest affairs of state. She had come a long way in five years; her future appearances on the public stage were to be very different from those of the past.

What the people of Constantinople thought of Justinian's marriage to Theodora is not recorded. If Procopius's account of her early life has any truth in it at all, there must have been many who saw it as a disgrace to the Empire. One suspects, none the less, that there were others prepared to adopt a less censorious attitude. Justinian had never acquired the common touch: he had always seemed somehow remote from his future subjects, chilly and withdrawn. Here at last was a sign that he was human, just like anyone else.

But to be human is not necessarily to be popular. However splendid the games in the Circus, however open-handed the largesse scattered to the crowds celebrating his second Consulship in the year following his accession, however generous the financial aid made available to cities stricken by earthquakes – there were nearly 5,000 casualties at Antioch in 528, and half as many again at Laodicea in 529 – Justinian was never loved. His extravagances were all very fine, but they all had to be paid for. So did the war with Persia, which began when he had been only a few months on the throne and smouldered fitfully on till after the death of King Kavadh in 531; so did the 'Everlasting Peace' with which it ended, signed with Kavadh's successor Chosroes in September 532, which provided for the payment by the Empire of an annual tribute – though it was never so described – of 11,000 pounds' weight of gold a year. So too did the monumental construction programme, which Justinian had begun in his uncle's reign with the great church dedicated to Mary the Mother of God at Blachernae, where the Walls of Theodosius ran down to the Golden Horn, and which he had continued with the rebuilding of no less than seven others – many of them originally founded by Constantine – commemorating early Christian martyrs who had met their deaths in and around Byzantium. This alone would have been an impressive achievement; but it proved to be only the beginning. In the first days after his succession he continued with a foundation of his own, erected in grateful memory of two more martyrs, St Sergius and St Bacchus – a church which, by the originality of its architecture and the sumptuousness of its carved decoration, ranks in Constantinople second only to St Sophia itself.[1]

For all these purposes and many others, the necessary funds could be raised – and indeed were – by a tightening-up and general streamlining of the system of tax collection. But such measures are never welcomed by those called upon to pay, and the widespread popular discontent was still further increased by the official appointed by the Emperor to put them into effect. This was a certain John of Cappadocia. We know nothing about his background, except that he came from Caesarea in Asia Minor and that he had little formal education. He was rough and uncouth, utterly devoid of any social graces; but Justinian recognized a superb administrator when he saw one, and in 531 promoted him to be Praetorian Prefect. In this capacity he instituted stringent economies in the provisioning of the army, launched a determined campaign against corruption, introduced new taxes – John of Lydia, one of our most valuable sources for the period, lists twenty-six of them – which fell, perhaps for the first time, as much on the rich and powerful landowners as on the poor peasantry, and did much to centralize the government, dramatically reducing the power of the senior provincial officials. Most of these reforms were long overdue, and John certainly

---

1 This exquisite building, now a mosque known as Little St Sophia – *Küçük Ayasofya Camii* – still survives below the southern end of the Hippodrome, just behind the Sea Walls. Its two patrons, Roman centurions converted to Christianity and subsequently martyred for their faith, had been particularly dear to Justinian since his youth, when he had been condemned to death after a plot against Anastasius and they, appearing to the Emperor in a dream, had obtained his release.

left the financial machinery of the Empire in very much better shape than he found it. Unfortunately, he combined with his industry and efficiency a degree of moral depravity that aroused universal contempt. Those whom he believed to possess hidden and undeclared riches he thought nothing of subjecting to imprisonment, flogging or even torture; he was, moreover, a glutton, drunkard and debauchee who, according to his Lydian namesake, not only drained the province of Lydia of all its wealth but 'left behind to the wretched inhabitants of the country not a single vessel of any kind; neither was there any wife, any virgin, or any youth free of defilement'.[1] His activities in these fields are unlikely to have been confined to a single province, and it is small wonder that by the beginning of 532 John was the most hated man in the Empire.

One other official, however, ran him close; and that was the jurist Tribonian, who in 529 was appointed Quaestor of the Sacred Palace, the highest law officer in the government. John of Cappadocia, nightmarish as he may have been in other respects, was at least a Christian, and personally incorruptible; Tribonian, a Pamphylian from Side, was an unashamed pagan and venal to boot: Procopius remarks that 'he was always ready to sell justice for gain and every day, as a rule, he would repeal certain laws and propose others, according to the requirements of those who bought his services'.[2] On the other hand – also unlike the Cappadocian – he was a man of quite irresistible charm, who astonished all with whom he came into contact by his immense erudition and the breadth of his learning. It must have been this last quality that appealed to Justinian; a considerable scholar himself, he had long contemplated an almost superhuman undertaking, and in Tribonian he found the one man capable of bringing it to fruition. This was a complete recodification of the Roman law. Such an attempt had already been made by Theodosius II in 438; but a century had passed since his day, and Justinian's plan was in any case far more ambitious: where his predecessor had contented himself with making a simple compilation of the imperial edicts, he aimed to produce an entirely new code, removing all repetitions and con-tradictions, ensuring that there was nothing incompatible with Christian teaching, substituting clarity and concision for confusion and chaos.

Under Tribonian's chairmanship and guided by his encyclopaedic

---

1 Herodotus (writing admittedly nine centuries earlier) tells us that the Lydians had the unfortunate habit of prostituting their daughters before marriage – although, he adds, 'apart from that, their way of life is very like our own'. But the *moeurs* of the ladies of Lydia had presumably changed since his day.

2 *History of the Wars*, I, xxiv, 16.

knowledge, the special commission appointed by the Emperor pressed forward with almost unbelievable speed. On 8 April 529, less than fourteen months after work began, the new *Codex* was ready; and a week later it came into force, the supreme authority for every court in the Empire. A fuller edition, including Justinian's own laws, appeared five years later; already in 530, however, a second commission under Tribonian began another codification, this time of the principal writings of all the ancient Roman jurists. Known as the *Digest* – or sometimes as the *Pandects* – it was the first attempt ever made to bring these also into the framework of a methodical system. The commission was said to have 'condensed the wisdom of nearly two thousand treatises into fifty books, and recast three million "verses" from the older writers into 150,000': an astonishing achievement in only three years. Finally in 533 there appeared the *Institutes*, a handbook of extracts from the two main books designed for use in the imperial law schools. All these were written in Latin – still the language of law, but of very little else. The Empire had changed much since the days of Constantine; the Hellenization of his city was almost complete.

In comparison with the immense weight of Tribonian's contribution to the imperial law, the irregularities of his professional life seem insignificant enough – particularly when we make allowance for Procopius's inveterate tendency towards exaggeration. There is no doubt, however, that he and John of Cappadocia were together largely responsible for the growing disaffection that marked the first five years of Justinian's reign. Few memories rankle so much as those of lost lawsuits that should have been won; and to the voices of disappointed litigants we must also add those of men who had been deprived of their positions (whether sinecures or not) and of those who, as a result of the tax reforms, had found their various sharp practices exposed and stopped. The latter were naturally somewhat less vocal; but any reticence in this respect was more than made up for by yet another class of malcontents: the Blues and the Greens. Once Justinian felt himself secure on his throne, he found that he no longer needed Blue support and so embarked on a policy of repression directed against both parties indiscriminately, limiting their powers and privileges and curbing their excesses with harsh, at times even savage, punishments. Thus, when the two factions came to blows after the races in the Hippodrome on 10 January 532, he did not hesitate to send in troops to restore order: and no less than seven of the ringleaders were condemned to death. Of these, five were executed without difficulty, but the remaining two were found to be still breathing when they were cut down. Rescued by a group of monks, they were hurried across the Bosphorus to sanctuary in the monastery of St Lawrence. There the City Prefect, Eudaimon, decided to starve them into submission and posted an armed guard outside the doors; meanwhile their followers demonstrated noisily, demanding that the two should be given their freedom.

The two men were, as it happened, a Blue and a Green; thus for the first time the two factions found themselves with a common cause. Three days later, as Justinian once again took his place in the Hippodrome and gave the signal for the games to begin, his appearance was greeted by uproar. At first it seemed nothing unusual, but then, suddenly, he realized that this demonstration was different to any he had witnessed before: the Greens and the Blues were united, and their clamour was directed not at each other but at him. '*Nikā! Nikā!*' they cried, using the normal word of encouragement – 'Win! Win!' – by which they were accustomed to cheer on the charioteers. In the past, however, they had invariably followed it with the name of the team they supported, each side trying to shout down the other. Now, in menacing chorus, they chanted the single word alone, over and over again. Factional differences had been forgotten. The crowd was speaking with one voice; and that voice was not pleasant to hear.

The races began, but failed to reduce the tension and were soon abandoned. The mob poured out of the great circus, hell-bent on destruction. Their first objective was the palace of the City Prefect where, having forced an entrance by killing the guards who stood in their way, they released all the prisoners from the cells and set fire to the building. From there they passed on to the Praetorian Prefecture, then to the Senate House, the Baths of Zeuxippus and of Alexander, and even to the two great churches of St Irene and St Sophia, leaving a trail of flames behind them. By the end of the day all these buildings and countless others standing along the Mesē had been reduced to smoking ruins.

Meanwhile new fires were constantly being started, and for five days and nights the smoke lay thick over the city. On the second day the mob, returning to the Hippodrome, called for the immediate dismissal of John of Cappadocia, Tribonian and the City Prefect Eudaimon – a demand which Justinian, by now seriously alarmed, granted at once. On the third, their fury still unassuaged, they began shouting for a new Emperor – one of Anastasius's nephews, a man named Probus; when they found that he had left the city they set fire to his house and went rampaging on. At last, on 18 January, Justinian partly recovered his nerve and faced them in the Hippodrome, taking the entire blame for all the disturbances and promising a full amnesty if they all returned quietly to their homes. This tactic had been employed twenty years before by his predecessor with complete success; but the present situation was far more serious than anything that Anastasius had had to face. The few half-hearted cheers were soon drowned in catcalls, and the Emperor retreated hurriedly into the Palace.

By now the rioters had found a new favourite. Hypatius, another nephew of the former Emperor, could look back on a distinguished military career, having commanded Byzantine armies both in Persia and against the rebel Vitalian in Thrace. Now an old man, he had no imperial ambitions and had indeed done his best to hide when the mob began calling his name; but they somehow ran him to earth and carried him shoulder-high to the Hippodrome where, in default of a diadem, he was crowned with a gold necklet borrowed from a bystander and seated on the throne in the imperial box. Meanwhile, in the Palace behind, a desperate Justinian was conferring with his advisers. Already some days before, he had ordered preparations to be made for himself and his court to flee the capital at short notice if the need arose, and he now argued that that moment could no longer be delayed.

Suddenly, Theodora intervened. She did not care, she said, whether or not it was proper for a woman to give brave counsel to frightened men; in moments of extreme danger, conscience was the only guide. So far as she was concerned, the possibility of flight was not to be considered for a moment, even if it brought them safety. 'Every man', she continued,

who is born into the light of day must sooner or later die; and how could an Emperor ever allow himself to be a fugitive? May I myself never willingly shed my imperial robes, nor see the day when I am no longer addressed by my title. If you, my Lord, wish to save your skin, you will have no difficulty in doing so. We are rich, there is the sea, there too are our ships. But consider first whether, when you reach safety, you will not regret that you did not choose death in preference. As for me, I stand by the ancient saying: the purple is the noblest winding-sheet.[1]

After that, there could be no question of departure; the crisis, it was agreed, must be resolved by force of arms. Fortunately, two of the Empire's best generals were present in the Palace. The first, Belisarius, was still in his twenties. A Romanized Thracian like Justinian, he had

1 Procopius, *History of the Wars*, I, xxiv, 33–7.

recently been recalled from the Persian front and had been promoted to Commander-in-Chief. The second, Mundus, was an Illyrian who found himself only by chance in the capital, but who happened to have with him a sizeable force of Scandinavian mercenaries. The two quickly decided on a plan of action.

Secretly they slipped out of the Palace, rallied their soldiers and, by separate and circuitous routes, marched on the Hippodrome. Then, at a given signal, they burst in simultaneously on the shouting, screaming mob, taking it completely by surprise. No quarter was given: Greens and Blues were slaughtered without discrimination. Meanwhile the Commander of the imperial bodyguard, an elderly and deceptively frail-looking Armenian eunuch named Narses, had stationed his men at the principal exits with orders to cut down all who tried to escape. Within a few minutes, the angry shouts in the great amphitheatre had given place to the cries and groans of wounded and dying men; soon these too grew quiet, until silence spread over the entire arena, its sand now sodden with the blood of the victims.

As the mercenaries, exhausted by their butchery, picked their way among the 30,000 bodies, finishing them off where necessary and relieving them of such valuables as they possessed, the trembling Hypatius was led before the Emperor. Justinian, who probably realized how his old friend had been swept up in events beyond his control, was inclined to be merciful; but Theodora stopped him. The man, she pointed out, had been crowned by the people; despite his grey hairs, he might at any time serve as a focus for further rebellion. Her husband, as always, bowed to her will. On the very next day Hypatius and his brother Pompeius were summarily executed and their bodies cast into the sea.

The Nika revolt (as it came to be called) taught Justinian a salutary lesson. Within a few weeks he felt sufficiently confident to reinstate Tribonian and John of Cappadocia in their former positions; but thereafter he was more circumspect, and though taxation remained heavy it no longer went beyond the bounds of reason. His subjects, too, were chastened. Thirty thousand of them indeed were dead, and there must have been countless others who attributed to divine providence alone their absence from the Hippodrome on that fateful afternoon. Emperors, it now appeared, could not be made and unmade as easily as they had thought. With Anastasius they had been able to do more or less as they liked; Justinian had shown that he was not to be trifled with.

Meanwhile, for Emperor and people alike, there was work to be done.

Their capital lay in ruins around them; whatever the cost, it must be rebuilt – where possible, on a yet grander and more impressive scale than before. Primarily, this was the responsibility of the City Prefect and his staff; but the central buildings of the capital were obviously too important to be left to subordinates, and first among them was St Sophia itself. This, Justinian resolved, was to be his own creation, and he lost no time. On 23 February 532, just thirty-nine days after the destruction of its predecessor, work began on the third and final Church of the Holy Wisdom.

Although the earliest of the three churches to be built on the site had been conceived by Constantine himself, it was not actually erected until the reign of his son Constantius, around the year 360, and lasted for less than half a century before being burnt down during the riots following the banishment of St John Chrysostom in 404.[1] The second church, re-dedicated eleven years later by Theodosius II, was almost certainly a near-replica of the first, designed once again on the traditional basilican plan. Justinian's building, however, was to bear no resemblance to these. It was to be infinitely larger, for one thing – far and away the largest religious building in the entire Christian world.[2] It would also be square rather than rectangular, reaching its climax not with its apsed sanctuary at the eastern end but with its high central dome. So revolutionary was the concept, indeed, that it seems likely that Justinian was already planning it with his two chosen architects, Anthemius of Tralles and Isidore of Miletus, long before the Nika rising made it necessary; for all their undoubted genius, they could hardly have prepared their working drawings in under six weeks.

Of these two architects we know little. Anthemius, a Greek from Asia Minor – Tralles, now Aydin, was a small town in the valley of the Meander – was primarily a mathematician and engineer, who is thought to have studied in Alexandria before finding his way to Constantinople. Once there, he worked for Justinian on St Sergius and St Bacchus, so impressing his master that he was later given technical authority over all the new building work in the capital. His colleague Isidore came from the same region, and may also have travelled to Egypt for his education: he is known to have written a brilliant commentary on a famous treatise on vaulting by the first-century mathematician Heron of Alexandria. By the time he received the imperial summons, he was already celebrated as the foremost teacher of his day.

1 See p. 130.
2 It would remain so until the building of Seville Cathedral some 700 years later.

From the outset Justinian seems to have given the two men *carte blanche*, regarding both the design and the cost of the building. His only stipulations were that it should be of unparalleled magnificence, and that it should be erected in the shortest possible time: he was already fifty years old and was determined to see it complete before he died. Procopius tells us[1] that he gathered artisans and craftsmen 'from the whole world'; according to another authority, he appointed a hundred foremen, each with a hundred men under him, setting 5,000 to the north side and 5,000 to the south, so that each of the two teams should strive to work faster than the other. Meanwhile an imperial rescript was circulated to all the provinces of the Empire, requiring their governors to examine all the ancient sites and to send at once to the capital any surviving classical remains that might be suitable for incorporation in the new structure. In response, we are told, eight porphyry columns, once part of a temple of the Sun, were received from Rome and eight of green marble from Ephesus. More marble, of every colour and kind, was especially quarried, for use on the walls and pavements:

... the fresh green from Carystus, and many-coloured marble from the Phrygian range, in which a rosy blush mingles with white or shines bright with flowers of deep red and silver. There is a wealth of porphyry too, powdered with brilliant stars, that once weighed down the boats of the broad Nile. You may see an emerald green from Sparta, and the glittering marble with the undulating veins which the tool has worked from the deep bosom of the Iassian hills, showing slanting streaks of blood-red and livid white ... Stone too there is that the Libyan sun, warming with his golden light, has nurtured from the dark clefts of the Moorish hills, of crocus colour sparkling like gold; and that product of the Celtic crags, a wealth of crystals, like milk splashed over a surface of shining black. There is the precious onyx, looking as if gold were glowing through it, and the marble that the land of Atrax yields ... in parts a fresh green like the sea or emerald stone, or again like blue cornflowers in grass, with here and there a drift of fallen snow ...

So wrote a certain Paul the Silentiary, whose long poem in praise of the new church – one might almost call it a rhapsody – was composed for an *encaenia* held there on Christmas Eve, 563, when the building was reconsecrated after being damaged in two successive earthquakes. Despite his flowery Homeric language, he is immensely detailed and astonishingly accurate – so accurate indeed that one feels that he must have written the poem in the building itself. 'The vaulting,' he continues, 'is

1 *Buildings*, i, 1.

formed of countless little squares of gold cemented together. And the golden stream of glittering rays pours down and strikes the eyes of men, so that they can scarcely bear to look. It is as if one were to gaze upon the mid-day sun in spring, when it gilds every mountain height.'

Interestingly, neither the Silentiary nor any of his contemporaries mention the existence of figurative mosaics. One would not in fact expect any such work of Justinian's time to have survived, since it would certainly have been destroyed by the iconoclasts in the eighth century; had there ever been any, it is inconceivable that neither Paul nor Procopius – to say nothing of other writers – would have said a word about it. The latter, on the other hand, echoes the former when he remarks that the interior of the great church was so full of light and sunshine as to suggest some inner radiance of its own, and there can be no doubt but that virtually the whole surface of the interior above the marble revetments – an area estimated at some four acres – was completely covered with mosaic, either in uniform gold or in decorative patterns in which red, blue and green *tesserae* were added. The vast majority of this original work is still in place, though we have regrettably lost the huge jewelled cross on a background of stars that once spread itself across the dome.[1]

But the splendour of the church was not confined to its surface decoration: architecturally, too, it seemed to its earliest visitors little less than a miracle. To Evagrius the historian, it was 'a great and incomparable work' whose beauty 'surpassed all powers of description'; to Procopius it seemed to soar up to heaven, rising above the surrounding buildings 'like a huge ship anchored among them'. But to most observers the most magical feature of all was that extraordinary dome, 107 feet across and 160 above the pavement, several times broader and higher than any other dome ever previously attempted, a shallow saucer pierced around its rim with forty windows so that it appeared to be 'suspended from heaven by a golden chain'.

And then there was the furniture: the fifty-foot iconostasis in solid silver, hung with sacred images of angels and apostles, the Holy Virgin occupying the place of honour in the centre; the high altar, encrusted with gold and precious stones, covered by a silver ciborium resting on four richly decorated columns; the immense circular ambo for the

1 The first dome collapsed on 7 May 558, after being severely weakened by earthquakes in 553 and 557. It was rebuilt by the nephew and namesake of Isidore who gave it a slightly steeper pitch, raising its crown some twenty feet higher than that of its predecessor; but this second dome collapsed with the western arch in 989, as did the third when the eastern arch fell in 1346. The present dome is the fourth, now reinforced with the iron chains inserted by the Italian architect Gaspare Fossati in the course of his major restoration during the 1860s.

preacher, ablaze with polychrome marble and mosaic; the gold lamps innumerable. The relics, too, were such as no other church could match, dominated as they were by the True Cross itself, brought back from Jerusalem by the Empress Helena with the other instruments of the Passion, among them were Christ's swaddling clothes and the table at which he and his Apostles sat for the Last Supper. Also to be revered were the chains of St Peter, the carpet of St Nicholas, the head of St Pantaleimon and the arm of St Germanus, which was laid upon each succeeding Patriarch at his induction. No wonder that Justinian, entering the completed building for the first time on 27 December 537 – just five years, ten months and four days after the laying of the first stone – stood for a long time in silence before being heard to murmur: 'Solomon, I have surpassed thee.'

10

Belisarius

[532–40]

His lofty stature and majestic countenance fulfilled their expectations of a hero ... By the union of liberality and justice he acquired the love of the soldiers, without alienating the affections of the people. The sick and wounded were relieved with medicines and money, and still more efficaciously by the healing visits and smiles of their commander ... In the licence of a military life, none could boast that they had seen him intoxicated with wine; the most beautiful captives of Gothic or Vandal race were offered to his embraces, but he turned aside from their charms, and the husband of Antonina was never suspected of violating the laws of conjugal fidelity. The spectator and historian of his exploits has observed that amidst the perils of war he was daring without rashness, prudent without fear, slow or rapid according to the exigencies of the moment; that in the deepest distress he was animated by real or apparent hope, but that he was modest and humble in the most prosperous fortune.

Gibbon, *The Decline and Fall of the Roman Empire*, Chap. XLI

In the period of relative domestic tranquillity that followed the Nika revolt and the peace concluded with Persia eight months later, Justinian was at last able to turn his mind to what he had always determined was to be the primary objective of his reign: to recover the Empire of the West. Like the vast majority of his subjects, he believed the Roman Empire to be one and indivisible, the political manifestation of Christendom; that half of it should have fallen into alien and heretic hands was an offence against the Will of God, and it was therefore his Christian duty to regain his lost heritage. During the previous century such a reconquest had been impossible: the Empire had been hard put to protect itself from the Germanic and Slavic tribes forever pressing on its frontiers, while the barbarian infiltration of the army itself made its very loyalty uncertain. But by Justinian's time these problems were largely solved; moreover, as it happened, he had found in Belisarius one of the most brilliant generals in all Byzantine history – the one man, he believed, to whom this sacred task could confidently be entrusted.

To this end he had recalled him from Mesopotamia in the autumn of 531. Already two years before, the young commander had been promoted to be *magister militum per orientem*, in which capacity he had inflicted an overwhelming defeat on a far superior Persian army at Dara, some twenty miles north-west of Nisibis. His military gifts were unquestioned: his personal courage had been proved again and again, and he was a natural leader of men. He had but one liability: his wife, whom he married soon after his return from the East. Antonina's background was not unlike that of her Empress. She too had been brought up in the theatre and the circus and her past, if not as lurid as Theodora's, was certainly far from stainless. At least twelve years older than her husband – Procopius says twenty-two – she had already had several children, in or out of wedlock. Unlike Theodora, she made no attempt to reform her character after her prestigious marriage, and in the years to come was to cause her husband much embarrassment and not a little anguish; but Belisarius, it seems, continued to love her and – perhaps to keep his eye on her as much as for any other reason – was accustomed to take her with him on all his campaigns.

The first territory to be singled out for reconquest was the Vandal Kingdom in North Africa. Much had happened in the sixty-five years since that humiliating fiasco when the expedition under Basiliscus had been annihilated by King Gaiseric. The latter had died in 477, having given his Kingdom a constitution in which the succession was decreed by the laws of primogeniture – putting it, in this respect, well in advance of any other Germanic state and even of the Roman Empire itself – and the throne of Carthage had accordingly passed to Gaiseric's grandson, an elderly and mildly homosexual bachelor named Hilderic. The offspring of Princess Eudocia, that daughter of Valentinian III who had been brought back to Africa with her mother and sister after the Vandal sack of Rome and subsequently married off to Gaiseric's son,[1] he was a Roman on his mother's side who had so far adopted Roman ways as to renounce the Arian heresy of his forefathers and embrace the orthodox faith; and his hatred of war was such that, if Procopius is to be believed, he would never allow the subject to be mentioned in his presence. All this was of course welcome news to Justinian, who understandably believed that with a little quiet diplomacy he could bring the Vandal Kingdom back into the imperial fold without the loss of a single Roman

[1] See p. 163.

soldier. Unfortunately, he had less time than he thought. In 531 Hilderic's distant cousin Gelimer finally lost patience, and with the enthusiastic support of most of the Vandal nobility seized the throne for himself – replying to the Emperor's immediate protest with a letter pointing out that 'nothing was more desirable than that a monarch should mind his own business'.

Gelimer had, it must be admitted, a point; but to Justinian these were fighting words. His advisers, remembering the earlier débâcle, advised strongly against war, John of Cappadocia most insistently of all:

You propose, O Emperor, to launch an expedition against Carthage, to which the land journey is one of a hundred and forty days. If you entrust your army to ships, you must cross a wide waste of waters to the utmost limits of the sea. Should misfortune overtake your forces, it will be a full year before the news is brought back to us. Even if you are victorious, you will never hold Africa while Italy and Sicily are in the hands of others, while if you are defeated your breach of the treaty will put the whole Empire in jeopardy. Success, in short, will bring you no lasting gain, while failure will risk the ruin of your flourishing and well-established state.[1]

For Justinian, however, Gelimer's insult continued to rankle; and after an Eastern bishop had informed him of a dream in which the Almighty had promised his assistance in a holy war against the Arian Vandals he needed no further prompting. Belisarius was given his orders; and on or about Midsummer Day 533 the Emperor stood at the window of the Palace to watch the departure of the expedition. It consisted of 5,000 cavalry and twice as many infantry – at least half of them barbarian mercenaries, mostly Huns but with a strong admixture of Heruli from Scandinavia. They travelled in a fleet of 500 transports, escorted by ninety-two *dromons*.[2] On the flagship, together with the commander himself, were his military secretary Procopius and, as usual, his wife Antonina.

The journey began inauspiciously, when two drunken Huns – and the Huns, notes Procopius, were the most intemperate drinkers in the world – murdered one of their comrades and were summarily hanged by Belisarius on the hill above Abydos. After that the fleet made good time to

---

1 Procopius, *History of the Wars*, III, x, 14–16.

2 The *dromon* was the smallest type of Byzantine warship, designed for lightness and speed. It carried a crew of some twenty rowers at a single bank of oars, and was roofed over to protect them from enemy missiles.

Methoni, at the south-west corner of the Peloponnese; but disaster struck when the sacks of ship's biscuit provided by John of Cappadocia were found to be mouldy – not, unfortunately, before 500 men had been severely poisoned. (Procopius claims that John, wishing as always to economize, had sent the dough not to a proper bakery but to the furnace which heated the baths of Achilles in Constantinople, with the result that it had been only half-baked.) Many days elapsed before the ships could be revictualled with local produce and were able to continue, via Zacynthus (Zante), to Catania.

After a brief period of Vandal rule, Sicily had been bought back by Odoacer in return for an annual subsidy. Since the Ostrogothic Kingdom of Italy was still, as in the days of Theodoric, friendly to Byzantium, Catania provided a useful vantage-point from which Belisarius could prepare his fleet for the final attack, while simultaneously gathering what intelligence he could about the enemy dispositions. To this end Procopius was sent south to Syracuse – where, as luck would have it, he soon ran into an old friend from his boyhood, one of whose slaves had returned only three days previously from Carthage. The information that this man was able to give him could hardly have been more welcome: the Vandals had heard nothing of the approaching fleet, and had indeed recently dispatched a major expedition of their own to put down a rising – inspired, though they did not know it, by Justinian himself – in Sardinia.

Belisarius, when he heard the news, gave orders to sail at once; and after touching briefly at Malta the fleet arrived safely in North Africa, disembarking the army on the open beach at what is now Ras Kaboudia, the easternmost point of the Tunisian coast where it swells out between Sousse and Sfax. From here both the cavalry and the infantry set off to the north towards Carthage, the ships keeping pace with them offshore. The distance, some 140 miles, is optimistically described by Procopius as being 'five days' journey for an unencumbered traveller'; but the Byzantines, with all their baggage and equipment, took twice that time and were still at the tenth milestone from the capital when, on 13 September, the Vandal army struck.

Once the Roman ships had been sighted off the coast, Gelimer had acted quickly. His fleet and part of his army were indeed away in Sardinia, but he still had plenty of men under arms at home, and by the time the invaders had disembarked his plans were already laid. The place he had chosen for the confrontation was a point near the tenth milestone, where the road from the south entered a narrow valley. The attack itself was to be threefold: his brother Ammatas would attack the vanguard while his nephew Gibamund swept down on the centre from the western hills and he himself dealt with the rear. It was an ambitious plan, which depended for its success on careful timing; unfortunately for Gelimer, his communications let him down. Ammatas moved too early; the Byzantines, forewarned, were ready and waiting for him. In the battle that followed, the Vandal prince was killed, though not before he had accounted for a dozen Romans; his own soldiers, seeing their leader fall, soon lost heart. Some were cut to pieces around him; the remainder fled.

The flanking attack was no more successful, and a good deal less glorious. By now the element of surprise had been lost, but if Gibamund had moved in quickly enough to the assistance of Ammatas, the two divisions might yet have saved the day. Instead, he hesitated, ordered a halt, and began carefully drawing up his troops in line of battle. He was still doing so when Belisarius's cavalry charged. They were Huns, hideous, savage and implacable. The Vandals took one look at the advancing horde and ran for their lives. All now depended on Gelimer himself. He started well, somehow contriving to cut Belisarius and his generals off from the main bulk of their army; at this point, however, he suddenly came upon the body of his brother – and the fight went out of him. For some time he remained motionless, refusing to leave the spot until the corpse had been carried from the field and arrangements made for its proper burial. Once again, Belisarius saw his chance. Swiftly regrouping, he bore down upon the Vandal host and scattered it to right and left. The battle was over. The defenders fled, not to the north whence they had come – for that road was already under Roman control – but westward into the deserts of Numidia. Carthage lay open.

Two days later, on Sunday 15 September, Belisarius – with Antonina at his side – made his formal entry into the city. Since the day of their first landing in Africa, his men had been under strict orders to respect the lives and property of the local people, who despite a century of barbarian occupation remained Roman citizens like themselves. There was no swagger, no insolence or arrogance, no braggadocio; everything bought in the shops was paid for, promptly and in full. As for Belisarius, he went straight to the palace where, seated on the throne of the Vandal King, he received the leading citizens and later dined in state with his officers – off dishes, Procopius tells us, that had been prepared for Gelimer himself.

But Gelimer had not given up the struggle. From his temporary refuge at Bulla Regia in Numidia, some hundred miles west of Carthage, he had sent an urgent message to his surviving brother Tzazo, who was in command of the Sardinian expedition, summoning him and his forces back at once to Africa. Meanwhile he settled down to reorganize and regroup his own army, and to rally support among the local Punic and Berber tribes, offering them generous rewards for every Roman head that they could lay before him. Thus, little by little, he built up his position; and when Tzazo and his men joined him early in December he felt himself strong enough once more to take the offensive. The new Vandal army was certainly not ten times the size of the Roman, as Procopius claims that Gelimer boasted to his followers; but it was nevertheless an impressive force that marched out of Bulla with the two brothers at its head, and took the road to Carthage – pausing on the way to demolish the great aqueduct on which the capital chiefly depended for its water supply.

Although Belisarius had spent the weeks since the Battle of the Tenth Milestone strengthening the Carthaginian defences, he had no wish to face a siege – particularly since he was beginning to suspect the loyalty of the Huns and other barbarians under his command. They had, he knew, been secretly approached by agents of Gelimer, who had appealed to them as fellow-Arians to transfer their allegiance; if they intended to betray him, he preferred that they should do so in the open field rather than surreptitiously in a besieged city. He too gave the order to march, and met the Vandal army at Tricamarum, thirty miles west of Carthage.

The battle was fought on 15 December. The Romans, with their vastly superior training and leadership, immediately took the initiative, charging three times into the thick of the Vandal ranks; and in the hand-to-hand fighting that followed the third charge Tzazo was cut down under the eyes of his brother. Once again Gelimer hesitated; his soldiers, seeing his indecision, began to draw back; and only then did the Huns – who, as Belisarius had suspected, had been waiting to see which way the battle would turn – make up their minds to enter the fray. Spurring their horses forward in a single thundering charge, they quickly turned the Vandal retreat into a rout. Gelimer fled back into his Numidian fastness, his army pell-mell after him. This time it was the end. Belisarius advanced to the city of Hippo – which opened its gates to him at once – and took possession of the royal treasure. Then, with a train of Vandal prisoners behind him and his wagons loaded with plunder, he returned to Carthage.

Gelimer, though well aware that his Kingdom was lost, did not at first surrender. For some weeks he wandered in the mountains, sheltered by Berber tribesmen. Early in 534 he found himself surrounded by a Roman force whose commander, Pharas the Herulian, encouraged him to give himself up – with assurances that Justinian bore him no grudge, that he would treat him as the king he was and arrange for him a dignified and comfortable retirement. But still Gelimer refused, asking only to be sent a sponge, a loaf of bread and a lyre – requests which caused the Romans some bewilderment until the messenger explained that his master needed the sponge to bathe an infected eye and the loaf to satisfy a craving for real bread after weeks of unleavened peasant dough. As for the lyre, he pointed out that Gelimer had devoted his time in hiding to the composition of a dirge bewailing his recent misfortunes, and was eager to try it out.

We are not told whether his wishes were granted; but in March, after a long and extremely disagreeable winter, the King of the Vandals finally surrendered. As he was led into the presence of Belisarius, those in attendance were surprised to see him shaking with uncontrollable laughter. Procopius suggests that his mirth was a cynical comment on the vanity of human ambition. Perhaps it was; there were, however, others present who concluded – more plausibly perhaps – that the unsuccessful usurper, after all his sufferings, was no longer quite right in the head.

It was high summer when Belisarius was recalled to Constantinople. Africa was not entirely pacified – some years were to elapse before the Berber tribes eventually became reconciled to imperial dominion – but that was a task that could be left to the Praetorian Prefect charged with the responsibility for the seven new provinces – they included Corsica, Sardinia and the Balearic Islands – which had been set up in the former Vandal territories. For his victorious general the Emperor had other, more ambitious plans.

First, however, he must be properly rewarded; and it was typical of Justinian's love of ancient customs and traditions that he should have accorded Belisarius a Triumph. Since the earliest days of the Empire these ceremonies had been the prerogative of the Emperor himself – or, very occasionally, members of his immediate family – and in recent centuries the practice had almost died out, even for them: the last non-imperial recipient of the honour had been Lucius Cornelius Balbus the younger in 19 BC. Now, 553 years later, the Roman populace cheered to the echo as Belisarius marched[1] into the Hippodrome at the head of his

---

1 Procopius makes it clear, however, that even Belisarius was obliged to enter the Hippodrome on foot, rather than in the *quadriga*, the four-horse chariot that he would certainly have been given in ancient times.

soldiers, followed by Gelimer, his family, and all the tallest and best looking of the Vandal prisoners. The procession continued with a seemingly endless succession of wagons, creaking under the weight of the spoils of war – including the *menorah*, that sacred seven-branched candlestick that had been brought by the Emperor Titus in AD 71 from the Temple in Jerusalem to Rome, whence in 455 Gaiseric had taken it to Carthage.

Later, after representations by the Jewish community – who emphasized the bad luck that would inevitably fall on Constantinople if it were allowed to remain – the ever-superstitious Justinian returned the *menorah*, together with the other vessels from the Temple, to Jerusalem. For the time being, however, objects that were at once so famous and so venerable lent additional lustre to the Triumph of Belisarius. The climax of the ceremony came when he and Gelimer – the latter's purple cloak now torn from his shoulders – prostrated themselves before the imperial box, where Justinian and Theodora sat in state. 'Vanity of vanities, all is vanity', the last King of the Vandals is said to have murmured as he grovelled in the dust beside his conqueror. In a subsequent private conversation with the Emperor, however, while refusing the offer of Patrician rank – which would have obliged him to abandon his Arian faith – he gratefully accepted Justinian's offer of rich estates in Galatia where, safely out of the way, he could live in quiet retirement with his family and worship as he liked. His fellow-prisoners were less fortunate: rounded up and formed into five imperial regiments known as the *Vandali Justiniani*, they were marched off to the Persian front, there to fight unwillingly for the Empire and to survive as best they could.

But neither Justinian nor Belisarius were to pay them much attention. Their minds were now fixed on the next stage of the Emperor's grand design to restore his Empire to its ancient glory: the reconquest of Italy.

Ever since he first came to power in his uncle's day, Justinian had cherished the dream of bringing the entire Italian peninsula back into the imperial fold. A Roman Empire that did not include Rome was an obvious absurdity; an Ostrogothic and Arian Kingdom that did, however well-disposed it might be, could never be anything but an abomination in his sight. Henceforth, too, it could be politically dangerous: now that Theodoric was dead, it was far from certain whether the friendly relations that he had always sought to maintain towards Constantinople would be continued by his successors – who could cause the Byzantine authorities all manner of trouble in the Balkans if they chose to do so.

Clearly, then, the Kingdom must be destroyed; the only question to be settled was the manner of its destruction. The situation in Italy was altogether different from that which had prevailed in Vandal North Africa. Where Gaiseric and his successors had arrogantly asserted their independence, the Ostrogothic King ruled – theoretically at any rate – in the Emperor's name as his Viceroy. Where they had cruelly persecuted the orthodox church, he – while himself remaining staunchly Arian – took immense pains to cultivate the friendship and support of the Pope and the leading Romans. In consequence he enjoyed great popularity among the citizens of the Empire whom he governed; and Justinian was well aware that those citizens, satisfied as they were with the status quo, might well resent the increased regimentation – to say nothing of the far heavier taxation – that would be sure to follow Italy's reintegration in the Empire.

Shortly before his death in 526, Theodoric had summoned the leading Gothic chieftains to his bedside and had presented to them as their future King his eight-year-old grandson Athalaric. The boy was the son of his only daughter Amalasuntha, now four years a widow and one of the most remarkable women of her time – as remarkable in her own way as Theodora herself, possessed of the same driving ambition and love of power for its own sake but at the same time an intellectual, fluent in Latin and Greek, enjoying a breadth of culture rare in any woman of the sixth century and unique among the Goths. Unfortunately for her, however, she had no Justinian to rely on for strength and support; and Gothic society was far more male-orientated than Greek. From the moment her father died and she assumed the regency on behalf of her son, she was conscious of the growing resentment of those around her – a resentment aggravated by her insistence on giving Athalaric a thorough classical education similar to that which she herself had received. Barely a year later, a body of influential Gothic nobles – almost all of whom were illiterate themselves – forced a showdown and, claiming that Athalaric should be studying the arts of war instead of spending his time with greybeard grammarians and philosophers, removed the young King altogether from his mother's control.

Amalasuntha had no choice but to yield. From that moment on she renounced all responsibility for Athalaric, who almost immediately fell into undesirable company and soon began, while still little more than a child, a decline into drunkenness and dissipation that was to kill him before he was seventeen. Meanwhile his mother, conscious of the increasing danger of her own position, entered into secret correspondence with Justinian. Over the next few years, although they never met, their relations grew steadily closer until finally a plot was hatched according to which Amalasuntha would flee across the Adriatic to the imperial port of Dyrrachium, where she would formally seek asylum and call on the Emperor to restore to her the power that was rightfully hers.

With the great Theodoric's daughter at his side, Justinian knew that he would be able to count on a large measure of support among the Goths themselves; given a modicum of good luck, he might even regain Italy for the Empire without bloodshed. But – just as in Africa three years before – events moved too fast for him. On 2 October 534 young Athalaric, exhausted by his debauches, died at Ravenna; and the throne passed to the last surviving male member of Theodoric's line, his nephew Theodahad. The new King was an unattractive figure, whose greed for vast territorial estates and lack of scruple in their acquisition had already made him the largest land-owner in the Kingdom; but he took no interest in power, preferring to lead the life of a Platonic gentleman-scholar in one of his innumerable villas. Amalasuntha was almost certainly unaware that he too had been in secret contact with Justinian; but with his accession she saw her chance. Let the two of them, she proposed, divide the sovereignty between them. Theodahad would thus be able to enjoy all the pleasures and privileges of kingship with none of its attendant responsibilities, while she herself took over the regulation of affairs. She was not, she emphasized, suggesting marriage – apart from anything else Theodahad had a wife already – merely a joint monarchy, with King and Queen working harmoniously together on an equal footing.

Theodahad agreed, and the new dispensation was duly proclaimed; almost at once, however, he regretted his decision and began to plot his cousin's overthrow. Amalasuntha still had many enemies in high places, plenty of them only too happy to enter into a new conspiracy against her. In April 535 she was seized and shut up in a castle on an island in Lake Bolsena, where she was shortly afterwards strangled in her bath. Theodahad vehemently disclaimed all complicity in the crime, but the rich rewards which he lavished on the murderers were enough to persuade most of his subjects otherwise.

Procopius tells us that Justinian, the moment he heard of Amalasuntha's imprisonment, sent Theodahad a message through his ambassador, Peter the Patrician, warning him that if the Queen were not immediately restored to the throne he would be forced to intervene; but that at the same time another message arrived secretly from the Empress, containing secret assurances that her husband would do no such thing and that Theodahad could feel free to deal with his prisoner in any way he saw fit. Whether this second message was prompted, as Procopius suggests, by jealousy or whether Theodora – perhaps with Justinian's connivance – was deliberately acting as an *agent provocateur* we do not know; in any event, by his murder of his cousin Theodahad played straight into Byzantine hands, giving the Emperor precisely the *casus belli* he needed. As soon as the news reached him in Constantinople, Justinian issued his orders. Mundus, the *magister militum per Illyricum*, was to occupy Dalmatia, which formed part of the Ostrogothic Kingdom; meanwhile Belisarius, fresh from his Triumph, was commanded to sail with an army of 7,500 men to Sicily.

The expeditions started well enough, but soon ran into difficulties. Gothic resistance in Dalmatia proved a good deal more stubborn than had been expected, and within a few weeks Mundus was killed in battle. Belisarius took Sicily with scarcely a struggle,[1] but was then called urgently to Africa to deal with a serious mutiny by the imperial army of occupation. This delayed him for many weeks, and on his return he found that dissatisfaction had spread among his own troops. By the time their morale had in turn been restored, winter was approaching and the campaigning season was at an end. It was not until the late spring of 536 that his army was finally able to land on Italian soil. Meanwhile Theodahad – who had panicked on first hearing of the Byzantine expeditions and had actually concluded a secret treaty with Justinian, according to which he undertook to hand over the entire government of Italy in return for the promise of 1,200 pounds of gold a year and a high position at Constantinople – had reneged on the agreement and, in an uncharacteristic burst of courage, ordered the striking of new coins depicting himself alone, bearing the imperial insignia.

But his elation was short-lived. One night in April or early May, Belisarius crossed the Straits of Messina, landed his army at Reggio and pressed onward up the peninsula. He met no resistance until he reached Naples, whose citizens defended it stoutly for three weeks; they would have held out still longer had not one of the Isaurians in the besieging army accidentally stumbled upon an ancient water-conduit, through which 400 picked men were able to crawl beneath the fortifications and

---

1 The only show of resistance was made by the Gothic garrison in Panormus – the present Palermo, but then a small port of relatively little importance. Belisarius massed his fleet so close inshore that the masts of his ships rose above the town walls. He then filled the ships' boats with men and hoisted them up to the yard-arms, whence they were able to fire their arrows down on the defenders and then leap directly on to the battlements. The garrison soon capitulated.

into the city. At a given signal from them, the remainder of the army then set up its scaling-ladders and launched a concerted attack on the walls. The defenders, finding themselves simultaneously assailed from within and without, were obliged to surrender and Naples was regained for the Empire.

Or what was left of it. Belisarius had warned the Neapolitans at the beginning of the siege that if they put up any resistance he would be unable to restrain his army – which, he reminded them, was largely composed of semi-savage barbarians – from the murder, rapine and pillage which they would consider their just reward after the capture of the city. But the warning had been ignored, and the miserable citizens now paid the price of their heroism. It was many hours before Belisarius was able to persuade his motley hordes of Alans and Isaurians, Herulians and Huns – these last the most terrifying of all since, being pagans, they had no compunction in burning down the churches in which their intended victims had sought asylum – to put up their swords and spears and return to their various camps. Soon, he explained, they would be on the march again; and their next objective would be Rome itself.

The Byzantine capture of Naples dealt a severe blow to the morale of the Goths, who unhesitatingly laid the blame for their defeat on Theodahad. He had long been detested by his subjects for his avarice and his extortions; more recently, persistent rumours of his secret correspondence with the enemy had done still more harm to his reputation. The fact that he had not dispatched a single soldier to the relief of Naples seemed to confirm these rumours: such apparent apathy could mean only that he had been bribed by Justinian to betray his people. Accordingly, at a vast assembly near Terracina, the Gothic leaders solemnly declared him deposed and, in the absence of any male descendant of Theodoric, nominated as his successor an elderly and not particularly impressive general named Vitiges. The first command issued by the new King of the Goths was for the execution of the old one: Theodahad had fled to the north, but was captured near Ravenna and dispatched on the spot.

Meanwhile Belisarius was about to march on Rome; and many of the Gothic chieftains must have wondered whether they had been wise in their choice of King when Vitiges announced that he would not be defending the city. Its people must look after themselves as best they could while he withdrew to Ravenna, there to consolidate his forces, draw up his long-term strategy and – somewhat more controversially –

divorce his wife of many years in favour of Athalaric's sister Matasuntha. There were, it must be admitted, sound political reasons for such a marriage. Vitiges was of humble origins and needed to improve his social status; he knew, too, that any other husband of the young princess might prove a dangerous rival. Finally there was the consideration that, with the granddaughter of Theodoric on the throne, Justinian would have less cause for intervention in Italy. But the marriage, as might have been expected, was an unhappy one from the start, and seems to have done the old man's reputation more harm than good.

With the retreat of Vitiges to Ravenna, Belisarius might have been expected to march with all speed on Rome. In fact, he showed himself to be in no particular hurry, preferring to spend the summer and autumn consolidating his hold on South Italy. Only in December did he move northward, ostensibly in answer to an invitation from Pope Silverius[1] to occupy the holy city; and one is tempted to conclude that the intervening months had been passed in arranging for such an invitation – which must have greatly strengthened his diplomatic position – to be sent. There is no reason to believe that Silverius was any more favourably disposed to the invaders than were his fellow-Romans: the Goths might be Arians, but they had always been tolerant and considerate rulers, whereas the Byzantines were widely mistrusted and their barbarian troops universally feared. But the formidable reputation of Belisarius himself – to say nothing of memories of the recent fate of Naples – would have been more than enough to persuade the Pope to do as he was told. Whatever the truth may be, on 9 December 536 Belisarius led his army north from Naples,[2] entering Rome by the Porta Asinaria near the Basilica of Constantine (now St John Lateran) as the Gothic garrison marched out through the Porta Flaminia.

But if Silverius and his flock imagined that by opening the gates to the imperial army they had avoided the miseries of a siege, they were to be disappointed. Belisarius himself entertained no such delusion. He knew that the Goths would be back soon enough; and the strength of the opposition encountered by the advance units that he had sent to

1 Silverius, who had been raised to the pontificate only six months before, was probably the only Pope in history to be the legitimate son of another. His father was Pope Hormisdas, who took orders only after the early death of his wife.

2 It is intriguing to reflect that had Belisarius stopped for rest and refreshment at the great abbey which he must have seen dominating the road from a high hill on his right, he would have found himself face to face with St Benedict in person, who had established his monastery – and the Order that still bears his name – on Monte Cassino only eight years before.

capture other strategic points in Umbria, Tuscany and the Marches suggested that they would fight a hard battle. Immediately he set his men to
the task of repairing and strengthening the Aurelian walls; meanwhile he
requisitioned immense quantities of corn from the surrounding
countryside and ordered additional shiploads from Sicily, until the huge
public granaries of Rome were full to overflowing. Once the Goths
arrived and surrounded the city he could not be sure of keeping open
his supply lines to the port of Ostia; and the coming siege, he knew,
might be a long one.

And so it was. After a fierce encounter near the Milvian Bridge in
which the Byzantines, though fighting with supreme courage, were
unable to stem the Gothic advance, Vitiges and his men took up their
positions around the city in the middle of March, 537. They were to
hold them for a year and nine days – an agonizing time for besiegers and
besieged alike, at the very beginning of which the Goths cut all the
aqueducts, thereby dealing Rome a blow from which it was not to recover for a thousand years. The history of the aqueducts stretched
almost as far back into the past: it had been as early as 312 BC that the
Romans, no longer prepared to make do with the murky insufficiency of
the Tiber, built the first of these magnificent conduits; over the eight
centuries that followed they were to construct ten more, the better to
supply not only their domestic needs but the innumerable fountains and
public baths for which their city was famous. And those aqueducts
provided something else as well: the hydraulic power which drove,
among other things, the mills on which the people depended for their
bread. It was, we read, Belisarius himself who now had the idea of
mounting millstones on small boats, suspending water-wheels between
them and then tethering them beneath the arches of a bridge where the
current was strongest, thereby ensuring a regular supply of flour throughout the siege.

Meanwhile he had applied to Justinian for reinforcements, the first of
which arrived before the end of April – some 1,600 Slavs and Huns,
who broke through the blockade and for the first time made it possible
to launch occasional sorties outside the walls. But the stalemate continued, and as summer drew on the sufferings increased on both sides – for
those within the city, famine; for those outside, disease and pestilence.
Only in November did the balance begin to shift in favour of the Byzantines, when 5,000 more men, both cavalry and infantry, arrived from the
East under the command of John, nephew of that rebellious Vitalian
who had given so much trouble to old Anastasius twenty years before.

Soon afterwards the Goths asked for a three-month truce, during which they offered peace proposals which Belisarius would have rejected out of hand had he not been obliged to transmit them to Constantinople for the Emperor's consideration. While awaiting a reply, he dispatched John with 2,000 horsemen on a punitive campaign along the eastern slopes of the Apennines. Leaving a trail of devastation behind him, John advanced rapidly up the peninsula, ignoring the fortified hill-towns of Urbino and Osimo but occupying the low-lying port of Rimini (then known as Ariminum) where he set up his advance headquarters.

The knowledge that the invaders were now in possession of an important city 200 miles in his rear and only thirty-three from Ravenna was enough to persuade Vitiges to raise the siege of Rome. Although there had been as yet no reply from Constantinople he was by now practically certain that his peace proposals had been rejected; he knew, too, that Belisarius had succeeded in bringing in fresh provisions during the early days of the truce and would therefore be able to hold out in Rome almost indefinitely. One early morning in the middle of March 538 his troops, sick, demoralized and dispirited, methodically set fire to their seven camps around the city and headed northwards along the Via Flaminia. But even now their humiliation was not over: Belisarius and his men came pouring out of the gates, fell on them from behind and, after yet another engagement at the Milvian Bridge, left several hundred more Goths dead on the river banks or drowned, weighed down by their armour, in the spring flood of the Tiber.

After this battle the surviving Goths were allowed to retreat in peace. A few days later, however, leaving only a small garrison in Rome, Belisarius himself set out to the north, occupying towns and mopping up isolated pockets of resistance as he went. Spoleto, Perugia and Narni had been taken by his advance parties even before the siege of Rome; to these he now added Ancona, together with a whole chain of strong-points linking those towns and Rome with the Adriatic. One thing only worried him: the knowledge that John with his large force of cavalry was still dangerously exposed in Rimini. He therefore sent two of his trusted officers up the coast with orders to the general to withdraw and to rejoin him, with his men, in Ancona.

And John, who seems to have inherited his uncle's rebellious streak, flatly refused. He had ambitions of his own; besides, he was in secret communication with Queen Matasuntha, a pro-imperialist like her mother, who was by now longing to do down her detested husband in any way that she could. The two officers had no choice but to return and report this flagrant piece of insubordination; and hardly had they done so when the Gothic army appeared beneath the walls of Rimini. A few days later the siege began, and the prospects for those within looked grim indeed. Unlike Rome, which had been able to hold out thanks to its splendid walls and the immense quantity of provisions laid in by Belisarius before the arrival of the Goths, here was a small town in a dead-flat plain, ill-protected and poorly stocked with food. The fury of Belisarius when he heard the news can be imagined. The loss of John he could probably by now contemplate with equanimity; but his 2,000 horsemen were less easily spared. On the other hand any relief expedition would be fraught with difficulty and danger, particularly since Auximum (Osimo) was still held by the Goths. Was he, for the sake of a single regiment of cavalry, to put his entire army in jeopardy? Should not John, who was after all solely responsible for his own misfortunes, now be left to pay the price of his disobedience?

Belisarius was still considering his next move when fresh troops arrived from Constantinople, headed by the most powerful figure at the imperial court: the eunuch Narses, who has already made a brief appearance in this story when as commander of the imperial bodyguard he played a decisive part, with Belisarius and Mundus, in putting down the Nika revolt. Born some sixty years before in that part of eastern Armenia that had been transferred to Persia in the partition of 387, he had risen steadily through the palace hierarchy to be *Praepositus Sacri Cubiculi* or Grand Chamberlain, a position which gave him the rank of *illustris* and made him an equal of the Praetorian Prefects and *magistri militum* – although, being constantly at the Emperor's side, he probably wielded more influence than any of them.

But he was no soldier. His life had been spent in the Palace, and even his command of the bodyguard was more of a domestic appointment than a military one. The question therefore arises, why he was given the leadership of the new expeditionary force; and to it there can be but one answer. Justinian was beginning to have his doubts about Belisarius. The general was too brilliant, too successful – and, being still only in his early thirties, too young. He was the stuff of which Emperors were made; worse, he was the stuff of men who made themselves Emperors. In short, he needed watching; and who better to watch him than Justinian's most intelligent and trusted confidant, a man whose age and condition alike debarred him from any imperial ambitions of his own? Even the eunuch's instructions from

Justinian gave a hint as to the real reason for his presence in Italy: he was to obey Belisarius in all things, *so far as seemed consistent with the public weal*. In other words, he must accept the general's orders in military matters, but could overrule him on all major decisions of state policy.

Within days of his arrival, Narses found himself taking part in a council of war summoned by Belisarius at Firmium – now Fermo – to discuss whether or not to mount an expedition to relieve Rimini. The majority of those present (who included, as always, Procopius) were hostile to John, on the grounds that 'he had been moved by insensate recklessness and a desire for large financial gain' – this last motive is not explained – 'to occupy the dangerous position in which he found himself; and that he had refused to allow his commander-in-chief to conduct the campaign according to his own ideas of strategy'. After all the junior commanders had had their say, Narses arose. Readily admitting his own lack of military experience, he pointed out that the Goths were deeply dispirited after the succession of reverses that they had suffered over the past two years. The capture of Rimini, however, and of so important a Byzantine force within its walls, would be hailed by them as a major victory, perhaps as the turning-point of the whole war. 'If,' he concluded, turning to Belisarius, 'John has treated your orders with contempt, it is in your power to deal with him as you like once the city is relieved. But see that in punishing him for the mistakes that he has made through ignorance you do not exact a penalty from the Emperor himself and from us his subjects.'[1]

The suggestion that John had acted 'through ignorance' can perhaps best be explained by Procopius's statement that 'Narses loved him above all other men'; at any rate, the eunuch's counsels prevailed and Belisarius, who seems wisely to have kept silent so that he should not appear to be overruled, began to make his plans accordingly. A week or two later, by means of a brilliantly executed amphibious operation in which he contrived to suggest to the Goths outside Rimini that they themselves were surrounded – and by a far more numerous force than in fact existed – he put the entire besieging army to flight and entered the city just in time to save the defenders from starvation. His natural resentment of his new rival, however, cannot have been diminished when John, instead of apologizing for his conduct and expressing gratitude for his rescue, attributed it exclusively to Narses and refused absolutely to thank anyone else. Between the general and the eunuch the seeds of dissension had

1 Procopius, *History of the Wars*, VI, xvi.

been sown; but neither could have imagined how bitter the harvest was to be.

Belisarius was a supreme strategist and, thanks to his immense physical courage, a superb commander in the field. As a general, however, there was one quality that he lacked: the ability to inspire the unquestioning loyalty of those under him. One of his chief lieutenants had already disobeyed his orders; now, after the relief of Rimini, a considerable portion of the army made it clear that, in the event of a split in the high command, they would follow Narses rather than himself. He knew that he was powerless to change matters, and it may have been as much to save his own face as for any other reason that he divided the army into two for the mopping-up operations that followed. At the start, the system worked well enough: the Byzantines took Urbino, Imola and Orvieto and re-annexed the province of Emilia. But now, suddenly and unexpectedly, there came disaster. The cause of it was the growing hostility between the two commanders; the place Mediolanum – better known to us as Milan.

The previous spring, at the time of the three-month truce during the siege of Rome, Archbishop Datius of Milan had appeared in the city and implored Belisarius to send troops to deliver his diocese from alien – and Arian – occupation; and the general had agreed. Why he did so is not altogether clear – it seems to have been just the same kind of mistake as that which had led John to occupy Rimini, dangerously over-extending his lines of communication and supply – but he had nevertheless dispatched 1,000 troops back with the archbishop to the north. They went by sea to Genoa, used the ships' boats to cross the Po, and decisively defeated a Gothic army beneath the walls of Pavia. To their disappointment they failed to take the city, but on their arrival at Milan the citizens immediately opened the gates. Bergamo, Como, Novara and several other towns gave them a similar welcome. Each, however, required a small garrison of imperial troops – which effectively reduced the force in Milan to some 300 men.

Now Milan was already the largest and most prosperous of all the cities of Italy, its population considerably greater than that of Rome itself; and its voluntary surrender came as a bitter blow to the Goths. Immediately he heard the news, Vitiges sent an army to recover it under his nephew Uraias. At the same time, and to the additional discomfiture of the Byzantine garrison, there arrived a body of some 10,000 Burgundians, sent by the Frankish King Theudibert. Thus, by the high summer of 538, the Milanese found themselves besieged by a far larger force than that which had threatened Rimini, and defended by so few soldiers that all able-bodied male citizens were obliged to take their turn on the ramparts. On this occasion – for which he may well have felt himself to be at least partially to blame – Belisarius unhesitatingly sent two of his best commanders to the relief of Milan, with an army which he believed to be similar in size to that of Uraias. These commanders, however, realized on reaching the Po that they would be hopelessly outnumbered, and refused to advance further without the support of John – who, probably through the influence of Narses, had escaped all punishment for his earlier disobedience – and Justin, who had succeeded Mundus as *magister militum per Illyricum*.

Belisarius at once issued the necessary instructions, but John and Justin refused point-blank to obey them, claiming that they now took their orders from no one but Narses; and by the time the eunuch had confirmed the command it was too late. The garrison, who had already for some time been reduced to a diet of dogs and even mice, had had enough. Ignoring a stirring exhortation by their commander, Mundilas, they gratefully accepted the terms offered them by Uraias, who gave them his word that they would be allowed to leave the city unharmed.

And so they were; but the offer, as they well knew, did not extend to the people of Milan, who in the eyes of the Goths had betrayed the city. All the male citizens – whose numbers Procopius improbably estimates at 300,000 – were put to the sword, the women being reduced to slavery and presented to the Burgundians in gratitude for their alliance. As for Milan itself, not a house was left standing.

Milan fell in the first months of 539. It was a catastrophe, but it had one useful consequence. On learning what had happened, Justinian recalled his chamberlain at once to Constantinople. The departure of Narses in its turn resulted in the withdrawal of the 2,000 wild Herulians who had accompanied him to Italy and who refused to serve under any other leader; but even this was a small price to pay for a single and undisputed command. No longer troubled by dissension within his ranks, Belisarius was able to concentrate on the capture of Auximum and Fiesole, the last two pockets of resistance south of Ravenna itself. The two towns would have fallen a good deal earlier than they did had it not been for the irruption of a huge Frankish army, this time under Theudibert himself, in the early summer. The Goths, to whom the Franks were bound by treaty, assumed that they had come as allies like the Burgundians in the previous year, opened the gates of Pavia to them and helped them to cross the Po; only then did they reveal themselves in their true colours, suddenly turning on their unsuspecting hosts and slaughtering them wholesale. As the surviving Goths fled towards Ravenna the Byzantines, similarly deceived, now also approached the Franks as new allies; but the barbarians, with a fine lack of discrimination, greeted them with a hail of flying axes – their favourite weapon – and put them in their turn to flight. For a moment it looked as though all Belisarius's careful work was to be undone; then, fortunately, dysentery struck the Frankish camp, accounting for as much as a third of Theudibert's men. The King gave the order to withdraw, and within days his savage, shambling host had dragged itself back across the Alps. The Byzantines, shaken but not seriously weakened, returned to their tasks, and by the end of the year the two stubbornly defended towns had given in.

It was now nearly four years since the imperial forces had first landed on Italian soil: four years during which the peninsula had been fought over, ravaged and laid waste from end to end. The farms had been burnt, the crops destroyed. The land had become a wilderness again, Italians and Goths alike suffering all the miseries of famine. Meanwhile Belisarius was gathering his strength for a final assault on Ravenna which, if successful, would put an end to the Ostrogothic Kingdom once and for all. For Vitiges, the situation was desperate.

One hope only was left to him. Some months before, he had received reports suggesting that Justinian was in difficulties on his eastern frontier, where the Persian King Chosroes I was threatening invasion; if the danger of this were such as to oblige the Emperor to throw his entire military strength against Persia, the cause of Gothic Italy might yet be saved. Vitiges had accordingly sent a letter to Chosroes by the hand of two secret agents, purporting to be a bishop and his chaplain travelling to the East on Church affairs. In it he pointed out to the Great King that the Roman Empire would be a far more redoubtable adversary if it had all the manpower and resources of Italy to draw on. If Chosroes were to strike at once, he would force the Byzantines to fight on both fronts simultaneously and immeasurably increase his own chances of success.

The two agents never returned to the West. Their Syrian interpreter, however, was caught as he tried to slip back across the frontier, brought to Constantinople and interrogated; and gradually the truth was revealed. For a long time Justinian had been worried by the worsening situation in Persia; now he grew seriously alarmed. It would be heartbreaking to have to call off the Italian campaign just as he was on the brink of victory, and to renounce – perhaps for ever – his life's dream of reuniting all Christendom under his aegis. On the other hand he could not possibly afford to take any chances with Chosroes; if the Great King was truly bent on war, the imperial army must be ready for him. The choice was agonizing, but at last he made up his mind. He would have to come to terms with the Goths, in order to free the most brilliant of his generals for another period of service in the East.

By the time the Emperor's orders reached Italy, Belisarius had moved in on Ravenna. The city was already surrounded – to the landward side by his army, to the seaward by the imperial fleet, which had set up a virtually impenetrable blockade. Its surrender could only be a matter of time; all that was required was patience. Then, one day towards the end of 539, ambassadors arrived from Constantinople empowered to sign a treaty with the Goths by the terms of which, in return for capitulation, they would be allowed to retain half their royal treasure and all Italy north of the Po. Belisarius was horror-stricken. This was betrayal indeed; but he could see no way of preventing the proposed agreement and was just about to accept the inevitable when, suddenly and unexpectedly, the Goths played straight into his hands. As astonished, presumably, as he was himself at their apparent good fortune, and perhaps fearing some sort of diplomatic trick, they made it clear that they would accept the treaty as valid only if it bore his own signature as well as those of the imperial plenipotentiaries.

Belisarius seized his chance. The proposed concessions, he thundered, were not only an insult to his soldiers, they were also unnecessary: total victory was imminent, for within a few weeks at the most the Goths could be made to surrender unconditionally. In such circumstances he refused absolutely to sign the treaty, and would agree to do so only on receipt of a personal command from the Emperor himself. For the moment there was stalemate. Then, one night, a secret emissary arrived from the Gothic court, bearing a new and extraordinary proposal: Vitiges would resign his throne and deliver up his crown to Belisarius, on the understanding that the latter should then proclaim himself Emperor of the West. Many an imperial general would have seized such an opportunity; the bulk of the army would probably have supported him, and with the Goths at his back he would have been more than capable of dealing with any punitive expedition from Constantinople. But Belisarius, whatever his long-term ambitions may have been, did not waver in his loyalty. In the words of Procopius, 'he hated the name of usurper with a perfect hatred', and it is unlikely that he gave the Goths' proposal a moment's serious consideration. On the other hand, he saw in it an ideal means of bringing the war to a quick and victorious end. All he had to do was to tell the Goths that he accepted their offer, and the gates of Ravenna would be opened to him.

First he sent away on foraging expeditions those commanders who had formerly allied themselves with Narses: he did not want them making trouble in advance, or claiming the credit afterwards. Then, summoning those on whose loyalty he could rely, he sought their approval for one last effort – an effort which promised to win back all Italy for the Empire and bring the whole Gothic nobility, with the royal treasure, captive to Constantinople. Once they had given their agreement – which they did without hesitation – no further preparations were necessary. Messengers sped to the Gothic court, with word that the great general looked favourably on their proposals and would formally invest himself with the diadem of the Western Empire after entering his capital. Duly the gates were flung open, and the imperial army marched in.

We do not know exactly when the Goths realized that they had been deceived. It may be that Belisarius never told them in so many words that he had no intention of setting himself up as a rival to Justinian, and that it was only gradually that there came upon them an understanding of the true state of affairs. As they watched the Roman soldiery loading their royal treasure on to the ships while Vitiges, Matasuntha and the chief nobles were all taken off into captivity, they must have reflected bitterly indeed on the perfidy of the general who had betrayed them. But there is no indication that Belisarius's conscience gave him any trouble. The Goths' proposal had been in itself perfidious; besides, were they not all of them rebels against the Emperor's lawful authority? War was war; and, by occupying Ravenna as he had done, he had saved untold blood-shed on both sides. One promise, in any case, he had kept to the letter: there had been no looting of private houses, no rapine and no killing. As he himself took ship for the Bosphorus in May 540 he felt no shame, only elation and pride. His Triumph after the capture of Carthage had been magnificent; how much more splendid might be his reward for returning the whole Italian peninsula, including Ravenna and even Rome itself, to the Empire?

Alas, he was disappointed. Perhaps he would have been doomed to disappointment in any event, for every victory that he won increased the Emperor's jealousy, together with his fears that one day his brilliant young general might take the law into his own hands and usurp the throne. But there was no feeling of victory in the air when he returned to Constantinople, and neither Justinian nor his subjects were in any mood for celebration. In June 540, only a few weeks after the fall of Ravenna, the troops of King Chosroes had invaded the Empire and captured Antioch, demolishing the city, massacring most of its inhabitants and sending the rest into slavery. The presence of Belisarius would be required, not at the Hippodrome but on the eastern front.

I I
Totila the Goth

[540–49]

Surely in these evil days you must sometimes remember the benefits that you
were wont to receive, not so very long ago, at the hands of Theodoric and
Amalasuntha ... My Roman friends, only compare the memory of those rulers
with what we now know of the conduct of the Greeks towards their subjects.
Do not think that I speak with youthful presumption or barbarian arrogance
when I tell you that we shall change all this and deliver Italy from her tyrants –
and not through our valour alone, but in the sure belief that we are ministers of
divine justice against these oppressors ...

Totila, in his letter
to the Roman Senate, 545 [1]

The Great King Chosroes I of Persia – known to his subjects as *An-
ushirvan*, 'of the Immortal Soul' – had occupied the throne since 531. Of
all the great Sassanian Kings, perhaps of all the Persian rulers throughout
history, he was the most illustrious and is still the best remembered. As
a statesman, he reformed and reorganized every branch of government
and completely revised the fiscal system; as a general, he created the first
standing army loyal to the King alone and pushed forward his frontiers
till they extended from the Black Sea to the Yemen, from the Oxus
River to the shores of the Mediterranean; as an intellectual, he had given
– even before his accession – an enthusiastic welcome to those pagan
Greek scientists and philosophers who had drifted to Persia after Justinian's closure of the School of Athens in 529. He founded his country's
great medical academy at Gondeshapur, codified the *Avesta* – the sacred
book of Zoroastrianism – compiled the first collection of the myths and
legends of his people and introduced from India the game of chess. He
was, in short, a worthy match for Justinian, his adversary and rival for
over thirty years.

1 Trans. Hodgkin. In fact, a fairly free translation when compared with the text given by Procopius
(*History of the Wars*, VII, ix, 7–18); but at least an admirable précis, which faithfully preserves the
tone of the original.

And yet, progressive as he was in many ways, in others Chosroes was very much the child of his time. His wars with the Byzantine Empire, for example, were fought not for conquest but, unashamedly, for plunder. Thus, studiously ignoring first a letter from Justinian in which he was sternly reminded of his treaty obligations under the 'Eternal Peace' and, later, one from Theodora – addressed to a minister but clearly intended for the Great King to see – promising rich rewards in return for non-intervention ('for my husband will do nothing without first seeking my advice') he crossed the imperial frontier in March 540 and captured the town of Sura on the upper Euphrates, whose handful of defenders took one look at the size of the army marching against them and sensibly withdrew. From there he passed on to Beroea (the modern Aleppo), setting fire to the city when the populace failed to raise the 4,000 pounds of silver he had demanded as a ransom, and so in early June found himself before the walls of Antioch – politely drawing his army aside to allow the newly arrived garrison, 6,000 strong but panic-stricken, to flee for its life. The citizens, however, did not give in so easily. They fought with determination and courage, Greens and Blues standing side by side on the ramparts and many of them dying where they stood. Sheer force of numbers allowed Chosroes finally to carry the day; but when he did so he made the people of Antioch pay dearly for their resistance. The great cathedral was stripped of all its gold and silver, and even of the polychrome marbles that adorned its walls; the other churches were similarly pillaged – except that of St Julian, which owed its salvation to its privileged position among the foreign embassies. Meanwhile the Persian soldiery satisfied its various lusts in the traditional manner, to the point where at least two distinguished ladies are said to have flung themselves into the Orontes to escape its attentions.

With all the wealth of Antioch loaded on to his baggage wagons, and before setting out on a triumphal tour of northern Syria during which he proposed to exact heavy tribute from every city he visited, Chosroes could afford to be generous; he therefore offered peace to Justinian in return for only a little more blood money: 5,000 pounds of gold to be paid at once, plus 500 more each succeeding year. The Emperor had no choice but to accept and pay up; and Chosroes returned to Persia, profoundly satisfied with his campaign. But he was back the following year, when an opportunity arose which, even if it meant a further breach of his treaty obligations, he could not possibly miss.

At the far south-eastern corner of the Black Sea lay the small, semi-autonomous kingdom of Lazica, sometimes known as Colchis. Its ruler,

King Gobazes, had in the past been content to be a vassal of the Byzantine Emperor, who had caused him and his immediate predecessors little trouble; but Justinian had recently sent in a personal representative, who had established various imperial monopolies and so antagonized the people that Gobazes in despair appealed to the Persian King. Lazica was a poor country, and would normally have offered Chosroes little temptation; on the other hand, as Gobazes was not slow to point out, it would provide him with a bridgehead on the Black Sea from which he could sail directly against Byzantium and make contact with other potential allies, notably the Huns. So it was that the spring of 541 saw Chosroes once again invading the Empire at the head of his army and marching into Lazica – where, after a pitched battle with the defenders which exacted a heavy toll on both sides, he captured its principal port, the strongly fortified city of Petra.[1] The summer would probably have been still more disastrous for Byzantium had it not been for a simultaneous expedition by Belisarius; even this proved, however, to be an oddly lacklustre affair. Ignoring Lazica altogether, he headed straight for Mesopotamia, crossing into Persian territory near Nisibis; but, deciding that this great fortress was too strong for him, he bypassed it and captured only one relatively unimportant town, Sisaurani, before the Mesopotamian summer and an outbreak of dysentery among his soldiers forced him to retire.

There seemed to be little in him of the old Belisarius: little of the energy, the cunning and the infinite resourcefulness that had brought him, while still under thirty, to the top of his profession and made his name famous throughout the known world. In 540, after his return from Italy, he had been expected to head straight for the East as ordered; instead, he had remained in his palace at Constantinople, showing himself little in public and seeing only a few close friends. When he did at last set out on campaign he seemed unable to take even minor decisions without seeking the advice and approval of his associates, to whom he appeared somehow distant and preoccupied; and so indeed he was. He had become obsessed by the infidelity of his wife Antonina – infidelity in which she was being abetted and protected by the Empress herself.

Theodora and Antonina had long been friends; but their friendship was further cemented in the course of 541 by their joint conspiracy against the Empress's most hated enemy, the Praetorian Prefect John of Cappadocia. John was well known to have imperial ambitions; and it was an

1 Not, of course, to be confused with the caravan city of southern Arabia, which was by this time already deserted and in ruins.

easy matter for Antonina to entice him to a secret meeting and persuade him to talk about how he planned to achieve his objective, while Theodora's spies remained in hiding, listening to every word. He was arrested, found guilty and dispossessed of his enormous wealth, but he was not condemned to mutilation or execution. His fate – the compulsory taking of holy orders, followed by exile in the comfortable diocese of Cyzicus on the Marmara – was, it was generally agreed, a good deal better than he deserved.

As a result of this intrigue, Antonina was able to call on the Empress for help in a domestic drama of her own, which reached a crisis at this time. For several years she had been involved in a passionate liaison with a young man named Theodosius – an indiscretion made more reprehensible by the fact that he was the godson of her husband and herself, and their adopted child. The extent to which Belisarius knew of this affair and condoned it is uncertain: Procopius's account – the only one that we have [1] – is a positive minefield of improbabilities and obvious exaggerations. But the young general possessed his full share of personal vanity and had no wish to be shown up publicly as a cuckold. He had raised no objection when Antonina told him that for the first time in their married life she would not be accompanying him on his new campaign, since he was well aware that she was at that moment engaged on delicate business with the Empress; but he was shattered when, a month or two after his own departure, he received reliable information that Theodosius – who had sought temporary refuge from the scandal by attaching himself to a monastery at Ephesus – had now returned to the capital and was living once again under his godmother's roof.

Belisarius's informant was none other than his stepson Photius – the son of Antonina by an earlier association – who had accompanied him to the Persian front. Photius cordially detested his mother, whom he suspected (with some justification) of having plotted to kill him; and when he received the news of her recent behaviour from a friend newly arrived from Constantinople he lost no time in passing it on to his stepfather. Together, the two decided on a plan of action. By this time the intrigue against the Cappadocian had been satisfactorily concluded and Antonina had announced her intention of coming east. When she did so, it was reasonably certain that Theodosius would return to Ephesus; at that moment Photius, taking advantage of his mother's absence, would follow him there and abduct him, putting him away in some remote and secret prison where he could cause no further trouble.

1 *Secret History*, i–iii.

Antonina arrived, and to her astonishment found herself immediately under arrest; meanwhile Photius had set off for Ephesus, taking with him one of his mother's eunuchs from whom he had gathered, with morbid satisfaction, further intriguing information about her private life. On reaching the city he found that Theodosius had been warned of his approach and had taken refuge in the church of St John; but the local archpriest, in return for a small bribe, handed him over without a word. Photius sent him off to a remote castle in Cilicia, and himself returned to the capital.

In doing so he made a grievous mistake; for by the time he reached Constantinople Antonina had somehow contrived to send the Empress an appeal for help. Photius was arrested in his turn, together with a number of other close friends of his stepfather; several of them, Procopius tells us, suffered imprisonment and even death for no other reason than their friendship. Photius himself was subjected to unspeakable tortures, but steadfastly refused to reveal the whereabouts of Theodosius. He was to languish in the palace dungeons for three years before he succeeded – with the unexpected assistance of the Prophet Zechariah, who appeared to him in a dream – in escaping to Jerusalem. Procopius bitterly reproaches Belisarius for having made no move to help his stepson after his own return to Constantinople; he may be right to do so, and the accusation has certainly left a stain on the general's character. But with Antonina – to whom, on the Empress's orders, he had become officially reconciled – and Theodora herself in league against him, it is not easy to see what he could have done.

Eventually Theodora tracked down the young man by other means, and restored him to the arms of his mistress; soon afterwards, however, Theodosius died of dysentery – foul play was not, as far as we know, suspected – and a great weight was lifted off Belisarius's spirit. Back in the East in 542, he was plainly himself again. Procopius delightedly describes how he received an ambassador from Chosroes:

... He set up a tent of heavy cloth known as a *pavilion*, and seated himself within it ... and he arranged his soldiers as follows. On either side of the tent were Thracians and Illyrians, with Goths behind them, and next to these Herulians, and finally Vandals and Moors. And their line extended a great distance across the plain, for they did not remain standing always in the same place, but stood apart from one another and wandered about, looking casually and without the least interest upon the envoy of Chosroes. And not one of them had a cloak or any other outer garment on his shoulders, but they sauntered about in linen tunics and trousers, tied loosely with girdles. And each one carried a horse-whip, but for weapons one had a sword, another an axe, another an uncovered bow. And all gave the impression that they were eager to be off on the hunt, with never a thought for anything else . . .

And when Abandanes [the envoy] came to Chosroes he advised him to take his departure with all possible speed. For he said that he had met a general who in manliness and wisdom surpassed all other men, and soldiers such as he had never seen.[1]

So the Great King turned back and, concludes Procopius, 'the Romans were loud in their praises of Belisarius, who seemed to have achieved greater glory in their eyes by this affair than when he brought Gelimer or Vitiges captive to Byzantium.' As usual he exaggerates; but it is clear that the old Belisarius touch was once more in evidence.

As it happened, the 542 campaign proved indecisive, owing to an out-break in both camps not of the usual dysentery or typhoid but of bubonic plague – an outbreak that was to prove one of the worst in Byzantine history. Beginning in Egypt, it quickly spread across all the lands of the Eastern Mediterranean to Constantinople, where it raged for four months, the toll rising to some 10,000 a day and, on one particular day, 16,000 – as many as the entire army in Italy. The proper burial of the dead soon became impossible; the corpses were carried off to a huge, long-abandoned fortress where they were piled up until they reached the roof. Daily life in the city came to a standstill; the surrounding fields lay unharvested, the markets were closed, the mills and bakeries fell idle with no one to work them. In consequence, plague was succeeded by famine. By the time the disease had run its course, the number of its victims was estimated at 300,000 – perhaps two out of five of the population.

Among those stricken was Justinian himself. For weeks during that nightmare summer he lay between life and death – leaving the supreme authority of the state in the hands of his wife and simultaneously intro-ducing a new and urgent question to be considered – that of the suc-cession. Theodora knew that her whole future was at stake. She and Justinian were childless; if her husband were to die, her only chance of retaining her power lay in arranging for him to be succeeded by a ruler of her own choice: a trusted courtier, perhaps, or some faithful old general with whom she could go through a ceremony of marriage, just as her predecessor Ariadne had done with Anastasius half a century before.

1 *History of the Wars*, II, 21.

Traditionally, however, the choice of Emperor lay with the army, most of whose senior officers were away in the East. By the time they heard of Justinian's illness, it seemed to them more than likely that he was already dead; and at a hastily convened meeting in Mesopotamia they agreed that they would refuse to recognize any ruler chosen at Constantinople in their absence and without their consent. Reports of this meeting in their turn were brought back to the capital, but not before Justinian was out of danger; and Theodora, feeling herself once again secure, flew into a fury. Two generals in particular were believed to have instigated the meeting. One of them, Buzes, a former Consul and *magister militum per orientem*, was flung into the by now notorious dungeons, where he languished in total darkness for twenty-eight months, emerging, it was said, more like a ghost than a man.

The other was Belisarius. He was too popular, and too powerful, to be dealt with in the same way as his subordinate, and Procopius asserts that none of the charges levelled against Buzes could conclusively be brought home to him. How this can be is not altogether clear: it may be that he was not physically present at the fateful meeting – though he must surely have endorsed its decisions. In any case, another pretext had to be found; and he was now accused of having enriched himself unduly with Vandal and Gothic treasure that should properly have been delivered to the Emperor. Here at least Theodora might be said to have had a case: Belisarius certainly made no secret of his immense wealth. His passage through the streets of Constantinople, mounted on a sumptuously caparisoned charger and followed by a regiment of his private barbarian bodyguards, had for some years savoured more of some royal progress than of a citizen of the Empire about his lawful occasions. On his return to the capital after the premature close of the 542 campaign, the Empress struck. First, the general found himself relieved of his Eastern command; next, his magnificent household was disbanded, his picked spearmen and footguards being distributed among his brother-officers and the palace eunuchs, who drew lots for them. Finally, his accumulated treasure was confiscated at Theodora's command – by the simple expedient of sending round one of her personal attendants with orders to bring everything of value straight to the imperial palace.

It was not till the following year, 543, that Justinian recovered sufficiently to reassert his authority. Soon afterwards Belisarius was pardoned and partially restored to favour; his treasure, too, was returned to him – with the important exception of thirty hundredweight of gold, which Theodora had graciously bestowed on her husband as a present – and the seal was set on the reconciliation by the betrothal of Joannina, his and Antonina's only child, to the Empress's grandson Anastasius. In a letter to him at this time, Theodora emphasized that she had forgiven him because of her close friendship with his wife; but it seems reasonably clear that there was another reason, far more cogent, for the general's reinstatement. In the outlying provinces of the Empire, the situation was deteriorating fast. Across the Mediterranean, an insurrection started by the Moorish tribes was spreading with terrifying speed throughout the province of Africa; in Italy, the Goths under Totila were also striking back and had already recaptured Naples. Only in the East had the year begun on a note of hope, King Chosroes's warlike intentions having been frustrated by a renewed outbreak of plague as well as by a rebellion fomented by one of his sons. But even here, the late summer brought disaster: an immense Byzantine army of some 30,000 men – the largest that Justinian had ever raised – marched into Persian-held Armenia and was annihilated by a far smaller Persian force.

This was, in short, no time to keep the Empire's one general of genius dishonoured, disarmed and humiliated in Constantinople; he was desperately needed in the field. Belisarius for his part asked nothing better. He at first hoped to go back to the Persian front, but this prospect was firmly blocked by Antonina: never again, she insisted, would he return to that part of the world in which she had been so grossly insulted. Theodora, predictably, supported her; and Belisarius received instead the supreme command of the imperial army in the West. But here again disappointment awaited him. Old scores, it seemed, had not yet been entirely settled. It was not with the rank of *magister militum* as he had assumed, but merely with that of *comes stabuli*, Count of the Stable, that he returned in May 544 – sadder, wiser and, though still only in his fortieth year, infinitely more tired – to Italy.

There is no more convincing testimony to the brilliance of Belisarius than the collapse of Byzantine power in Italy after his departure in 540. With his triumphal entry into Ravenna that spring it must have seemed to everyone – Greek, Goth and Italian alike – that the whole peninsula had been recovered for the Empire. True, there were one or two small pockets of resistance, notably in Verona and Pavia, where the Gothic nobles acclaimed a young chieftain named Hildebad as their new King; but Hildebad's effective army amounted to no more than 1,000 men, and it seemed inconceivable that he could hold out longer than a few more weeks at most.

Nor would he have done so, if Belisarius had remained in Italy – or even, in all likelihood, if Justinian had appointed a competent successor. But the Emperor did no such thing. Instead, he left five subordinate generals jointly to consolidate the Byzantine hold on Italy as best they might, giving no single one of them authority over the rest. With the arguable exception of John, nephew of Vitalian, who for all his other faults was an excellent commander in the field, these generals were all distinctly second-rate: one, also named John, was known as *Phagas*, the Glutton; another, Bessas, was a turncoat Goth; the other two, Vitalius and Constantian, were relatively recent arrivals from Dalmatia. On Belisarius's departure, they divided up the territory between them and gave themselves over to a single object – plunder. Within weeks, the demoralization of the Byzantine army was complete. By the end of the year Hildebad had built up a considerable force of his own – it included a good many deserters from the imperial ranks – and was in effective control of all Italy north of the Po.

The reason for the Emperor's disastrous decision is not far to seek: he had clearly been informed of the Goths' offer of the throne to Belisarius – a fear that the latter might change his mind and accept it must almost certainly have been a factor in his recall – and he was terrified lest any successor might succumb to the same temptation. So compelling was this fear that for over two years he was to watch the situation in Italy steadily deteriorate before naming a Praetorian Prefect, and was then to pick on a feckless nonentity whom he knew to be incapable of rebelling against him but who unfortunately proved equally incapable of anything else. It was another two years before he reluctantly brought himself to return to Belisarius – not only the most inspired but also the most unswervingly loyal of all his generals – the command that he should never have lost.

King Hildebad meanwhile had not lasted long, having in May 541 been beheaded at dinner by one of his guards, Velas, whose bride-to-be he had unthinkingly bestowed on another.[1] His successor Eraric attempted to come to terms with Justinian and after only five months was murdered in his turn; and so the way was clear for the young man who was to prove himself the greatest, as well as the most attractive, of

---

1 'So when he had stretched out his hand to the food as he lay reclining upon his couch, Velas suddenly smote him on the neck with his sword. And so, while the food was still grasped in the man's fingers, his head was severed and fell upon the table, and filled all those present with great consternation and amazement.' So Procopius, *History of the Wars*, VII, i, 47–9.

all the Gothic rulers. His name, according to the evidence of every one of his coins, was Baduila; but even in his lifetime he seems to have been universally known to his subjects as Totila, and it is thus that he has gone down to history.

Totila was Hildebad's nephew; the date of his birth is not known, but he can hardly have been out of his middle twenties. He too had been secretly negotiating with the imperial generals, who were probably not unduly alarmed at the news of his elevation; once in the seat of power, however, he declared an out-and-out war against them, galvanizing the Goths as none of his predecessors could have hoped to do. Nor did he limit his attentions to his own people. He never forgot that the vast majority of his subjects were not Goths but Italians; their support too was vital if he were ever to expel the Byzantines from Italian soil. In Theodoric's day, and under his immediate successors, relations between Italian and Goth had been cordial – particularly among the governing classes, since the Gothic rulers needed Roman administrative and financial skills for the smooth running of their kingdom. Since Belisarius's victories, however, the Italian aristocracy had thrown in its lot with the Empire; and so it was to the humbler echelons of society – the middle class, the urban proletariat and the peasants – that young Totila now appealed.

And they responded, as he knew they would. They no longer felt any natural loyalty to the Empire which, though it still called itself Roman, was by now almost entirely Greek; furthermore, they were already suffering appallingly from Byzantine rapacity. That of the various generals had been bad enough; more recently, however, they had been forced to submit to the attentions of Justinian's own tax-gatherers, a new class of high officials whom he called Logothetes. The reputation of these men can best be indicated by the nickname given to their chief, a certain Alexander, who was universally known as *Psalidon*, 'the Scissors', for his notorious ability to clip round gold coins, retaining the clippings for himself. He and his subordinates were paid by results, the imperial treasury allowing them a commission of one-twelfth on all that they collected; and they bled the country white.

Totila's call promised an end to oppression. The slaves would be liberated, the great estates broken up, the land redistributed among the tenant farmers and the peasants; no longer would Italian taxes be used to maintain a vapid and corrupt court, to build vast palaces a thousand miles away that none of the contributors would ever see, or to pay protection money to barbarian tribes beyond the remotest frontiers of the Empire. It was hardly surprising that the people listened to him – and followed.

So indeed did many of the imperial soldiery, for they too were feeling the Scissors' edge. Within months of his accession Totila was strong enough to drive back one imperial army of 12,000 men from the gates of Verona, and to annihilate another in pitched battle outside Faventia (Faenza). In the spring of 542 came yet another victory, in the Mugello valley some fifteen miles north of Florence, in which he completely routed the army of John, nephew of Vitalian, the ablest of all Justinian's generals in the peninsula. Now the whole of the centre and the south lay open to him. On he went; and by the late summer of the same year he had effectively subjugated all Italy apart from Ravenna, Rome, Florence and a few fortified coastal cities. Chief among these was Naples; and it was to Naples, defended as it was by a largely Isaurian garrison of 1,000 men, that he now laid siege.

It is significant, if hardly surprising, that not one of the imperial generals in Italy should have made any attempt to relieve the city. Now, and only now, did Justinian steel himself to appoint a Praetorian Prefect with supreme powers in the province; but this man, Maximin, delayed till the end of the year on the coast of Epirus and, having finally landed at Syracuse, refused absolutely to leave it. By this time one naval relief expedition, launched on his own initiative by an old colleague of Belisarius, had been destroyed by Totila; a second, dispatched in January 543 by Maximin – who took care, however, not to join it himself – was overtaken by a sudden storm and dashed against the rocks.

Meanwhile the Gothic blockade of the city was total; and in May the Neapolitans were starved into surrender. Totila's terms were characteristically generous: the soldiers of the Byzantine garrison were allowed to leave in peace with all their possessions, and even had ships put at their disposal to take them wherever they liked. They chose Rome, and when contrary winds made the sea journey impossible they were given horses and beasts of burden and sent on their way with an escort. Typical too was the consideration shown by the young King to the Neapolitans themselves. Well understanding the danger of giving too much food too quickly to starving men, he first sealed off the city and then had a relatively small amount of food distributed to each household; the next day the ration was increased, and so on succeeding days until the people had once again returned to their normal diet.

The fall of Naples – for the second time in seven years – dealt a further blow to Byzantine morale. For the rest of the year Totila con-

tinued to mop up pockets of resistance and to consolidate his hold on
the peninsula, and by January 544 the Greek generals in their various
redoubts decided that they had had enough. A letter to Justinian was
drafted by Constantian in Ravenna – Maximin, if he was around at all,
seems to have been universally ignored – and signed by his fellow-
commanders, declaring that they could no longer defend the imperial
cause in Italy; it was this letter, almost certainly, that decided the Emperor to send back Belisarius. Meanwhile, in the hope that he might
be able to gain control of the city without bloodshed, Totila addressed a
passionate appeal to the Senate in Rome, an extract from which, condensed and somewhat freely translated, will be found at the head of this
chapter.

It received no answer. John, who was commanding in Rome, forbade
the Senate to send a reply – much as they would probably have liked to
do so. Totila then tried a direct appeal to the Romans. He arranged for a
number of copies to be made of a shortened version of his letter and
smuggled in under cover of darkness; and the populace awoke one
morning to find these posted up in prominent places all over the city,
assuring them that the Gothic King wished only to bring them freedom,
and that he promised to respect the lives and property of all those Romans
who were prepared to give him their support. John, now seriously
alarmed, persuaded himself that the Arian clergy had been responsible
for the propagation of the letter and went so far as to expel them
wholesale; but the true culprits were never identified.

Nor, however, was there a spontaneous uprising by the people of
Rome that Totila may have hoped for: if he wished to occupy the city he
could do so only by force. By now he was far away to the south, besieging the little Apulian port of Hydruntum (Otranto) which he feared
might be used as a bridgehead for a Byzantine relief expedition; but its
resistance proved fiercer than he had expected; leaving a small force
beneath the walls to continue the siege, in the early summer of 544 he
set off at once with the bulk of his army on the long march up the
peninsula to Rome.

He might, conceivably, have been one degree less confident had he
known that, while he was marching, Belisarius was already on his way
to Italy. The next round of the long contest between Greek and Goth
could not be much longer delayed.

From the moment he left Constantinople, Belisarius had known that he
would have to fight his second Italian campaign with, effectively, one

hand tied behind his back. Justinian had entrusted him with the reconquest of the peninsula, but had given him only a handful of inexperienced troops, little authority and no money at all. It was even
rumoured that the Emperor had extracted a promise from his general not
to request funds from the imperial treasury, but to provide both the men
and the necessary equipment at his own expense. In former days Belisarius
would probably have accepted such charges willingly enough; with
a private fortune greater than that of any other citizen of the Empire
outside the imperial family he would hardly have noticed them, and a
few victories would soon have replenished his coffers. But now, with
much of his wealth expropriated by the Empress and fully conscious that
in the existing situation there might be no victories at all, he was
powerless; and the few extra soldiers that he had managed to recruit on
his way to Italy were not such as to inspire any greater confidence in the
future.

He did his best. Within a year of his arrival in the summer of 544, he
had relieved Otranto and Osimo and rebuilt the defences of Pesaro,
which subsequently withstood a determined attack by Totila. During
this time, however, he had also seen several defections by imperial troops,
many of whom had received no pay for well over a year, and had understood all too clearly how radically the situation had changed in the four
years that he had been away. It was no longer just the Goths who were
actively hostile to the Empire; it was virtually the whole population.
With the forces at his command he might just succeed in maintaining an
imperial presence in Italy; but he could never reconquer it.

Such were the considerations in his mind when he wrote in May 545 to
Justinian, telling him of his desperate need of men, horses, arms and money:

A man who has not a sufficient supply of these cannot, I believe, wage war. It
is true that after laborious searches in Thrace and Illyria I was able to collect
some soldiers there; but they are few in number, wretched in quality, have no
weapons worth speaking of and are altogether inexperienced in fighting. As for
the soldiers whom I found here, they are discontented and discouraged, de-
moralised by frequent defeats, and at first sign of a foe are so bent on flight that
they slip at once from their horses and hurl their arms to the ground. To find
money in Italy for the war is impossible, since the country has been largely
reconquered by the enemy. Thus we cannot give the soldiers their long overdue
arrears of pay, and this knowledge of our indebtedness makes it hard for us to
speak freely to them.

Sire, you must be plainly told that the greatest part of your army has enlisted
and is now serving under the enemy's standards. If the mere sending of Beli-

sarius to Italy were all that were necessary, your preparations for war would be perfect; but if you would overcome your enemies you must do something more than this, for a general is nothing without his officers. First and foremost you must send me my own guards, both cavalry and foot-soldiers; secondly, a large number of Huns and other barbarians; and thirdly, money with which they may all be paid.

Belisarius entrusted this letter to John, whom he naturally expected to return as soon as possible with whatever military and financial help the Emperor might have been persuaded to provide. John, however, delayed for several months in Constantinople; it was not until late autumn that he returned, to find Belisarius awaiting him impatiently in Dyrrachium. The latter's irritation at the delay can hardly have been diminished by the news that his subordinate had taken advantage of his stay in the capital to woo and marry the daughter of Germanus, the Emperor's first cousin; henceforth, with his new imperial connections, he would be more insufferable than ever. On the other hand he had brought with him a considerable army, a mixed force of Romans and barbarians under the joint command of himself and an Armenian general named Isaac. They all crossed at once to Italy, landing there not a moment too soon: almost simultaneously, the army of Totila reached Rome and laid siege to the city.

To the Byzantines, the prospects looked bleak. Totila controlled all the territory between Rome and the sea, while his fleet was already drawn up at the mouth of the Tiber. Moreover the commander of the imperial garrison, Bessas, was of Gothic origin and uncertain loyalty. He had made no effort to lay in emergency food supplies; provisions were already found to be short when the siege began, and as it progressed he showed himself less interested in defending the city than in lining his own pocket by selling off what little was left to the highest bidder. As famine took hold, the saintly deacon Pelagius – Pope Vigilius being, for reasons shortly to be explained, under imperial arrest in Sicily – attempted negotiations with Totila, but they came to nothing. Belisarius saw at once that the only hope lay in sailing quickly to the mouth of the Tiber, running the gauntlet of the Gothic fleet, then landing his men and falling on the besieging army from behind; but John, though technically his junior, once again refused to obey. The first priority, he insisted, must be to recapture the south; only then could the army advance northwards to Rome. The result of this disagreement was probably the worst expedient of all: a division of the limited forces available, with each commander pursuing his own plan of action.

But Belisarius did not despair. By the time he reached Portus, where the Tiber flowed out into the sea, he had already laid his plans. While Bessas kept the Goths occupied with diversionary sorties, he proposed to lead an amphibious attack against their rear, marching part of his army along the south bank of the river while the rest, embarked on 200 ships, would smash the enemy fleet and then sail upstream in support. During the entire operation, the Armenian general Isaac was to remain in charge at Portus, looking after the reserves, the provisions, the remaining vessels and – by no means the least important – his wife Antonina, who had recently arrived to join him. Under no circumstances whatever, he emphasized – not even if it was reported that he himself had been captured or killed – was Isaac to leave his post.

In the event Bessas made no sorties, nor indeed the slightest effort of any kind to help his chief. Belisarius launched his expedition regardless. Keeping at bay the Gothic defenders along the banks with streams of arrows fired from the decks, his ships slowly forced their way up the river. After four miles, he easily smashed through the great iron chain and wooden boom that Totila had flung across as an additional protection, and was just about to attack the heavily fortified bridge that constituted the last obstacle before Rome itself when an urgent message was brought to him: Isaac had been taken prisoner. As Belisarius saw it, this could mean one thing only: the Goths had launched a surprise attack on Portus, seized the town and cut him off from the sea. And there was something else, still more terrible to contemplate: if Isaac had been captured, so too had Antonina. Calling off the attack at once, he dashed back to the coast – only to discover that Isaac, chafing at his enforced inactivity, had attacked the Gothic garrison at Ostia in flagrant disobedience of his orders and had been overcome by his intended victims. Apart from himself and the few soldiers who had accompanied him, everything and everyone else – including Antonina – was safe.

The last chance had been lost: Rome's fate was sealed. And yet, sick and starving as the Romans were, it was neither sickness nor starvation that caused the city's fall. It never surrendered; but on the night of 17 December 546 a group of four discontented Isaurian soldiers of the garrison opened up the Asinarian Gate, and the Goths flooded in. Whether the traitors had been among those Isaurians to whom Totila had shown such unusual consideration after his capture of Naples three and a half years before, we shall never know; but the young King certainly had little cause to regret his generosity.

Bessas took flight at once, together with most of the garrison, leaving all his ill-gotten treasure behind to swell the Gothic coffers. Several of the Roman nobles – those of them who had not been obliged to eat their horses – rode off with him. The remainder sought refuge in the churches till Totila had brought his men under control, then slowly emerged to resume their desperate search for food until such time as supplies in the city returned to normal. Of the populace, Procopius[1] tells us that only 500 citizens were left. Some of us may agree with Gibbon in finding this figure hard to accept; in fact, however, there seems nothing particularly improbable about it. There can in any case be no doubt that although, strategically speaking, the fall of Rome was of little real significance, as a symbol it was all-important; and Totila understandably saw its capture as an opportunity to send ambassadors to the Emperor, offering him peace on the basis of a return to the status quo of happier days. 'You will have learned,' he wrote,

of what has occurred in the city of the Romans; this I propose to pass over in silence. Why I am sending you these envoys, however, I shall explain. It is our wish that you should accept for yourself the blessings of peace, and that you should grant them also to us. Of these blessings we have most excellent examples and reminders in Anastasius and Theodoric, who ruled not long ago and whose reigns were given over to peace and prosperity. If this should be also your desire, I shall look upon you as my father, and you may henceforth count on us as your allies against all your enemies.

But Justinian would have none of it. To accept Totila's proposals would have been effectively to write off ten years' campaigning and to admit the defeat not only of his armies but also of his most cherished ambitions. Belisarius, he pointed out, was his commander in Italy, and was possessed of complete plenipotentiary authority. If the King of the Goths had anything he wished to communicate, it was to him that his words should properly be addressed.

It is unlikely that Totila even approached Belisarius as Justinian had suggested; and it is unlikelier still that, even had he done so, he would have received a remotely encouraging reply. The fall of Rome was soon forgotten – the Byzantines even managed briefly to reoccupy it in April 547, though they were to lose it again less than three years later – and after a few more months of desultory fighting up and down the peninsula it became clear that the two sides had reached a stalemate, with neither strong enough to eliminate the other. Belisarius decided on one last

1 His full account of Totila's siege of Rome will be found in his *History of the Wars*, VII, xv–xx.

appeal to his Emperor. He knew that for Justinian the international situation had improved since his last attempt: peace had finally been concluded – though at a considerable price – with King Chosroes, and the rebellion in Africa, which had been raging for the past five years and had made formidable demands of money and manpower, had finally been put down. Perhaps, in the calmer conditions now prevailing, he might at last get what he wanted.

His emissary on this occasion was his wife Antonina. She had seen for herself the difficulties that he was having to face, and could speak of them from first-hand experience. She had, moreover, direct access to the Empress, and through her to Justinian himself; she would not allow herself to be fobbed off with underlings. Around midsummer, 548, she left for Constantinople – only to find the city plunged into deepest mourning. Just a few days before, on 28 June, Theodora had died of cancer. Antonina saw at once that her mission was doomed: the Emperor, prostrated with grief, would see no one and was incapable of taking decisions. All that she managed to obtain from those in temporary control was the recall of her husband; if failure in Italy was now inevitable, she was determined that he should not carry the blame.

Early in 549 Belisarius returned to the capital. After the glory of his first Italian campaign, his second had brought him only five years of frustration and disappointment. But he had saved Italy, at least temporarily, for the Empire. Had it not been for his energy and resolve, in the face of the most discouraging conditions imaginable, there is little doubt that the Byzantines would have been expelled in 544; thanks to him the foundations for reconquest were laid for the second time, making it relatively easy when the moment came for his old rival Narses – possessed of all the resources for which he, Belisarius, had appealed in vain – to win the victories and the acclaim that should rightfully have been his own.

The Last Years of Justinian

[549–65]

The natural course for a high-souled Emperor to pursue is to seek to enlarge the Empire, and make it more glorious.

Procopius

Justinian greeted his general like a long-lost friend – which, in a sense, he was. For years the two men had been kept apart by the intrigues of Theodora, who had continually poisoned her husband's mind with fabricated stories about Belisarius – his faithlessness, his duplicity, his imperial ambitions. The Emperor had never really believed her; yet the doubts that she implanted in his mind were enough to produce a vague feeling of mistrust which endured for as long as she lived. With her death, however, this feeling was quickly dissipated; by the time Belisarius returned to Constantinople, Justinian had recovered from the initial shock of his bereavement – though he continued to mourn his wife until the day he died – and welcomed him with open arms, adopting him as his closest confidant and going so far as to erect a gilded statue of him, next to that of his uncle Justin, in the Augusteum.

Even Belisarius, however, seems to have been unable to persuade the Emperor to provide the men and money for a final all-out attack on Totila. It was not that Justinian lacked determination to regain Italy for the Empire. This had, after all, been his primary objective ever since his accession, and his categorical refusal to receive Totila's ambassadors after the latter's capture of Rome is clear enough indication that he had in no way weakened in his resolve. But for the past six years he had had a major theological problem on his hands – a problem which the death of his wife had rendered, if anything, still more intractable; and the hiatus which now occurs in the story of the Italian reconquest – following the recall of Belisarius and preceding the brief final act of the drama – provides us with a welcome opportunity to see what had occurred.

At the root of the trouble there lay the same old enigma that had caused all the previous disputes – the identity of Christ. The orthodox view was that laid down nearly a century before by the Council of Chalcedon: that the Saviour possessed, in his one person, two natures inseparably united, the human and the divine. But this view had never been accepted by the monophysites, according to whom the divine nature alone existed and who consequently saw Christ as God rather than man; and these, heretics as they might be, were far too numerous and too widespread to be eliminated. Egypt, for example, was monophysite through and through; in Syria and Palestine, too, the doctrine had taken a firm and potentially dangerous hold. In the West, on the other hand, such heresy as existed at all was Arian rather than monophysite and was to be found almost exclusively among the barbarians. The Roman Church was staunchly orthodox and quick to protest at any deviation from the Chalcedonian path. Justinian therefore had a difficult and delicate course to steer. If he dealt too harshly with the monophysites, he risked rebellion and the possible loss to the Empire of valuable provinces – Egypt was one of its chief sources of corn. If he treated them with too much consideration, he incurred the wrath of the orthodox and split his subjects more than ever. Fortunately Theodora had strong monophysite sympathies, even going so far as to maintain a discreet monastery in the Great Palace; her husband could thus on occasion afford to take an outwardly rigid line in the knowledge that she would secretly be able to temper its severity.

Thanks to this somewhat disingenuous policy, the Emperor had managed to curb most of the monophysite communities – outside Egypt, where he left them firmly alone – with considerable success; but then, suddenly, there emerged a charismatic new leader. Jacob Baradaeus ('the Ragged') was a Syriac-speaking monk from Mesopotamia. He had already spent fifteen years in Constantinople – where he may well have been one of the Empress's protégés – during which time he had caused the authorities little trouble; but in 543 the exiled monophysite Patriarch of Alexandria chose to consecrate him Bishop of Edessa. The fact that he had no hope of ever setting foot in his see, which was already safely held by a perfectly sound Chalcedonian, worried him not a bit: for him the important thing was the consecration itself, and its effect on him was electric. Disguised as a poor beggar – hence his name – he embarked on a mission to revive monophysite sentiment throughout the East, travelling constantly and at prodigious speed the length and breadth of Syria and Palestine, Mesopotamia and Asia Minor, consecrating some thirty bishops as he went and ordaining several thousand priests.

Unable to stamp out the flames of fanaticism that sprang up everywhere in the wake of Baradaeus, Justinian found himself in a quandary. The monophysites in their present mood needed still more careful treatment than before; at the same time he was already being criticized in the West for weakness and inertia in the face of the new threat. Some kind of positive action was clearly required; and so, for want of any better solution, he decided on a public condemnation – not of the monophysites but of those who occupied the other end of the theological spectrum, professing the humanity rather than the divinity of Christ: the Nestorians. This by now half-forgotten sect had been anathematized as early as 431 at the Council of Ephesus; afterwards the majority had fled eastward, to Persia and beyond, and few if any of them now remained within the imperial frontiers. It thus mattered little whether they were attacked again or not; but they had the advantage of being detested by monophysites and orthodox alike, and an *ex cathedra* pronouncement of the kind the Emperor intended would, he hoped, do something to defuse the increasing hostility between the two. Early in 544 he published an edict, condemning not the heresy itself but three particular manifestations of it, soon to become notorious as the 'Three Chapters': the person and writings of Nestorius's teacher, Theodore of Mopsuestia, and certain specific works of two other, still more obscure theologians, Theodoret of Cyrrhus and Ibas of Edessa.

It was a foolish idea, and it fully deserved the response it received. Only the orthodox clergy in the East agreed – in some cases a trifle unwillingly – to toe the imperial line. The monophysites, who had hoped for genuine concessions, were unappeased; in the West, the Roman bishops made no attempt to conceal their fury. Any attack on the Nestorians, they thundered, could only be a blow in favour of the monophysites; besides, had not the Council of Chalcedon examined the writings of Theodoret and Ibas and found them blameless? They refused absolutely to condemn the Three Chapters; and Stephen, the papal legate in Constantinople, made known his master's displeasure by pronouncing the ban of the Church on Patriarch Mennas himself.

Justinian was first surprised by these reactions, and then seriously alarmed. In Italy, during the four years that had passed since the first recall of Belisarius, the Byzantine position had grown steadily worse; now, at a moment when he needed their support more than ever before, he had managed to antagonize Pope Vigilius and the entire Church of Rome. The sooner the whole thing were forgotten, the better. He made no protest when the Pope failed to condemn the Three Chapters, but settled down quietly to mend relations.

For a year and a half he pursued this policy, and would presumably have continued to do so had circumstances allowed; but by the autumn of 545 Totila's army was at the gates of Rome. Were he to capture the city, there was nothing to prevent his holding the Pope hostage, with consequences that could only add further fuel to the flames. Justinian acted quickly. On 22 November an officer of the imperial guard with a company of excubitors arrived in Rome, seized Vigilius just as he was leaving the Church of St Cecilia after mass, loaded him on to a boat waiting in the Tiber and carried him off down the river.

The Pope, who had no particular wish to remain in the city during what promised to be an unpleasant and protracted siege, made no complaint when told that he was being taken to Constantinople – though he may not altogether have relished the prospect of renewing his acquaintance with Theodora. Some years before, while serving as papal legate at the imperial court, he had made a secret agreement with her, by the terms of which Belisarius would depose Pope Silverius and instal him, Vigilius, in his place; in return, he would denounce the principles laid down at Chalcedon and proclaim his acceptance of the monophysite creed. The Empress had fulfilled her side of the bargain, but the Pope had reneged on his; back in Constantinople, he might have a certain amount of explaining to do.[1] As things turned out, however, his meeting with the imperial couple did not occur as soon as he had expected; he remained for a whole year as their guest at Catania in Sicily – during which he dispatched several ships, laden with grain, for the relief of Rome – and only in January 547 reached the capital.

At this stage Vigilius was still firm in his refusal to condemn the Three Chapters. Though the Emperor had greeted him warmly on his arrival and even put at his disposal the old Palace of Placidia as a residence, the Pope lost no time in making his authority felt, immediately placing Patriarch Mennas and all the bishops who had subscribed to the imperial edict

---

1 A writer known as Anastasius Bibliothecarius – the Librarian – maintains that it was not Justinian but Theodora, bent on vengeance for this and other pretended offences (including murder) on the part of the Pope, who engineered the arrest of Vigilius. But the story as he tells it is too improbable to be taken very seriously.

under four months' further sentence of excommunication.[1] Before long, however, the constant pressure exerted by the Emperor and Empress – who seemed to have forgotten her previous grievances but who on this issue was every bit as zealous and determined as her husband – began to wear him down. On 29 June he was officially reconciled with the Patriarch, and on the same day he handed Justinian his signed condemnation of the Chapters, stipulating only that it should be kept secret until the end of a formal inquiry by certain Western bishops – whose findings, he hinted, were a foregone conclusion; and on 11 April 548 he published his *Judicatum*, in which he solemnly anathematized the Three Chapters, while emphasizing that his support for the doctrines of Chalcedon remained unshaken.

Thus, when the Empress died eleven weeks later, it might have been thought that she and her husband had triumphed, and had succeeded at last in restoring unity to the Church. In fact, the split was soon revealed to be deeper than ever. Theodora had always been more feared than her husband; while she lived, many distinguished churchmen – including several of her former protégés – had preferred to keep a low profile rather than incur her displeasure. After her death, they came out publicly in opposition to the imperial edict, and gradually others followed suit across Europe. Whatever Vigilius might have said to the contrary, there could be no doubt that his anathemas had dangerously undermined the authority of Chalcedon; and the Pope was now generally reviled throughout Western Christendom as a turncoat and an apostate. In Africa, indeed, the local bishops went further still and excommunicated him.

Only in Italy was there no real opposition to Vigilius; poor, beleaguered Italy – sacked, plundered, ravaged and now half starving – had little time to spare for abstruse theological niceties. The long struggle between Roman and Goth for mastery over the peninsula was now entering its final phase.

Justinian's anxieties over the Three Chapters, though largely of his own making, had turned his mind away from his Italian problems. He always tended to underestimate the Goths; it may well be, too, that the recovery of Rome by the Byzantines in April 547, only four months after its capture by Totila, had confirmed him in his belief that, given only a little more time, the Gothic opposition would crumble of its own accord.

---

1 No less an authority than Pope Gregory the Great claims that he also excommunicated Theodora herself. But Gregory was then still a child in Rome, and his story sounds highly unlikely. If Vigilius had taken so bold a step, we should surely have heard about it at the time – though he himself would not, one suspects, have lasted very long.

Unfortunately, it did no such thing. On 16 January 550, history repeated itself and another group of disaffected Isaurians in the Roman garrison opened the gates – this time those of the Porta Ostiensis, near S. Paolo fuori le Mura – to Totila's men. But whereas in 546 the Goths had entered the city as invaders, they now showed every sign of staying. Many of them appropriated empty houses and settled in with their families; the Senate was reopened; refugees were encouraged to return to their old homes; damaged buildings were repaired and restored. The following summer, Totila gave still more conclusive evidence of his intentions where Rome was concerned: he staged a full-scale revival of the Games in the Circus Maximus, and personally presided over them from the imperial box. Meanwhile his fleet was ravaging both Italy and Sicily, to return in 551 loaded to the gunwales with plunder. These two insults finally stung Justinian to action. The first he could see only as a deliberate challenge to his authority; the second was the more galling in that Sicily had, since its reconquest by Belisarius, been part of the Emperor's personal patrimony, its revenues passing directly to him rather than through the imperial exchequer. He immediately looked for a new commander-in-chief to send to Italy; and his choice fell on his own first cousin, Germanus.

In Theodora's day the appointment would have been unthinkable; she had detested Germanus even more than Belisarius, and had done him down wherever she could. But Theodora was gone; Germanus was an able soldier of long experience, without any of his predecessor's brilliance but reliable, efficient and absolutely loyal. He possessed, moreover, another advantage that promised to strengthen his position considerably once he reached Italy, for he had recently married Matasuntha, widow of that luckless King Vitiges who had died a captive in Constantinople eight years before. As granddaughter of the great Theodoric, she could be expected to attract the allegiance of most of the Gothic nobility, just as Germanus might, with any luck, win the support of the Italian land-owners.

Was Justinian consciously working towards a restored Empire of the West, with Italians and Goths finally united and Germanus reigning in Ravenna as his Caesar and ultimate successor? Something of the sort may well have been in his mind as he bade farewell to his cousin, now at the head of an army considerably larger than any ever allowed to Belisarius, his beautiful young wife – still only about thirty and pregnant for the first time – at his side. Whether this objective would ever have been achieved, we cannot tell. In the autumn of 550 Germanus was stricken with fever and died at his camp in Sardica (now Sofia). He never set foot in Italy, and never saw his son.

The news of his cousin's death came as another severe blow to Justinian. He was now sixty-eight, and childless. Thoughts of possible successors were beginning to occupy his mind, and Germanus, whatever the outcome of the Italian campaign, had been the obvious candidate. But the Italian situation was more pressing still, with a huge army now leaderless in the field. Its withdrawal at this stage would be worse than its defeat – tantamount to an open acknowledgement of Totila's sovereignty over the peninsula. A new commander must be found, and quickly. Did the Emperor turn, as he had turned twice before, to Belisarius? If so, Belisarius must have refused point-blank; for the man chosen for this last attempt to bring Italy back into the imperial fold was none other than the eunuch Narses, now well into his seventies.

The choice was, to say the least, unexpected; on examination, however, it was seen to be less perverse than might have been thought. Narses was admittedly old, but he had lost none of his energy or his decisiveness. He was relatively inexperienced in the field; but there were several excellent tacticians – notably his old friend John – already in Italy. What was needed above all was a superb organizer, strong-willed and determined, able to dominate a team of ever-squabbling rivals and inspire them with new purpose and spirit. And for such a task Narses was ideally qualified.

He had no delusions as to the magnitude of his task; by now only four cities in all Italy – Ravenna, Ancona, Otranto and Crotone – remained in Byzantine control. But Narses had not spent a lifetime in the imperial palace for nothing. He knew Justinian better than any man alive, and easily persuaded him to make available an even greater army than that he had given to Germanus – at least 35,000 men, most of them barbarians: Lombards, Gepids, Herulians and Huns, together with a number of Persians captured in the recent war. He left Constantinople in the spring of 551, but spent the rest of the year in Thrace and Illyria, touring military establishments, recruiting still more troops and generally working himself in. The coming campaign was to be the culminating achievement of his career. He could not afford to fail.

Only in the early summer of 552 did he and his men begin their march into Italy. They came by land, advancing around the head of the Adriatic to Ravenna, where Narses was able to provide what was left of the local troops with their long overdue arrears of pay; thence, after nine days' consolidation, they continued across the Apennines and down the Via Flaminia towards the south, Totila meanwhile advancing northward up the same road to block their path. So it was that, one day towards the end of June, at Taginae (somewhere between the little towns of Scheggia and Gualdo Tadino) the Roman and Gothic armies met for what was to prove the decisive encounter of the entire war.

Though no longer an eye-witness – he had returned to Constantinople with his master Belisarius – Procopius is still able to give us a remarkably detailed account of the battle. He tells us, for example, how Totila tried to deceive Narses by first saying he wished to delay the fighting for a week and then attacking on the following day, but how Narses suspected a trick and was ready for him; how later the Gothic King, learning that a further 2,000 of his men were on their way, genuinely played for time, going so far as to treat the two armies to a display of horsemanship and Gothic *haute école* in his efforts to win a few additional hours – incidentally providing, one would imagine, a memorable contrast with the shrivelled old eunuch who watched impassively from the opposing ranks; and how, when battle had at last been joined, the Gothic army was progressively outflanked and outfought until, as the sun was sinking, it fled in panic and disorder, the Byzantines in hot pursuit. Totila himself, mortally wounded, took flight with the rest and died in the little village of Caprae – now Caprara – a few hours later.

For the Goths, all hope was now lost; but they did not surrender. Unanimously they acclaimed Teia, one of the bravest of Totila's generals, as his successor and continued the struggle. An attempt to forge an alliance with the Franks, who controlled much of Italy north of the Po, came to nothing. The Frankish King Theudibald preferred to let the two protagonists fight it out together while he remained on the sidelines; he accepted Teia's presents, but lifted not a finger to help him. Narses meanwhile continued his advance to the south, while city after city opened its gates to the conquerors. Rome itself fell after a brief siege – changing hands for the fifth time since the beginning of Justinian's reign – but the old eunuch marched on. Totila, he had learnt, had deposited vast reserves of treasure and bullion at Cumae, at the far northern end of the Bay of Naples; he was determined to lay his hands on it before it was spirited away. Teia, similarly resolved that he should do no such thing, sped to relieve the garrison; for some reason, however, he and his army emerged from the mountains at the southern end of the bay, near Nocera; and it was there in the valley of the river Sarno (then known as the Draco) to the south-east of Vesuvius – a mile or two from the already long-forgotten Pompeii – that, at the end of October 552, Romans and Goths met for the *coup de grâce*. Teia himself fought heroically, until felled by a well-aimed javelin; but even after his head had been impaled on a lance and raised aloft for all his men to see, they still battled on. It was only on the evening of the following day that the few still surviving agreed to negotiate. By the terms of the consequent treaty, the Goths undertook to leave Italy and to engage in no further warfare against the Empire, receiving in return the guarantee that they would be permitted to take all their movable property with them and that they would never be forcibly conscripted into the imperial army.

A few pockets of resistance remained. The garrison at Cumae held out for a few months longer and – thanks largely to belated Frankish support – one or two cities north of the Po remained at least technically in Gothic hands for longer still; not for another nine years was Narses able to send his master the keys of Verona. But it was that desperate battle beneath Vesuvius that marked, for all practical purposes, the defeat of the Goths in Italy. Justinian's grandest ambition was realized at last.

History offers few examples of a campaign as swift and decisive as that of Narses being successfully concluded by a general in his middle eighties; nor, surely, any more persuasive argument in favour of castration. Almost unbelievably, however, just as that ancient Armenian was marching his men into Italy in the spring of 552, another, smaller Byzantine expeditionary force had landed in Spain under the command of a general who was older still. His name was Liberius, and he is recorded as having been Praetorian Prefect of Italy sixty years before, in Theodoric's day; at the time of which we are speaking, therefore, he cannot possibly have been less than eighty-five.

Compared with the reconquest of Italy the Spanish campaign was never more than a side-show, and its story can be quickly told. By now Spain was firmly in the hands of the Visigoths, who had first arrived there in the early fifth century and who in 418 had made a pact with Rome by the terms of which they agreed to recognize the sovereignty of the Empire. The position was thus very much the same as it had been in Italy under Theodoric, with a Roman land-owning aristocracy living comfortably on its estates, perfectly satisfied with the status quo and doubtless grateful that the immense distance separating them from Constantinople reduced imperial interference to the point of imperceptibility. For them and their Visigothic masters, the first warning of the approaching storm came with Belisarius's recovery of Vandal North Africa in 533, and his eviction of a Visigothic garrison from the port of Septem – now Ceuta – the following year. An attempt by the Visigothic King Theodis to seize it back in 547 ended in disaster; his protests that the Romans had cheated by attacking on a Sunday while ne was at church did not alter the fact that his army had been annihilated, and he himself met his death shortly afterwards at the hands of an assassin.

Then, in 551, Theodis's second successor, King Agila, found himself faced with two simultaneous rebellions: one by the Romans of Cordova and one, larger and far more serious, by his own kinsman, Athanagild. He fought back with courage and determination, and it was not long before Athanagild appealed to the Emperor for help.[1] Here was precisely the opportunity Justinian had been waiting for. Despite the exigences of the Italian campaign and his chronic shortage of manpower, he ordered that a small force – perhaps one or two thousand at the most – should be detached from Narses's army and sent under Liberius to Spain for the support of Athanagild and the protection of the Roman insurgents. Landing on the south-east coast, they met with little resistance: the Visigothic army was already hopelessly divided between those who were loyal to Agila and those who had thrown in their lot with the rebellion. Before long Liberius effectively controlled the whole area south of a line drawn from Valencia to Cadiz, including Cordova. In 555 Agila was murdered by his own troops and Athanagild assumed the throne without opposition.

Had the new King agreed to rule as an imperial vassal, all would have been well; such, however, had never been his intention and he soon made it clear to Liberius that he expected him and his army to withdraw as soon as they conveniently could. The old man – who was clearly every bit as good a diplomat as he was a general – agreed in principle, but gradually persuaded Athanagild to negotiate; and finally an agreement was reached between them according to which the Empire kept much of the territory it had conquered. But its soldiers were few, and its lines of communication dangerously long; and Justinian was obliged to acknowledge that a good seven-eighths of the peninsula lay beyond his power. On the other hand, he retained the Balearic Islands which, together with Corsica and Sardinia (reconquered respectively by Belisarius and Narses) gave him a firm base in the western Mediterranean, and he could boast that the Empire now once again extended from the Black Sea to the Atlantic Ocean. The expedition may not have been a complete success; but it was certainly not a failure.

*

1 The Visigoths, like almost all the barbarian tribes, were devout Arians; according to Bishop Isidore of Seville, however, Athanagild was secretly a Catholic – in other words, an orthodox Christian. If he is right, Justinian would doubtless have been even more eager to go to his assistance.

When the army of Narses drove the Goths out of Rome for the last time, Pope Vigilius was not present to preside over the services of thanksgiving. He was still in Constantinople, ever more inextricably enmeshed in the dispute over the Three Chapters. The hostility aroused by his *Judicatum* had compelled him to revoke the offending document in 550; and though in August of that year he had secretly sworn to Justinian a written oath that he would continue to use all his influence on his behalf, his efforts to regain the control – and, more difficult still, the respect – of the Western Churches had inevitably led him further and further away from the Emperor's own position. Relations between the two became still more strained the following year, when Justinian published a second edict, in the form of a long treatise in which he set forth – as if he himself were a one-man Ecumenical Council – his own interpretation of the basic tenets of Christianity, ending up with yet another violent condemnation of the Chapters. Prompted, no doubt, by many of the Western churchmen in the city, Vigilius protested that the edict went against the principles of Chalcedon and called upon the Emperor to withdraw it. Justinian, predictably, refused; whereupon the Pope summoned a meeting in his palace of all the bishops from both East and West who were present in the city. This assembly pronounced unanimously against the edict, solemnly forbidding any cleric to say mass in any church in which it was exhibited. When, a few days later, two prelates ignored this decree they were immediately excommunicated – as was (for the third time) the Patriarch himself.

On hearing the news, Justinian flew into a towering fury; and the Pope, suspecting that he was no longer safe from arrest, sought refuge in the Church of St Peter and St Paul, which the Emperor had recently built next to the Palace of Hormisdas.[1] Scarcely had he reached it, however, when there arrived the Praetor of the People, who commanded the city police, with a company of the imperial guard. According to a party of Italian churchmen, who were eye-witnesses of what took place and who subsequently described it in detail to the Frankish ambassadors,[2] they burst into the church with swords drawn and bows ready-strung and made straight for the Pope. He, seeing them, made a dash for the high altar; meanwhile the various priests and deacons surrounding him

---

1 This was a Constantinian building looking out on to the Marmara immediately to the south of St Sophia. It took its name from one of its first residents, a fugitive Persian who became one of the chief advisers to the Emperor Constantius.

2 Their letter will be found in Migne, *Patrologia Latina*, Vol. 69, Cols. 113–19.

remonstrated with the Praetor, and a scuffle ensued during which several of them were injured, though not seriously. The soldiers then seized hold of the Pope himself, who was by this time clinging tightly to the columns supporting the altar, and tried to drag him – some by the legs, some by the hair and others by the beard – forcibly away. But the more they pulled, the tighter he clung – until at last the columns themselves came loose and the altar crashed to the ground, narrowly missing his head.

By this time a considerable crowd, attracted by the commotion, had begun to protest vehemently against such treatment being accorded to the Vicar of Christ; the soldiers, too, were manifestly unhappy, and the Praetor wisely decided to withdraw, leaving a triumphant though badly shaken Vigilius to survey the damage. The next day there arrived a high-powered delegation, led by Belisarius, to express the Emperor's regrets for what had occurred and to give the Pope a formal assurance that he could return to his residence in the capital without fear of violence or apprehension.

The Pope returned at once, but soon found that he was being kept under so close a surveillance as to amount to something approaching house arrest. He realized, too, that if he were to break the present dead-lock and maintain the prestige that he had striven so hard to recover among the Western Churches, he must once again take decisive action. Two nights before Christmas, in the late evening of 23 December 551, he squeezed his considerable bulk through a small window of the palace and took a boat across the Bosphorus to Chalcedon, where he made straight for the Church of St Euphemia. It was a clever move, and also a symbolic one in that he was deliberately associating himself with the scene of the Great Council of 451, distancing himself from the Emperor who was questioning its authority and taking refuge from him in the very building in which its sessions had been held exactly a century before. Once again a delegation under Belisarius came to plead with him, but this time he stood firm; and when a detachment of soldiers called a few days later they were content to arrest some of his priests, but made no attempt to lay hands on the Pope himself. Vigilius meanwhile composed a long letter to Justinian known as his *Encyclica*, in which he answered accusations made by the Emperor by giving his own account of the controversy as he saw it and once again proposing negotiations. In a less conciliatory mood, he also published his sentences of excommunication on the Patriarch and the two bishops who had incurred his wrath the previous August.

Negotiations were resumed in the spring, and in June Justinian decided on a major tactical concession: the Patriarch and other excommunicated bishops were dispatched to St Euphemia to apologize and humble themselves before Vigilius, after which the Pope returned to his palace. It was also agreed to annul all recent statements on both sides covering the Three Chapters, including the Emperor's edict. To the papal supporters it must have seemed like victory: if recent statements were annulled it was hardly likely that any more would be made, and with any luck the whole issue might now be allowed to fade back into the obscurity it deserved. But Justinian was not yet beaten. He now decreed a new Ecumenical Council to pronounce upon the matter once and for all, and invited Vigilius to preside.

In theory an Ecumenical Council of the Church was a convocation of bishops from every corner of Christendom. When all were gathered together it was believed that the Holy Spirit would descend on them, giving a sort of infallibility to their pronouncements. Their judgement was supreme, their decisions final. In practice, however, attendance was inevitably selective. If therefore the Church was split on any given issue, the outcome of the Council's deliberations would depend less on divine intervention than on the number of bishops from each side able to attend; and both Emperor and Pope knew full well that bishops were considerably thicker on the ground in the East than they were in the West, and that – particularly if the meetings were held in Constantinople – the Easterners would thus command a substantial majority. Vigilius accordingly suggested that the question should be put to a small committee composed of an equal number of representatives from both East and West, but Justinian refused; and after various other possibilities had been put forward and similarly rejected the Pope decided that his only chance lay in boycotting the assembly altogether. In consequence, when the Fifth Ecumenical Council eventually met in St Sophia on 5 May 553, under the presidency of Eutychius, Mennas's successor as Patriarch – of the 168 bishops present only eleven were from the West, and nine of these were African. Justinian too had elected to stay away since, he explained, he did not wish to influence the assembly; but his letter to the delegates, read aloud at the opening session, reminded them that they had already anathematized the Three Chapters. No one present could have had any doubt as to what was expected of him.

For over a week the deliberations continued; then, on 14 May, after repeated invitations to attend, the Pope produced what he described as a

Constitutum, signed by himself and nineteen other Western churchmen. It was to some degree a compromise, in that it allowed that there were indeed certain grave errors in the writings of Theodore of Mopsuestia; but, it pointed out, the other two writers accused had been pronounced 'orthodox fathers' at Chalcedon. In any case, it was not proper to anathematize the dead. The present agitation over the Three Chapters was therefore unfounded and unnecessary, and itself to be condemned. Vigilius concluded by forbidding – 'by the authority of the Apostolic See, over which by the Grace of God we preside' – any ecclesiastic to venture any further opinion on the matter.

It was not till 25 May that the Pope formally sent a copy of his paper to the Palace. He cannot have expected it to be well received; neither, however, had he reckoned with the changed situation in Italy. Totila was dead; the Goths were defeated; no longer was it necessary to woo the Roman citizens in Italy for their support. Justinian had had more than enough of Vigilius, and now at last he could afford to treat him as he deserved. He made no reply to the *Constitutum*; instead, he sent one of his secretaries to the Council with a packet containing three documents. The first was the text of the Pope's secret declaration of June 547, anathematizing the Three Chapters; the second was his written oath of August 550, swearing to do everything in his power to bring about their condemnation; and the third was a decree that his name should be forthwith struck from the diptychs. This was tantamount to a sentence of excommunication on the Pope himself – though Justinian stressed that in repudiating Vigilius personally he was not severing communion with Rome.[1] At its seventh session on 26 May the Council formally endorsed the Emperor's decree and condemned the Pope in its turn, 'until he should repent his errors'; and at its eighth and last, on 2 June, echoing the Emperor's second edict almost verbatim, it anathematized a whole series of heretics including Theodore and Theodoret. (Ibas escaped, on the grounds that the offending letter attributed to him had in fact been written by someone else.)

For Vigilius, it was the end of the road. Banished to an island in the Marmara, he was told that until he accepted the findings of the Council he would never be permitted to return to Rome. Not for another six months – by which time he was suffering agonies from kidney-stones – did he capitulate; but when at last he did so his surrender was absolute. In a letter to the Patriarch of 8 December he admitted all his previous errors, and two months later – almost certainly at Justinian's insistence –

1 *Non sedem sed sedentem*, 'not the seat but the sitter'.

he addressed to the Western Churches a second *Constitutum* in which he formally condemned the Three Chapters and all who dared uphold them; as for himself, 'whatever is brought forward or anywhere discovered in my name in their defence is hereby nullified'. He could not say more. By now too ill to travel, he remained another year in Constantinople and only then, during a brief respite from the pain, started for home. But the effort was too great. On the way, his condition suddenly grew worse. He was obliged to interrupt his journey at Syracuse; and there, broken alike in body and spirit, he died.

It is an almost universal characteristic among autocrats that they cling compulsively to power, to the detriment alike of their subjects and their reputation. If death had come to Justinian at the same time as it came to Pope Vigilius, he would have been genuinely mourned. By the reconquest of Italy he had restored to his Empire its former frontiers and had made the Mediterranean once again a Roman lake; by the Council of Constantinople he had brought at least a semblance of unity to the Christian Church. His work was done, all his dominions at peace. He was seventy-three years old, his beloved Theodora was dead and it was time for him to follow her to the grave. But death did not come; indeed, it delayed its coming for another ten years. And the Empire suffered.

All through that last, unhappy decade of his life Justinian persistently refused to delegate his authority, while it became clearer and clearer to those around him that he no longer possessed either the ability or the appetite to wield it properly himself. 'The old man no longer cared for anything,' wrote a contemporary, 'his spirit was already in heaven.' Money – always a problem – was shorter than ever; but whereas in the old days the Emperor would have taken steps himself to find at least part of what he needed, now he left it to his ministers to do the best they could. The defence of the frontier had always been one of his primary concerns: he had raised literally hundreds of walls and ramparts, of castles and strongholds, from the Euphrates to the Guadalquivir. But by 555 he had allowed the imperial army, which had once numbered 645,000 men, to shrink to a mere 150,000, while the great frontier fortresses stood desolate and abandoned. War, money, defence, even conquest – all these things had begun to bore him. Nowadays he cared only for religion, for the state of the Church – *his* Church – and for the endless theological disputations in which, true Byzantine that he was, he found both stimulus and relaxation.

Hostile neighbours were to be bought rather than fought, even though the exchequer had no funds with which to buy them. Thus the payment in 556 to the Great King of 30,000 gold *solidi* obtained a fifty-year peace treaty with Persia – well worth it, from Justinian's point of view, for the renunciation of all Persian claims on Lazica and for the opportunity for him to stand down his army along the seemingly endless eastern frontier. Unfortunately, protection money has always been a poor guarantee for the future; he who starts to pay it usually finds it very hard to stop. Sometimes, too, such methods proved impracticable. Only three years afterwards, in 559, meeting little resistance from the Danubian defences or from the long inner chain of forts that Justinian had erected behind them, a Hunnish tribe known as the Kotrigurs swarmed deep into imperial territory, striking southward into Thessaly and advancing eastward through Thrace to within twenty miles of the capital.

This was not the first invasion that the Empire had suffered in recent years – in 548 and again in 550 the Slavs had overrun the Balkan peninsula as far as the Gulf of Corinth, the Adriatic and the shores of the Aegean – but for the people of Constantinople it was by far the most terrifying, many of them in their panic taking flight with their families and all their movable possessions across the Bosphorus. Justinian himself was not unduly alarmed; the invaders had been able to approach so close only because the Anastasian Walls, which ran some thirty miles west of the city from Selymbria on the Marmara to the Black Sea, had recently been severely damaged in an earthquake. On the other hand the Walls of Theodosius, which formed the inner line of defence, had survived intact and were still fully manned. In such circumstances he knew that they could be trusted to keep out any army in existence, let alone so primitive and ill-equipped a horde as the Kotrigurs.

What he did feel was humiliation: that he, who had destroyed the Ostrogothic and Vandal Kingdoms in Italy and Africa and had re-established the imperial presence in Spain, should have allowed a rough barbarian tribe of which few people had ever heard to approach to his very doorstep, plundering and laying waste everything in their path. This time there was no alternative but to fight. As so often in the past at moments of crisis, he sent for Belisarius.

The general was still only in his middle fifties. Although it was now ten years since he had seen action in the field, he had lost none of his energy, nor any of his astonishing tactical imagination. With only a few hundred men at his disposal he organized a brilliant guerrilla campaign, in the course of which he drew the Kotrigurs into a carefully planned ambush and left 400 dead where they had fallen before driving the remainder back to their base camp near Arcadiopolis (Lüleburgaz). Doubtless he could have driven them further if Justinian had allowed him; with a few more men he could probably have destroyed them utterly. But that was not the Emperor's way. He preferred diplomacy, backed up where necessary with bribes. And so he bought the Kotrigurs just as he had bought the Persians, promising them a generous annual subsidy on condition that they returned to their homeland and made no further incursions into imperial territory.

After so encouraging a start, this was not a very creditable outcome to the affair; it certainly did not merit Justinian's triumphal procession into his capital when he returned that August from Selymbria, whither he had made one of his rare excursions from Constantinople to super-intend the reconstruction of the Anastasian Walls. This extraordinary ceremony, in which Belisarius took no part, was apparently intended to convince his subjects that the Kotrigurs had been annihilated after a great and glorious victory for which the Emperor himself had been alone responsible; that old jealousy for his brilliant commander that had always smouldered in his heart had suddenly flared up again, for the first time since Theodora's day.

Belisarius doubtless took note, and retreated once more into the background. Even then, no one was probably more surprised than he when, in the autumn of 562, several distinguished citizens were accused of plotting against the Emperor's life and one of them named him as being among those implicated. Nothing, of course, was ever proved; but he was shorn of all his dignities and privileges, and lived for eight months in a state of disgrace until Justinian, finally persuaded of his in-nocence, reinstated him. It was presumably this unfortunate incident that gave rise to the legend according to which the Emperor had his old general blinded and thrown out into the streets with a begging-bowl; but the earliest authority for this story dates from more than five cen-turies later and can safely be rejected.[1] After his return to favour Belisarius lived out his life in tranquillity and comfort, dying in March 565 at the age of about sixty. Antonina, now probably well into her eighties, survived him.

That same month saw Justinian's last item of legislation, the end of a long series of enactments on ecclesiastical affairs – they included a law

---

1 Strangely enough, the work in question – a late-eleventh-century account of Constantinople ten-tatively attributed to Michael Psellus – refers on the very same page to the continued existence of the gilded statue of Belisarius that Justinian had erected in 549. This would surely have been taken down had the general suffered the fate described.

fixing the official dates of Christmas and the Epiphany – to which, as he grew older, he devoted more and more of his time. He continued through the summer and early autumn, working at his desk, granting audiences and holding theological discussions; then, on the night of 14 November, quite without warning, he died – of a heart attack presumably, or a stroke. The only official with him at the time was the Patrician Callinicus, Praepositus of the Sacred Bedchamber, who subsequently reported that the Emperor had, with his last breath, designated his successor: his nephew Justin, son of his sister Vigilantia.

There may have been some who doubted this story, but no one was in a position to contradict it. The account of what happened next is also somewhat suspect, relying as it does on the testimony of a third-rate African poet named Corippus who was obviously anxious to ingratiate himself with the new Emperor; but since it was intended to be read by several eye-witnesses to the events it describes, it is probably true in its essentials at least. Corippus sings of how the Patrician quickly summoned a number of senators and how together they hurried to Justin's mansion. There they found the prince, accompanied by his wife Sophia – who was Theodora's niece – in a beautiful room overlooking the sea, and hailed him as their new Emperor. The whole party then repaired to the Palace, where Justinian had been laid out on a golden bier and where Sophia, producing a golden cloth on which she had embroidered scenes from her uncle's life, draped it reverently over the body.

The following morning the imperial pair rode in state to St Sophia where Justin, having been ceremonially raised on a shield in the old Roman manner and crowned with the imperial diadem, made an inaugural speech in which he swore to his orthodox beliefs, undertook to rule with piety and justice and – somewhat ungraciously, it may be thought – expressed his regret that his predecessor in his old age had neglected or mismanaged so many important departments of state. He and Sophia then continued to the Hippodrome, where they received the acclamation of their new subjects and paid off, then and there, all Justinian's debts left unsettled at his death. Only when all these formalities had been completed could they proceed to the funeral itself. The body, now raised on a high catafalque glittering with gold and jewels, was carried slowly from the Palace and through the densely packed but silent streets, followed on foot by Justin and Sophia, the Senate and senior officers of State, the Patriarch, bishops and clergy, the soldiers and the Palace Guard. On arrival at the Church of the Holy Apostles it was borne up the nave to the tomb of Theodora, next to which stood a vast porphyry sarcophagus, empty and waiting. Into this it was gently lowered, while a mass was said for the repose of the old Emperor's soul.

An age had ended. The Empire had passed from an uncle to a nephew, in as smooth and undisputed a succession as had ever been known; but there is no mistaking the fact that, far from inaugurating the glorious new era of which he had dreamt, Justinian was the last Roman Emperor to occupy the throne of Byzantium. It was not simply that he had been born a Latin, and that – if Procopius is to be believed – he spoke barbarous Greek all his life; it was that his mind was cast in a Latin mould, and that throughout his reign he devoted the greater part of his prodigious energies to the restoration of the old Roman Empire. What he never understood was that that Empire was by now an anachronism; the days when one man could stand in undisputed universal authority were gone, and would not return. He had dealt the Vandals and the Ostrogoths their respective death-blows; but the barbarian tribes that pressed along his northern frontiers were as numerous as ever, and ever more eager to enjoy for themselves the warmth and fertility of the Mediterranean lands. No longer moreover were they prepared, as their predecessors had been, to accept the role of barbarians. Already the Slavs had begun their slow but relentless infiltration into the Balkans. As for Italy, in the reconquest of which Justinian had spent almost half his lifetime and which he had regained only at the cost of many thousand lives and untold human misery, it was to remain in imperial hands, after his death, for just three years.

Of all the Emperors of Byzantium, he is the one whom we find the easiest to imagine – thanks to the great contemporary mosaic in the choir of the Church of S. Vitale in Ravenna, dating from 546 when the building was completed. Justinian looks younger than his sixty-four years, but his face – in striking contrast to the imperial diadem that he is wearing and the golden nimbus that frames his head – is plain and unidealized: a portrait clearly taken from the life, as is that of Maximianus, Archbishop of Ravenna, who stands next to him. It is not a fine face – the Macedonian peasant is there for all to see – nor indeed a particularly strong one. Certainly it bears no comparison with that of Theodora on the opposite wall, frowning menacingly from between pendant ropes of pearls as she extends a great jewelled chalice – in a gesture that echoes those of the Three Kings, embroidered along the bottom of her purple robe. No wonder, one feels, that her husband was easily led – if it was she who was doing the leading.

And yet, weak-willed and vacillating as he could often be, Justinian was – with anyone except his wife – an autocrat through and through. He possessed in full measure the faults which are all too frequently associated with absolute power: the vanity, the quickness of temper, the occasional bursts of almost paranoid suspicion, the childish jealousy of anyone – though it was usually Belisarius – who he feared might threaten his prestige. On the other hand his energy astonished all who knew him, while his capacity for hard work was apparently without limit. Known within his court as *akoimētos* – 'the sleepless' – he would spend whole days and nights together pondering on affairs of state, attending personally to the minutest details, wearing out whole successions of secretaries and scribes as the sky darkened, then lightened, then darkened again outside the palace windows. Such, he believed, were the duties imposed by God upon an Emperor; and he performed those duties with conscientious dedication and – at least until the very last years of his life – with unfailing efficiency.

But there were other sides, too, to an Emperor's life. He could not always remain closeted in the imperial chancery. He must also move out among his people, dazzling them with a majesty and magnificence that reflected the glory of the Empire itself. Hence the sumptuous processions, the high ceremonial pomp with which he was surrounded on all public occasions. Hence also his passion for building. The Empire's splendour, he believed, must be made manifest in its capital. Justinian transformed Constantinople; and though many of his most extraordinary monuments – such as the Great Palace, which he entirely rebuilt for himself and his successors, with its famous 'Bronze Gate', the *Chalkē*, ablaze with polychrome marble and mosaic, or his own immense equestrian statue on a column in the Augusteum – have long since crumbled away to dust, the great churches of St Sophia and St Irene and the little miracle of St Sergius and St Bacchus have somehow survived and still have the power to catch the breath. So, even more surprisingly, have certain of his public works – above all the vast columned cisterns now known as the Yerebatansaray and the Binbirdirek, constructions as remarkable in their way as any that can be seen in the city. But – despite the fact that he so seldom left it himself – Justinian did not confine his tremendous building projects to his capital. Roads were laid, sewers were sunk, bridges and aqueducts sprang up in every corner of the Empire; not one but several new cities were founded and given the name of Justiniana in his honour. Antioch, after its sack by Chosroes in 540, was rebuilt on a far more lavish scale than formerly, as were the Syrian towns destroyed in the succession of earthquakes that, in 551 and again in 554, shook the province to its foundations.

One reason for Justinian's compulsive building operations may be that here at least he could be reasonably certain of the outcome of each new enterprise. Not all his other endeavours were equally successful – often through his chronic inability to come to terms with the world as it was, rather than as he would have liked it to be. In his desire for religious unity, as we have seen, he succeeded only in deepening the rift between East and West, orthodox and monophysite, since having once taken a decision it never occurred to him that he might be wrong. Similarly his immense efforts to reform the administration and to purge it of corruption were repeatedly sabotaged by his own extravagance: so great was his need of money that he simply could not afford to be too particular about how it was obtained. Even his conquests had disappointing results. He had hoped, by restoring the conquered lands to the Empire, to bring them peace, prosperity and good government; in fact, the depredations of the imperial soldiery, followed by those of the swarms of tax-collectors and logothetes, left the local populations in misery and destitution. And although vast expenditure in Africa – including a magnificent rebuilding of the city of Carthage – ultimately replaced that economy on a sound footing, in Italy such similar attempts as were made ended in failure, leaving its desperate people all too ready to welcome the Lombard invaders.

But there were successes too, particularly in the field of industry and commerce. By Justinian's day, Constantinople was already the principal centre of the entrepôt trade between Europe and Asia, and carrying on a brisk business with both the Mediterranean world and the Orient. The West, however, was by now sadly impoverished; it was to Cathay and the Indies that the Byzantines looked for their commercial prosperity – and for the silks, spices and precious stones by which they set so much store. But there was one perennial problem which beset all merchants trading in such commodities: the presence of Persia. Caravans taking the land route from the East passed without hindrance as far as the oases of Samarkand and Bokhara and the Oxus River; thereafter, however, they were in Persian territory, where the Great King exercised a strict control over all their transactions – often, in time of war, suspending them completely. The sea route presented the same difficulty, since all cargoes had to be landed in the Persian Gulf. Huge tolls were levied, especially on silk – the most sought-after item of all – and direct trading was forbidden. Sales could only be effected by Persian middlemen, and they too took exorbitant commissions.

This was the stranglehold that Justinian had determined to break. First, he opened up new routes designed to bypass Persia altogether: a northern one via the Crimea, Lazica and the Caucasus – where his subjects were already carrying on a flourishing trade in textiles, jewellery and wine, which they exchanged for leather, furs and slaves – and a southern one which used the Red Sea rather than the Gulf and which involved him, already in the early 530s, in negotiations with the Ethiopian kingdom of Axum. The first of these attempts was partially successful; the latter failed, owing to the firmness of the Persian grip on the Indian and Ceylonese ports. The real breakthrough came only in 552, when a party of orthodox monks sought an audience with the Emperor and offered to obtain through certain contacts in Soghdiana – that distant land beyond the Oxus – a quantity of silkworm eggs, together with enough technical knowledge to establish an industry. Justinian leapt at the chance; before long there were factories not only in Constantinople but in Antioch, Tyre and Beirut (and later at Thebes in Boeotia) and the imperial silk industry – always a state monopoly – became one of the most profitable in the Empire.

After thirty-eight years on the throne, a personality as powerful as that of Justinian could not fail to be missed by his subjects; but he was not deeply mourned. Even in his early days he had never won their love. By the time he had grown old, the tyranny of his tax-gatherers had created dangerous discontent; of the last ten years of his reign, no less than six saw serious rioting in the capital. Economically, despite all his efforts, he left the Empire prostrate: for that reason alone, he cannot be considered a truly great ruler. On the other hand, he also left it infinitely richer in amenities, services and public works, and incomparably more beautiful. He extended its frontiers, he simplified and streamlined its laws. He worked ceaselessly, indefatigably, as few rulers in history have ever worked, for what he believed to be the good of his subjects. When he failed, it was almost invariably because he attempted too much and set his sights too high; never the reverse. More than any other monarch in the history of Byzantium, he stamped the Empire with the force of his own character; centuries were to pass before it emerged from his shadow.

13
The Downward Drift

[565–610]

En Avares Francique truces Gipidesque Getaeque
Totque aliae gentes commotis undique signis
Bella movent. Qua vi tantos superabimus hostes
Cum, virtus Romana, jaces?

Lo, the Avars and the wild Franks, the Gepids and the Getae,[1] and so many other nations, their standards waving, make war on us from every side. What strength shall we find to overcome such fearsome enemies when you, O Roman virtue, lie forgotten?

Justin II, quoted by Corippus,
In Laudem Justini, I, 254–7

Byzantium was indeed beset by its enemies; and whether or not the Emperor Justin II, standing beside the bier of his predecessor, actually lamented the passing of the old Roman virtues as Corippus would have us believe, he certainly did his best to resurrect them. Proud, arrogant, unshakeable in his self-confidence, he believed implicitly that with wisdom and determination, with prudence and fortitude and above all with courage, those enemies could and would be scattered – and that he was the man to do it. He was soon to be painfully, even pitifully, disillusioned.

Justin gave proof of his new philosophy within a week of his accession, when he received an embassy from the Avars, a race of unknown but probably Tartar origin that had made its first appearance in the West only a few years before. His uncle, as might have been expected, had agreed to pay them an annual subsidy in return for their undertaking to keep various other hostile tribes away from the imperial frontiers; but in 562 they themselves had invaded Thrace and had categorically declined to accept the alternative homeland that he offered them in Pannonia. Clearly they were not to be trusted; and when their representatives,

1 A barbarian tribe by then extinct. The reference is presumably to their successors, the Slavs.

having offered formal congratulations to the new Emperor, requested payment of the money due to them under the former agreement it was Justin's turn to refuse. In the course of the following year he showed that he intended to take a similar line with the several other recipients of Justinian's bounty, including the Great King Chosroes himself. Such a display of firmness much increased his popularity, particularly as it seemed to offer prospects of reduced taxes; it soon revealed, however, that Justinian had not been paying out his subsidies for nothing.

Ironically enough, the race that dealt the Empire the severest blow of the many it sustained during Justin's reign was one which had previously caused no trouble and which had never received a penny of Byzantine protection money. The Lombards were a Germanic people who, in the fourth and fifth centuries, had slowly drifted southwards from their homes around the lower Elbe to the region that we should now call Austria. In 567, allied with the Avars, they inflicted an annihilating defeat on their neighbours the Gepids, and in the spring of the following year they crossed the Julian Alps into Italy. It says much for the effects of the wars of Belisarius and Narses that after fifteen years the greater part of the country was still in ruins, its people stunned and demoralized. The Lombards encountered no real resistance anywhere except Pavia, which they captured only after a three-year siege; but they made no move against Ravenna – where the imperial commander Longinus also refrained from opposition, contenting himself with securing the city and its immediate surroundings. Meanwhile the conquerors continued their southward advance. Their King, Alboin, went no further than Tuscany, but many of his nobles pressed on further to set up independent duchies in Spoleto and Benevento which were to survive for another five centuries.[1]

Thus, from the start, the Lombards came to Italy not as raiders but as permanent settlers. They intermarried with the Italians, adopted their language, absorbed their culture and doubtless intended to make the whole peninsula their own. The fact that they made no attempt at this time on Byzantine Ravenna, nor on the cities of the Venetian lagoon associated with it is probably explained by their lack of numbers;

---

1 There is a venerable legend according to which the Lombards had been invited into Italy by Narses, in revenge for an insult that he had received from the Empress Sophia who, so the story goes, had sent him a distaff in a pointed reference to his emasculation. 'I will weave her such a skein,' the old eunuch is said to have muttered, 'that she will not unravel in her lifetime.' It is a good story – but, alas, nothing more.

doubtless for the same reason Naples, Calabria and Sicily also remained in imperial hands. It would be a mistake therefore to see the Lombards as destroyers of everything that Justinian, Belisarius and Narses had achieved; what they did was to impose severe limits on Byzantine authority in Italy and to introduce a powerful new element into the political scene. For over two centuries they were to flourish as an independent kingdom – until at last they were swallowed up in the new-founded Empire of the West and Charlemagne himself assumed their crown.

It might have been expected that so staunch an upholder of the Roman tradition as was the Emperor Justin would have lost no time in sending an army to expel the Lombards from his dominions; but he was fully occupied with the Avars. They too had profited vastly from the victory that the Lombards, with their help, had won over the Gepids. The former having moved into Italy and the latter having been virtually wiped out, the old Lombard territories now lay open to settlement; and once installed in their new homeland the Avars were at last in a position to take their revenge on Justin for his refusal to continue their subsidy. In 568, only a few months after the Lombard invasion, they burst into Dalmatia in a frenzy of wholesale destruction. This time the Emperor reacted quickly, sending as large a force as he could muster under the command of his Count of the Excubitors, Tiberius; but after three years of warfare the exhausted general could continue no longer and was obliged to seek a truce. The ensuing treaty cost Justin 80,000 pieces of silver, a sum far greater than the original subsidy; the blow to his pride must have been greater still.

That same year, 571, saw a dangerous development in the East. Justin was not the only ruler who had difficulties with his neighbours. For King Chosroes, the perennial problem was that of Armenia. It was not so much the fact that the Armenians, having lost not only their independence but also their political unity, were now split between the Byzantine and the Persian Empires; rather was it the fierce pride that they took in their Christianity, which constantly impelled those of them who were under the sway of the Great King to escape from the Persian yoke and, if they could no longer have a Kingdom of their own, to join their compatriots as subjects of the Christian Emperor. Now, suddenly, this chronic disaffection exploded into open revolt and the insurgents appealed to Justin for support – a request which as a Christian monarch he could not possibly ignore. Neither, however, could he hope that Chosroes, already furious at his refusal to continue the tribute promised by his uncle, would any longer restrain himself. Early in 572 the Persian War was resumed. It was to continue, with brief interruptions, for twenty years.

From the outset, things went badly for Byzantium. In November 573 the Persians seized Dara on the Tigris, one of the most important Christian bishoprics in the East; and at much the same time they invaded and ravaged Syria – whence, the chroniclers assure us, they returned with no less than 292,000 captives. Of these, 2,000 of the most beautiful Christian virgins were personally selected by Chosroes for presentation to the Khan of the Turks, whom he hoped to enlist as an ally; but the maidens, when they reached a great river within fifty leagues of the Khan's camp, sought permission from their heavy military escort to bathe, separated themselves a little from the soldiers on grounds of modesty and then, rather than face the simultaneous loss of their religion and their virtue, deliberately drowned themselves.[1]

By this time the Emperor had abandoned his earlier policy of guarded toleration of monophysitism in favour of open persecution – a decision made more reprehensible by the fact that he and Sophia had both been monophysites themselves in their youth, having later adopted the orthodox faith for purely political reasons. There were, so far as we know, no executions or tortures, but monks and nuns were driven from their monasteries and convents and the monophysite clergy were no longer recognized. This abrupt change of attitude occurred in 571, and some historians have attributed it to the beginnings of the mental disturbance which, over the next three years, reduced Justin to a state of hopeless insanity. In his calmer moments, John of Ephesus tells us, his chief amusement was to sit in a little cart and be dragged round his apartments by his keepers; but he was often subject to fits of extreme violence, during which he would attack anyone who approached him[2] and try to hurl himself out of the windows, which had to be fitted with bars for his protection. In these moods there was only one way to pacify him: to

---

1 John of Ephesus, *Ecclesiastical History*, VI, i. This period marks the first appearance of the Turks in the history of the West. In 568 or 569 they had sent an embassy to Constantinople, and a treaty of allegiance in the event of renewed hostilities with Persia had been signed the following year; but Chosroes was evidently not unhopeful of winning them over.

2 'They selected strong young men to act as his chamberlains and guard him; and when these youths were obliged to run after him and hold him, he, being a powerful man, would turn upon them and seize them with his teeth, and tear them; and two of them he bit so severely about the head as to do them serious injury; and they took to their sick beds, and the report spread about the city that the Emperor had eaten two of his chamberlains' (John of Ephesus, III, iii).

speak the name of Harith, the leader of a minor Arab tribe known as the Ghassanids. For reasons that were never altogether understood, this relatively unimportant chieftain inspired him with such terror that he instantly became quiet.

Sophia had meanwhile taken over the government of the Empire, and in 574 she persuaded Chosroes to grant a year's truce in return for a payment of 45,000 *nomismata*; but at the end of that same year, finding the burdens of state too heavy to bear alone, she took advantage of one of her husband's brief spells of lucidity to persuade him to raise Tiberius – whose defeat by the Avars had not, apparently, affected his reputation – to the rank of Caesar. From that moment the two of them acted as joint regents; and when Justin died on 4 October 578 his former Count of the Excubitors was his uncontested successor.

For Tiberius, it had not been an easy regency. The Turks, furious at the peace with Persia about which they had not been consulted and which they considered a betrayal, had repudiated the alliance and seized a Byzantine stronghold in the Crimea; and in 577 a vast horde of Slavs – their numbers were conservatively estimated at a hundred thousand – had poured into Thrace and Illyricum and settled there, the few and insignificant imperial garrisons being powerless to stop them. A more immediate problem than either, however, was that presented by Sophia herself. Not for nothing was she Theodora's niece. Having secured her colleague's promotion, she immediately began to show a marked reluctance to share her authority with him – especially in financial matters, in which he was, she claimed, unnecessarily extravagant. For as long as her husband lived, she insisted on keeping the keys of the imperial treasury herself, granting the unfortunate Caesar only the most meagre of allowances on which to keep himself and his family; she also jealously refused to permit his wife Ino or his two daughters to set foot in the Palace. Only after Justin's death did Tiberius finally dare to assert himself: Sophia, despite several unsuccessful plots to dethrone him, suddenly found herself deprived of her court and placed under close surveillance, in which unhappy condition she was to remain for the rest of her natural life while Ino, now rechristened Anastasia, was at last able to enjoy the privileges so long denied her.

The new Emperor, who assumed on his accession the additional name of Constantine, was – in marked contrast to his two predecessors – outstandingly popular with his people. He was also a pragmatist who, throughout his short reign, did his utmost to stem the steady decline in Byzantine fortunes. Persecution of the monophysites was stopped at once; being himself a Thracian, he instinctively understood that with Greek influence everywhere on the increase it was above all the Greek-speaking provinces of Asia that must be kept loyal and contented, and if that meant antagonizing the West it could not be helped.[1] At the same time, in a deliberate reaction to the haughty aristocratic style favoured by Justinian and Justin, he tried to broaden the base of government by increasing the powers both of the previously moribund Senate and of the demes – the Greens and the Blues – which had been suppressed by Justinian after the Nika riots. The principal focus of his attention, however, was the army. The moment he had control of the Exchequer he set out to strengthen it by every means within his power, and in 581 he established a new elite corps of 15,000 barbarian *foederati*[2] which, centuries later, was to evolve into the famous Varangian Guard.

With all his excellent intentions and his unremitting effort, Tiberius Constantine might have proved a great Emperor. The fact that he failed to do so can be attributed in a large degree to the fatal weakness against which Sophia had so forcibly reacted – his uncontrolled liberality. Not content with remitting, soon after his accession, one quarter of all taxes levied throughout the Empire, at various times in his reign he dispensed huge amounts of largesse in every direction. In his first year alone he gave away no less than 7,200 pounds of gold – 800 of them to the army in Asia – to say nothing of silver, silk and other luxuries in almost insane abundance. The next three years saw further distributions on a similar scale; and it was perhaps just as well for the imperial treasury that by the end of the fourth he was dead – of poison, it was rumoured, taken in a dish of early but particularly succulent mulberries.

Tiberius Constantine died on 13 August 582, in his palace of the Hebdomon.[3] A week before, he had appointed as his successor a young Cappadocian named Maurice, to whom he had simultaneously given his second daughter Constantina in marriage. Maurice could already boast a distinguished military record; he had just returned from four years at the Persian front, during which time he had largely reorganized the army, breathing new life and hope into its dispirited ranks. 'Make your reign my finest epitaph,' were the last words of the dying Emperor; and for

1 It must, however, in justice be recorded that he was a good deal less sympathetic to Arianism – presumably because, being a heresy favoured almost exclusively by barbarians, it did not in his view deserve similar respect.
2 See p. 108.
3 A suburb of the city which lay at the seventh milestone.

the next twenty years Maurice was to rule the Empire with a firm and competent hand.[1] Coming to the throne during one of those brief lulls which occasionally interrupted the long drawn-out war with Persia, he was able to give serious thought to the situation in the West and to what was left of Justinian's conquests in Italy and Africa. The result was the two great Exarchates which he created – Ravenna and Carthage; organized on strict military lines under an Exarch who wielded absolute power over both the military and the civilian administration, they were long to remain the principal western outposts of imperial authority.

All too soon, however, hostilities with Persia flared up again. Old Chosroes had died in 579, a few months after Justin, and had been succeeded by his son Hormisdas, who had inherited to the full his father's love of battle. He had sustained a grave defeat at the hands of Maurice in 581, after which he had needed time to rebuild his shattered army; but by the end of the following year he had returned to the attack. A detailed account of the subsequent course of the war would be tedious for writer and reader alike, and is in any case unnecessary; suffice it to say that, despite a serious mutiny of their army in 588, the Romans somehow managed to hold their ground for two more years, until a *coup d'état* in Persia led to a civil war. Hormisdas was killed; his son Chosroes II fled into Byzantine territory and appealed to Maurice for help. Despite the almost unanimous advice of his ministers, the Emperor saw a chance and seized it: he told the prince that he would be happy to provide the assistance he needed – but only in return for a treaty of peace between the two Empires, by the terms of which both Persian Armenia and eastern Mesopotamia, including the two great cities of Dara and Martyropolis on the Tigris, would be restored to Byzantium. In 591, with his support, young Chosroes overthrew the opposition – and kept his promises to the letter. The Persian War was over, sooner and on more favourable terms than anyone had dared to expect.

Now at last Maurice could fling the whole weight of his army against a foe which, during the past two years, had become every bit as dangerous as the Persians had ever been. In 571, the Avars had won their first major victory over Tiberius – by then Caesar and effective co-regent of the Empire. Next, in 581, they had captured by trickery the key city of Sirmium on the river Sava, which they were soon able to use as a base for the mopping up of several poorly-defended Byzantine

---

1 Our main primary source for the reign of Maurice is the *History* of Theophylact Simocatta, an Egyptian whose name literally means a flat-nosed cat and in whose style – I quote Professor Bury – 'bombast, in all its frigidity, is carried to an unprecedented extreme'.

fortresses along the Danube. Meanwhile they continually increased their demands for tribute, until by 584 Maurice – whose propitiatory presents of an elephant and a golden bed had been contemptuously rejected by the Avar Khagan – was obliged to agree to a revised figure of 100,000 pieces. By this time the Emperor had appointed as general of his army in the West a former commander of his bodyguard named Comentiolus; but the army itself amounted to a mere 10,000 men, of whom only slightly more than half were capable soldiers; and apart from one significant victory at Adrianople he had little success in stemming the barbarian tide.

The peace with Persia meant that Maurice suddenly found himself with a far greater force at his disposal for deployment in the West;[1] and such was his exhilaration that he announced his intention of taking the field in person. The Patriarch and Senate, to say nothing of his own family, implored him not to risk his life in such a manner; he refused to listen. As it happened, they need not have worried. The Emperor had got no further than Anchialus – on the Gulf of Burgas, in modern Bulgaria – when the unexpected arrival of a Persian embassy in Constantinople recalled him hurriedly to the capital; and by the time the ambassadors had departed he had lost interest in joining his army. Perhaps it was just as well. Despite his new-found strength the war was to continue, against both the predatory Avars and the immigrant Slavs, for the rest of his reign; and was to prove, indirectly, the cause of his death.

Maurice's difficulties in the West were further complicated by the fact that his relations with the Papacy were deteriorating fast. There had been several minor points of contention over the years, but the serious trouble began only in 588, when the Patriarch of Constantinople, John the Faster, adopted the title of 'Ecumenical' – thereby implying universal supremacy over all other prelates, including the Pope himself. John was not the first Patriarch to make this claim; the title had been used at various times for the best part of a century and until now had passed apparently unnoticed. This time, however, there were angry expostulations from Pope Pelagius; and still more vigorous protests followed two years later, when Pelagius was succeeded by one of the most formidable

1 As Theophylact puts it: 'And so, now that the day smiled upon affairs in the East, and made not her progress mythically, in Homeric fashion, from a barbaric couch, but refused to be called "rosy-fingered" inasmuch as the sword was not crimsoned with blood, the Emperor transferred his forces to Europe' – a fair enough example of the literary style admired at the time, through which the luckless historian is compelled to wade.

characters ever to assume the throne of St Peter: Gregory the Great. Gregory at once fired off two letters. The first was to Maurice demanding, for the sake of the peace of the Empire, that he call his recalcitrant Patriarch to order; the second he addressed to the Empress Constantina, begging her to intervene with her husband; John's arrogant assumption of the ecumenical title was, he claimed, a clear indication that the age of Antichrist was at hand.

Whether Constantina ever replied we do not know; but her husband did, and he fully supported his Patriarch. From that time forward, Gregory's irritation is plain to see; even so reasonable a measure as Maurice's law forbidding serving soldiers to desert on the grounds that they wished to enter monasteries was denounced by him as a further blow struck against the Church. But the Byzantines were irritated too, and it may well have been as a result of the Pope's protests that the fatal word soon became a regular part of the Patriarchal style. Gregory's successors wisely decided to ignore it; but what both sides must have known well enough was that the incident, trivial as it might seem in retrospect, marked another stage in the steadily growing rivalry between the Eastern and Western Churches – a rivalry which, four and a half centuries later, was to end in schism.

From the moment that he assumed the throne of Byzantium, Maurice had had to face one overriding problem: lack of money. Thanks to his predecessor's extravagance he had inherited a virtually bankrupt state, and the almost incessant warfare in both East and West – to say nothing of the vast subsidies which he was obliged to pay to his potential enemies – made it impossible for him to replenish the imperial coffers as he would have wished. The result was a parsimoniousness which, in his later years, became an obsession – making him not only unpopular with his subjects but oddly insensitive to what they would or would not tolerate. Already in 588 his proclamation that all military rations were to be reduced by a quarter had led to a widespread mutiny among the army of the East; in 599 he is said to have refused – once more on grounds of economy – to ransom no less than 12,000 prisoners taken by the Avars, who consequently put them all to death; and three years later, in 602, he issued the most disastrous decree of all: that the army should not return to base for the coming winter, but should sit it out in the inhospitable and barbarous lands beyond the Danube.

The reaction was immediate and dramatic. The army had been fighting hard for eight months, and was physically and mentally exhausted.

During that time the men had acquired considerable amounts of booty, which was however useless to them until they could sell it in the markets of the capital. There was, in any case, a generally accepted tradition that soldiers returned for the winter to their wives and families. Instead, they were now being ordered to endure the intense cold and discomfort of a winter under canvas on the plains of Pannonia, living as best they could off the local populations and in constant danger from marauding barbarian clans, all because their miserly Emperor claimed that he could not afford to send them home. When they reached the fortress of Securisca (now the Bulgarian town of Nikopol) at which they were to cross the Danube, they flatly refused to go another step. Their general, Peter – whose position was scarcely improved by the fact that he was the Emperor's brother – argued and pleaded with them in vain. Turning their backs on him in scorn, they raised one of their own centurions, a certain Phocas, on their shields and proclaimed him their leader.

Peter, doubtless considering himself lucky to have escaped with his life, hurried back to Constantinople with news of the revolt, bearing with him a message to the Emperor from the rebels, who were even then preparing to march on the capital. There was no question, they emphasized, of Phocas being made Emperor. Maurice himself they would no longer tolerate, but they had not withdrawn their allegiance from his family: they would be happy to acclaim either his seventeen-year-old son Theodosius (who would be the first Emperor since Theodosius II to have been born in the purple), or failing him his father-in-law Germanus, as successor to the throne.

Both men chanced to be away together on a hunting expedition, but were immediately recalled by Maurice and accused of treason. Theodosius was flogged; Germanus, fearing (with good reason) that his life was in danger, fled for refuge to St Sophia where – with the help of numerous adherents – he successfully resisted several attempts by the imperial guard to drag him out by force. The Emperor meanwhile had turned for support to the demes – the two popular factions of the Hippodrome, brought out of their temporary obscurity by Tiberius and once again influential forces in the city. He had hoped to ensure the allegiance of both the Blues and the Greens, and had been relieved when both had agreed to man the Theodosian Walls against the mutineers' advance; but he soon discovered that while he could rely on the loyalty of the 900 active Blues, that of the 1,500 Greens was dangerously uncertain. By now riots had broken out all over the capital, and an angry crowd had gathered in the square outside the Palace, hurling imprecations at the Emperor and baying for his blood.

That night – it was 22 November – Maurice, his wife Constantina and their eight children, together with Constantine Lardys, the Praetorian Prefect of the East whose house had been burnt down by the mob, crept out of the Palace in disguise and took a small boat across the Marmara to Asia. A violent storm carried them far off their course, but they landed at last on the shore of the Bay of Nicomedia, near the Church of St Autonomus the Martyr. Here the Emperor, incapacitated by a severe attack of gout, was obliged to remain with Constantina and the rest of his children; Theodosius and the Prefect, however, headed east to the court of the Persian King. Chosroes owed his throne to Maurice's support; now was his opportunity to repay the debt.

In Constantinople, Germanus had meanwhile emerged from his refuge in St Sophia and, encouraged by the popular support he had received, now made his bid for the throne. Everything, he knew, depended on the attitude of the demes. He himself had always favoured the Blues, but it was clear that his cause would be hopeless without the backing of the far more numerous and influential Greens – in return for which he promised their leader, Sergius, rich rewards once the Empire were his. The offer was carefully considered, but refused. Convinced in their hearts that despite his protestations he would never really abandon their rivals, the Greens cast in their lot with Phocas, who had by now reached the out-skirts of the capital.

Phocas too had made up his mind. His early disclaimer of any imperial ambitions may have been sincere at the time, but now the situation had changed: of the two candidates for the throne, Theodosius had fled and Germanus, it appeared, was no longer acceptable. From his headquarters in the Hebdomon he sent an emissary into Constantinople with a message to be read from the high pulpit of St Sophia, requiring Patriarch, Senate and people to come out at once to the Church of St John the Baptist; and there, a few hours later, 'that impudent centaur' (as Theophylact[1] describes him) was crowned Emperor of the Romans. The following morn-ing, in a chariot drawn by four white horses, he rode in triumph into his capital, scattering showers of gold to the populace as he passed; the day after, he made the traditional donations to the soldiers and, with still greater pomp, invested his wife Leontia with the rank and title of Augusta. During this last ceremony a scuffle broke out between the Blues and

1 The full story of Maurice's downfall is given by Theophylact (*History*, VIII, vi–xii).

the Greens, in the course of which several Blues were heard to shout: 'Beware, beware! Remember that Maurice is not dead!' Phocas is unlikely to have forgotten; but it was a state of affairs that he was determined to remedy. A troop of soldiers was dispatched to Asia, where it quickly ran the fugitives to earth. The Emperor made no attempt to escape; there was no fight left in him. Indeed he appeared almost to welcome his captors, even sending a messenger to recall Theodosius and Constantine Lardys and dissuading the children's nurse from her attempt to substitute another child for one of the imperial princes. He is said to have watched impassively as his four younger sons were butchered before his eyes, only murmuring, 'Thou art just, O Lord, and just are thy judgements,' again and again. Then without another word he himself faced the executioner who dispatched him at a stroke. The bodies were cast into the sea, and Theophylact tells us that huge crowds came down to the shore to gaze on the corpses as they floated on the still waters of the bay. The troop commander, Lilius, meanwhile returned with the five heads to Constantinople, where they were later exposed at the Hebdomon.

As a ruler, Maurice had his faults. He was too much given to nepotism, a tendency which led him to advance worthless men like his brother Peter to positions far beyond their capabilities and to bestow large estates on members of his family and other favourites. His subjects, too, were surprised – in view of the parsimoniousness for which he was famous – to see the vast sums that he spent on his birthplace, the insignificant little Cappadocian town of Arabissus, in his determination to transform it into a rich and splendid city.[1] We have seen, finally, his curious insensitivity to the feelings of his subjects and his inability to judge how far an unpopular policy could safely be pursued. In other ways, however, he proved a wise and far-sighted statesman. Quite apart from his newly established Exarchates of Carthage and Ravenna, he redrew the administrative map of the Empire, incorporating the scattered imperial possessions in both East and West into a new provincial system far simpler and more logical than the old. He was careful, too, always to place the ultimate responsibility for any given province in the hands of the military rather than those of the civil authorities. It was the former *magister militum* who was now accorded the new title of Exarch, effectively the imperial viceroy and answerable to none but the Emperor himself. Had

---

1 Now the still more insignificant village of Yarpuz, a little to the north of Maraş. When an earthquake destroyed all that Maurice had built, he immediately began all over again.

such firm organization existed in Justinian's day, Italy would surely have been conquered a good deal more expeditiously than it was, and might even have succeeded in turning the Lombard tide.

Thus the tragedy of Maurice's overthrow, even though he brought it largely on himself, was one that he had done little to deserve. By a combination of determination, clear-sightedness and sheer hard work he left the Empire immeasurably stronger than he found it – which was more than could have been said of any of his three immediate predecessors. Had he allowed his soldiers only a little more bread, or his people just a few more circuses, he would easily have escaped the fate he was called upon to suffer. Even as things were, it was only a matter of weeks before his subjects were mourning his death, asking themselves how they could ever have sacrificed him for the depraved and sadistic monster who took his place.

The chronicler George Cedrenus has left us a physical description of the Emperor Phocas. It hardly predisposes us in his favour. Under a tangle of red hair his thick, beetling eyebrows met across his nose; the rest of his face was deformed by a huge, angry scar that turned crimson when he was aroused, giving it a still more hideous aspect than that which it normally bore. He was not, however, as pleasant as he looked. Debauched, drunken and almost pathologically cruel, he loved, we are told, nothing so much as the sight of blood. Until his day, torture had been rare in the Byzantine Empire; it was Phocas who introduced the gallows and the rack, the blindings and the mutilations which were to cast so sinister a shadow over the centuries to come.

His eight-year reign saw the Empire at the nadir of its fortunes: a depth of abasement, humiliation and despair unequalled at any previous moment in its history. It was not the first time, nor would it be the last, that a popular revolution had given place to a reign of terror. The deaths of Maurice and his sons proved to be only the beginning; thereafter, executions and judicial murders followed thick and fast – among them those of the Praetorian Prefect Constantine Lardys; of Comentiolus; of the Emperor's brother Peter; and, almost certainly, of his son Theodosius – though a persistent rumour that he had escaped to Persia seems to have been believed by Phocas himself, who soon afterwards had one of his principal henchmen put to death on a charge of having accepted bribes to assist the young prince's flight. Of those principally concerned in the drama the only survivors – apart from the new Emperor and his friends – were Germanus, who swore loyalty to Phocas and whose life was accordingly spared on condition that he became a priest, and the Empress Constantina, who was dispatched with her three daughters to a nunnery. All those suspected of continuing loyalty to Maurice, whatever their rank or station, met their deaths by the axe, the bowstring or, more frequently, slow torture.

King Chosroes, meanwhile, had found in the fate of his friend and benefactor the pretext he had long been awaiting, and in 603 launched a huge army against Byzantium. Now the Empire had at that time only one first-rate general in the East, a certain Narses – he was, so far as is known, no relation of his more famous namesake – who had distinguished himself in the previous phase of the war and at whose name, we are told, every Persian child cringed in terror. For Maurice, Narses would have sprung to arms and, quite probably, driven back the invader; for Phocas he refused to budge. He had heard enough of the upstart Emperor to be determined to unseat him, even at the cost of a Persian victory. Rallying his men to his own standard, he rose in rebellion, seized Edessa (the modern Urfa) and appealed to Chosroes for help. That part of the army that had remained loyal to Phocas thus found itself obliged to fight two enemies simultaneously and soon took flight. Narses and Chosroes met in Edessa, together – if an Armenian chronicler is to be believed – with a young pretender who claimed to be Theodosius, and began planning their joint attack upon the usurper.

It was now plain to Phocas that if he were to save his skin he would need every soldier he possessed on the eastern front. He quickly concluded a truce with the Avars – promising them a huge annual tribute in return – and flung the whole weight of his army against the advancing Persians. But it was of no avail. Narses was lured to Constantinople under a guarantee of safe conduct, ostensibly to discuss peace terms. If only the Emperor had acted in good faith, he could probably have come to some arrangement and even won back his general's allegiance. Instead, the moment Narses reached the capital he was seized and burnt alive. At a stroke, Phocas had deprived himself of his best commander. Only two others remained of comparable quality; and of those one died of wounds after a battle, while the other was recalled on suspicion of treason and cast into prison in Constantinople. Supreme command of the army passed to the Emperor's nephew, one Domentziolus, a callow and inexperienced young soldier who proved no match for his brilliant adversaries. Over the next four years the Persians overran much of western Mesopotamia and Syria, Armenia and Cappadocia, Paphlagonia and Galatia in a steady, relentless tide, until in 608 their advance guard was encamped at Chalcedon, within sight of the capital. Meanwhile the Slavs and the Avars – the latter oblivious of the protection money they had received – continued to flood into the Balkan peninsula.

Desperate crises of the kind that the Empire was now facing tend to arouse strong feelings of national solidarity, the threatened people forgetting its political, social or even its confessional differences in its determination to present a united front against the common enemy. If Phocas had any chance left to him of averting disaster, it would have been to encourage such an attitude among his subjects. Instead, he chose this of all moments to initiate an all-out campaign for the persecution and forcible conversion of the Jews. Most of his intended victims lived in the eastern provinces – in the front line, as it were, in face of the Persian attack; to alienate them at such a time was an act of barely credible folly. The result was as might have been expected. The Jews of Antioch rose in revolt and began in their turn to massacre the local Christians, inflicting a particularly horrible and obscene death on the Patriarch, Anastasius. Thousands of terrified citizens, Christian and Jewish alike, fled the butchery and sought refuge in Persian-held territory. The whole Empire, it seemed, was rapidly sinking into anarchy.

Meanwhile, plot succeeded plot in swift succession. In one of them, Phocas was to be murdered in the Hippodrome, his place taken by the Praetorian Prefect of the East, Theodorus; in another, the Prefect was to be supplanted by Germanus – still as ambitious as ever, despite the holy orders he had reluctantly assumed. Both of these conspiracies were betrayed and reported to the Emperor, who had all those involved immediately executed – including the ex-Empress Constantina and her three daughters. More executions followed as Phocas, seeing the Empire tottering about him, grew more and more paranoically unstable. In the capital, the Greens revolted and set fire to several public buildings; in the eastern provinces there was chaos. Christians and Jews were now everywhere at each others' throats, while the latter openly allied themselves with the Persians – who, not surprisingly, received them with open arms. Even as far away as Palestine, what had begun as faction fighting between the Blues and the Greens in Jerusalem was now assuming the dimensions of civil war.

It was, of all places, from Africa that deliverance came at last. Ruling as Exarch in the city of Carthage was a certain Heraclius, who had been one of Maurice's principal generals in the war with Persia some twenty years before. With him as his second-in-command was his brother Gregorius. The two men were both by now in their late middle age –

too old, certainly, to take any decisive action themselves beyond breaking off communications with Constantinople and cutting off the grain supplies on which the capital depended; but in the course of the year 608 they raised a considerable army and prepared a fleet of warships, which they placed under the command of their respective sons: the army under Nicetas, son of Gregorius, and the fleet under the son of Heraclius, who bore the same name as his father. Towards the end of the year, Nicetas set out overland for Egypt, where he soon succeeded in capturing Alexandria before continuing his advance on Constantinople;[1] and in 609 the young Heraclius sailed for Thessalonica, receiving a rapturous reception at all the ports at which he called on his way. Once arrived in the city, he spent the best part of a year rallying all the European malcontents to his banner and collecting further ships to swell his expedition; then, in the summer of 610, he set off on the last lap of his journey.

Even now, he was in no particular hurry. There were plenty more stops along the route to Constantinople, each one providing its quota of new adherents; and it must have been a formidable force indeed that, on Saturday 3 October, sailed confidently through the Marmara to anchor at the mouth of the Golden Horn. Heraclius was not expecting opposition. For some time now he had been in secret correspondence with Priscus, the Emperor's son-in-law and another one of Maurice's old commanders, who had himself narrowly escaped execution a year or two before[2] and who had assured him that he would be welcomed in the city as its deliverer; he knew, too, that in the unlikely event of trouble he could rely on the entire faction of the Greens to intervene on his behalf. In fact, no intervention was necessary. Two days later the captive Emperor, already shorn of his imperial robes, was rowed out to his ship and dragged into his presence.

'Is it thus,' asked Heraclius, 'that you have governed the Empire?'

'Will you,' replied Phocas, with unexpected spirit, 'govern it any better?'

It was a good question; but it was hardly calculated to incline Heraclius

---

1 Owing to his delay in Egypt, Nicetas was to reach Constantinople some time after his cousin, but Gibbon tells us that 'he submitted without a murmur to the fortune of his friend, and his laudable intentions were rewarded with an equestrian statue and a daughter of the Emperor'.

2 Priscus had been conspiring against his father-in-law ever since the leaders of the demes had erected statues of his wife and himself next to those of the Emperor and Empress in the Hippodrome; Phocas, in a paroxysm of fury, had ordered them to be removed and had been with difficulty restrained from executing Priscus on a charge of treason. Two years after his accession Heraclius, having rather better cause to doubt Priscus's loyalty, ordered him forcibly tonsured and removed to a monastery, where he died a year or two later.

towards clemency. One of our sources, John of Antioch, tells us that he had Phocas chopped into pieces to make 'a carcase fit for hounds'; others suggest that he was delivered up to the combined mercies of the Blues and the Greens, to much the same effect. His henchmen and cronies suffered similar fates; and that very afternoon, in the Chapel of St Stephen within the Great Palace, Heraclius underwent two separate, though near-simultaneous, religious ceremonies. First he was married – to a lady to whom he had long been betrothed. Formerly known as Fabia, she now changed her name to Eudocia. Immediately afterwards, he was crowned Emperor.

14

The First Crusader

[610–41]

Noblest of the Gods, King and Master of the whole Earth, Son of the great
Hormisdas, CHOSROES, to Heraclius his vile and insensate slave:

Refusing to submit to our rule, you call yourself lord and sovereign. You
seize and distribute our treasure, you deceive our servants. You never cease to
annoy us with your bands of brigands. Have I not destroyed you Greeks? You
say that you trust in God; why then has he not delivered out of my hand
Caesarea, Jerusalem, Alexandria? . . . Could I not also destroy Constantinople?

Letter from Chosroes II
to Heraclius, *c*. 622

Now in the prime of life – he was probably about thirty-six – fair-haired
and broad-chested, still glowing with his triple triumph of conquest,
marriage and coronation in a single day, Heraclius must have appeared
something of a demi-god when, on the evening of Monday 5 October
610, he stepped out of the Great Palace, his lovely young wife on his
arm. And yet, among all his cheering subjects, there were surely many
who feared lest this twenty-first Emperor of Byzantium might also
be the last.

Never had any of his predecessors inherited so desperate a situation.
To the west, the Avars and the Slavs had overrun the Balkans, their
raiding parties regularly approaching the very gates of Constantinople; to
the east the Persian watch-fires at Chalcedon, immediately across the
Bosphorus, were clearly visible from the windows of the imperial palace.
The capital, he knew, was safe for the moment: the Theodosian Walls
were in good repair, while the Persians had no ships by which to pass
over the straits, which were in any case ceaselessly patrolled by his own
fleet. Constantine the Great had chosen the site for its impregnability,
and he had chosen well. But though the centre of the Empire might
remain secure, the extremities were fast falling away. The entire Balkan

peninsula was by now effectively lost to the Slavs; and the Persian advance, halted as it might be at the frontiers of Europe, was continuing in Asia unchecked – and was now receiving additional momentum all the time, thanks to the enthusiastic support of the Jewish communities. Within a year of Heraclius's accession, the brilliant Persian general Shahr-Baraz – the 'Royal Boar' – had seized Antioch. In 613 he added Damascus, and in 614 Jerusalem.

Of the many catastrophes that have befallen this unhappiest of cities during its long history, the capture of Jerusalem by the Persians was one of the most hideous. The tale begins innocently enough: the citizens accepted the quite reasonable terms offered them – including a Persian garrison – and for a month all was well. Then, without warning, the Christians suddenly rose up and slaughtered every Persian and Jew on whom they could lay their hands. Those fortunate enough to escape hurried at once to Shahr-Baraz, who had by now continued his advance with the army. He turned back, only to find that Jerusalem had once more closed its gates against him. For the best part of a month it held out; only after the Persians had mined the walls were they able to smash their way into the city.

What followed was a massacre – and one of quite unprecedented savagery. It lasted for three long days, at the end of which hardly a Christian was left alive, hardly a house standing. The Church of the Holy Sepulchre was burnt to ashes, together with most of the other principal Christian shrines; the Patriarch Zacharias was taken prisoner; the True Cross was seized, together with all the other most sacred relics of the Crucifixion, including the Holy Lance and Sponge, and carried away to Ctesiphon. Nor, it appears, were the Persians the only – or even the worst – aggressors. Many Jews had survived the first uprising; many more had taken service with the Persian army; and more still, we may assume, when they heard of what was going on in Jerusalem, hurried up from the neighbouring towns and villages to settle old scores. According to one of our principal sources for the period, the monk Theophanes – who was, however, writing 200 years later, and from a strongly Christian viewpoint – no less than 90,000 of his co-religionists met their deaths at Jewish hands during those nightmare days. None, he maintains, were spared – least of all the monks and nuns, who were often singled out for especially brutal treatment.

The news of the destruction of Jerusalem, and above all of the removal of the True Cross, was received with horror in Constantinople. No clearer mark of divine displeasure could be imagined. But it was not the end of the Empire's tribulations. Three years later the Great King turned his attention to Egypt; and before long one of the most indispensable sources of the imperial corn supply had become a Persian province. With the entire Greek peninsula now lost to the Slavs and the rich wheatfields of Thrace in Avar hands, the inevitable result was famine, bringing pestilence in its train. It began to look as though the Romans might, after all, be brought to their knees – though by starvation rather than conquest.

Already in 618 Heraclius had virtually decided on a drastic and unprecedented step – that of abandoning the capital altogether and falling back on his home city of Carthage, there to prepare a major offensive against his enemies similar to that which had led to the elimination of Phocas. From the point of view of the Empire as a whole, such a course would have had much to recommend it. It would have enabled him to make his dispensations in a way that was impossible in beleaguered Constantinople; it would have rid him of the inhibiting and frequently destructive influence of the Byzantine aristocracy and Senate, which had grown dangerously powerful since the death of Justinian; and it would have spared him the expense of maintaining the imperial palace and the court ceremonial that went with it, liberating huge sums of money for the raising of manpower and the provision of equipment and supplies. The citizens of Constantinople, on the other hand, were predictably horrified. Led by Sergius the Patriarch, they came to the Emperor in a body and implored him to remain with them; and Heraclius gave in to their entreaties. It may be that he feared a revolution if he stood firm; perhaps he interpreted as a sign from heaven the recent shipwreck, in a violent storm, of the vessel bound for Carthage on which he had secretly entrusted an advance consignment of the palace treasure some weeks before. In any case, he must have seen in this appeal the perfect opportunity of renewing the covenant with his subjects. If he remained with them, they in turn must be ready to accept whatever sacrifices he might demand of them, whatever hardships he might impose. Unhesitatingly, they accepted; and a day or two later, in the Church of St Sophia and in the presence of the Patriarch, he gave them a solemn oath that he would never desert the city.

By this time Heraclius had already been eight years on the throne – eight years about which our chief sources for the period are unusually silent; and more than one modern historian has expressed surprise at so long a period of apparent inactivity on the part of a young and energetic

Emperor, at a time when the Empire was facing one of the most awesome crises in its history. Was it really necessary – so the argument runs – for him to wait twelve years after his accession before leading his army into battle? The answer, surely, is that it was. He had found the Empire in a state of chaos: the treasury exhausted, the army demoralized and dispirited, the civil administration incompetent and hopelessly corrupt. Confronted as he was by two such formidable enemies, there could be no question of victory until he had subjected the whole state to a thorough reorganization, moulding it once again into an efficient fighting machine. Meanwhile, he refused to be hurried. The walls of Constantinople and the waters of the Bosphorus would keep his foes at bay for as long as was required, if not a good deal longer. Let Chosroes whittle away at the eastern provinces if he must; once he were defeated, all the lost territory would be regained at a stroke. But to march against him without adequate preparation would be to risk the defeat not only of the Roman army but – since he was resolved to lead it in person – of Heraclius himself. And that, almost certainly, would be the end of the Empire.

Therefore, the very day after his coronation, he had set to work. His first task was to make those of his dominions as were still within his control properly ready for war. His years at Carthage – one of the two great exarchates established by Maurice some thirty years before – had shown him the wisdom of running the outlying provinces on strict military lines; and it was on just such a basis that he now began to reorganize all that part of Asia Minor that had not been lost to the Persians. This consisted, roughly speaking, of the land that lay west of a jagged line running north-east from Seleucia (the modern Selifke) on the Mediterranean coast to Rhizus (Rize) on the Black Sea;[1] and Heraclius now divided it into four Themes – the Opsikion to the north-west, the Armeniakon to the north-east, the Anatolikon in the centre and finally the Carabisiani, which covered most of the southern coast and its hinterland. The new designation was significant in itself: *thema* was the normal Greek word used to describe a division of troops, so the warlike character of the scheme was emphasized from the start. Not only was each theme placed under the supreme command of a *strategos*, or military governor; but considerable numbers of soldiers, or potential soldiers, were settled in each, receiving inalienable grants of land on condition of hereditary military service.

1 The Persian camp at Chalcedon had been merely a temporary outpost; all the land around it had remained loyal to the Emperor.

This new arrangement was to prove of immense value for the defence of the Empire in the years to come. It laid the foundations for a well-trained and on the whole reliable native army, and it effectively put an end to the old hit-and-miss system whereby the Emperor was obliged to recruit bodies of barbarian or other foreign mercenaries who all too frequently betrayed him. Well before the end of the seventh century there had grown up, all over western Anatolia, a whole new class of soldier-farmers who maintained themselves on their own land and, in return for a nominal stipend, were expected to present themselves for duty, armed and mounted, when summoned. The former provincial administration with its Praetorian Prefectures – dating largely from the days of Diocletian and Constantine and in some respects older still – soon withered away.

Then there were the imperial finances to be restored – another task which could not be accomplished overnight. Heraclius tackled it in a number of ways – through taxation, forced loans and the imposition of crippling fines on former members of Phocas's notoriously corrupt bureaucracy; he was also able to arrange for large subsidies from his family and friends in Africa. But by far the most significant single source of revenue was – for the first time in its history – the orthodox Church. For Patriarch Sergius, the coming war was to be a war of religion, a war which would signal the final victory of the forces of Christ over the pagan fire-worshippers; and he was resolved to back his Emperor to the hilt. Relations between himself and Heraclius had recently been under strain. The Empress Eudocia had died, apparently of an epileptic seizure, soon after the birth of her second child in 612; and her husband had shortly afterwards gone through a ceremony of marriage with his niece Martina, thereby causing much scandal in religious circles. Sergius had made a violent protest at the time; but now, in the national interest, he was prepared to overlook any irregularities in the Emperor's private life. Unhesitatingly he put all the ecclesiastical and monastic treasure, from every diocese and parish under his authority, at the disposal of the State. Heraclius accepted it at once. At least for the moment, his financial worries were over.

Before he could march against the Persians, however, there were the Avars to be dealt with. In 619 it looked as though some accommodation might be reached, when their Khagan proposed a conference with the Emperor at Heraclea on the Marmara. Heraclius eagerly accepted the invitation, and decided to dazzle the barbarian horde with elaborate pageantry and theatrical performances, all designed to show off the

magnificence of the Empire. It was while he was planning these manifestations at Selymbria that he suddenly received word that a detachment
of Avar troops was even then taking up its position in the wooded
heights above the Anastasian Walls.[1] Clearly the whole thing was a plot:
his line of retreat to Constantinople was to be cut off, after which it
would be an easy matter to take him prisoner. Delaying only long enough
to throw off his imperial robes and to disguise himself as a poor peasant,
he leapt on to his horse and galloped back at full speed to the capital;
minutes later, the Avars were in hot pursuit. They found the Theodosian
Walls closed against them, but departed only after having destroyed
several churches in the outer suburbs.

How Byzantine–Avar relations were patched up after this regrettable
incident we do not know; our sources are once again silent. All that can
be said for certain is that by the spring of 622 Heraclius was ready for
the war which would, he was determined, put an end to the Persian
threat once and for all. On Easter Monday, 5 April, he boarded his
flagship – the first Emperor since Theodosius the Great personally to
lead his forces into battle[2] – and set sail to the south-west, his war fleet
crowding behind him. Already, had he but known it, he had taken the
Persians by surprise. They had expected him to move up the Bosphorus
and into the Black Sea, ultimately launching his attack through Armenia.
Instead, he headed in precisely the opposite direction: through the
Marmara and the Hellespont, down the Ionian coast to Rhodes, then
east along the southern shore of Asia Minor to the Bay of Issus. Here –
only a few miles from where Alexander had routed the Persian host
nearly a thousand years before – he landed his army, and here he spent
the entire summer in an intensive programme of tactical exercises and
manoeuvres, testing his own generalship and building up the endurance
and stamina of his men until he felt that together they would be a match
for anything the Great King could hurl against them. All the time, too,
he was working steadily on their morale. It was their privilege, he told
them, to be the chosen instruments of God by which he would destroy
the forces of Antichrist. They were fighting not just for the Empire but
also for their Faith, and must comport themselves accordingly. The
Emperor's court poet, George of Pisidia, who accompanied the expedition, describes somewhat sanctimoniously the contrast between the two

1 See p. 260.
2 In 487 the Emperor Zeno, in one of his rasher moments, had undertaken to march against
Theodoric the Ostrogoth, and a century later Maurice had wished to take the field against the
Avars; but both had thought better of it.

camps. In the Persian, he claims, the air was loud with cymbals and every kind of music, as the naked houris danced for the generals' delectation; in the Roman, 'the Emperor sought delight in psalms sung to mystical instruments, which awoke a divine echo in his soul'.[1]

Only as autumn was closing in did Heraclius begin his advance to the north towards Pontus and the Black Sea; and it was probably somewhere in the Cappadocian highlands that the Roman and Persian armies came finally face to face. The latter were once again under the command of Shahr-Baraz, their greatest and most experienced general. Heraclius, by contrast, had never before commanded an army in the field; but the encounter ended in the precipitous flight of the Persians, while the imperial troops pursued them through the rocks and gullies – for all the world, wrote George of Pisidia, as if they were hunting wild goats. Hugely elated by his victory, Heraclius hurried back by sea from Trebizond to Constantinople – where the Avars were again giving trouble – leaving his army to pass what remained of the winter in Pontus. There were no protests this time from the soldiers that they were not being permitted to return to their families. They were, after all, soldiers of the Cross – and victorious ones at that.

The second year of the campaign was even more successful than the first. After settling the Avar problem and spending Easter with his family in Nicomedia, the Emperor took ship back to Trebizond, accompanied this time by his beloved Martina. There he found the army awaiting him, eager to march. South-eastward they went, through Armenia and over the Persian frontier into the region we now know as Azerbaijan, the 'land of fire' that was the centre of Zoroastrian fire-worship. Presently the news reached him that Chosroes himself was nearby, in his magnificent palace at Ganzak; and having previously received reports suggesting that the True Cross and the other holy relics from Jerusalem might be there also, Heraclius now advanced directly on the city.

With a garrison estimated at 40,000, the Great King might have been expected to make a stand; instead, he immediately took flight towards Nineveh, leaving the great palace and the fire-temple adjoining it to the mercy of the invaders. Heraclius, however, was not in merciful mood. One glance at the temple, with its central statue of Chosroes surrounded by winged figures representing the sun, moon and stars, was enough to throw him into a fury. The building was razed to the ground, and the palace too; after which the army passed on to the neighbouring town of

1 *Exp. Pers.*, iii, 1; Bury, op. cit., V, iii.

Thebarmes, birthplace of Zoroaster himself, and reduced it to ashes in its turn. To their sorrow, there was no sign of the holy relics; but at least the Persian sack of Jerusalem had been properly avenged.

On they marched, almost due south now, towards the Persian capital at Ctesiphon, leaving a trail of ravaged fields and burning cities behind them. Had Heraclius driven his men just a little harder, they might have reached their goal before Shahr-Baraz arrived from the west with his newly recruited army – and the war might have ended four years earlier than it did. But the winter was approaching – and he had moreover other, more personal, reasons for wishing to call a halt. He told his men that he had resolved upon a *sors evangelica*: they would all fast for four days, after which he would open the gospels at random and be guided by whatever verse first met his eye. Which passage this proved to be we are not told; but it comes as no great surprise to hear that it confirmed the Emperor's own inclinations. Even the most bellicose of his lieutenants could hardly object to an order that could boast the Almighty's own seal of approval; but there must have been more than a few knowing glances when, a month or two later, the Empress Martina was safely delivered of a child.

The region to which Heraclius and his army withdrew – rather confusingly known as Albania – lay just beyond the confines of the Persian Empire, on the western shore of the Caspian. It was at that time inhabited by various barbarian tribes, mostly of Hunnish origin, who hated the Persians and were correspondingly well-disposed towards their enemies; many of them, indeed, eagerly enlisted under the imperial standards. Thus it was with a considerably larger army than before that Heraclius was able to launch the campaign of 624 – a campaign which centred almost exclusively on that territory, part Albania, part Armenia, lying between the Cyrus and the Araxes Rivers.[1] There the Romans gained a victory even more decisive than that of two years before, this time over the combined armies of Shahr-Baraz and his colleague Sarablagas, who was killed in the course of the fighting. No sooner was the battle over than a third Persian general, Shahin,[2] arrived at the head of yet another force in the hopes of turning the tide. But he was too late – and by the time he realized the fact, he found that he was also too late to retreat. His army in its turn, tired after a long march and appalled by the unexpected scenes of carnage, was quickly smashed to pieces.

The Emperor wintered on Lake Van; with the coming of spring, however, he decided to leave the high Armenian plateau. The local tribes

1 Now the Kura and the Aras.
2 He was also known as Saes, a name by which he appears in several of the chronicles.

were beginning to distrust his increasing strength, and could no longer be relied upon; while the Persians, after their defeats of the previous year, would certainly not wish to give battle there again. It was far likelier that Shahr-Baraz would return to Asia Minor and, perhaps, press on to Chalcedon as he had before – particularly since the Avars were known to be preparing a major offensive from the west. And so, on 1 March 625, Heraclius led his army away on what was to be the longest and hardest journey that they had yet undertaken. Heading north past the eastern shore of the lake, they met the Arsanias River – now the Murat – among the foothills of Ararat, then followed it some 200 miles to the west before dropping down southward again to the neighbouring cities of Martyropolis and Amida (Diyarbakir), both of which he captured. From Amida it was only another seventy or eighty miles to the Euphrates, which they reached without, as yet, having had sight or sound of the enemy.

But he had been right about Shahr-Baraz, who had been following his every movement and who reached the great river just in time to cross it by a rope bridge – the only one existing for many miles on either side – and to cut it behind him. Heraclius had no alternative but to turn south, where he was fortunate enough to find a ford near Samosata (Samsat); it was then a relatively easy march on to the swiftly flowing Sarus – now the Seyhan – which he met just north of Adana. Here at last he found the Persian army, awaiting him across the river and drawn up ready for battle. There was, as it happened, a modest bridge nearby and the Romans, despite the fatigues of their long march, immediately flung themselves into the attack; but Shahr-Baraz, feigning retreat, cunningly led them into a carefully prepared ambush. Within a matter of minutes, the vanguard of the Emperor's hitherto invincible army was utterly destroyed.

The Persians meanwhile, overjoyed by the success of their plan and now busily engaged in pursuing and finishing off the survivors, had allowed their attention to become momentarily distracted from the bridge; and Heraclius saw his chance. Spurring his horse forward, he charged across, his rearguard close behind him. A Persian giant blocked his path, but the Emperor cut him down with a stroke of his sword and sent him plunging into the river. Shahr-Baraz, suddenly aware of what was happening, ordered his archers to defend the bank; but Heraclius pressed on, oblivious of the hail of arrows around him – several of which had found their mark on his own body. The Persians watched him in amazement. Not even their general could conceal his admiration:

'Look at your Emperor!' he is said to have exclaimed to a renegade Greek nearby. 'He fears these arrows and spears no more than would an anvil!'[1]

By his courage alone, Heraclius had saved the day. Early the next morning the Persians struck camp and began the long, weary journey back to their homeland, all the spirit gone out of them. Still, it had been a hard-fought battle; and the Emperor may well have reflected, as he led his sadly diminished army back through Cappadocia to its winter quarters outside Trebizond, on the dangers of over-confidence. Despite the heavy casualties, morale remained high; and thanks to the heroism that he had shown, his own personal prestige was higher still. But this year, for the first time, he had looked defeat in the face – and he had not liked what he saw. The war was not yet over. All the signs suggested that the enemy – both enemies – would renew the offensive in the spring; and that Constantinople itself would be their objective.

The city of Trebizond was ideally placed to receive intelligence from both east and west; and from neither quarter were the reports favourable. The Great King, determined to bring the war to a quick conclusion, had ordered a mass conscription of all able-bodied men, including foreigners, within his dominions and had entrusted Shahin with 50,000 hardened troops, ordering him to pursue Heraclius and cut his army to pieces. Should he fail, his own life would be forfeit. Shahr-Baraz, on the other hand, was to march an army of new recruits, untried and untrained, across Asia Minor to Chalcedon, there to give all possible assistance to the Avars in their projected attack. This too was now almost ready for launching. Meanwhile the Avar Khagan had managed to assemble virtually all the barbarian tribes from the Vistula to the Urals, and was already dragging his huge siege engines towards the walls of Constantinople. To what extent he had been able to coordinate his plans with those of the Persians is hard to assess; but some degree of collusion is beyond a doubt – the result, in all likelihood, of Shahr-Baraz's long sojourn at Chalcedon before his recent campaigns.

Heraclius was now faced with a difficult decision. If he and his army remained in Anatolia, his capital might fall through lack of manpower to protect it; if on the other hand he were to rush to its defence, he would be obliged to abandon positions on which the whole containment of the Persian menace depended, to say nothing of all hope of recovering the True Cross. At a stroke, he would be throwing away everything that he

1 Theophanes, *Chronographia* in M.P.G., Vol. 108, p. 654.

had worked so hard, through four exhausting campaigns, to achieve. He decided therefore to stay where he was, but to divide his available forces into three. The first left at once by sea for Constantinople; the second, which he placed under the command of his brother Theodore, he sent off to deal with Shahin, whom he knew to be in Mesopotamia; the third – and by far the smallest – would remain under his command, hold Armenia and the Caucasus and, he hoped, ultimately invade a relatively defenceless Persia.

This decision did not, however, mean that the Emperor intended to leave Constantinople and its defenders to look after themselves. On the contrary, Patriarch Sergius and the Patrician Bonus, to whom he had jointly entrusted the city's defence, found themselves deluged with orders, instructions, advice and messages of encouragement. These last were posted publicly in the streets and had an immediate effect, firing the whole population with determination and enthusiasm for the struggle ahead. Heraclius himself meanwhile turned his attention to one of the principal Hunnish tribes of the Caucasus, the Khazars, intercepting them as they returned from a raiding expedition in Azerbaijan and dazzling their Khagan, Ziebil, by the splendour of his court, which he maintained even when on campaign, and by the richness of his presents. In the course of one of their several conversations, he showed the Khagan a picture of his daughter Epiphania and promised him her hand in marriage. Ziebil, enchanted by the picture and flattered beyond measure both by the treatment he was receiving and by the prospect of himself joining the imperial family, offered Heraclius 40,000 of his best men in return. (Fortunately for Epiphania, he was dead by the end of the year; the poor girl was thus spared the grim fate to which her father had unhesitatingly consigned her.)

While Heraclius and his new Khazar army were ravaging Azerbaijan, his brother Theodore scored a crushing victory over Shahin in Mesopotamia. We know little about the battle, save that it was fought in a driving hailstorm, which unleashed its entire fury on the Persian army – the Romans being in some mysterious way sheltered or protected from it. In consequence of his defeat, the Persian commander fell into a deep depression and shortly afterwards died – whether by his own hand, to forestall the promised vengeance of his master, or of sheer despair is not recorded. When Chosroes heard of his death, he ordered the body to be packed in salt and brought to him at once; on its arrival, he watched grimly while it was stripped and scourged until it was no longer recognizable.

For some time now, there had been those at the Persian court who were beginning to doubt the Great King's sanity. After this exhibition they doubted no longer.

It was 29 June 626. The night sky glowed red with the light of blazing churches as Persians and Avars signalled to each other across the Bosphorus, confirming that they had arrived in their prearranged positions and that they were ready to mount their concerted attack. The inhabitants of the suburbs outside the walls hastily loaded their possessions on to barrows and carts and sought refuge within the gates, which were closed and bolted behind them; and the long-threatened siege began. As the barbarian hordes dug themselves in along the walls, the Avar Khagan made one last offer to spare the city, in return for a huge ransom; but morale in Constantinople had never been higher, and his proposals were rejected with contempt.

The barbarian host – Avars and Huns, Gepids and Bulgars, Scythians and Slavs – numbering about 80,000, were now spread out along the whole seven-mile length of the Theodosian Walls from the Marmara to the Golden Horn – in the upper reaches of which, a mile or two to the north of the city, a fleet of small dug-outs, manned by Slavs of both sexes, stood ready to give sea-borne assistance as necessary to the besiegers. The walls were defended by rather more than 12,000 Byzantine cavalry; but these in their turn were supported by every citizen of Constantinople, the entire population having been worked up by Patriarch Sergius to a positive frenzy of religious enthusiasm. Day and night, the pressure was maintained; one after another, the great catapults and mangonels were trundled into position, hurling huge rocks against, and occasionally over, the ramparts. But the walls held, and the defenders stood firm. Surprisingly, perhaps, the Persians had still made no attempt to cross the Bosphorus. It was true that they had no siege engines, and they may well have reasoned that for the moment they could make no useful contribution to the proceedings; but to the people of Constantinople it seemed that they were playing an unusually passive role.

All through a sweltering July the siege continued, Patriarch Sergius making a daily procession with his clergy along the whole length of the walls, carrying above his head a miraculous icon of the Virgin which, it was claimed, struck terror into the hearts of the barbarians below. Then, on the evening of Saturday 2 August, the Khagan invited the Patrician Bonus to send a deputation to his camp, giving it to be understood that he might be ready to call off the attack on more favourable terms than those previously offered. The delegates duly arrived at his tent, where they were furious to find three silk-robed envoys from Shahr-Baraz also present; and they felt still more insulted when the Persians were offered seats, while they themselves were obliged to remain standing. A violent argument ensued, after which the Byzantines repeated once again that they had no intention of surrender, then turned angrily on their heel and returned to Constantinople. That night they took their revenge. The boat carrying the three Persians was intercepted as it returned to Chalcedon. One of the three, who had attempted to hide under a pile of blankets, was beheaded on the spot; the second had his hands cut off and was returned to the Khagan; the third was carried to a point off Chalcedon and there executed in full view of the Persian camp. His severed head was then hurled ashore with a message attached. It read: 'We and the Khagan are now reconciled. He has taken charge of the first two of your ambassadors. As for the third, here he is!'

It may be that the luckless Persians, in a final attempt to save their own lives, had revealed to the Byzantines details of their army's future plans; for, on the following Thursday, 7 August, a fleet of rafts and dugouts which was moving quietly across the Bosphorus to the Asiatic shore, there to pick up Persian troops and ferry them back over the straits, suddenly found itself surrounded by Greek ships. Their crews, hopelessly outnumbered, were either killed outright or thrown into the sea to drown, while their crude vessels were towed triumphantly back to Constantinople. Almost immediately afterwards, a collection of similar craft which the Slavs had gathered in the upper reaches of the Golden Horn was also pressed into action: their orders were to wait for a pre-arranged signal – a beacon fire at the foot of the walls, where they ran down to the water at Blachernae – and then to row *en masse* down the Horn and force their way through to the open sea. Once again, Bonus received advance warning of what was planned. Quickly he brought all his available biremes and triremes up to Blachernae; then, the moment they were in position, he himself lit a signal fire. The Slavs, who had not been expecting it for some hours, were taken by surprise; nevertheless, they obediently started on their way – only to run straight into the Byzantine ambush. Within an hour, their whole fleet was destroyed.

After this second disaster the besiegers seem to have been overcome by a sort of panic. The siege engines in which they had put so much trust had been proved useless, their most subtle stratagems had been effortlessly thwarted. At this moment, too, the news reached them of Theodore's victory over Shahin and Heraclius's new alliance with the

Khazars. There could be but one explanation: the Empire was under divine protection. Had not a richly dressed woman – whom many believed to be the Blessed Virgin herself – been seen pacing to and fro along the ramparts? The next morning, the barbarians began to strike their camps; the day after, they were gone. Face, as far as possible, was saved: one or two more churches were burnt as they retreated, and there were the usual threats of vengeance and an early return to renew the siege. But to the Byzantines these words must have had a hollow ring. As the last of the horde disappeared from sight, with one accord they all hurried to Blachernae where, just outside the walls, stood the great church dedicated to the Virgin. To their joy, they found it untouched – yet another proof of her miraculous powers, to which they unhesitatingly ascribed their salvation.

The year 626, so memorable for the people of Constantinople, was for the Emperor Heraclius boring in the extreme. His Khazar alliance, by which he had set such store, proved a disappointment – after the death of Ziebil, the tribesmen quietly drifted away to the steppes of Turkestan whence they had come – and after Theodore's victory over Shahin there had been no major engagement with the Persians. Early in 627, therefore, the Emperor decided to make the long journey south to the palace of the Great King himself – at Dastagird, some twenty miles north of Ctesiphon. The journey took him most of the year; he was in no particular hurry, and it was in his interest to devastate as much of the countryside as he could *en route*. He knew, too, that he must move with caution. An immense Persian army was not far away; it might strike at any time, and he could not risk being caught off his guard.

But the Persian army was also biding its time. Its new commander was a general named Razates; he too had been ordered by Chosroes to conquer or die, and he was determined not to meet Heraclius until he was ready to do so, and then on his own terms. The moment came only at the very end of the year, when he finally caught up with the Roman army by the ruins of Nineveh. Even then, there was no surprise attack. Both commanders had ample time to choose their positions and dispose of their forces as they thought best; both placed themselves in the front line; and early in the morning of 12 December battle was joined. It continued for eleven hours without a break, every man involved knowing full well that he was almost certainly fighting the decisive encounter of the war. At its height, Razates suddenly challenged Heraclius to single combat. The Emperor accepted, spurred on his dun charger

Dorkon, and – if George of Pisidia is to be believed – struck off the general's head with a single thrust. Two more Persian commanders are said to have suffered similar fates. Heraclius himself was wounded more than once, but refused to sheathe his sword. He and his men were still fighting when the sun set. Only then did they realize that there was virtually no enemy left to oppose them. The Persian army had been annihilated; all its commanders lay dead on the field.

It was morning before they could collect the spoils. The Emperor himself claimed the shield of Razates, set with 120 plates of gold, together with his gauntlets and his superb saddle. The general's head, impaled on a lance, was exhibited at the centre of the Roman camp, surrounded by twenty-eight captured Persian standards. Meanwhile the victorious soldiers were similarly helping themselves to helmets and swords, bucklers and breastplates. Few were to return to the west without some proud trophy of that memorable day.

But the time had not yet come to turn back. Chosroes had still to be sought out and toppled from his throne. After a few days' rest the army continued its march to the south, now heading towards Dastagird along the left bank of the Tigris. The river's two mighty tributaries, the Great Zab and the Little Zab, were crossed without incident, and Heraclius was able to celebrate Christmas in the oasis of Yezdem, while the priests of Zoroaster looked helplessly on. It was at about this time that he had the supreme good fortune to intercept a messenger from Chosroes bearing a letter to Shahr-Baraz in Chalcedon, ordering him to return at once. Here was an opportunity not to be missed. The Emperor quickly dictated another message, which was translated and substituted for the first. It announced a major Persian victory over the Romans, and instructed Shahr-Baraz to remain where he was. At least one potential danger had been deftly averted.

The Great King, meanwhile, had fled. He, his wife and his children had slipped out of the palace at Dastagird through a hole in the wall, unbeknownst to his ministers or even to his guards. He went first to Ctesiphon, the ancient capital in which he had not set foot for twenty-four years, only on his arrival remembering the prophecy of the Magi that any return to the city would portend his inevitable downfall; there was nothing for it but to continue his flight eastward into Suziana, the modern Khuzistan. Heraclius arrived at Dastagird to find the vast palace deserted. It was, by all accounts, of a beauty and sumptuousness incomparable; indeed, as the chief residence for a quarter of a century of the most magnificent of all the Sassanian monarchs, it could hardly have been otherwise. But the Emperor and his soldiers showed it no mercy or respect. They could not take it with them; and so in January 628 they committed it, and everything within it, to the flames – just as Alexander and his followers had fired Persepolis a thousand years before.

From the safety of Suziana, King Chosroes rejected a Roman offer of peace, calling instead on women and children, old men and eunuchs, to rally to the defence of Ctesiphon. But no one listened. The Persians had lost patience with their King; they were no longer prepared to tolerate his irrational behaviour, his folly or his by now legendary cruelty. Anyone could see that flash-point was not far off. For Heraclius, there was no purpose in besieging the old capital, or even in finally overthrowing a ruler whose own subjects were obviously about to do the job very effectively themselves. He may, too, have remembered his distant predecessor, the Emperor Julian who, returning nearly three centuries before from another expedition to the East, had been cut down in the desert by a Persian army within a few miles of Ctesiphon. He had no wish to suffer a similar fate. While still at Dastagird, therefore, he ordered his men to make themselves ready to march; and a week or two later he headed for home.

The subsequent downfall of Chosroes is not really part of our story; suffice it to say that the revolt, when it came early in 628, was led by the King's own son, Kavadh-Siroes; by Gundarnasp, the general commanding at Ctesiphon; and by Shahr-Baraz, who had by now returned from his long spell of inactivity at Chalcedon after discovering that Chosroes, furious that he had not come back earlier as instructed, had ordered his execution.[1] The Great King was seized and flung into what was known as the Tower of Darkness, being allowed only as much bread and water as would keep him alive and so prolong his agony. All his children by his beautiful young second wife, Shirin – one of whom he had tried to make his successor – were then executed by their half-brother in his presence. Finally, on the fifth day of his incarceration, he was shot slowly to death with arrows.

The news reached Heraclius at Tauris (now Tabriz). The Persian ambassadors who brought it had encountered on their way, frozen in the mountain snows, the corpses of 3,000 of their compatriots, victims of

---

[1] The discovery was made as a result of the interception by the Byzantines of another Persian messenger. This time they naturally passed his message on to Shahr-Baraz, having first added a list of four hundred other senior Persian officers also purportedly condemned – thereby ensuring plenty of support for the revolt when it took place.

the Emperor's last campaign. Only after Gundarnasp agreed to accompany them did they find the courage to complete their mission, and it was 3 April when they at last reached the Roman camp. Siroes's letter, announcing that he had succeeded to the throne 'without difficulty, by the grace of God', would have turned the stomach of a lesser man; but Heraclius gave as good as he got, addressing his reply to his 'dear son' and protesting that he had never dreamt of overthrowing Chosroes and that, had he captured him, he would immediately have restored him to power. The result was a treaty of peace, by the terms of which the Persians surrendered all the territories they had conquered and all the captives they had taken, together with the True Cross and the other relics of the Passion.

On Whit Sunday, 15 May, Patriarch Sergius ascended the high ambo in St Sophia and read the Emperor's message to his people.[1] Beginning with the *Jubilate* – 'Be joyful in the Lord' – it was, predictably, more a hymn of thanksgiving and a religious exhortation than a proclamation of victory; and though there was much vilification and abuse heaped on the dead Chosroes ('He has gone by the same path as Judas Iscariot, of whom the Almighty said that it were better he had never been born') it is noteworthy that there is not a word of disapproval of Siroes and his particularly revolting parricide. But the people of Constantinople did not care. While the Senate passed a resolution granting Heraclius the honorific title of *Scipio*, one and all began to prepare a reception worthy of the conqueror.

Leaving the signing of the peace treaty to Theodore, Heraclius had meanwhile begun the long journey home with his army. When at last he arrived at his palace of Hiera, opposite Constantinople across the Bosphorus, it was to find what appeared to be the entire population of the capital waiting to greet him, olive branches and lighted candles in their hands. In the palace itself was his family: his sixteen-year-old elder son Constantine, who had already distinguished himself by his courage during the siege; his daughter Epiphania – all unconscious, one hopes, of the fate she had so narrowly escaped; his younger son by Martina, Heraclonas, now thirteen; and Martina herself, who had returned from the East with her new-born baby some months before.

It was, according to Theophanes, a happy if tearful reunion, after which the family might have been expected to pass on at once to Constantinople. Heraclius, however, had resolved not to enter his capital without the True Cross, which Theodore had been charged to bring as

1 The full text is preserved in the Paschal Chronicle.

quickly as possible. There was some initial delay, since for some time it could not be found; it was Shahr-Baraz who, in return for an assurance of the Emperor's goodwill towards him, eventually revealed its hiding-place. With this holiest of relics at last in his possession, Theodore hurried back; but it was well into September before he arrived at Chalcedon and arrangements could be made for the imperial home-coming.

The Golden Gate of Constantinople, that great ceremonial arch erected by Theodosius the Great in about 390 and incorporated into the newly built Land Walls some thirty years later, is a sad sight today. The plates of solid gold which covered it and to which it owed its name have long since disappeared; gone too are the sculptures, both marble and bronze, which adorned the façade. Worse still, its three openings have been bricked up so that it is no longer even a gate at all. It now stands, half-hidden by the long grass surrounding the *yediküle* – the Castle of the Seven Towers, a few hundred yards along the walls from the Marmara shore – ignored and forgotten. It must, however, have looked very dif-ferent on the morning of 14 September 628, when Heraclius entered his capital in triumph. Before him went the True Cross; behind, surrounded by his victorious soldiers, lumbered four elephants who had also made the long journey from Persia – the first, we are told, ever seen in Con-stantinople. Among the cheering crowds there were many who remarked how their Emperor had aged during his years of campaign: certainly, there was little now to remind them of the stalwart young demi-god who had made his first entry into the city on his arrival from Carthage, eighteen years before. The years of anxiety and hardship had taken their toll: though still only in his middle fifties he looked old and ill, his body prematurely stooping, his once-glorious mane of blond hair now reduced to a few grey strands. But if he had worn himself out, he had done so in the service of the Empire; thanks to him Sassanid Persia, though it would struggle on for a few more years, would never again prove a threat to Byzantium.

The procession threaded its way slowly through the streets to St Sophia, where Patriarch Sergius was waiting; and, at the solemn mass of thanksgiving that followed, the True Cross on which the Redeemer had died was slowly raised up until it stood, vertical, before the high altar. It was, perhaps, the most moving moment in the history of the Great Church, and it could well have been seen as a sign that God's enemies had been scattered and that a new golden age of Empire was about to dawn.

Alas, it proved to be nothing of the kind. Just six years before, in September 622 – the very year in which Heraclius had launched his Persian expedition – the Prophet Mohammed had taken flight with a few followers from the hostile city of Mecca to friendly Medina, thereby marking the starting-point for the whole Muslim era; and just five years afterwards, in 633, the armies of Islam would begin the advance that was to take them, in the course of a single century, to within 150 miles of Paris and to the very gates of Constantinople. Christendom's most formidable rival – and for the next thousand years its most implacable enemy – was already born, and would soon be on the march.

Until the second quarter of the seventh century, the land of Arabia was *terra incognita* to the Christian world. Remote and inhospitable, productive of nothing to tempt the sophisticated merchants of the West, it had made no contribution to civilization and seemed unlikely ever to do so. Its people, insofar as anyone knew anything about them, were presumed to be little better than savages, periodically slaughtering each other in violent outbreaks of tribal warfare, falling mercilessly upon any traveller foolhardy enough to venture among them, making not the slightest attempt towards unity or even stable government. Apart from a few scattered Jewish colonies around the coast and in Medina and a small Christian community in the Yemen, the overwhelming majority practised a sort of primitive polytheism which, in the city of Mecca – their commercial centre – appeared to be somehow focused on the huge black stone that stood in their principal temple, the *Ka'aba*. Where the outside world was concerned they showed no interest, made no impact and certainly posed no threat.

Then, in the twinkling of an eye, all was changed. In 633, showing a discipline and singleness of purpose of which they had previously given no sign and which was therefore totally unexpected by their victims, they suddenly burst out of Arabia. After three years they had taken Damascus; after five, Jerusalem; after six, all Syria. Within a decade, Egypt and Armenia had alike fallen to the Arab sword; within twenty years, the whole Persian Empire; within thirty, Afghanistan and most of the Punjab. Then, after a brief interval for consolidation, the victorious armies turned their attention to the West. In 711, having occupied the entire coast of North Africa, they invaded Spain; and by 732, less than a century after their first eruption from their desert homeland, they had crossed the Pyrenees and driven north to the banks of the Loire – where, after a week-long battle, they were checked at last.

History provides few parallels for so dramatic a saga of conquest, and only one explanation: that the Arabs were carried forward on a great surge of religious enthusiasm, implanted in them by their first and greatest leader, the Prophet Mohammed. So, indisputably, they were; it is worth remembering, however, that this enthusiasm contained scarcely any missionary zeal. Throughout their century of advance, their attempts at the mass – or even individual – conversion of their defeated enemies were remarkably few; and they tended at times to show an almost embarrassing respect for the religion of the Jews and Christians who, as 'People of the Book', could normally count on their toleration and goodwill. What their faith gave to them was, above all, a feeling of brotherhood, of cohesion and of almost limitless self-confidence, knowing as they did that Allah was with them, and that if it were His will that they should fall in battle they would be immediately rewarded in paradise – and a delightfully sensual paradise at that, whose promised delights were, it must be admitted, a good deal more alluring than those of its Christian counterpart. In this world, on the other hand, they willingly adopted a disciplined austerity that they had never known before, together with an unquestioning obedience whose outward manifestations were abstinence from wine and strong drink, periodic fasting and the five-times-daily ritual of prayer.

The founder of their religion was himself never to lead them on campaign. Born of humble origins some time around 570, orphaned in early childhood and finally married to a rich widow considerably older than himself, Mohammed was that rare combination of a visionary mystic and an astute, far-sighted statesman. In the former capacity, he preached, first, the singleness of God and second, the importance to mankind of total submission (*islam*) to his will. This was not a particularly original creed – both Jews and Christians, inside Arabia as well as out, had maintained it for centuries – but it seemed so to most of those who now heard it for the first time; and it was Mohammed's skill to present it in a new, homespun form, clothed in proverbs, fragments of desert lore and passages of almost musical eloquence, all of which were combined in that posthumous collection of his revelations which we know as the Koran. He was clever, too, in the way in which – although he almost certainly considered himself as a reformer rather than a revolutionary – he managed to identify his own name and person with the doctrine he preached: not by ascribing any divinity to himself as Jesus Christ had done, but by putting himself forward as the last and greatest of the

Prophets, in whom all his predecessors – including Jesus – were subsumed.

He was a statesman, above all, in his pragmatic approach. Despite his genuine spiritual fervour, he was never a fanatic. He perfectly understood the people among whom he lived, and was always careful not to push them further than they would willingly go. He knew, for example, that they would never abandon polygamy: he therefore accepted it, and indeed himself took several more wives after the death of his first. Slavery was another integral part of Arabian life: this too he tolerated. He was even prepared to come to terms with features of the old animist religion; as early as 624 he decreed that the Faithful should turn towards the *Ka'aba* in Mecca when praying, rather than towards Jerusalem as he had previously enjoined. He never ceased to stress, on the other hand, one entirely new and distinctly unpalatable aspect of his creed – the inevitability of divine judgement after death: often, it seemed, he described the torments of hell even more vividly than the joys of paradise. And the fear of retribution may well have proved useful when he came to weld his followers into a political state.

Mohammed died of a fever in Mecca – to which he had triumphantly returned – on 8 June 632; and the leadership, both religious and political, passed to his oldest friend and most trusted lieutenant Abu-Bakr, who assumed the title of Caliph – literally, 'representative' of the Prophet. In the year following, the Muslim armies marched. But Abu-Bakr was already growing old; he in turn died soon afterwards – according to tradition in August 634, on the very day of the first capture of Damascus – and it was under the second Caliph, Omar, that the initial series of historic victories was won. In one respect in particular, luck was on the side of the Arabs: the recent war between Byzantium and Persia had left both Empires exhausted, no longer capable of any serious resistance. For the former, the situation was further aggravated by the fact that the peoples of Syria and Palestine felt no real loyalty towards the Emperor in Constantinople, who represented an alien Graeco-Roman culture and whose lack of sympathy for their monophysite traditions had periodically led to active persecution. The Muslim tide, composed as it was of Semites like themselves, professing a rigid monotheism not unlike their own and promising toleration for every variety of Christian belief, cannot have seemed to them substantially worse than the regime it swept away.

The Arab invasion of Syria in 633 found Heraclius already back in the East. He had stayed in Constantinople only six months after his triumphant homecoming, conscious all the time of the tasks that awaited him in the lands that he had so recently left. The provinces, for example, that he had reconquered from Persia – they must be re-established and reorganized, given a firm military and economic base to protect their future security. The doctrinal problems with the Eastern churches – they must be studied, thoroughly discussed and, if possible, resolved. Most important of all, the True Cross must be returned to Jerusalem where it belonged. With the coming of spring in 629, accompanied by his wife Martina and his eldest son Constantine, he had set off across Anatolia for Syria and Palestine. On reaching the Holy City, he had personally carried the Cross along the Via Dolorosa to the rebuilt Church of the Holy Sepulchre, where Patriarch Zacharias was waiting to receive it back into his charge.

It was a measure of the good government that he had given the Empire – to say nothing of the security of his own position – that Heraclius was able to spend the next seven years in these eastern provinces, moving constantly from place to place, setting up his court in Damascus or Antioch, Edessa[1] or Emesa[2] or Hierapolis,[3] stamping out incompetence and inefficiency, reducing the power of the rich land-owners, improving and streamlining the administrative machine. Meanwhile, in the theological field, he made himself the champion of a new formula, recently developed by Patriarch Sergius in Constantinople, in the hopes that it might prove acceptable to the orthodox and monophysite communities alike, thus healing the rift which was assuming ever more dangerous proportions.

Sergius's proposal was, essentially, that although Christ had two separate natures, the human and the divine, these natures possessed a single active force, or energy. To put it another way, all that the monophysites would now be asked to accept was that the unity which they very properly perceived in the Saviour was one of energy rather than of nature. From the first this solution to the problem had been enthusiastically supported by Heraclius, who had proposed it to an Armenian bishop as early as 622; and during these later years we find him returning to it again and again – with, it must be said, most encouraging results. At Hierapolis in 629 the monophysite Bishop Athanasius had endorsed it in return for being appointed Patriarch of Antioch, and in the following year the new Patriarch of Alexandria reported further notable successes. From Rome, meanwhile, Pope Honorius had intimated that he had no

1 Urfa.　　2 Homs.　　3 Mambij.

objection – although he made it clear that he took little interest in the matter one way or the other.

There was, nevertheless, a good deal of opposition from other quarters; and this opposition was led and orchestrated by a fanatically orthodox monk by the name of Sophronius. If Sophronius had remained in his monastery all might have been well, but in 634 an ironic fate decreed that he should be elected Patriarch of Jerusalem. Immediately, with all the authority of his new rank, he redoubled his attacks. The new doctrine, he thundered, was nothing but a bastard form of monophysitism, thinly disguised; as such, like the older heresy, it was a betrayal of all that had been achieved at the Council of Chalcedon. Suddenly, support for the theory of the single energy began to fall away. Erstwhile enthusiasts began to see fallacies and inherent contradictions, and the Emperor watched powerless while all that he had so patiently and painfully built up crumbled away to dust.

Nor was this the only blow that he was called upon to bear. In that same disastrous year of 634, the armies of the Prophet first poured into Syria; soon afterwards, news reached Heraclius in Antioch that the modest Byzantine force sent against them had been utterly annihilated. A few months later the Muslims had occupied Damascus and Emesa and were laying siege to Jerusalem. Now it was no longer just the results of long and patient diplomacy that had been undone overnight; it was all that had been achieved in six years' hard campaigning. Shattered as he was by these events, Heraclius at once applied himself to the task of raising a full-scale army; and a year later no less than 80,000 men were drawn up outside Antioch, including several thousand Armenians and a large detachment of Christian Arab cavalry.

In face of this threat the Muslims withdrew their garrisons from Emesa and Damascus and fell back on the Yarmuk River, a tributary of the Jordan which meets it just south of the Sea of Galilee. In May 636 the imperial army advanced southward to meet them – but, instead of launching an immediate attack, waited for three months in apparent indecision. The delay was fatal. The Christians, exposed to the increasingly merciless heat of the Syrian summer, grew restive and demoralized while the brilliant young Muslim general Khalid harassed them with incessant forays while awaiting the reinforcements he had ordered from Arabia. Soon after these had arrived, on 20 August, a violent sandstorm swept up from the south; Khalid saw his chance and charged. The Byzantine troops, caught unawares and blinded by the flying sand blown full in their faces, gave way under the impact and were massacred almost to a man.

The struggle, such as it had been, was over. Emesa and Damascus were reoccupied, and have ever since remained under Muslim rule. Jerusalem, under the governorship of Patriarch Sophronius, resisted stoutly for as long as it could; but food supplies were running low, all the surrounding countryside was in Arab hands and, apart from a small garrison at Caesarea, there was no Christian army nearer than Egypt. By the autumn of 637, the Patriarch agreed to capitulate – stipulating, however, one condition: that the Caliph Omar should be present to receive his surrender in person. Thus it was that, in February 638, the Caliph himself rode into Jerusalem. He was mounted on a snow-white camel, but his robes were tattered and threadbare in keeping with the austerity enjoined by the Prophet. Sophronius received him on the Mount of Olives and showed him every courtesy, taking him personally on a tour of the principal Christian shrines;[1] only when he saw the ragged but majestic figure standing in silence on the site of the Temple of Solomon – whence, it was believed, his friend Mohammed had ascended into heaven – did the Patriarch's self-control momentarily desert him. 'Behold,' he murmured, 'the Abomination of Desolation, spoken of by the Prophet Daniel, that standeth in the Holy Place.'

And what, during this hideous chain of disasters, of Heraclius himself? True, he had ordered the mobilization of his ill-fated army; but neither before nor afterwards did he personally take any part in the fighting. How, one wonders, can it possibly be that this heroic soldier-Emperor, scourge of the Persians, the first to lead his subjects into battle for over 200 years, should have remained inactive while these new and terrible enemies carried all before them – that this stalwart defender of Christendom, recoverer of the True Cross, should have stood by while Jerusalem itself fell into the hands of the infidel, lifting not a finger to save it?

The answer to these questions becomes painfully clear as we follow the Emperor through the last tragic years of his life. Already stricken by the disease that was ultimately to kill him, he was also rapidly approaching a state of both mental and spiritual collapse. Even before the battle of the Yarmuk, as he watched while the soldiers of the Prophet

1 The Caliph is said to have been in the Church of the Holy Sepulchre when the hour came for prayer, but to have refused to spread his prayer-rug within the church lest the building should be claimed by his followers for Islam. He therefore withdrew to the outer porch and prayed there. His fears proved justified: the porch – but only the porch – was immediately taken over, and remains in Muslim hands to this day.

overran the lands that he had fought so hard to regain, he had been tormented by fears that God had abandoned him – that the Almighty had perhaps even transferred His support to this new tribe of conquerors. After the battle, he had given up all hope. His life's work, his long struggle with Persia, his tireless efforts to settle the theological controversies – all had been in vain. Pausing only to slip into beleaguered Jerusalem, thence to remove once again the True Cross that he had so recently restored, he turned his back on Syria for ever and set off on the long, weary road to Constantinople.

By the time he reached the Bosphorus his mind was seriously affected. Somehow, on the journey, he had developed an unreasoning terror of the sea; and once arrived at the palace of Hiera, nothing would induce him to make the mile-long journey across the strait. He remained, trembling, in his apartment, refusing to receive the anxious delegations from the capital that begged him to delay his return no longer, occasionally sending his sons to represent him at the games or at important feasts of the Church. Meanwhile he began to behave with quite uncharacteristic brutality. Hearing rumours of a conspiracy within the city in which his nephew Theodore and his bastard son Athalaric were said to have been implicated, he had them both sent away into banishment – but not before their noses and hands had been cut off at his command. When Theodore arrived at his place of exile on the Maltese offshore island of Gozo, it was to discover that the governor had been ordered to remove one of his feet as well.

Only after a delay of several weeks did his wife and his entourage hit upon a way of getting the Emperor home. If we are to believe the history of Theophanes – who, it must be remembered, was writing nearly two centuries after the event – a bridge of boats was thrown across the Bosphorus and fenced with green branches so as to form a sort of artificial hedge along each side, preventing him from seeing the water; Heraclius then mounted his horse and rode across 'as if he were on land'. Given the width of the strait and the strength of the currents, the story seems hardly likely; perhaps, as certain more recent historians have suggested, he travelled on a boat similarly disguised. Whatever the truth may be, the last return of the Emperor to his capital could not have been other than a sad, pathetic contrast to his previous entry, less than nine years before.

By this time it was plain to all that he was a dying man; and his superstitious subjects were not slow to explain the cause of his decline. Clearly, they whispered, he had incurred the wrath of God by his incestuous marriage to his niece. Of the nine children that Martina had borne him, four had died in infancy, one had a twisted neck and another, Theodosius, was deaf and dumb: could there be any more unmistakable indication of divine displeasure? The Emperor's steadily deteriorating mental and physical condition was only additional corroboration. Martina, never popular in Constantinople, now found herself hated and publicly reviled.

It is uncertain, however, whether she greatly cared, for all her energies were now fixed on a single objective: to ensure the succession of her own first-born, Heraclonas,[1] as co-Emperor with Constantine, her husband's son by his first wife Eudocia. The task was scarcely daunting. Young Constantine, despite the heroism he had shown during the siege of the capital in 626, had grown up a sad and sickly young man, almost certainly consumptive; although there is no cause to think that his reason was impaired, he is known to have needed constant attention. And Heraclius no longer possessed the strength to resist his wife, even had he wished to do so. Thus it was that on 4 June 638, in the Palace of the Bosphorus, he tremulously lowered the imperial diadem on to the head of Heraclonas, while Martina and Constantine stood by. Both sons – now twenty-three and twenty-six respectively – were thenceforth co-rulers with their father, accompanying him (when he appeared at all) at occasional state ceremonies, but more and more often representing him in his absence.

The most important of these ceremonies, occurring within a few weeks of his son's coronation, was Heraclius's promulgation of what was known as his *Ekthesis*, in which he made one last attempt to heal the still-raging monophysite controversy. The doctrine of the single energy of Christ had, as we have seen, been exploded by Sophronius of Jerusalem four years previously; in Constantinople, however, Patriarch Sergius had refused to give up, and had now slightly amended his formula. The question of energies, it seemed, was no longer relevant: the important thing was that Christ, while possessing the two natures that had been confirmed at Chalcedon, had but a single *will*. If only this proposition could now be universally accepted, peace would at last return to the tormented Church.

And so the principles of monothelitism, the doctrine of the Single Will as set forth in the *Ekthesis*, were circulated to all the bishops of Christendom. A copy was posted up in the narthex of St Sophia; and

1 His real name was Heraclius, but he was generally known as Heraclonas to distinguish him from his father.

when Patriarch Sergius died in December 638 its prospects looked distinctly promising, with all four of the eastern Patriarchs signifying their assent. Only two years later did the blow fall, and then from a most unexpected quarter. Early in 641, the newly elected Pope John IV condemned the whole thing out of hand. An issue which had been virtually confined to the Eastern Church, and to which the Pope in Rome had till now shown himself to be largely indifferent, had suddenly been inflated into a major schism between East and West.

It led, too, to the final humiliation of the Emperor Heraclius. His body by now distended and near-paralysed with dropsy and plagued by other symptoms almost as unattractive,[1] he spent the days groaning on his litter, brooding on the frustration of his efforts, the hopelessness of his life and the torments that he confidently expected after his death. In December 640 he had been informed of the arrival of the Saracen army at the gates of Alexandria; and now, just two months later, came the news of the Pope's condemnation of monothelitism. Had it been just a little longer delayed, the Emperor would have been beyond its reach; coming as it did, it added yet further to his despair. He was too tired, now, for courage: with his last breath he denied having had any part in the *Ekthesis*. It was all the fault of Sergius, he muttered; only at the Patriarch's request had he given it his unwilling approval. Thus, on 11 February 641, with a transparent lie on his lips, one of the greatest of Byzantine Emperors expired in misery and shame.

He had lived too long. Could he only have died in 629, with the Persian Empire on its knees and the Holy Cross restored to Jerusalem, his reign would have been the most glorious in the Empire's history; those last twelve years brought him only disappointment, disillusion and, ultimately, dishonour – with all the pain and indignity of a loathsome disease. Yet his record, despite its tragic end, remains a magnificent one. Without his energy, determination and inspired leadership, Constantinople might well have fallen to the Persians – in which case it would almost inevitably have been engulfed a few years later by the Muslim tide, with consequences for western Europe that can scarcely be imagined. As it was, he left Byzantium stronger than it had been for centuries, thanks to the military and administrative organization that he conceived and created and that was to become the backbone of the medieval Empire. The survival of that Empire for another 800 years, during which

1 'Every time that he voided water, he was obliged to lay a board across his stomach to prevent its spurting into his face' (Nicephorus, VII, xi). Thus, his subjects whispered, was the organ primarily responsible for his incestuous union singled out by the Almighty for special punishment.

it was to reach its highest and most brilliant apogee, was due in a very large measure to him.

Culturally, too, his reign marked the beginning of a new era. If Justinian had been the last of the truly Roman Emperors, it was Heraclius who dealt the old Roman tradition its death-blow. Until his day, Latin was still regularly used by the civil service and even by the army – despite the fact that it was incomprehensible to the overwhelming majority of his subjects. At a moment when efficiency of communications was of paramount importance, such a state of affairs was clearly ridiculous; and it was Heraclius who decreed that Greek, for long the language of the people and the Church, should henceforth be the official language of the Empire. Within a generation, even among the educated classes, Latin became virtually extinct. Finally, by way of marking the end of the old Empire and setting the seal on the new, he abolished the ancient Roman titles of imperial dignity. Heretofore, like his predecessors, he had been formally hailed as *Imperator Caesar* and *Augustus*; all these were now replaced by the old Greek word for 'King', *Basileus* – which was to remain the official title for as long as the Empire lasted.

For three days after his death the body of the Emperor lay, grotesque and misshapen, on an open bier guarded by the Palace eunuchs, while those of his subjects who remembered him in the years of his greatness filed slowly past it in silent homage. It was then laid in a sarcophagus of white onyx and buried, near that of Constantine the Great, in the Church of the Holy Apostles. Heraclius's sufferings were over at last; one further indignity, however, was reserved for him. Barely three months after his entombment, on the order of his first-born son, the sarcophagus was reopened and the jewelled diadem with which he had been buried was wrenched from his head.[1] Spite, rather than cupidity, seems to have been the motive: Constantine had probably never forgiven his father for obliging him to share a crown that should have been his alone. None the less, as we read of those hideous last years of this most tragic of Emperors, it is hard not to feel that he – more perhaps than any other occupant of the Byzantine throne – should have been allowed to rest in peace.

1 Cedrenus, I, p. 753.

15

The Heraclian Line

[641–85]

Mais le VIIe siècle n'en marque pas moins pour l'Orient grec la fin du monde
antique; et, à ce titre, peut-être vaut-il la peine de montrer par quelques exemples
ce que furent les âmes, déséquilibrées et troubles, des hommes qui virent
s'accomplir cette grande évolution.

Charles Diehl,
Choses et Gens de Byzance

The death of Heraclius, long expected as it was, threw Byzantium into
chaos; and the cause of all the trouble was Martina. Not content with
persuading her husband to crown their son Heraclonas co-Emperor, she
had also forced him to draw up a will entrusting the Empire jointly to
his eldest son and true heir Constantine III, to Heraclonas and to herself.
One of the first acts of her widowhood was to hold a public rally in the
Hippodrome, at which she announced the terms of the will, making it
clear to all present that it was she who proposed to exercise the effective
power.

But the Byzantines would have none of it. They had long mistrusted
Martina for her scheming ambition; many, too, held her responsible for
her husband's decline and death. Their worst suspicions now seemed
confirmed. How, they demanded, could a woman receive or reply to
foreign ambassadors, let alone administer an Empire? The very idea was
preposterous. They would be happy to accord her the respect due to an
Empress Mother, but their obedience would be given only to her son
and stepson. Martina, baffled and furious, had no alternative but to
retreat into the palace; but she was not beaten yet. Soon afterwards
Constantine, the senior Emperor, fell sick. Possibly for a change of air,
but more likely to distance himself from his stepmother, he crossed the
Bosphorus to the palace at Chalcedon, but the move was of no avail:
he died on 25 May 641, after a reign of just three and a half months.

Was he killed by Martina? We cannot say for certain. In the absence of any contemporary records we are obliged to rely, for what little information we have, principally on Nicephorus and Theophanes, both writing in the early ninth century; and of these Nicephorus (whose account is the more detailed of the two) makes no such suggestion. Constantine had long been in ill health, and could well have died of natural causes. On the other hand the circumstances and above all the timing of his death are, at the very least, suspicious. Moreover, as we shall very shortly see, his son and successor did not hesitate to accuse the Empress, in the strongest possible terms, of his murder.

It also seems undeniable that Constantine himself had felt threatened. Why, otherwise, having first moved to the Asiatic shore, should he have appealed to the army from his deathbed to protect his infant heir, Heraclius, and his other children, and to uphold their rights of succession? As it happened, he need not have worried. The people of Constantinople, already overwhelmingly in favour of the senior branch of the family, were outraged by the way in which Martina, scarcely before her stepson's body was cold, openly sent all his ministers into exile and, ignoring her own son, assumed full imperial authority; and they were still more incensed by her enthusiastic support of monothelitism, a by now plainly unsuccessful doctrine which had never found popular favour and which Constantine had been doing his best to sweep away. In the summer of 641, in response to increasingly insistent demonstrations, little Heraclius had been crowned Emperor, and his name – presumably to avoid confusion with his grandfather – changed to Constans; and in September of the same year, by command of the Senate, Martina and Heraclonas were suddenly arrested. Her tongue was cut out; his nose was slit;[1] and the two were exiled to the island of Rhodes, never to return to the capital. If the Empress's only crime was her overweening ambition, she had paid a heavy price for it; if she and her son were regicides, they were lucky to have escaped so lightly.

My father Constantine reigned with Heraclius, his father and my grandfather, for a considerable time; but after the latter's death for only a very short period. For the envy of his stepmother Martina brought his high hopes to nothing and deprived him of his life – and all for the sake of Heraclonas, the son of her incestuous union with Heraclius. Your vote above all contributed to the just

---

1 The slitting – effectively the amputation – of the nose was an ancient oriental practice, introduced for the first time in Byzantium when Heraclius had thus punished Theodore and Athalaric for their suspected conspiracy a few years before (see p. 308). Its purpose was to invalidate the victim's claim to the throne since an Emperor, in the Byzantine view, must be free of all obvious physical imperfections.

deposition of her and her son from the imperial dignity, in order that the Roman Empire should not be obliged to countenance so grave an insult to the Law. Of this your noble eminences are fully aware; and I therefore invite you to assist me by your advice and judgement, in providing for the general safety of my subjects.[1]

With these words the eleven-year-old Constans II, now sole ruler of Byzantium, addressed the assembled Senate early in 642, entrusting it with the care of the Empire during his minority. During the years following the death of Justinian the Senate had grown rapidly in power and prestige. It was now as influential as ever it had been, serving both as adviser to the sovereign and as the supreme court of justice; and it was, in the absence of any senior member of the imperial family, the obvious body to assume the regency. But Constans was to mature into a determined and self-willed autocrat; he was not to accept its tutelage for long.

His twenty-seven-year reign was overshadowed from beginning to end by his constant struggle with the seemingly invincible Saracens. Already at the time of his accession they were advancing relentlessly through Egypt, which his stepmother during her brief period of power had virtually surrendered to them; and in 642 the Byzantine garrison sailed obediently out of Alexandria, leaving the country in the hands of the great Arab general Amr. When, two years later after the death of the Caliph Omar, his successor Othman recalled Amr to Medina, the Byzantines saw an opportunity for a counter-offensive and sent out a fleet, which managed briefly to recapture Alexandria; but as soon as the news reached Amr he hurried back to Egypt, and by the summer of 646 was once again in control. Razing the walls of Alexandria to the ground, he established a new capital, at the southern end of the delta and consequently less vulnerable to attack, in a village known as Fostat, later to be renamed Cairo. The popular tradition that the Muslim armies put the torch to the famous Library of Alexandria – the greatest in the world of late antiquity – is unfounded; that had already been destroyed by the Christians, in the anti-Arian riots of 391. Nor did they take any vengeance on the local populations – most of whom, like their Syrian and Palestinian neighbours, seem to have found their conquerors a welcome change from the Byzantines. Having thus successfully deprived the Empire of its richest and most valuable province, they then drove westward along the North African coast – in 647 inflicting a disastrous defeat on Gregory, Exarch of Carthage, who had advanced against them with an army (we are told) of 120,000 men.

The new Caliph Othman was a weaker, less effectual leader than the

1 Theophanes, 6134.

austerely magnificent Omar; in one respect, however, he proved considerably more far-sighted. Omar, with the desert-dweller's deep-rooted mistrust of the sea, had steadfastly refused to allow the building of a fleet; Othman, at the continued insistence of Muawiya, the Arab governor of Syria, gave his consent. Inevitably, the ship-building programme which was immediately initiated took several years to complete: Muawiya filled in the time leading major offensives into Armenia and – in 647 – as far west as Cappadocia, where he captured Caesarea (now Kaiseri). Only two years later, however, his fleet was ready, his seamen trained; and he at once flung the full force of it against Cyprus, with himself in command. The target was well chosen: Cyprus was one of the Empire's chief naval bases, and though Muawiya had not sufficient manpower to occupy it permanently he was able to take its capital Constantia[1] by storm, sack the city, destroy the port and harbour installations and ravage vast tracts of the surrounding country.

In 650 it was the turn of Aradus (now Ruad), a prosperous merchant city on an island off the Syrian coast, which was burnt to ashes and left uninhabitable, its people driven away to seek refuge where they might. After that, Constans was able to negotiate a two-year truce; but this only freed Muawiya to concentrate on more ship-building, so that in 654 he was able to launch a still more formidable expedition against the island of Rhodes. The extent of the damage wrought on this occasion is not recorded, though it must have been considerable; our best source, Theophanes, is understandably more interested to tell us of the fate of the celebrated Colossus. This hundred-foot-high bronze statue of Helios the sun god – one of the Seven Wonders of the World – had been commissioned from a local sculptor, Chares of Lindos, in 304 BC, and proudly set up beside the entrance to the harbour;[2] but alas, only a century later an earthquake brought it crashing to the ground. The heartbroken Rhodians never tried to re-erect it, but left it for nearly nine more centuries lying where it had fallen. It was only now, during the temporary Arab occupation of the island, that Muawiya had it broken up and sold for scrap. The metal was ultimately sold to a Jewish merchant from Edessa; he needed 900 camels to carry it away.

---

1 Better known nowadays by its original Greek name of Salamis, Constantia lies about 5 km north of Famagusta. Although later rebuilt and refortified, it was to suffer several further raids and a serious earthquake, as a result of which the harbour silted up and became unusable. It was then abandoned, its ruined buildings making it a convenient quarry for Famagusta in its fourteenth-century heyday.

2 Contrary to the popular legend, never straddling it.

The capture of Rhodes – and of its neighbour Cos soon afterwards – persuaded Constans that he must take the initiative: left to himself, Muawiya would obviously continue to add island after island to his chain of conquests until it extended to Constantinople itself. In 655, therefore, an imperial fleet sailed out of the Marmara and southward down the coast. It met the Saracens off Phoenicus – the modern Finike – in Lycia, and immediately battle was joined. This was the first of a whole millennium of sea fights between Christian and Muslim, and it was a catastrophe. The Byzantine navy was shattered, and Constans himself escaped only by changing clothes with one of his men – who was subsequently killed in the fighting.

The situation now looked grave indeed; but the next year saw a momentous event which prevented Muawiya from following up his advantage. On 17 June 656 the Caliph Othman was assassinated in his house at Medina, while reading the Koran. Ali, the Prophet's son-in-law, was elected his successor on the spot, and was supported by the tribesmen of Mesopotamia; Muawiya, on the other hand, who had been simultaneously proclaimed in Syria, accused Ali of complicity in the murder and, hanging Othman's bloodstained shirt on the *mimber*[1] of the Great Mosque of Damascus, swore vengeance. The ensuing strife continued until 661, when Ali's own assassination left Muawiya supreme. For the next five years the Muslim world would be in ferment – and Byzantium could breathe again.

The Emperor – whose heavily hirsute appearance had by now earned him the nickname of *Pogonatus*, 'the Bearded'[2] – doubtless welcomed the respite, and in 659 was more than happy to accept Muawiya's offer of 1,000 *nomismata* in return for a cessation of hostilities, with the additional bonus of a horse and a slave for every day that the peace between them should last. The question arises, all the same, why he had waited fourteen years after his accession, until the year 655, before taking any action at all against his enemy. Much the same question, it will be remembered, had been asked of his grandfather Heraclius, and to some extent the same

---

1 The hooded pulpit, reached by a long flight of steps, from which the Friday sermon is delivered.

2 This nickname was long mistakenly attributed to Constans's son, Constantine IV. The confusion was finally cleared up by E. W. Brooks in his monograph 'Who was Constantine Pogonatus?' in *Byzantinische Zeitschrift*, Vol. xvii (1908), pp. 460–62. All the Emperors at this period wore beards; a glance at their coins, on the other hand, makes it clear that the luxuriant growth on the face of Constans was, even by seventh-century standards, something rather special.

answer can be given: he needed time to prepare his forces. But for Constans there was another requirement too. The ill feeling engendered by the monothelite controversy and the intrigues of Martina had left Constantinople dangerously split. It was of the first importance that he should somehow re-establish – at least so far as he could – religious and political unity.

He himself had never had any time for theological speculation: of the doctrine of the Single Will he probably understood little and cared less. Originally intended as a constructive compromise, it had only added to the prevailing bitterness and confusion. The sensible thing, clearly, would be to forget all about it and pretend that it had never been put forward. Unfortunately, however, it still had influential adherents in the capital, led by the Patriarch Paul in person, while a vociferous opposition had been organized in Africa by an alarmingly articulate monk known as Maximus the Confessor. Early in 646 Maximus arranged for a manifesto condemning the heresy to be endorsed by a synod of African bishops and forwarded to Pope Theodore; and the Pope, understandably irritated that his predecessor's action of only six years before should have had so little effect, wrote to the Patriarch demanding a full statement of his beliefs. Paul replied, defending the offending doctrine in the strongest possible terms, whereupon Theodore promptly excommunicated him.

Constans was still only seventeen, but his reaction was so characteristic of him that it must clearly have been his own initiative. Whereas his grandfather would have defended his Patriarch in a long and closely reasoned document – as Paul doubtless urged him to do – he remained determinedly impartial, while contriving at the same time to be both firm and decisive. Early in 648 he published an edict known as the *Typos*, or *Type*. It did not seek to weigh the pros and cons of monothelitism, still less to pronounce on its validity; it simply decreed that the whole dispute should be consigned to oblivion, and that the state of affairs that had prevailed before it began should continue 'as if the issue had never arisen'. If a bishop or a clerk should dare even to raise the subject, he would be immediately deposed; if a monk, he would be excommunicated; if a member of the army or civil service, he would be deprived of his rank or office; if a senator or the equivalent, he would lose his property; if a private person, he would be flogged and banished.

It is hard not to sympathize with Constans; at the same time he should have known, even at his age, that it is impossible to put back the clock. The problem would not go away, and the *Typos* satisfied nobody. In

October 649 Pope Theodore's successor, Martin I, summoned a Council of 105 bishops in the Lateran Palace which duly condemned it; he then sent the Emperor a full report of the Council's findings, considerately translated into Greek for his benefit, under cover of a letter of studied politeness in which he required him formally to express his abhorrence of the monothelite dogma.

Constans, it need hardly be said, had no intention of doing any such thing. Little did Pope Martin know that before his letter was even written the newly appointed Byzantine Exarch of Ravenna, Olympius, was on his way to Italy with a small armed force, bearing orders to arrest the Pontiff – on the somewhat shaky grounds that his recent election had not been submitted to Constantinople for approval. Anastasius, Pope Martin's biographer, claims that Olympius had decided to kill the Pope rather than take him prisoner but, being continually thwarted in his attempts to do so, concluded that his intended victim was under divine protection and made a complete confession to him; what is beyond doubt is the fact that he then tried to take advantage of the widespread anti-Byzantine feeling in Italy to detach the whole province from the Empire and seize the secular power for himself. He did not succeed, but retired with his army to Sicily where he died three years later.

One year after his death, however, in June 653, his successor as Exarch, a certain Theodore Calliopas, landed in Italy. Theodore had similar instructions, and was determined to carry them out. Within days of his arrival, Pope Martin – already a sick man – had been duly arrested and put on board the ship that was to carry him to face trial in Constantinople. For some unexplained reason he was not taken there directly, but was held for a year on the island of Naxos; only in September 654 did he reach the Bosphorus – to find that his tribulations had hardly begun. Arriving early in the morning, he was obliged to remain on board till sunset, being subjected throughout the day to the jeers and mockery of the populace. At nightfall he was taken off to the prison of Prandearia, where he was held for the next ninety-three days. Finally, half-starving, freezing cold (for it was now mid-winter) and unable to walk, he was brought before the tribunal.

To the original charge of having assumed the Papacy without imperial consent, a new and graver one had now been added: the Pope was accused of having conspired with Olympius against the Emperor. He naturally denied all the allegations, but the outcome was a foregone conclusion: he was found guilty, sentenced to death and led out into a

large open courtyard where, in the presence of a dense crowd, his papal
robes were torn from his shoulders. Even his undershirt was ripped
from top to bottom, 'so that he was naked in several places'. An iron
chain was then flung around his neck and he was marched through the
streets to the *Praetorium* – the imperial prison – with the executioner's
sword carried before him. On arrival there he was obliged to share a cell
with murderers and common criminals, and was treated with such brutality that his legs were badly cut and the floor of the cell was stained
with his blood.

Patriarch Paul, meanwhile, was on his deathbed. There he was visited
by Constans, who gave him – presumably in an attempt to raise his
spirits – a full account of Martin's trial and his subsequent sufferings. To
the Emperor's surprise, the dying man was much distressed. 'Alas,' he
murmured, 'this too must I answer for'; and he begged the Emperor as
his last wish that the Pope should be subjected to no further ill treatment
and that his life should be spared. His request was granted – though
only after Martin had spent another eighty-five days in prison – and the
sentence commuted from death to banishment. The old man was sent off
to Cherson in the Crimea where, less than six months later, on 16 September 655, he died. Nor was he the only martyr to the doctrine of the
Single Will: soon after his condemnation it was the turn of Maximus the
Confessor. He too was brought from Italy to stand trial in Constantinople, where he was subjected to unspeakable brutalities – including
the removal of his tongue and the cutting off of his right hand – in
attempts to force him to recant. But like Martin he stood firm and –
thanks largely to his immense reputation as a theologian[1] – also escaped
execution, finally dying a natural death in 662 in his place of exile, at the
age of eighty.

As the eastern provinces of his Empire fell one by one to the Arab
invaders, Constans began to turn his thoughts increasingly towards those
of the West. In the past half-century they had given his predecessors and
himself little enough trouble; his grandfather Heraclius had hardly
needed to spare them a thought. He knew, however, that this happy
state of affairs could not last. In the Balkans, the Slav settlers were

---

1 Maximus, even more than Pope Martin, had been the spiritual leader of the opposition both to the
Ekthesis and the *Typos*. Indeed he had gone even further, maintaining that the Emperor as a layman
had no right to pronounce on theological matters. The author of no less than ninety major works,
he was in many respects the forerunner of those medieval fathers who were to uphold the claims of
the Church against the State in centuries to come.

growing restive and making difficulties over their annual tribute; in Italy, especially after the arrest and trial of Pope Martin, Byzantium was more unpopular than ever it had been; Sicily, meanwhile, was in very real danger from the Saracens, who had first attacked it as early as 652 and had since occupied still more of the North African coast, from which they would doubtless be launching further expeditions before long. If, in short, preventive measures were not taken, the western provinces might drop away from the Empire just as surely as those in the East had done.

The respite afforded by Muawiya's preoccupations with the Caliphate gave the Emperor precisely the chance he needed. Already in 658 we find him leading a punitive expedition against the Balkan Slavs, large numbers of whom he transported and resettled in Asia Minor; but it was only in 662 that he took the decision which might have changed the whole future history of the Roman Empire: to leave Constantinople for ever and establish his court permanently in the West. His grandfather Heraclius had had the same idea nearly half a century before, and had been dissuaded only by the combined entreaties of Patriarch and people. Heraclius, however, had been an outstandingly popular ruler; his grandson was not. Constans had antagonized the monophysite and monothelitist communities by refusing to give them the support they had hoped for, and the orthodox by his treatment of Martin and Maximus; worse still, in 660 he had shamelessly ordered the murder of his brother Theodosius, having previously forced him into the priesthood – not, as he claimed, because Theodosius had been conspiring against him but, as everybody knew, because he was under pressure to crown him co-Emperor and could not bear to contemplate any sharing of his own authority.

We can probably discount the suggestion by later historians that the Emperor fled his capital to escape from the hideous visions of his bloodstained brother which haunted his midnight hours; nor, surely, can his decision be attributed to his unpopularity in the city – even though this may go some way to explain why the inhabitants seem to have raised no objections.[1] He had never made any effort to be popular and, so long as his position remained secure, the degree to which he was loved by his subjects was a matter of supreme indifference to him. In any case his primary purpose in leaving was a far more honourable one: to protect Italy, Sicily and what was left of his African province from Saracen

---

[1] Another reason for their apathy may have been that they did not know his true intentions and simply assumed that he was leaving on an extended tour of his western dominions rather than deserting them for ever.

conquest. If in addition he could drive the Lombards from Italy – or at least from the southern half of the peninsula – then so much the better.

Leaving his wife and three sons in Constantinople, the Emperor sailed in early 662 for Greece, where he seemed to have found more to do than he had expected. He remained there, first in Thessalonica and then in Athens, for a full year; and it was not until the spring of 663 that he finally crossed the Adriatic and landed with his army at Tarentum – now Taranto. The Lombards put up what opposition they could, but their local militias were small: Constans was able to advance without too much difficulty as far as Benevento, to which he laid siege. Unfortunately for him, the city had already sent an urgent appeal for aid to the Lombard King Grimuald in his capital at Pavia, and Grimuald had at once dispatched a relief force of considerable strength; if Benevento could hold out until its arrival, it would be the Byzantines who found themselves outnumbered.

At this point, as the Lombard army was advancing rapidly southwards, a messenger who had been sent on ahead by Grimuald to inform the Beneventans of its approach was captured and brought before Constans. Cunningly, the Emperor offered to spare his life if he would deliver a contrary message, to the effect that no help was to be forthcoming. The messenger – his name was Sesuald – agreed; but when he was brought beneath the walls he shouted, before his captors could silence him, that the army was indeed on its way and had already reached the Sangro River. He barely had time to add a plea for the protection of his wife and children before his head was struck from his shoulders; shortly afterwards it was loaded into a catapult and hurled over the walls.

But Sesuald had saved Benevento, and the imperial army had no course but to go on to Naples – which was a Greek city, and therefore friendly – and thence to Rome where Constans, despite his treatment of Martin, was accorded a formal welcome by Pope Vitalian and solemnly escorted into the city – the first Emperor to set foot in it since the fall of the Western Empire nearly two centuries before. The *Liber Pontificalis* describes approvingly how he spent the next twelve days visiting all the major churches; but the Romans were a good deal less gratified when he began stripping their city of what few valuables it still possessed – including even the copper from the roof of the Pantheon – and shipping them back to Constantinople. Great must have been their relief when, on 12 July, he returned to Naples.

In the autumn, having marched slowly south through Calabria, Constans crossed the Straits of Messina to Sicily; and for the next five years he kept his court at Syracuse. For the Sicilians, those five years were one protracted nightmare. The honour, such as it was, of finding their island selected for the capital of the Roman Empire was as nothing in comparison with the extortions of the imperial tax-gatherers – for the satisfaction of whom, we are told, husbands were sold into slavery, wives forced into prostitution, children separated from their parents. Nor can we tell how long these depredations might have continued had not the Emperor unexpectedly come to a sudden, violent and somewhat humiliating end. There was, so far as we know, no preconceived plan to assassinate him, far less any deeply hatched conspiracy; but on 15 September 668, while he was innocently lathering himself in his bath, one of his Greek attendants – in what we can only assume to have been a fit of uncontrollable nostalgia – felled him with the soap-dish.

During the Emperor's long absence from Constantinople, the remaining eastern provinces had been administered by the eldest of his three sons, who now succeeded him as Constantine IV. Owing to our continued – and deeply frustrating – lack of contemporary historians, we know little about his appearance or character; an incident occurring soon after his accession, however, hardly predisposes us in his favour. In 669 certain regiments from Asia Minor marched on the capital, demanding that Constantine should crown his two younger brothers co-rulers with himself, on the curious grounds that since Heaven was ruled by a Trinity, so should the Earth be also. The firmness and promptness of the Emperor's reaction showed, as clearly as anything could, how he intended to govern: he invited the leaders to a conference in his palace, and immediately on their arrival had them seized and summarily executed – after which, as Gibbon tells the story, 'the prospect of their bodies hanging on the gibbet in the suburb of Galata reconciled their companions to the unity of the reign of Constantine'. Opinions differ as to whether or not the two young princes had instigated the uprising; but their brother was not in the mood to give them the benefit of the doubt. In conformity with the practice now growing distressingly frequent in Byzantine political life, their noses were slit – not just a punishment and a warning for the future, but a silent proclamation, to army and people alike, of their unfitness to rule.

Such a charge, despite his periodic outbursts of brutality, could never be levelled against Constantine. On the contrary, he was to prove a wise statesman and, like his great-grandfather, a born leader of men. Admittedly he had inherited from Heraclius a superbly organized state –

at least where its Anatolian heartland was concerned; one might argue, too, that he enjoyed more than his fair share of good luck. But what cannot be questioned is the fact that the first decade of his reign marked a watershed in the history, not only of the Byzantine Empire, but of all Christendom: the moment when, for the first time, the armies of the Crescent were checked, turned and put to flight by those of the Cross.

The brief respite was over. In 661 the Caliph Ali had been assassinated outside the mosque at his headquarters in Kufa; since then, Muawiya had reigned supreme. One of his first decisions had been to establish his capital at Damascus, where he founded the dynasty of Omayyad Caliphs that was to endure for the next eighty years. An old and venerable city, it was moreover incomparably better placed than the remote townships of the Arabian Hejaz for the achievement of his prime objective: the annihilation of the Roman Empire. With the vastly increased resources now at his command, he had resumed those tactics that had served him so well in the previous decade, every year dispatching a new army into Anatolia and a new fleet up the Ionian coast, plucking off the imperial cities and islands one by one. After Cos came Chios; after Chios, Smyrna; finally, in 672, the Saracens sailed up the Hellespont and into the Marmara, where they captured the peninsula of Cyzicus on the Bithynian shore – only some fifty miles across the water from Constantinople itself – and began to fortify it as their principal bridgehead. Two years later the siege began.

Most of the previous attacks against the city of Constantine had been launched from the landward side: this one came from the sea. The Saracen ships carried heavy siege engines and huge catapults with which to bombard the walls and their defenders alike. But the fortifications, both along the Marmara and the Golden Horn, were proof against all their assaults – while the Byzantines for their part were able to create havoc among the attackers by means of a secret weapon invented a few years before by a certain Callinicus, an architect and chemist from the Syrian city of Heliopolis (more familiar to us nowadays as Baalbek). It was a secret so well guarded that to this day we are uncertain of the precise composition of what was known throughout the middle ages as 'Greek fire'.[1] Sometimes it was sprayed, by means of a pump or syphon, over an enemy vessel; sometimes it was poured into long, narrow

1 Marcus Graecus, a writer of the tenth century, gives a rough recipe: 'Take pure sulphur, tartar, sarcocolla [Persian gum], pitch, dissolved nitre, petroleum [obtainable from surface deposits in Mesopotamia and the Caucasus] and pine resin; boil these together, then saturate tow with the result and set fire to it. The conflagration will spread, and can be extinguished only by urine, vinegar or sand' – a property which, if true, would give a completely new dimension to the technique of fire-fighting.

cartridges and catapulted against its objective. The results were almost invariably catastrophic – particularly since the flaming liquid, being oil-based, would float upon the surface of the sea, frequently igniting the wooden hulls of the ships and causing an additional hazard to those who tried to save themselves by jumping overboard.

But the Muslims, unaccustomed to such opposition, refused to admit defeat. Retiring with the approach of winter to Cyzicus, they called up further reinforcements from Syria and spent the next few months repairing and refitting their ships. With the coming of spring they returned to the attack; but the second year of the siege did not prove any more successful than the first. Nor did the third, nor the fourth; it was only after the fifth year of frustration, in 678, that the siege was finally raised and the battered remnants of the Saracen fleet turned about and headed for home. Even then their tribulations were not over; returning along the coast of Pamphylia, they ran into a freak autumn storm which accounted for yet further losses.

While Muawiya's navy was hammering in vain against the walls of Constantinople, his army had sustained similar reverses nearer home. Here his enemies were not the Byzantines but the so-called Mardaites – bands of Christian freebooters who, from their original redoubts high in the Taurus Mountains, had spread south into Syria and Mount Lebanon, where they were waging a ceaseless guerrilla war against the Arabs as far south as Jerusalem and even the Dead Sea. To the Caliph, already seriously worried by his inability to control these brigands, the news of the humiliation of his fleet came as a shattering blow. The Empire, it seemed, was invincible after all, under the divine protection of its Christian God. In 679, discouraged and demoralized, he accepted Constantine's offer of peace – under terms which, a few years before, he would have considered ignoble: the evacuation of the Aegean islands that he had so recently conquered, plus an annual tribute to the Emperor of fifty slaves, fifty horses and 3,000 pounds of gold. A year later he was dead.

Constantine, on the other hand, was at the height of his popularity and prestige. He had inspired his subjects with the courage and the morale to withstand five years of siege by a power hitherto considered irresistible, and in doing so he had saved Western civilization. Blocked from Europe by the impregnable walls of Constantinople and the un-yielding spirit of the Emperor and his people, the armies of the Prophet were obliged to travel the entire length of the Mediterranean to the Straits of Gibraltar before they could invade the continent – thus extending their lines of communication and supply almost to breaking point and rendering impossible any permanent conquests beyond the Pyrenees. Had they captured Constantinople in the seventh century rather than the fifteenth, all Europe – and America – might be Muslim today.

And Western civilization recognized its saviour. It was not only the Khagan of the Avars and the Slav tribal leaders in the Balkans who sent Constantine embassies of congratulation, with requests for assurances of peace and friendship: it was also the Lombard and Frankish princes of the West. He was, after all, the sole Emperor of the Christian world: a ruler with whom they might disagree or even on occasion wage war, but whose precedence they would never have questioned; and he had shown himself worthy of his title.

With the Saracens finally in retreat, Constantine could turn his attention to another, lesser, enemy – the Bulgars. These warlike pagan tribesmen were not in fact Slavs – as their descendants, largely for linguistic reasons, are generally considered today – but of Turkic origin; they had, however, left their ancient home in the lands between the lower reaches of the Volga and the Don and had migrated westward to the north bank of the Danube, whence more and more of them were trickling across the river into imperial territory. In 680 a large squadron of Byzantine ships, with the Emperor himself in command, sailed up the Bosphorus into the Black Sea and landed an army just north of the Danube delta. Unfortunately, the region had not been reconnoitred in advance: the swampy terrain made any organized advance impossible, while Constantine himself suffered an agonizing attack of gout which obliged him to retire for a few days to Mesembria nearby. Such a minor incapacity should not have affected the campaign unduly; for some reason, however, the rumour spread through the army that the Emperor had taken flight. In the ensuing panic his men turned and fled – while the Bulgars, seeing their chance, pursued them across the Danube into the former province of Moesia, killing all those whom they captured.

The net result of the expedition was thus precisely the opposite of what had been intended: instead of forcing back the Bulgars, it facilitated and encouraged their further penetration of the Empire. The invaders quickly realized that the new region in which they found themselves, an unusually fertile land protected by the Danube to the north, the Balkan Mountains to the south and the Black Sea to the east, was far preferable to that which they had just left. Easily subduing the seven Slavonic tribes who had already settled there, they rapidly established a strong

Bulgar state – which, in a somewhat different form, survives to this day – and even obliged the Emperor to agree to the annual payment of protection money to their King.

It was, in fact, more of a humiliation than a real disaster. Given the strength of the Bulgars along the frontier, some such arrangement would sooner or later have been inevitable. It had, moreover, the advantage of cementing a general peace which was to endure to the end of Constantine's reign and which allowed him to tackle the most stubborn of all his internal problems. The doctrine of the Single Will of Christ had sustained several severe blows during his father's time, but had obstinately refused to die. Already in 678 the Emperor had written to the Pope, proposing an ecumenical council of the Church to settle the matter once and for all; and the Pope, after summoning a preliminary synod in Rome to ensure that the Western representatives at least should speak with one voice, enthusiastically agreed. All through the early autumn of 680 the delegates poured in – 174 of them, from every corner of the Christian world. The Italian party, which consisted of the Bishops of Palermo, Reggio and Porto and their suites, together with a priest named Theodore representing the Greek Church of Ravenna, were received with particular honours and accommodated in the Palace of Placidia at the Emperor's expense. By the beginning of November most of them had arrived, and a week later the Sixth Ecumenical Council of the Church held its first session in the *Trullos*, or Domed Hall, of the imperial palace.

The Council was to hold eighteen plenary sessions, spread out over the next ten months. Constantine himself presided over the first eleven of them – though he was careful to remain impartial throughout and to express no opinions of his own – and again over the last, when on 16 September 681 he formally endorsed the almost unanimous findings. The doctrine of the Single Will, the Council decided, was incompatible with that of the humanity of the Saviour – who possessed, on the contrary, 'two natural Wills and two natural Energies, without division, alteration, separation or confusion'. Those who had maintained otherwise were condemned and cursed – including the now defunct Pope Honorius, who had given his somewhat lukewarm approval half a century before.

The problem of a canonically elected Pope being anathematized by his own successors has been a perennial source of embarrassment to Roman Catholic theologians – particularly those who have had to defend the later doctrine of papal infallibility; but it caused no anxiety to those gathered in the Domed Hall who, after the Emperor's closing speech, cheered him to the echo – hailing him as the Light of the World, the new Constantine the Great, the new Marcian,[1] the new Justinian, and the Destroyer of all Heretics. None of these accolades were altogether justified, least of all the last; but when, four years later, Constantine died of a sudden dysentery at the age of just thirty-three, he could congratulate himself not only that he was leaving his Empire stronger, more peaceful and more united than at any time in the century, but that he had dealt the monothelite heresy a blow from which it would never recover.

---

1 It was Marcian who summoned the Council of Chalcedon in 451, when the monophysites were first condemned (see Chapter 7).

16
The Emperor who Lost his Nose

[685-711]

Non cuicunque datum est habere nasum.

It is not given to just anyone to have a nose.

Martial

Constantine IV was barely seventeen when his wife Anastasia had given
birth to their first-born son. Had he been a little older and wiser, he
might not have named the baby Justinian; for the arrogant and ob-
streperous youth who, just sixteen years later, became lord and master of
the Roman Empire was from the outset determined to model himself on
his tremendous namesake and to leave, as Justinian I had left, the indelible imprint of his personality on every facet of the State. In some
respects he was to succeed; intelligent, shrewd and politically perceptive,
with all the driving energy of his great-great-grandfather, he showed in
his youth all the makings of a capable and gifted ruler – perhaps even of
a great one. His tragedy was to have inherited also, and in full measure,
that streak of mental imbalance that had so clouded the last years of
Heraclius and that was again apparent in the behaviour of the ageing
Constans. If there was little sign of this defect in Constantine IV, this
may be only because he died before it could become manifest; in his son
Justinian, on the other hand, it appeared early and rapidly established its
hold, robbing him of judgement and moderation alike and transforming
him into an inhuman monster whose only attributes – apart from his
spirit and undoubted courage – were a pathological suspicion of all those
with whom he came in contact and an insatiable lust for blood.

The beginning of his reign was promising enough. Successful military
expeditions to Armenia, Georgia and Syria led the fifth Caliph, Abdul-
Malik – who had assumed supremacy over the Faithful in the same year
as Justinian's own accession – to seek in 688 a renewal of the treaty
concluded by Constantine IV with Muawiya. This new settlement was,

from the Byzantine point of view, a distinct improvement on the old: in addition to the down payment of 1,000 *nomismata*, the tribute of horses and slaves was increased to one of each every Friday. It was also agreed, with regard to the revenues of Armenia and Iberia[1] on the one hand and Cyprus on the other, that these should in future be divided equally between the two signatories – an arrangement that resulted in the demilitarization of Cyprus and a state of enviable autonomy for its people which was to endure for the best part of the next three centuries.[2] A more dubious provision of the treaty was that the marauding Mardaites should be evacuated from Mount Lebanon and resettled in Anatolia. For years these wild tribesmen had been a continual thorn in Saracen flesh, and had served the Empire well; and there were many Byzantines who feared that their removal would result in a dangerous weakening of the Syrian frontier. But Justinian believed – probably rightly – that by transferring them to Attalia (Antalya) and several other key points along the southern coast he was in fact strengthening his defences rather than the reverse.

Besides, he saw it as an integral part of a far larger and more ambitious plan: the repopulation of Anatolia, which had never really recovered from the depredations of his namesake Justinian the Great. This policy was not new; it had been spasmodically pursued ever since the introduction by Maurice of 30,000 Armenian cavalry a century before. But Justinian gave it new impetus, and it is in this light that we should probably see his large-scale military expedition of 688–9 into the Slav lands of the West. Having made a triumphal entry into Thessalonica, he somehow arranged for the transportation across the Aegean of vast numbers of Slav villagers and peasants, and for their resettlement in the Theme of Opsikion – the old Bithynia, occupying the entire south coast of the Sea of Marmara together with a considerable hinterland. In the year following he ordered several other similar transplantations of whole communities, from outlying lands in both East and West: it has been estimated that he was responsible, in the space of some five or six years, for the establishment of perhaps a quarter of a million new immigrants in Asia Minor.

Such immense movements of population could hardly fail to bring radical changes in their train. The backbone of the administrative structure remained the Themes, first introduced by Heraclius; but within

1 The region immediately to the north of Armenia, between the Black Sea and the Caspian.
2 They were, *inter alia*, exempt from compulsory military service, and would also be unaffected by the iconoclast persecutions of the eighth century.

them the social conditions were very different from those of his day. At the beginning of the century, the dominant influence was that of the great land-owners – the prototypes of the feudal barons of Western Europe; by the end, the emphasis is on the new class of free and independent peasants, cultivating their own fields but bound to their neighbours by the woods, meadows and pastures held in common. So sudden an improvement in living conditions led, predictably, to a rising birthrate and a steady increase in the amount of land under cultivation; and the growing population produced in its turn – since Heraclius's institution of compulsory military service for the head or eldest son of each family was firmly maintained – an ever-stronger provincial militia ready for action at short notice. This social revolution – for it was nothing less – is reflected in one of the two most revealing pieces of legislation to have come down to us from the period: the so-called 'Farmers' Law', which most modern scholars date to Justinian (though it may be slightly later). Though the punishments laid down for various misdemeanours in the village community are often savage – flogging or blinding for the theft of corn, loss of a hand for setting fire to a barn or granary – it gives a wonderfully vivid picture of rural life in the otherwise shadowy seventh century.[1]

By this time, too, it is clear that taxes were levied not on the individual villager but on the village as a whole. There was nothing wrong with this principle in itself; each man paid his share, in a proportion decided by the community. The trouble came only when Justinian began – as he very soon did – to make demands far above the ability of his subjects to fulfil. The majority of these subjects, it must be remembered, were foreigners recently arrived, uprooted against their will from their homeland and with no inborn feelings of loyalty to their Emperor. It was doubtless for this reason that, after the outbreak of fresh hostilities with the Arabs in 691, we find some 20,000 Slav soldiers deserting to the enemy – so ensuring a major defeat for the Empire at Sebastopolis[2] in the following year and the consequent loss of Armenia. It was on this occasion, according to Theophanes, that Justinian gave the first proof of the savagery that was to make his name infamous. He is said to have rounded up all the Slav families in Bithynia – many hundred miles from the scene of the betrayal – on the shore of the Gulf of Nicomedia and then to have ordered a general massacre, with men, women and child-

[1] An English translation may be found in the *Journal of Hellenic Studies*, Vol. XXXII (1912), pp. 87–95.

[2] The present Sulusaray, between Sivas and Amasya.

ren by the thousand being slain in cold blood and flung into the sea.

It is only fair to record that some doubts have been cast on this allegation, as a result of the discovery of a lead seal datable to 694–5 – that is, two or three years *after* the massacre – and identifying its owner as an administrator of the Slav mercenaries in Bithynia. This certainly suggests that the Slavs in the region were not *all* murdered; on the other hand, it could equally easily be explained by a new influx of settlers, brought in to replace those who had been killed. One modern historian goes so far as to state categorically that 'Theophanes cannot be believed';[1] alas, everything we know of the Emperor's later life suggests that his story may be all too true.

Fascinating as are the provisions of the Farmers' Law, there is one other document that tells us even more about the manners and customs prevailing in Justinian II's day: the record of the great Synod of 165 Eastern bishops, summoned by the Emperor in 691 and known as the Quinisextum. The proclaimed purpose of this gathering – which explains, incidentally, its rather curious name – was to regulate all those matters left outstanding after the Fifth and Sixth Ecumenical Councils; but it was also yet another example of the Emperor's determination to leave his mark on ecclesiastical affairs as on every other branch of government. Thus, in the absence of any major issues to be discussed, the delegates were compelled to spend much of their time on matters of little real importance – and sometimes, indeed, of quite astonishing triviality.

They are, however, not a jot less interesting on that account. We read, for example, in Canon 3 that second marriages for the clergy are forbidden, and that no man who, after his baptism, has married a widow, a prostitute, a slave or an actress may enter the priesthood; in Canon 11, that no priest might consult a Jewish physician or take a bath in company with a Jew; in Canon 24, that the clergy were banned from the races and the theatre, and that if invited to weddings they must retire 'before the games began'; in Canon 42, that 'those hermits who dress in black, wear their hair long and go about the towns visiting laymen and women' must cut their hair and enter a monastery and, if they refuse, must be chased away to desert places; in Canon 50, that playing at dice, even for laymen, was punishable by excommunication; in Canon 61, that six years of penitence were to be imposed on all who consulted fortune-tellers, 'showed bears or other animals to deceive the simple', or sold lucky

1 Ostrogorsky, in the 1st ed. of translation; in the 2nd ed., the sentence has been amended (pp. 131–2) to read: 'It is not of course possible to credit Theophanes . . .' The change of nuance is intriguing.

charms and amulets; in Canon 62, that all pagan festivals such as the Bota (in honour of Pan) or the Brumalia (in honour of Bacchus) were prohibited, as were all dances by women and all by either sex in honour of pagan gods, all comic, tragic or satyrical masks, all transvestites, and all invocations to Bacchus during the grape harvest; in Canon 65, that it was forbidden to dance round bonfires at the new moon; in Canon 79, that Christmas presents were forbidden; in Canon 91, that abortionists and their patients should be punished in the same way as murderers; and in Canon 96, that the ban of the Church would fall on all those who 'curled their hair in a provocative or seductive manner'.

Now most of this was harmless enough, and we may be sure that the deliberations of the Quinisextum made little or no difference to the habits and superstitions of the country folk of Anatolia and the Balkans, who have maintained many of them up to the present day. All might have been well had not Justinian – who had not troubled to invite any special representatives from Rome to his Synod – sent the 102 approved Canons to Pope Sergius I, with somewhat peremptory instructions to endorse them. Since several of these Canons – such as those permitting marriage among the secular clergy or condemning fasts on Saturdays in Lent – were directly contrary to Roman usage, the Pope very naturally refused;[1] whereupon Justinian ordered the Exarch of Ravenna, one Zacharias, to arrest him forthwith and bring him to Constantinople for judgement.

In doing so, he clearly had in mind his grandfather's treatment of Pope Martin and – even more, perhaps – the first Justinian, who had behaved in similar fashion to Pope Vigilius. But times had changed. Pope Sergius was a good deal more powerful, and more popular, than his two unfortunate predecessors. On receiving their orders, the imperial militias of both Ravenna and Rome flatly refused to obey. Soon after Zacharias reached the Lateran Palace, the building was surrounded; and the unfortunate Exarch found himself a prisoner of his own troops and of the Roman populace, all hurling imprecations on the Emperor and himself for presuming to lay hands on the Pontiff. Only, we are told, after Sergius had personally intervened on his behalf could he be persuaded to emerge from under the papal bed and make good his escape.[2]

When the news reached Constantinople, Justinian flew into one of those ungovernable rages for which he was already famous. It is unlikely,

---

1 Another Canon to which the Pope took particular exception was that which forbade the popular metaphor of Christ as a Lamb. Sergius, we are told, had a special affection for this image, and expressed his displeasure by deliberately adding the *Agnus Dei* to the Mass.

2 *Liber Pontificalis*, I, 373–4.

however, that the majority of his subjects felt much sympathy. In the seven years since his accession the young Emperor – he was still barely twenty-three – had acquired a degree of unpopularity previously equalled, perhaps, only by Phocas. His high-handed treatment of the recent settlers had already, as we have seen, resulted in a massive mutiny that had cost him Armenia. The old aristocracy, fully aware of his hostility, had been obliged to stand impotently by while he had steadily shorn them of their powers and privileges in favour of a free peasantry responsible only to himself; and even that peasantry had been antagonized by his insatiable demands for money.

Here was the one field in which Justinian II could equal, or even surpass, his great namesake. He too had a passion for building, on a scale which threatened to reduce his subjects to penury. His tax-collectors – above all his Grand Logothete (and defrocked priest) Theodotus and his *Sacellarius* Stephen of Persia, a huge and hideous eunuch never seen without a whip in his hand – had quickly shown themselves to be as brutal and merciless as John of Cappadocia at his worst, thinking nothing of torturing their victims (often by hanging them over a slow fire and smoking them into unconsciousness) if they could thereby extract a few additional pieces of gold for their master. Inevitably, it was the wealthy aristocracy that suffered most: Justinian made no secret of the fact that he hated them and was determined to destroy them as a class. They bore the extortions till they could bear them no more; then they rose in revolt.

Their leader was one of themselves, a professional soldier named Leontius who, after distinguishing himself in the Armenian and Caucasian campaigns, had been disgraced in 692 – he may have commanded the army that had been defeated at Sebastopolis – and thrown into prison. While there, so the story goes, he had been visited by two monks, one of whom had foretold that he would one day wear the imperial diadem. This prophecy had so preyed on his mind that when in 695 he was suddenly set at liberty and nominated military governor of the new Theme of Hellas, he marched on the *Praetorium*, overpowered the Prefect and released all the prisoners that were being held there – many of them his old comrades-in-arms, who declared for him at once. Together they then moved on to St Sophia, calling on all whom they passed to gather at the Great Church. On their arrival the Patriarch, who had recently given the Emperor some offence and was already fearing the worst, unhesitatingly declared in their favour, with the words, 'Here is the day which the Lord hath ordained!' By morning, thanks to the enthusiastic support of the Blues, Leontius had been proclaimed Basileus and the revolution was over. Justinian was taken prisoner and led in chains round the Hippodrome, while his erstwhile subjects screamed insults and abuse. In token of the new Emperor's long friendship with his father Constantine IV, his life was spared; he suffered instead the by now usual mutilations to nose and tongue[1] before being sent off to eternal exile in the Crimean city of Cherson. His rapacious ministers were less fortunate: tied by the feet to the backs of heavy wagons, they were then dragged down the Mesé from the Augusteum to the Forum Bovis – the modern Aksaray – and there burnt alive.

Ten years and two Emperors later, the people of Byzantium would have bitter cause to regret that they had not consigned Justinian II to a similar fate.

The deeply undistinguished reign of Leontius is notable for one thing only: the capture of Carthage by the Saracens and the consequent extinction in 698 of the Exarchate of Africa. The upstart Emperor had done his best to save the situation, sending the largest fleet he could muster to the relief of the beleaguered city; ironically enough, it was this very fleet that overthrew him. Rather than return and report their failure, its leaders decided instead to rebel, acclaiming as Basileus one of their own number, a *drungarius* – the rank roughly corresponded to vice-admiral – whose Germanic name of Apsimar was hastily changed to Tiberius. When the fleet reached Constantinople, the Greens – who had never liked Leontius – upheld the cause of the mutineers, and their support proved decisive. The unhappy man lost – all too predictably – his nose, together with as much of his hair as was necessary to provide him with a tonsure, and was sent off to the monastery of Dalmatus.

Tiberius, for his part, proved a good deal more effective. With the help of his brother Heraclius he strengthened both the land and the sea defences of Anatolia, and in 700 actually invaded Saracen-held Syria, going on to regain – though unfortunately only for a brief period – parts of Armenia. Later, in 703 and 704, he beat back successive Arab invasions of Cilicia, inflicting heavy losses as he did so; indeed, had he only retained the imperial diadem, he might well have achieved still greater things, earning for himself a distinguished place on the roll of Byzantine Emperors. But he did not retain it. In 705 he in his turn was

---

1 The slitting of the tongue seems on this occasion to have been more symbolic than anything else: Justinian remained, so far as we can judge, an unusually talkative man all his life. The damage to his nose, on the other hand, resulted in lasting disfigurement: he was ever afterwards known as *Rhinotmetus* – 'Cut-Nose'.

overthrown. Justinian, after a decade in exile and despite his hideous mutilations, had returned to the capital – with his ambitions as strong as ever and vengeance in his heart.

The city of Cherson – now known as Korsun – consists today of a few excavated streets with the remains of a central square, a theatre and some rather good mosaic floors of the sixth century. Thirteen hundred years ago, on the other hand, it was a considerable community: a semi-autonomous dependency of the Empire with its own independent Hellenistic traditions, its own governing magistrate and its own senate. The small imperial garrison stationed there existed more for its protection than for its control. It was, however, useful to Byzantium in two ways. First, it was a valuable observation post, from which a watchful eye could be kept on the barbarian tribes – Alans and Avars, Bulgars and Slavs, Khazars and Petchenegs – who still led their old wandering lives through South Russia and the Caucasus; second, its remoteness made it an admirable place of exile – for Pope Martin among many others, who had died there just thirty years before the arrival of Justinian.[1]

The Emperor – still, it must be remembered, only twenty-six at the time of his banishment – had made it known from the start that he considered his stay in Cherson to be strictly temporary. Gradually he gathered round him a circle of loyal adherents who, as time went on, grew steadily more outspoken in their hostility to Leontius. When the usurper was dethroned in 698 they made no secret of their delight; and by 702 or early 703 Justinian had become such a liability to the local authorities that they decided to return him to Constantinople. Learning of their intentions just in time, however, he slipped out of the city and appealed for protection to the Khazar Khagan Ibuzir, who welcomed him with enthusiasm and immediately gave him his sister for a bride. The lady's first impressions of her new husband are, perhaps fortunately, not recorded; he cannot have been a pretty sight. But it is significant that he immediately renamed her Theodora. The two then settled in Phanagoria, at the entrance to the Sea of Azov, to await developments.

Their married life was soon interrupted. Clearly it was only a matter of time before the exiled Emperor's whereabouts became known in Constantinople, and at some point in 704 one of Theodora's hand-maidens brought her the news that an imperial envoy had arrived at her brother's court, offering rich rewards for Justinian, dead or alive. Ibuzir, it appeared, had stood firm at first, but as the envoy's tone became

1 The Pope had hated it, and had complained bitterly about the living conditions. He even wrote to his friends asking them to send him bread, 'which is talked of, but has never been seen'.

threatening he had slowly weakened; his brother-in-law was now in imminent danger of his life.

This report was confirmed a few days later when a detachment of soldiers suddenly appeared at Phanagoria, purporting to be a newly formed bodyguard. Justinian did not believe them for a moment. He soon singled out two officers as his potential assassins. Before they could strike, he invited them separately to his house; and then, as they entered, he leapt upon them and strangled them with his own hands. The immediate danger was averted; but there was still no time to be lost. Theodora, now heavily pregnant, had no choice but to return to her brother; Justinian himself slipped down to the harbour, commandeered – or, more probably, stole – a fishing-boat and sailed off into the night, back round the Crimean coast to Cherson. In doing so he was aware that he was risking his life; he was well known throughout the city, disguise – for him of all people – was impossible, and the authorities would never allow him to escape a second time. Somehow, however, he managed to contact his supporters and to summon them to a secret rendezvous – whence they all set sail together under cover of night, westward across the Black Sea.

The story is told of how, on their journey, their frail vessel was caught in a fearful tempest; and of how one of their number suggested to the Emperor that the divine anger might be assuaged by a promise that, if he regained his throne, he would spare all those who had formerly opposed him. Justinian's reaction had been entirely characteristic: 'If I spare a single one of them,' he had replied, 'may I be drowned on this instant.' Nothing happened; the storm subsided; and the little boat was carried safely to the Bulgar-held lands around the Danube delta.

The Bulgar King Tervel received Justinian as warmly as had the Khagan of the Khazars a year or two before, and readily agreed to his proposal: that he should provide all the military assistance necessary for the Emperor to regain his throne, in return for the title of Caesar and the hand of his daughter[1] in marriage. Thus it was that in the spring of 705 the exiled Emperor appeared, at the head of an army of Slavs and Bulgars, before the walls of Constantinople. For three days he waited, while his peremptory demands for the gates to be opened to him were answered with derisive insults; then he took action. During those three days, his scouts had discovered an old water conduit, long disused, running beneath the walls into the city. On the night of the third day, accompanied only by a few picked volunteers, he managed to squeeze

1 The child of his first wife Eudocia, who had died young.

himself along it, finally emerging just outside the Palace of Blachernae at the northern extremity of the walls. The sleeping guards were taken by surprise, and within a few minutes the building was his. When the word spread the next morning that the Emperor had returned and had taken possession of his palace, Tiberius fled to Bithynia; and the citizens of Constantinople, faced with the alternatives of surrender or the immediate sack of their city at the hands of the barbarian hordes, very wisely chose the former.

If the Emperor had indeed sworn that fearful oath during his crossing of the Black Sea, those who had accompanied him would have had good cause to remember it in the days that followed. Tiberius himself was soon captured, and his predecessor Leontius was dragged, protesting, from his monastery; then, on 15 February 706, the two were paraded in chains through the city to the Hippodrome – just as Justinian had been ten years before – while their erstwhile subjects hurled abuse and pelted them with ordure. The prescribed circuit complete, they were flung down before the Emperor, who symbolically planted one purple-booted foot on the neck of each while the crowd chanted the Ninety-First Psalm, verse thirteen of which had seemed particularly appropriate:

> Thou hast trodden on the asp and the basilisk:
> The lion and the dragon hast thou trampled underfoot.[1]

Then they were taken away to the place of execution, where their heads were severed from their shoulders.

Meanwhile the Bulgar army was waiting at the gates. Not without difficulty had Tervel restrained his men from bursting into the city and giving themselves over to the rapine and looting to which they had been eagerly looking forward; and Justinian was well aware that his new ally would not lead them home before claiming his reward. Of the projected marriage of Tervel to his daughter nothing more is heard; since the chroniclers make no further mention of the girl herself, we can only conclude that she had followed her mother to an early grave. But the other half of the bargain was inescapable; and so it was that shortly after his return, in an impressive ceremony held before a vast concourse of spectators, he draped a purple robe across the shoulders of the Bulgar King, seated him at his side and formally proclaimed him Caesar. Many of those present were horrified: here was the highest title after that of the Emperor himself, one which had hitherto been invariably reserved

---

1 The point here is the play on words: 'the lion' is Leontius, 'the asp' Apsimar. (The English Authorized Version prefers 'adder' to 'asp', which rather spoils the joke – such as it is.)

for senior members of the imperial family; must they now be obliged to watch in silence while it was conferred not even on a citizen of the Empire, but on a barbarian brigand? Yes, was the short answer: they were. All too soon it was to be made plain to them that their Basileus was no respecter of tradition; and that whatever they felt about his decisions, they would do well to keep their opinions to themselves.

For now came the Terror: an orgy of blood-letting worse even than that initiated by Phocas a century before. As Paul the Deacon[1] unpleasantly put it (in a snide reference to the Emperor's noselessness), 'as often as he wiped away the drops of rheum from his nostrils, almost as often did he order another one of those who had opposed him to be slain.' Tiberius's brother Heraclius – the best general in the Empire, a brilliant soldier whom Justinian could ill afford to lose – was hanged with all his staff officers on a row of gibbets erected along the Land Walls; others were tied up in weighted sacks and thrown into the sea. Patriarch Callinicus, who had crowned both the usurpers, was blinded and exiled to Rome – as a warning, it was murmured, to Pope John VII if he did not ratify the Quinisextum – and the countless other cases of torture and mutilation were by no means confined to those who had opposed Justinian in the past. To his contemporaries only one explanation was possible; the Emperor was mentally unhinged. By now he seemed totally oblivious of state affairs, or of the ever-worsening situation along the imperial borders. He wanted only two things. The first was blood – and if that blood were the life-blood of the Empire itself, he cared not a jot. The other was his wife.

It was two years now since he had seen her; he may not even have known whether she and her baby were dead or alive. Nor could he be certain that her brother would allow her to leave his court. In the event, however, he need not have worried. On hearing of the Emperor's reinstatement the Khagan Ibuzir had repented of his former faithlessness; he was now eager to resume their former friendship and to enjoy the perquisites of an imperial brother-in-law. Theodora arrived safely in Constantinople with her little boy – named, rather unfortunately, Tiberius – the first foreign-born Empress ever to ascend the throne of Byzantium. Justinian was at the quayside to greet them; and now the watching crowd gasped again as the truth slowly dawned: this ogre who was their Emperor, this monster of inhumanity who seemed to breathe only bitterness and hatred, was in love. Inevitably, there were those who shook their heads as they watched the Emperor lower the diadems on to

1 *Historia Langobardorum*, VI, xxxii.

the heads of his wife and son in St Sophia. The woman was, after all, not just a foreigner – though that would have been bad enough. She was a barbarian to boot – and her son, whom Justinian had named co-Emperor at the same time, was half-barbarian too. *Mésalliances* of this kind, they whispered, would have been unthinkable in former times.

But then, so would an Emperor without a nose. Such old-fashioned prejudices were no longer acceptable in Justinian's Constantinople. It was significant that he had not cut the noses of either of the upstart pretenders; having proved by his own example that an Emperor could be an Emperor whether he possessed a nose or not, there was simply no point in doing so. The only way to make sure that they would cause no further trouble was to eliminate them completely – which was what he had done. In consequence of this, the abominable practice of *rhinokopia*, as it was called, is hardly ever heard of again. By the same token, Theodora the Khazar was only the first of many Empresses born beyond the furthest confines of the Empire.

The Byzantium of the eighth century would be, in short, a very different place from the Byzantium of the seventh; and for that difference Justinian II was, for all his violence and his brutality, to be very largely responsible.

Justinian's elevation of Tervel was not his only attempt to improve relations with his neighbours. Soon after his restoration he liberated 6,000 Arab prisoners of war taken by his two predecessors; and a year or two later he sent the Caliph Walid I a vast quantity of gold, a team of skilled workmen and a huge consignment of mosaic *tesserae* for the embellishment of the great Mosque of Medina, then a-building. In return, Walid is said to have bestowed on him a whole 'houseful' of pepper, valued at 20,000 dinars.

But alas, no amount of extravagant gestures could keep the peace for very long on the imperial borders. Justinian's neighbours to both east and west soon realized that by his wholesale purges he had eliminated all his best officers, and they were not slow to take advantage of the fact. In 708 the Byzantines suffered a serious defeat at the hands of certain Bulgar tribes (who were, however, almost certainly not subject to Tervel) at Anchialos near the mouth of the Danube; and in 709 they sustained an even graver blow: the loss of the key stronghold of Tyana in Cappadocia to the Arabs, whose victory was to encourage them to make further and still deeper incursions into imperial territory.

That same year, 709, saw another incident far more damaging to

Justinian's reputation than the loss of any number of fortresses. This was his punitive expedition against Ravenna. His motives remain a mystery. True, the city had defied him when he had tried to lay hands on Pope Sergius; but that was seventeen years before, and even his own ten-year exile is not quite enough to explain the delay. Our most vivid authority for this episode, a ninth-century Ravennate named Agnellus, suggests that it was certain of his fellow-citizens who had been responsible for the Emperor's *rhinokopia*; but this sounds even more unlikely.

There remains, however, a third possibility: that Ravenna was showing disturbing signs of rebelliousness towards Rome. Relations between the two were never entirely easy: as capital of the Exarchate, Ravenna always claimed a degree of ecclesiastical autonomy; she tended to resent Roman supremacy and, in particular, the special oath of obedience that all her archbishops, on their appointment, were required to swear to the Pope. Normally this resentment was allowed to smoulder quietly, doing little real harm; in 708, however, the new archbishop, Felix by name, categorically refused to sign the necessary undertaking. There followed a furious altercation, and it is this which may have persuaded the Emperor – or at least provided him with an excuse – to take the action he did. In the spring of 709 he sent a fleet to Ravenna under a certain Patrician named Theodore, with instructions to invite all the local dignitaries to a banquet in his name. Unsuspectingly, they presented themselves on the appointed day; whereupon they found themselves seized, fettered, loaded on to a ship and carried off to Constantinople, while Theodore's troops sacked and looted their city. On their arrival they were led before Justinian – seated, Agnellus tells us, on a throne of gold and emeralds and wearing a pearl-encrusted diadem fashioned for him by the Empress with her own hands – who unhesitatingly sentenced them to death. Only one life would he spare: that of the archbishop, in consequence of an admonitory dream that he had had the night before. Felix's sentence was commuted to one of blinding,[1] after which he was exiled to Pontus. Only after Justinian's death was he permitted to return to his see.

In Ravenna, Justinian's action proved predictably disastrous. The smouldering discontent flared up – as well it might – into open insur-

---

[1] The method employed was an interesting one: a huge silver dish was heated till it was red hot, after which 'the strongest vinegar' was poured over it. The Patriarch was obliged to stare directly into it for a long time, thereby utterly destroying his sight (Agnellus, p. 369).

rection, followed by a campaign of civil disobedience which was to prove
a source of considerable anxiety to succeeding Exarchs in the years to
come. In Rome, by contrast, it seems hardly to have been noticed. Any
Pope worthy of his tiara could have been expected to protest – and
protest vociferously – at such outrageous treatment of his flock, and in
particular of a consecrated prelate, insubordinate or not; from Pope
Constantine I, however, there came not a word of remonstration. Subsequent events were to reveal why: at long last, Emperor and Pope
together were hoping to solve the vexed question of the Quinisextum.

All through Justinian's exile, the 102 Canons approved by his Synod
had remained without papal endorsement; and one of his first acts on his
return had been to send two metropolitan bishops to the Pope (then
John VII) suggesting that he give his approval at least to those Canons
to which he had no objection. It was a reasonable enough request –
especially coming from an autocrat like Justinian – but not, apparently,
reasonable enough for the Pontiff, who refused his assent to the lot. The
consequent stalemate might have continued indefinitely, had not John
died in 707. His second successor – the first, an elderly Syrian called
Sisinnius, reigned only three weeks before expiring in his turn – fortunately proved better disposed. This was Constantine, another Syrian,
who in 710 accepted Justinian's invitation to come himself to the capital
and settle matters once and for all.

Constantine arrived with a numerous retinue in the early spring of
711. Having travelled the last leg of the journey by land, he was met at
the seventh milestone by an impressive delegation headed by the Patriarch and the co-Emperor Tiberius, Justinian's son, now aged six.
Richly caparisoned horses with harnesses of gold were put at their
disposal, and the combined party made its formal entry into the city
by the Golden Gate, before proceeding down the Mesē to the Palace
of Placidia, which had once again been made ready for a papal visitor.
The Emperor, oddly enough, was not in the capital to greet his guest,
being away in Nicaea; but he sent a cordial letter of welcome, suggesting
that the two might meet at the half-way point of Nicomedia. Whether
or not this was an attempt to gain a tactical advantage by forcing Constantine to come out to meet him must be a matter of conjecture; at
all events the Pontiff willingly agreed – and was rewarded, when the
meeting took place a day or two later, by the sight of Justinian, in full
regalia including the imperial diadem, prostrating himself to kiss his
foot. On the following Sunday the Basileus received the sacrament at the
papal hands and sought general absolution for his sins; the two then

returned together to Constantinople, where their discussions began.

Of the agreement that resulted, our knowledge is sadly sketchy: our two Greek sources obviously take no interest in the Western Church, while the author of the *Liber Pontificalis* dwells delightedly on the details of the Pope's reception and the ceremonies arranged in his honour, to the virtual exclusion of the theological and liturgical issues involved. All that can be said with any certainty is that concessions were made on both sides; that the Pope finally approved about half the Canons, on the understanding that the Emperor would drop the rest; that the two parted amicably, with Justinian 'renewing all the privileges of the Church' – whatever that might mean; and that the papal mission returned safely to Rome in October, just a year after it had set out.

It might have been expected – and, by the majority of his subjects, must devoutly have been hoped – that the Emperor, seeing the fury of the insurrection that had followed his punitive expedition to Ravenna, would have decided against any further adventures of the same kind. But Justinian was ever unpredictable, and early in 711 – it must have been just about the time he was conferring with the Pope – he struck again, this time against his former place of exile, Cherson in the Crimea. As with Ravenna, his reasons are hard to analyse. According to both Nicephorus and Theophanes, he was impelled solely by the desire to take vengeance on a city which had sought to surrender him to the usurping Emperor Tiberius; but if so, why did he wait six years after his reinstatement? There is, fortunately, another, more plausible, possibility. Some time after his departure from the Crimea, his brother-in-law the Khagan of the Khazars seems to have advanced to Cherson and – if he did not actually conquer the city – to have established a presence there in the person of a Khazar *Tudun*, or Governor. It may therefore have been this technical infringement of the imperial frontier – or at least of the Byzantine sphere of influence – that caused the Emperor to act as he did; in this event, his wrath would have been directed primarily at the Khazars rather than against the native inhabitants of the city.

Whatever his motives, his expeditionary force – which is reported to have numbered 100,000 men, though this is almost certainly an exaggeration – achieved its object well enough. Seven of the leading citizens were roasted alive, countless others were drowned in the approved manner (with weights attached) and some thirty – including the Tudun and the Greek mayor, Zoilos – were sent, with their families, in chains to Constantinople. An imperial Governor named Elias was appointed in the place of the Tudun and settled in the city with a much-enlarged garrison. But when the Emperor came to summon his army home, disaster struck: one of those storms for which the Black Sea has always been famous arose without warning and engulfed the entire fleet. Precise figures must, as always, be treated with suspicion, but the casualties were estimated at 73,000.

At this point both our sources report that Justinian, on being brought news of the catastrophe, burst into peals of laughter. If so, the most charitable interpretation is that he had suffered an attack of acute hysteria; otherwise it is hard to escape the conclusion that he had in turn fallen victim to the family madness. Almost immediately, he announced his intention of sending out a second expedition; before he could do so, however, he was pre-empted by messengers bringing further disquieting news: a Khazar army had arrived in Cherson to defend the city from Byzantine attack. Worse still, the imperial Governor Elias and the entire garrison, finding themselves hopelessly outnumbered and in imminent danger of their lives, had deserted *en masse* to the enemy.

Insane or not, Justinian now took the only possible course – that of diplomacy. He released both the Tudun and the mayor and sent them back, with an escort of 300 soldiers, to resume their former positions. With them went his own Grand Logothete, George of Syria, with instructions to present the Emperor's sincere apologies to the Khagan for all that had occurred. He was then to ask for the surrender of Elias, together with that of a leading Byzantine exile, a general of Armenian extraction named Vardan – Hellenized to Bardanes – whom, probably rightly, he blamed for the Governor's treachery.

But the citizens of Cherson were in no mood for conciliation. The Logothete and his entourage were put to death on their arrival; the Tudun, with his 300-strong escort, was dispatched to the Khagan. Unfortunately he died on the way; and the Khazars, taking the view that he would probably need his escort just as much on his journey to the next world as he had in this one, killed the lot of them. Cherson and the other cities of the Crimea now formally announced that they no longer recognized Justinian as their Emperor. Instead, they gave their allegiance to Bardanes the Armenian exile – who, adopting the fine old Roman name of Philippicus, forthwith proclaimed himself Basileus. Henceforth it was open war.

Justinian's anger when these developments were tremblingly reported to him was fearful to behold. At once he prepared a new armament under the command of the Patrician Maurus, with orders to raze Cherson to the ground, leaving no living thing within its walls. Thanks to the huge siege engines that he had brought with him, Maurus actually succeeded in destroying two of the city's defensive towers; but now a further body of Khazar troops arrived and he had no option but to make terms. Having done so, however, he knew that he could never return and report his failure to Justinian; he asked to be brought before Philippicus, and fell on his knees before him. The die was cast; there was no point in waiting any longer. The Byzantine fleet and what remained of the army sailed back to Constantinople with the new Emperor at its head.

Justinian, meanwhile, had made the cardinal mistake of leaving his capital – not in flight (for he had as yet no idea of these last developments) but in order to put down some minor rising in Armenia. He never got there: the moment the news was brought to him that a third would-be usurper of his throne was on his way across the Black Sea, he turned and, 'roaring like a lion', made all possible speed back to his capital. But he was too late. Philippicus arrived first, and the people of Constantinople received him with open arms. Justinian was arrested at the twelfth milestone by a body of troops under the command of Elias – the same officer, in all probability, whom he had appointed Governor of Cherson only months before – who claimed the privilege of performing the execution himself, striking off his head with a single blow and sending it to the new Emperor as a trophy. Subsequently, we are told, it was exhibited in Rome and Ravenna. Meanwhile the headless corpse, denied the dignity of a Christian burial, was flung unceremoniously into the Marmara.

When the news of Justinian's death was carried back to Constantinople his mother, the Empress Anastasia, seized her little grandson Tiberius and hurried him off to sanctuary in the Church of the Virgin at Blachernae. No sooner had they arrived there, however, than two agents of Philippicus presented themselves and demanded that the Prince be given into their custody. The old Empress tried to plead with them, and one of them seemed disposed to listen; but while he did so his companion – whose name was John Strouthos, 'the Sparrow' – advanced upon the terrified child, who stood clinging to the altar with one hand and clutching a fragment of the True Cross in the other. No Byzantine could possibly ignore so holy an object, but Strouthos was not to be deflected from his mission. Wrenching the fragment from Tiberius's grasp, he reverently laid it upon the altar. Next he untied a box of other saintly relics from the Prince's neck and transferred it to his own. Only then did he drag his small prisoner to the porch of a neighbouring church, where he stripped him of his clothing and, in the chronicler's graphic words, 'slaughtered him like a sheep'. Thus, with the cold-blooded murder of a little boy of six, was the Heraclian line extinguished for ever.

Running in direct succession through five Emperors, that line constitutes the first true dynasty in Byzantine history. It had begun magnificently; it ended, 101 years later, in butchery and shame. Justinian II was not, it must be emphasized, the unmitigated disaster that has often been suggested. In his first reign especially, he worked as hard as any of his predecessors to strengthen the defences of the Empire, still further developing the Theme system and, where necessary, moving whole populations in order to establish military colonies in strategic areas. Similarly, his Farmers' Law – if it was indeed his – did much to free the agricultural peasantry from their former bondage to the landed aristocracy, giving them independence, self-respect and, in future generations, the readiness to defend their territory against all comers. He strove, also, to improve relations with his two most dangerous neighbours, the Arabs on one side and the Bulgars on the other; and if in this field he was ultimately less successful, the attempts were nevertheless surely worth making. Finally, he left the Empire on excellent terms with the Church of Rome, living to receive the Pope as an honoured guest in his capital – the last elected Pontiff to set foot in the city for twelve and a half centuries.[1]

Such a record is far from contemptible, even if we leave aside the extraordinary courage and determination displayed by Justinian when, after nearly a decade of exile and horribly disfigured, he made his way back from the Crimea to reclaim his throne. Yet no amount of pleading can excuse the atrocities for which he was responsible nor diminish the incalculable number of his subjects, the majority of them completely innocent, who were put to death at his command. It has been plausibly suggested that the uncontrolled violence of his nature can be explained, at least in part, by the mutilation that he himself had suffered and the hideous – and humiliating – face which he was ever afterward obliged to present to the world: a face which can have been but little improved by the artificial nose of solid gold which he is said to have worn in his later years. That may be an explanation, but it is in no sense an excuse; it would certainly have been of small comfort to his victims and their

---

1 The next occasion was to be the visit by Pope Paul VI to Istanbul on 25 July 1967.

families, and it could not in any sense mitigate his conduct during his first reign which, though less unbridled than the second, was still intolerable enough to provoke a revolution.

His subjects, in short, were well rid of him. We may feel sympathy for his mother, Anastasia, who is said to have once been whipped by Stephen the *Sacellarius* without her son's lifting a finger in her defence or taking any punitive action afterwards; for his wife Theodora, of whose fate we know nothing but who was probably with her husband – since she was clearly not with her son – when the end came; and above all for his son: poor, frightened Tiberius, murdered for no good reason shortly before his seventh birthday. Justinian, on the other hand, was forty-two when he died; and of him it can only be said that his death, on 4 November 711, came not a moment too soon.

17

The First Iconoclasts

[711–75]

In the long night of superstition the Christians had wandered far away from the simplicity of the Gospel: nor was it easy for them to discern the clue, and tread back the mazes of the labyrinth. The worship of images was inseparably blended, at least to a pious fancy, with the Cross, the Virgin, the saints and their relics; the holy ground was involved in a cloud of miracles and visions; and the nerves of the mind, curiosity and scepticism, were benumbed by the habits of obedience and belief.

Gibbon, *The Decline and*
Fall of the Roman Empire,
Chap. XLIX

It was fortunate that Justinian II, during the days when he was still an effective ruler, had done so much to strengthen, both economically and militarily, the heartland of the Empire; because in Constantinople itself morale was now dangerously low. Less fortunate was the fact that his successor Philippicus Bardanes quickly proved himself a hopeless hedonist, who spent vast sums on his own amusement and, in his serious moments, seemed interested only in reviving the old theological disputes for which, over the years, the Byzantines had already paid so heavy a price. His innermost convictions probably tended towards monophysitism – that most inflammatory of heresies which, wisely, he did not attempt to revive. He did, however, make a determined effort to reimpose the monothelite compromise, even going so far as to issue an imperial edict on his own authority rejecting the decisions of the Sixth Ecumenical Council, which had condemned the doctrine only thirty years before. At the same time he ordered the removal of a picture in the imperial palace representing the Council in session, together with an inscribed plaque commemorating the event on the Milion Gate.

When the news of all this reached Rome, Pope Constantine – already horrified by the fate of his friend Justinian and implacably hostile to his successor – flew into a fury. The formal letter that Philippicus had addressed to him, notifying him of his accession in terms which struck the Pope as profoundly heretical, he rejected out of hand – replying with a decree of his own in which he made it an offence to stamp the new Emperor's portrait on coins, to refer to his reign in the dating of documents, or even to include his name in Church prayers. Finally, in obvious retaliation for the removal of the offending picture, he gave orders that a whole series of similar paintings – not just of the Sixth Council but of all the other five as well – should be specially painted for the walls of St Peter's.

In a more peaceful age, an Emperor might have been allowed to indulge himself in the quintessentially Byzantine combination of sensual pleasure and Christological speculation to his heart's content, leaving his subjects to get on with their own lives. Not, however, in 712; for the murder of Justinian had given the Bulgar King Tervel just the opportunity he needed. On the pretext that he was honour-bound to avenge his former friend, he now invaded the Empire for the second time and advanced once again to the walls of Constantinople, leaving a trail of devastation behind him. Perhaps because he trusted his Bulgar ally, Justinian had paid little heed to his Thracian defences, and his successor had cared for them even less. If the invaders were to be driven back, the Emperor had no choice but to summon additional troops from the Opsikian Theme across the Marmara.

Inescapable as it may have been, the decision proved his undoing. The Opsikians were notoriously self-willed, and felt no instinctive loyalty to an Armenian upstart who, having reached the throne by methods to say the least questionable, now seemed disposed to treat it like a plaything. They laid their plans with care; then, on Whit Saturday, 3 June 713, soon after the Emperor had settled down to a noon-day siesta after an agreeable morning spent banqueting with friends, a group of soldiers burst into his bed-chamber, seized him and hurried him away to the Hippodrome. There, in the changing room of the Green charioteers, his eyes were put out. He had reigned just nineteen months.

After the success of their coup, the Opsikians might have been expected to proclaim one of their own number the new Basileus. In some way, however, they were prevented from doing so; and the choice of the Senate and people fell on a certain Artemius, who had been Chief Secretary to the former Emperor. It may have been this background that persuaded him to choose for his imperial title the name of another former civil servant who had risen to the supreme power: on the following day,

Whit Sunday, he was crowned by the Patriarch in St Sophia as the Emperor Anastasius II.

Anastasius was a far abler ruler than his predecessor, and deserved to last a good deal longer than he did. He began, very sensibly, by rescinding Philippicus's monothelitist edict and restoring the memorials of the Sixth Ecumenical Council to their rightful places; then he settled down to the problem of imperial defence. Thanks to the Opsikian troops, the Bulgars had retreated back into their homeland; it was now the Arabs who were, once again, on the march – and who, as the Emperor's spies ominously reported, were preparing another full-scale attack on Constantinople. Anastasius at once began major operations on the Land Walls, repairing and reinforcing them where necessary. The state granaries were filled to bursting point, and every citizen was ordered to lay in enough food to last him and his family for three years; meanwhile the Byzantine shipyards were working harder than ever before. If the attack came, the Empire would not be caught unprepared.

But could the attack not be prevented altogether? Anastasius believed that it could, and early in 715 he decided to launch a pre-emptive strike against the Saracens, using Rhodes as a base for the operation. His chances of success looked excellent and, had he been allowed to proceed as he had planned, his subjects might have been spared much suffering. Alas, the Opsikian troops had developed a taste for rebellion. No sooner had they arrived in Rhodes than – barely two years after they had dethroned Philippicus – they turned on John, the General Logothete to whom Anastasius had given command of the expedition, and clubbed him to death. They then made their way to Constantinople, picking up *en route* an innocuous and inoffensive tax-gatherer named Theodosius whom, for reasons not entirely clear, they decided to proclaim Emperor. When Theodosius was informed of their intention he very sensibly fled into the mountains; but he was tracked down and forced at sword-point to accept – though still very reluctantly – an honour that was, to him, as undesirable as it was unexpected. Meanwhile the rebels had reached the capital where, after a few months of bitter strife, Anastasius was deposed in his turn and withdrew to a monastery in Thessalonica.

With the accession of Theodosius III, the Byzantines could look back on no less than six Emperors in the previous twenty years; five of their reigns had ended violently and the sixth was shortly to do so. Never since the foundation of Constantinople had there been so prolonged a period of restless anarchy. But salvation, although the people were not yet aware of it, was on the way; and it is to the future author of this salvation that we must now direct our attention. His name was Leo, and he is often known as 'the Isaurian'; in fact, he was almost certainly nothing of the sort.[1] His simple peasant family had originated, so far as we can tell, in the old Roman town of Germanica, in the district of Commagene beyond the Taurus Mountains – the present city of Maraş; later, as part of Justinian II's huge shifts of population, it had been resettled near Mesembria in Thrace.

From Leo's point of view, his new home could scarcely have been better chosen. Impelled, as he had been since early childhood, by a relentless determination to make his way in the world, he had ridden out to meet Justinian II when the Emperor was marching on Constantinople in 705 and, according to tradition, had offered him 500 sheep for the army; in return, he had been invited to join the imperial guard with the rank of *spatharius*. Before long his outstanding abilities (or, as some have less charitably suggested, his insufficiently concealed ambitions) persuaded Justinian to send him to the East on a delicate diplomatic mission among the various barbarian peoples and buffer-states in Syria and the Caucasus – principally the Alans, Abasgians and Armenians – sometimes inciting one against the other, sometimes cementing alliances between them in opposition to the Arabs. It was a task for which Leo was admirably suited, and for several years he performed it brilliantly. It therefore came as no surprise when, in 715, Anastasius appointed him Governor (*strategos*) of the Anatolikon, one of the largest and most important Themes in the Empire. He reached his new post just in time: early the following year two huge Saracen armies crossed the imperial border, one under the command of the Caliph's brother, Maslama, the other under a general named Suleiman; and the latter's first objective was the capital of the Anatolikon, the city of Amorium.[2]

What happened next is obscure. Theophanes produces a whole saga of picaresque incident, told with an abundance of detail suggesting that it may well be based on some lost diary written by Leo himself; unfortunately his account is so involved as to be largely incomprehensible. All that emerges with any degree of certainty is that Leo immediately entered into negotiations with the Arab leaders and that in consequence,

1 The confusion arises from an ambiguous passage of Theophanes (p. 391). Any reader wishing to investigate more deeply must refer to the formidably learned article by K. Schenk, *Kaiser Leons III Walten im Innern*, in *Byzantinische Zeitschrift*, Vol. V (1896), p. 296ff.

2 Once one of the key strongholds of the Empire, Amorium is now reduced to a few ruined buildings and the remains of a defensive wall. It is as yet unexcavated. It stands on a site now known as Ergankale, just outside the village of Asarköy, about fifty-five km south-west of Sivrihisar.

some time towards the end of 716, their armies retired once again behind the frontier. So bald a statement, on the other hand, raises more questions than it answers. How did Leo achieve such a remarkable result? What did he offer the Saracens in return for their withdrawal? Above all, perhaps, to what extent was there collusion between them? Our sources do not reveal; the most likely answer, however, is that Maslama and his colleague Suleiman tried to use Leo for their own ends, but were in fact outsmarted and used by him instead. They were already well aware that he was hostile to Theodosius and that he was generally expected, sooner or later, to seize the throne; and their intention was first to encourage his revolt and then, once he was safely established, to make him their puppet until such time as he could be obliged to surrender the whole Empire into the Caliph's hands. Theophanes records that Suleiman's forces, outside the walls of Amorium, were actually ordered to shout, 'Long Live the Emperor Leo!' and to encourage the city's defenders to take up the cry; and two separate Arab sources report that the *strategos* secretly promised to accept the generals as his paymasters and to do as they bade him.

So, very probably, he did – pointing out, however, that his path to the throne would be a good deal more difficult if he were seen to have Saracen support, and thereby persuading them to make their tactical retreat. There is not a shred of evidence to suggest that Leo ever had the slightest intention of betraying the Empire; his subsequent actions as Emperor are alone sufficient proof of that. But his profound understanding of Arab psychology and his easy fluency in Arabic – which, given his origins, may even have been his first language, with Greek only a later acquisition – enabled him to deceive and out-manoeuvre them at every turn.

Some months previously Leo had taken the precaution of obtaining the support of Artabasdus, Governor of the Armeniakon Theme, promising him in return the hand of his daughter in marriage and the rank of *curopalates* – one of the three highest in the Empire, usually reserved for members of the imperial family. Together, the two now marched on Constantinople. At Nicomedia they easily defeated a small army sent out against them under the command of Theodosius's son, taking him prisoner with his entire household. From there, knowing the defences of the capital to be virtually impregnable, Leo opened up negotiations with the Patriarch and Senate. They did not take much persuading. It was, they were well aware, only a matter of months before the Saracens renewed their offensive; if Constantinople were once again to be besieged, they were in little doubt as to whom they would rather have as their leader.

Early in 717 Theodosius, having received formal assurances that neither he nor his son would be harmed, abdicated the throne on to which he had been so unwillingly thrust and retired with relief to a monastery at Ephesus; meanwhile, on 25 March, the greatest Emperor since Heraclius entered the city in triumph by the Golden Gate and was crowned in St Sophia.

If we are right in our speculations, it may well have been in accordance with a carefully pre-arranged plan that, in the high summer of 717, Prince Maslama marched across Asia Minor. He captured Pergamum and pressed on to Abydos, whence he and his army crossed the Hellespont into Thrace; and on 15 August, with 80,000 men encamped around him, he stood before Constantinople. Just over a fortnight later, on 1 September, Suleiman entered the Marmara at the head of a fleet which the chroniclers estimate at 1,800 ships of war; and the blockade of the city began.

Leo III was ready – though not, perhaps, in quite the way that the Arab generals had expected. He had put to good account the five months that had elapsed since his coronation, pressing on with the various defence measures initiated by Anastasius and ensuring that his people had all they needed to defend themselves against the worst that the Saracens could hurl against them. As the siege progressed, it came more and more to resemble its predecessors of the 670s, when for five years Constantine IV and his subjects had fought off the Saracen onslaught. In those days, however, the fighting had been limited to the summer months; now it continued throughout the winter – and that winter proved the cruellest that even the oldest citizens could remember, with the snow lying thick on the ground for over ten weeks. Inevitably it was the besiegers who suffered the most, unaccustomed as they were to the treacherous Constantinopolitan climate and having no protection against the elements but their flimsy tents – a more effective shield from the desert sun than against the icy winds of Thrace. Soon, too, the food ran out; in such conditions scavenging was impossible and, if Theophanes is to be believed, the desperate Arabs were reduced to eating their horses, donkeys and camels and, finally, cakes of dead men's flesh, mixed with their own excrement and baked in the camp ovens. Famine, as always, brought disease; with the hardness of the ground putting burial out of the question, hundreds of corpses were flung into the Marmara. Suleiman himself was among the victims. On the sea, meanwhile, Greek fire exacted a daily toll among the Saracen ships. There was a bad moment in the early spring when the defenders were horrified to see on the horizon a second armada, almost as immense as the first, arriving from Egypt; fortunately the majority of them proved to be manned by Christian galley-slaves, who deserted *en masse* at the first opportunity.

It was, however, a Bulgarian army that delivered the *coup de grâce*. The Bulgars had no love for the Byzantines, but they preferred them to the infidel and were in any case determined that, if Constantinople were to be taken, it should fall into Bulgar rather than Arab hands. As spring turned to summer they marched down from the north, fell on the sick and demoralized Saracens and killed, we are told, 22,000 of them. Now at last Maslama decided that he and his men had had enough: early in August he gave the signal to withdraw. The land army – or what was left of it – dragged itself back to Syria without further mishap; but the remainder of the fleet, by now so damaged as to be dangerously unseaworthy, was almost annihilated in a series of summer storms. Only five vessels returned safely to their home ports.

This time the Byzantine victory was decisive. Over the years to come – indeed, throughout Leo's reign – the Arabs would make countless raids and incursions into Anatolia; but never again would they put the very survival of the Empire in jeopardy – and never again would they lay siege to its capital. As for the Emperor himself, he had amply justified his bid for power. He had, moreover, made a considerably larger contribution to his subjects' deliverance than most of them ever knew. As near-contemporary Arab accounts make clear, he had been in touch with Maslama and Suleiman from the start, making them endless promises that he had no intention of keeping and offering them copious advice that he knew would prove disastrous. Eventually, of course, the two leaders realized that they had been duped, and Leo cheerfully admitted as much; but by then it was too late. Meanwhile the Emperor had had plenty of time in which to indulge his penchant for intrigue: there are good reasons to suspect that both the mass desertion of the galley-slaves and the perfectly-timed arrival of the Bulgar army were due, at least in part, to his machinations.

In just a dozen years – he cannot even now have been much over thirty – Leo had risen from the status of a simple Syrian peasant to that of Emperor of Byzantium; and in doing so he had almost certainly saved his Empire from destruction. And yet, strangely enough, his chief claim to fame rests on neither of these achievements. The greatest and most fateful step of his career had yet to be taken.

*

Ever since the dawn of history, when man first became a religious animal and almost simultaneously – give or take a millennium or two – made his first clumsy attempts at adorning the walls of his cave, he has had to face one fundamental question; is art the ally of religion, or its most insidious enemy? Primitive societies often tended to take the easy way out by equating the two, first creating a fetish for themselves and then worshipping it; with the advent of theological speculation, however, and the idea of a universal deity unfettered to a piece of wood or stone, something better was required: and it thus became more and more essential to establish whether or not the visual depiction of the godhead was possible and, if so, whether it should be permitted.

Speaking in necessarily general terms of the world's great religions, it could be said that Judaism and – later – Islam set their faces resolutely against such practices, while the Hindus and the Buddhists saw no objection. As for Christianity, it has never quite made up its mind. For most of its history and among most of its adherents, pictorial or sculptural representations of Jesus Christ and even (though less frequently) God the Father have been enthusiastically encouraged, to the incalculable benefit of the artistic heritage of the world. In certain places and periods, however – England under the Commonwealth being an obvious example – opinion has swung sharply in the opposite direction; and never has such a reversal wrought more havoc, or caused more repercussions through the length and breadth of Christendom, than that which was instigated by Leo III – and was later to be carried on with even greater vigour by his son Constantine.

The sudden appearance of iconoclasm – the word means, literally, 'the smashing of icons' – on the Byzantine religious scene has often been explained by the proximity of the world of Islam, to which the very idea of a representation of the human form, whether religious or secular, was abhorrent; and it would be hard indeed to argue that Leo, with his Syrian background, was not to some extent at any rate influenced by Islamic beliefs and practices. On the other hand it should also be remembered that this new and revolutionary doctrine was in fact an obvious corollary to the monophysite belief: if we accept only the divine nature of Christ – which is by definition impossible to depict – and reject the human, we cannot logically approve of a two- or three-dimensional portrayal of him as a human being. It was therefore not surprising that most of the support for the new movement should come from the eastern provinces of the Empire, in which monophysitism had always been more prevalent and which had always been influenced by oriental mystical philosophy, rather than from the more down-to-earth, materialistic West.

None the less, the iconoclasts had a strong case. Ever since the beginning of the century the cult of icons had been growing steadily more uncontrolled, to the point where holy images were openly worshipped in their own right and occasionally even served as godparents at baptisms. It was thus as a protest against what they considered flagrant idolatry that a number of bishops in Asia Minor had adopted an iconoclast manifesto and were now intent on spreading their ideas more widely through the Empire.

Leo himself, despite his Syrian background, had given no early indication of similar tendencies: indeed, on several occasions during the recent siege he had made full use of one of Constantinople's most popular wonder-working icons, the Virgin *Hodegetria* ('She who shows the Way'), having it paraded up and down the city walls to give his men courage and to strike fear among the besiegers. On the other hand he had made no protest – as he had had every reason to do – when in 723 the Caliph Yazid, having been cured of a serious illness by a Jewish necromancer from Tiberias, was persuaded by the said necromancer to issue an edict ordering the immediate destruction of all Christian pictures in churches, markets or private houses throughout his dominions;[1] and there is some evidence to suggest that the same *éminence grise* had subsequently appeared in Constantinople and put similar pressure on the Emperor. In 725 the iconoclast bishops certainly did so. It seems, therefore, that Leo's change of heart was far from spontaneous; rather was it the result of a combination of Muslim and Jewish influences, together with others – perhaps the strongest of all – exerted by a number of his own Christian subjects. In the same year he went so far as to preach a series of sermons in which he pointed out some of the more flagrant excesses of the iconodules – as the image-worshippers were called – which he held to be in open disobedience of the Law of Moses as laid down in the Second Commandment. Then, in 726, he decided to set an example.

He could hardly have chosen a more striking one. Facing eastwards towards St Sophia across the broad open space of the Augusteum was the principal gateway to the imperial palace, known as the Chalkē. Destroyed by the mob during the Nika riots, it had been rebuilt by Justinian and was now a magnificent edifice in its own right. Procopius tells us[2]

---

1 The details are uncertain, since the text of Yazid's edict has not survived; but there is no doubt of the wholesale destruction that followed.

2 *Buildings*, i, 10.

that it was a tall, vaulted building with a central dome, the interior revetted with slabs of polychrome marble above which ran a cycle of dazzling mosaics representing the victories of Justinian and Belisarius and the capture of various cities of Italy and Libya. In the centre were full-length mosaic portraits of the Emperor and Theodora – presumably very much on the same lines as those in the still surviving Church of S. Vitale in Ravenna – with the Kings of the Goths and the Vandals standing bound before them and the Senate ranged solemnly to each side. The walls were lined with statues, some antique, some of former Emperors; outside, above the great bronze doors that gave the building its name, there rose a vast golden icon of Christ.

It was this tremendous icon – perhaps the largest and most prominent in the whole city – that Leo selected as the first to be destroyed. The popular reaction was immediate: the officer in charge of the demolition party was set upon by a group of outraged women and killed on the spot. As the news of the desecration spread, more demonstrations followed. Widespread mutinies were reported in the Aegean fleet, and others among the army in Thrace. Whatever the Eastern bishops might say, the Emperor's European subjects – inheritors as they were of the old Graeco-Roman tradition – had left their sovereign in no doubt of their own feelings. To them, iconoclasm meant nothing less than wilful sacrilege. They loved and revered their images, and they were prepared to fight for them.

Leo saw that he must advance with caution. Once he had dealt with the mutineers, he decided to give tempers time to cool. Unfortunately, they did nothing of the kind. In 727, his Italian subjects in the Exarchate of Ravenna rose in revolt, backed to the hilt by Pope Gregory who, quite apart from his natural feelings of revulsion at the destruction of the holy images, deeply resented the Emperor's presumption in arrogating to himself the supreme authority in matters of doctrine. The Exarch was murdered, his provincial governors put ignominiously to flight. Meanwhile the rebellious garrisons, all recruited locally, chose their own commanders and asserted their independence.[1]

These upheavals, it should be noted, were the consequence not of any imperial decree but of a single action by the Emperor: the destruction

---

1 In the communities along the shore of the Venetian lagoon, their choice fell on a certain Ursus, or Orso, from Heraclea, who was placed at the head of the former provincial administration and given the title of *Dux*. At that moment the Republic of Venice was born; and that title, transformed by the rough Venetian dialect into *Doge*, was to be passed down through 117 successors and over more than a thousand years until the Republic's end in 1797.

of the icon over the doors of the Chalkē. Once aware of the fury that he had aroused, Leo might have been expected to call a halt for fear of sparking off a full-scale civil war; but his resolution never wavered. For three years he tried unsuccessfully to negotiate with the Church leaders, both in the East and in the West, who opposed him; then, in 730 – having first taken the precaution of dismissing the iconodule Patriarch Germanus and replacing him with a weakly acquiescent cleric named Anastasius – he finally issued his one and only edict against the images.

The die was cast. All holy pictures were to be destroyed forthwith. Those who failed to obey would be subject to arrest and punishment; those who continued to cherish their images could expect relentless persecution. In the East, the blow fell most heavily on the monasteries, many of which possessed superb collections of ancient icons – to say nothing of vast quantities of holy relics, now similarly condemned. Hundreds of monks fled secretly to Greece and Italy, taking with them such of the smaller and more precious treasures as could safely be concealed beneath their robes. Others sought refuge in the deserts of Cappadocia, whose contorted outcrops of soft and friable volcanic tufa had, already for the best part of a hundred years, offered troglodytic sanctuary for other Christian communities threatened by the advancing Saracen. Meanwhile in the West Pope Gregory, seeing that an open breach could no longer be postponed, issued a public condemnation of iconoclasm and followed it up with two letters to Leo, setting out the orthodox view on images and suggesting that the Emperor leave the task of defining Christian dogma to those best qualified to perform it.

Leo's first reaction was to deal with Gregory in much the same way as Constans II had dealt with Pope Martin; but the ships sent to arrest the Pontiff foundered in the Adriatic, and before anything further could be done Gregory himself was dead. His successor and namesake took an equally determined line. Still further incensed by the Emperor's confiscation, early in 731, of the annual incomes from the Churches of Sicily and Calabria he summoned a synod in November which decreed excommunication for all who laid impious hands on sacred objects of any kind. Leo retaliated by transferring the Sicilian and Calabrian bishoprics, together with a considerable number of others throughout the Balkan peninsula, from the see of Rome to that of Constantinople. Henceforth the already strained relations between the Eastern and Western Churches were marked by a still more unconcealed hostility, which was to continue with only brief intermissions for more than three centuries until the final schism.

Of the last decade of Leo's reign we know little. The 730s were a relatively quiet time for Byzantium: apart from the regular Saracen raids in Anatolia which had become an accepted fact of life, they were probably to a large extent taken up with the consequences of the iconoclast decree, its further implementation and the pursuit and chastisement of those who elected to defy it. Quiet as they may have been, however, those years were certainly not happy. Leo III, like Heraclius before him, had saved the Western world; but whereas Heraclius had striven to put an end to religious strife, Leo seems almost deliberately to have encouraged it. When he died, on 18 June 741, he left behind him an Empire which, though finally secure against its Arab enemies, was more deeply and desperately divided than ever in its history.

Constantine V, his son and successor, was the last man to reunite it. Known during his own lifetime and to posterity by the unattractive nickname of Copronymus – a sobriquet acquired, Theophanes assures us, as a result of an unfortunate and embarrassing accident at his baptism – he had been crowned co-Emperor by his father in 720 at the age of two; and from an early age he had been closely associated with Leo in his iconoclast policy. It was almost certainly for this reason that his much older brother-in-law Artabasdus – Leo's principal ally in his bid for power, whom he had rewarded with the hand of his daughter Anna – in 742 launched a surprise attack on the young Emperor while he was marching eastwards on a campaign against the Saracens, soundly defeated him and, hurrying to the capital, proclaimed himself Basileus in his stead. He then immediately ordered the restoration of the icons – people were astonished at the quantity of holy images said to have been destroyed that suddenly reappeared safe and sound, just as they were at the number of former iconoclasts who now revealed that they had been secret iconodules all along – and for sixteen months Constantinople looked itself again, its churches and public buildings once more aglitter with gold.

But Constantine was not beaten. He had sought refuge at Amorium, the scene of his father's early successes, where the garrison – composed as it was entirely of local Anatolians – was iconoclast to a man, and where he was given an enthusiastic welcome. From there it was a simple matter to raise further troops of similar persuasion, with whose help in 743 he defeated Artabasdus at the ancient Sardis (Sardes), in Lydia, and marched on to Constantinople, which surrendered to him on 2 November. Artabasdus and his two sons were publicly blinded in the Hippodrome, their chief supporters executed or subjected to various mutilations; meanwhile the trembling Patriarch Anastasius, who had predictably turned his coat and crowned the usurping Emperor, was first flogged, then stripped naked and, sitting backwards on a donkey, ignominiously paraded round the arena. After this humiliation – which had been accurately predicted by his predecessor Germanus fifteen years before – he was, to everyone's surprise, reinstated in his former office. Here was one of Constantine's subtler moves. He was always anxious to reduce the influence of the hierarchy, in order to concentrate as much power as possible in his own hands; and a thoroughly discredited Patriarch was just what he wanted.

The rebellion of Artabasdus had two significant results. The first was to inflame the Emperor's hatred of icon-worshippers to an almost pathological degree. Once restored to the throne, he intensified his persecution of all who displayed the slightest sign of religious superstition; the citizens of Constantinople, in particular, felt themselves to be in the grip of a new reign of terror. And yet, surprisingly perhaps, about Constantine himself there was nothing remotely austere, any more than there had been about his father. Except where the images were concerned, the iconoclasts were far from puritanical – less so, indeed, than many an image-loving Western churchman. In one of his letters to Leo, Pope Gregory had accused him of trying to console those who missed their old icons with 'harps, cymbals, flutes and other such trivialities'; and even in the visual arts secular subjects continued to be actively encouraged. A near-contemporary[1] tells us, for example, that the mosaics portraying the life of Christ on the walls of the Church of St Mary in Blachernae were almost immediately replaced with others, just as fine, depicting landscapes with so many trees and birds and fruits as to make it look half-way between a provisions market and an aviary. More improbable still was the Patriarchal Palace, which was, we learn, richly embellished with representations of horse-races and scenes of the chase.

Constantine's own tastes, if our meagre (and, alas, exclusively iconodule) sources can be believed, bordered on the libertine. Shamelessly bisexual, he filled his court with exquisite young favourites; and although various accounts of unbridled orgies can probably be ascribed to the malicious tongues of his enemies, there was certainly plenty of music and dancing; the Emperor himself is said to have been an accomplished performer on the harp. None of this, however, should be taken to imply that he was not a fundamentally religious man. On the contrary, he had

[1] The anonymous author of the *Life of St Stephen the Younger*, written in 808 on the basis of earlier information provided by Stephen, deacon of St Sophia.

pondered long and deeply over the doctrinal issues raised by his policies
– during his life he wrote no less than thirteen theological treatises –
and had drawn his own conclusions, which he made no attempt to conceal. What evidence we have makes it clear that he was at heart a
monophysite: he abhorred the cult of the Virgin Mary and refused outright to allow her the title of *Theotokos*, Mother of God, since he held
that she had given birth only to the physical body of Jesus Christ, in
which his Spirit had been temporarily contained. For the worship of the
saints – and worse still, their relics – he showed a still greater contempt,
as he did for any form of intercessory prayer. Even the use of the prefix
'Saint' before a name would incur his wrath: St Peter could be referred
to only as 'Peter the Apostle', St Mary's church as 'Mary's'. If a member
of his court forgot himself so far as to invoke the name of a saint in
some exasperated expletive, the Emperor would immediately reprimand
him – not for the implied lack of respect for the saint in question, but
because the title was undeserved.

The second consequence of Artabasdus's coup was to impress upon
Constantine the full strength of the opposition to iconoclasm, especially
in the capital. It convinced him that Leo's decree of 730 was by itself
inadequate: what was required was a full Council of the Church. At the
same time he knew, like his father before him, that to press on too fast
might be fatal, since it could well provoke a revolution; and it was
another twelve years before he felt strong enough to summon what he
described as an Ecumenical Council to give its official approval to
iconoclast doctrines. Meanwhile he prepared the way with care. Bishops
whose views he considered unsound were quietly eased out of their sees,
and imperial nominees appointed in their place; new dioceses were established and given to trustworthy supporters.

Outside the Patriarchal see of Constantinople, however, the Emperor
had comparatively little influence – a fact made the more unfortunate in
that the Patriarchs of Alexandria, Antioch and Jerusalem had all declared
themselves in favour of images. Rather than risk any overheated discussions, with the attendant possibility of the Council's findings turning
out otherwise than he had intended, Constantine had therefore decided
that no representatives from these sees – or, of course, from that of
Rome – should receive invitations; and the relatively small assembly that
gathered in the Palace of Hiera, on the Asian shore of the Bosphorus, on
10 February 754 had thus no conceivable right to the title of 'Ecumenical'
that it so presumptuously claimed. It consisted altogether of 338 prelates,
meeting under the presidency of Bishop Theodosius of Ephesus, a son

of the former Emperor Tiberius II – Patriarch Anastasius having succumbed to a particularly revolting disease the previous autumn[1] and no
suitable replacement for him having yet been found. For seven months
they debated; but the results of their deliberations, as promulgated on 29
August in Constantinople, came as no surprise. Christ's nature, they
unanimously declared, was *aperigraptos* – not circumscribable, and consequently not to be represented as circumscribed by the limits of a figure
within a finite space. As to the images of the Virgin and saints, they
smacked of heathen idolatry and were thus equally to be condemned.

These conclusions were, predictably, enshrined within countless pages
of meticulous reasoning, backed up by much biblical and patristic quotation and any amount of pulverizing scholarship; but they were all that
the Emperor needed. The order for the destruction of every holy image
was reconfirmed, the leaders of the pro-icon party – who included the
deposed Patriarch Germanus, together with the party's chief polemicist
John of Damascus – excommunicated. And the persecutions continued
with renewed vigour. Henceforth, however, there becomes apparent a
gradual change of emphasis. The monasteries, as we have seen, had long
been a target of the iconoclasts – but principally, in the early days of the
movement, because of the quantity of icons and relics that they possessed.
After the Council, the Emperor began persecuting them for their own
sake, and with a fury that raises serious doubts as to his sanity. Referring
to them as 'the unmentionables', he would fulminate with maniacal passion against their cupidity, corruption and general debauchery: there
were, it seemed, no crimes of which they were not guilty, no depths of
degradation to which they had not sunk. The most famous of his victims
(since he is the subject of a still-extant biography) was Stephen, abbot of
the monastery of St Auxentius in Bithynia, who became the chief focus
of monkish resistance. Arrested on charges of every kind of vice – and,
most serious of all, of persuading, under false pretences, numbers of
innocent people to embrace the monastic life – he was first exiled, then
imprisoned and finally, like his namesake the Protomartyr, stoned to
death in the street.

But Stephen was only one of many hundreds – perhaps several thousands – of monks and nuns who in the last fifteen years of the reign of
Constantine suffered ridicule, mutilation or death (and sometimes all
three) in defence of their chosen way of life. In the Theme of Thracesion

---

1 A stoppage of the bowels, described by Theophanes as a *chordapsus*, which caused him to vomit up
their contents. His flock reflected on his undistinguished record as Patriarch and, as usual, drew
their own conclusions.

– which was nowhere near Thrace, but comprised the central section of the Ionian coast and its hinterland – the local Governor assembled every monk and nun and commanded them all to marry at once or face transportation to Cyprus. This same official, Michael Lachanodrakon, is also said to have impregnated the beards of those monks who opposed him with a highly inflammable mixture of oil and wax, and then set fire to them; in their abandoned monasteries he committed whole libraries to the flames, sold the consecrated vessels of gold and silver and sent the proceeds to the Emperor – who replied with an effusive letter of thanks, describing him as a man after his own heart. Of what happened in the other Themes we have rather less information; but the story is unlikely to have been very different.

For atrocities of this kind there can obviously be no excuse; but it is only fair to observe that in the course of the seventh and eighth centuries the monasteries in the Empire had multiplied in both size and number to the point where they were beginning to cause the administration serious concern. Despite all the ambitious resettlement programmes of Justinian II and others, there remained huge areas of Asia Minor which were still desperately underpopulated; and the situation became graver still between 745 and 747, when an epidemic of bubonic plague removed perhaps a third of the inhabitants. For reasons both economic and military, more manpower was urgently needed – to till the soil, to defend the frontiers and, above all, to reproduce. Instead, more and more of the population, male and female, rich and poor, young and old, were opting for a life which was both sterile and unproductive and which, however beneficial it might be to their immortal souls, was utterly useless to the State. It was this dangerous tendency, every bit as much as religious superstition in the narrower sense, that Constantine was fighting during his later years; we are told that few things angered him more than when members of his court or, worse still, officers of the army announced their intention of retiring to some distant cloister when their work was done. Ultimately, however, he lost the battle. His draconian measures could not fail to be effective in the short term; but within a few years of his death the monasteries were as full and flourishing as before. Indeed, the problem that they presented was never completely solved. For all their undoubted contribution to the civilization of Byzantium, they were to continue to drain its life blood for another seven centuries, until the end came.

The reign of Constantine Copronymus is so overshadowed by the spectre of iconoclasm that his military achievements are all too often overlooked. He was by no means the natural soldier that his father had been; nervous and highly strung, he had a chronically weak constitution and suffered from periodic bouts of depression and ill health. Few Emperors, in short, seemed worse equipped, physically or temperamentally, for the rigours of military life. And yet, against all expectations, he proved a courageous fighter, a brilliant tactician and a superb leader of men; and, of all his subjects, it was probably his soldiers who loved him the most.

In the first decade of his reign, once Artabasdus had been dealt with, his principal adversaries were the Arabs, weakened as they were by a long and bitter civil war which enabled Byzantium at long last to take the initiative. In 746, Constantine invaded northern Syria and captured Germanicia, the home of his ancestors; the larger part of the population he resettled in Thrace, where a colony of Syrian monophysites survived well into the ninth century. The next year brought a major victory at sea, when an Arab fleet from Alexandria fell victim, as so many others had done before it, to the ravages of Greek fire. Other triumphs followed in Armenia and Mesopotamia; but then, in 750, the situation underwent a radical change. At the battle of the Greater Zab River, the army of the Caliph Marwan II was smashed by that of Abu al-Abbas al-Suffah, and the Omayyad dynasty of Damascus came to an end. The Caliphate passed to the Abbasids of Baghdad, who were more interested in the East – in Persia, Afghanistan and Transoxiana – than in Europe, Africa or Asia Minor; and the Emperor in Constantinople was able to turn his attention to other, more immediate dangers nearer home.

Notably the Bulgars. For some years their attitude towards the Empire had been growing increasingly threatening, and in 756 matters came to a head. The immediate cause of the trouble seems to have been the sudden influx of Syrians into Thrace after Constantine's expedition, and the still more unwelcome arrival of a colony of Armenians a year or two later. This had necessitated the building of several fortresses, which may well have been a technical violation of a treaty concluded between Theodosius III and Tervel in 716; in any event it provided the Bulgars with an excuse for a new invasion of imperial territory. Riding out at once at the head of his army, the Emperor had little difficulty in putting the invaders to flight; but he could not prevent their returning again and again in the years that followed, and henceforth successive Bulgar campaigns became a regular feature of Byzantine military life. Constantine himself was to lead no less than nine of them; and one, in 763, brought him the most glorious – though also the most hard-won –

victory of his career, when on 30 June, in a battle which raged from dawn to dusk on one of the longest days of the year, he utterly destroyed the invading army of King Teletz, subsequently celebrating his success with a triumphal entry into his capital and special games in the Hippodrome.

And even that was not the end. There was another important campaign in 773, and yet another in 775. But this, for Constantine, was the last. As he was marching northward to the frontier in the fierce heat of August, his legs grew so swollen and inflamed that they could no longer support him. He was carried on a litter back to Arcadiopolis and thence to the port of Selymbria where, shortly afterwards, a ship arrived to take him home to Constantinople. It was not a long journey, but he did not live to complete it. His condition suddenly worsened, and he died on 14 September. He was fifty-seven.

It was unfortunate – perhaps, for Byzantium, disastrous – that Constantine should never have spared for his Western dominions even a fraction of the care and attention he lavished on those of the East. Within a few years of his accession, Italy had found itself under heavy pressure from the advancing Lombards, who were already whittling away at Byzantine territory. At that time a well-directed expedition – which the Empire was quite capable of launching – might have saved the situation; but instead of showing the solidarity that was so desperately needed, Constantine deliberately antagonized the Pope, and with him the vast majority of his Italian flock, by his clumsy attempts to enforce iconoclasm. Somehow the Exarchate survived – though only just – the events of 727; but in 751 Ravenna was finally captured by the Lombard King Aistulf, and the last imperial foothold in North Italy was lost, never to be regained. Rome, abandoned by the Emperor, was left naked to her enemies.

But not for long. Beyond the Alps to the west, a new and more benevolent power was rapidly rising to greatness. In the very year that Ravenna fell, the Frankish leader Pepin the Short had received papal approval for the deposition of the Merovingian King Childeric III – who had long been his puppet – and his own coronation. Pope Stephen II – to whom the Franks must have seemed considerably more desirable allies than the heretical and domineering Byzantines – thus felt himself in a strong position to seek assistance and personally set off for France where, at Ponthion, in 754, on the Feast of the Epiphany, he conferred upon Pepin the title of Patrician and anointed him, together with his two sons, Charles and Carloman, as King of the Franks. In return Pepin promised to transfer all those territories which the Lombards had captured from the Empire, not to their rightful sovereign but to the Pope.

He proved as good as his word. In response to a letter said to have been miraculously penned by St Peter himself, Frankish troops swept into Italy, bringing Aistulf to his knees; and in 756 Pepin forthwith proclaimed the Pope sole ruler of those lands formerly comprised by the imperial Exarchate, snaking across central Italy to embrace Ravenna, Perugia and Rome itself. His authority to do any such thing is, to say the least, doubtful. It was at one time suggested that he might have justified his action by the so-called Donation of Constantine, of which there will be more to say later; but recent evidence suggests that this shameless forgery was not concocted for another half-century. It remains true that the Papal States which he thus brought into being, however shaky their legal foundation, were to endure for over eleven centuries, providing a standing invitation to foreign adventurers up to and including Napoleon III, and constituting one of the principal obstacles to the realization of Italy's long-cherished dream of unity; while the Frankish alliance with the Pope was to lead, less than half a century later, to the establishment of the only Christian polity – apart from the Papacy itself – ever to put forward claims equal to those of Byzantium itself: the Holy Roman Empire.

18
Irene

[775–802]

An image, when the original is not present, sheds a glory like the original; but when the reality is there the image itself is outshone, the likeness remaining acceptable because it reveals the truth.

Clement of Alexandria,
quoted by Nicephorus

Despite his unorthodox sexual proclivities, Constantine Copronymus was three times married and succeeded in fathering, on two of his wives, six sons and a daughter; and it was the eldest of those sons, born of another Khazar princess, who on his death assumed the throne as Leo IV. Although far more balanced a character than his father, Leo proved to be nowhere near so capable a ruler; allowance, however, must be made for two cruel handicaps with which he had to contend throughout his short reign. One was the disease – probably tuberculosis – which was to kill him while he was still some months short of his thirty-second birthday. The other was his wife, Irene.

The second Athenian to become Empress of Byzantium, Irene could hardly have been more different in character from the brilliant young Athenais who had married Theodosius II three and a half centuries before. Scheming and duplicitous, consumed by a devouring ambition and an insatiable lust for power, she was to bring dissension and disaster to the Empire for nearly a quarter of a century, and to leave a still darker stain on her reputation by one of the foulest murders that even Byzantine history has to record. During her husband's lifetime she could operate only through him; but as he was both morally and physically weak while she was preternaturally strong, her influence is discernible from the moment that he assumed the supreme authority.

Why Leo – or, more probably, his father – chose her is a mystery. She was, it is true, startlingly beautiful; but the Empire was full of beautiful women and she possessed no other obvious advantage. Her family and antecedents were obscure; although she seems to have adopted the name of Irene only on her marriage, we know of no other. Her native city, too, had long since lost its old distinction. The former intellectual capital of the world was now a pious little provincial town: even the Parthenon had been converted into a church. Worse still from the imperial point of view, the people of Athens were known to be fervent supporters of images; and Irene was no exception. Her husband, left to himself, would have been an iconoclast like his father – in one of his rare moments of self-assertion he was to have a group of senior officials publicly scourged and imprisoned for icon-worship – but his wife made no secret of her own sympathy for such practices and constantly strove to bring about, once and for all, the defeat of iconoclasm and everything that it stood for.

Now there is no reason to think that Irene was not perfectly sincere in her beliefs, and for as long as her activities were limited to the exercise of a moderating influence on her husband they were plainly beneficial: thanks in large measure to her, the exiled monks were allowed back into their monasteries, the Virgin Mary was once again accepted as an object of veneration rather than the butt of ribald jokes, and the Emperor was actually hailed as 'Friend to the Mother of God' – a title that would have thrown his father into paroxysms. But during the high summer of 780 Leo's health took a sudden turn for the worse. Boils broke out all over his head and face, he was stricken with a violent fever and on 8 September he died, leaving a son just ten years old. This was Irene's opportunity. She immediately declared herself Regent on behalf of the boy, and for the next eleven years was the effective ruler of the Roman Empire.

Her position was not, however, undisputed. The army in Anatolia, still overwhelmingly iconoclast, mutinied within a matter of weeks, ostensibly in favour of one or the other of the late Emperor's five brothers, all hopelessly incompetent but providing a useful focus for discontents. The insurrection was quickly put down, and its ringleaders appropriately punished, the five brothers – who were quite probably innocent – being tonsured, forcibly ordained and then, lest anyone should have any further doubts about their religious status, obliged jointly to administer the sacrament at St Sophia on the Christmas Day following. For Irene, the lesson was not lost. Now more than ever she understood the strength of the opposition: every high office of Church and State and most of the army was in iconoclast hands. If she were to succeed in her purpose, she would have to pick her way with care.

The attempted insurrection provided her with an excuse to carry out a purge of the army; but the price she paid was a high one. In face of the dismissal of many of the best and most popular officers, those who had escaped the purge grew discontented and demoralized to the point where they could no longer feel any loyalty to the imperial throne. In Sicily, the Byzantine Governor declared himself independent and shortly afterwards threw in his lot with the Saracens of North Africa. In the East, when the Caliph's son Harun al-Rashid crossed the border in 782 at the head of an army estimated at 100,000, the Armenian general Tatzates immediately defected in similar fashion, his men following him without hesitation: Harun was eventually bought off by a humiliating and expensive truce, by the terms of which Irene agreed to pay him an annual tribute of 70,000 gold dinars for the next three years. Significantly, the Empress's only military success throughout the years of her regency was won in her native Greece, where the army was composed largely of westerners and iconoclasts were few. Thither in 783 she dispatched her chief minister and favourite, the eunuch Stauracius who, having first put down the rebellious Slavs in Macedonia and Thessaly, advanced deep into the still unsubdued Peloponnese, whence he returned loaded with plunder.

After this small triumph Irene felt strong enough to press on with her ecclesiastical policy. In 784 the iconoclast Patriarch resigned – the reason given was ill health, but some degree of persuasion does not seem unlikely – his place being taken by the Empress's former secretary Tarasius. In the circumstances, she could have made no better choice. The new Patriarch had never been a churchman; though he was well versed in theology – as were all educated Byzantines – his training had been that of a civil servant and diplomat. His approach to the iconoclast issue was consequently that of a practical statesman rather than a cleric. Even he, as we shall see, was to make mistakes; it remains true that much of the short-term success of the iconodule reaction was due to his wisdom and sound judgement.

The first priority, he decided, must be the restoration of relations with Rome. On 29 August 785 Irene and her son therefore addressed a letter to Pope Hadrian I, inviting him to send delegates to a new Council at Constantinople which would repudiate the findings of its heretical predecessor. The Pope replied with guarded enthusiasm. It was, he suggested, a pity that the Emperor and Empress had seen fit to appoint a layman to the Patriarchate, and had once again described him as 'Ecumenical'; on the other hand he greatly looked forward to the restoration of the South Italian, Sicilian and Illyrian bishoprics to his authority, and expressed his confidence that, if they dutifully followed his guidance as their spiritual father, young Constantine would grow up to be another Constantine the Great while Irene herself would prove a second Helena.

Thus, when the Council convened for its opening session on 17 August 786 in the Church of the Holy Apostles – the qualifying adjective, forbidden in the days of Constantine V, now happily reinstated – complete with delegates from Rome and all three Eastern Patriarchates, the cause of the icons seemed assured. But Tarasius, carefully as he had laid his plans, had underestimated the determination of the iconoclast diehards; they were not yet beaten, and they demonstrated the fact in the most forceful manner possible. Soon after the delegates had taken their seats, a detachment of soldiers from the imperial guard and the city garrison suddenly burst into the church and threatened dire penalties on all who did not leave at once. The meeting broke up in disorder verging on panic, and the papal legates, deeply shaken, at once took ship back to Rome.

Irene and Tarasius acted with decision. A few weeks later they announced a new expedition against the Saracens. The mutinous troops were mobilized for action and carried across into Asia; once there they were quietly but firmly disbanded, their place in the capital being taken by trustworthy units from Bithynia. Meanwhile the departed delegates were laboriously reassembled, and in September 787 the reconvened Seventh Ecumenical Council began its work at last, amid the strictest security precautions, in the Church of the Holy Wisdom at Nicaea – where the First Council had been held by Constantine the Great more than four and a half centuries before. As an earnest of its good intentions towards Rome, the two papal delegates – who had got as far as Sicily before their reluctant return – were given precedence over all the rest, including Patriarch Tarasius, in the attendance lists; the Patriarch served, however, as acting chairman – the true presidency being vested in Christ himself, represented (as was usual in Church assemblies) by the Book of the Gospels, laid open upon the presidential throne.

This time there were no interruptions. The business of the Council, it appeared, was not to discuss the pros and cons of iconoclasm; it was simply to ratify the return to the veneration of images. In the year that had passed since the abortive meeting in Constantinople, the entire opposition seems to have withered away. This is not, however, to say that matters proceeded entirely smoothly. Indeed, the very first issue to be discussed – the treatment of those formerly iconoclast bishops who were now prepared to admit their past errors – generated considerable heat, certain of the delegates almost coming to blows. The Council wisely decided that these bishops, once they had made full and public recantation, should be taken back into the bosom of the Church; but the motion was carried only in the teeth of violent opposition on the part of the representatives of diehard monasticism, who insisted that the offending prelates should be cast for ever into the outer darkness. There was much angry muttering as the former iconoclasts stood up one after the other, to acknowledge, as one of them put it, that they had been 'born, bred and trained in heresy', stigmatizing the Council of 754 as 'a synod gathered together out of stubbornness and madness . . . contrary to all truth and piety, audaciously and temerariously subversive of the traditional law of the Church by the insults that it hurled and the contempt that it showed towards the holy and venerable images'.

With relief, the Council now turned to a less divisive topic. Though all those present were agreed on the general desirability of the images, it was deemed essential to assemble a body of supporting evidence from the Scriptures and the early Fathers of the Church, thereby establishing the truth once and for all – and, it was hoped, ensuring that the same doctrinal mistake could not be repeated by generations to come. Some of the testimony adduced was of such footling triviality that it might have been better suppressed: the recanting Bishop Basil of Ancyra, for example, assured the assembly that he had frequently read the story of the sacrifice of Isaac and had remained unmoved, but that the moment he saw it illustrated he burst into tears. Another former iconoclast, Theodore of Myra, capped this neatly with a story of one of his archdeacons, who had had a vision of St Nicholas and was fortunately able to recognize him at once from his icon. But at last the task was completed to the general satisfaction, and by the seventh session the Council was ready to approve a new definition of doctrine. This condemned hostility to holy images as heresy; decreed that all iconoclast literature must be immediately surrendered to the Patriarchal office in Constantinople under pain of degradation from holy orders or, in the case of laymen, of excommunication; and formally approved the veneration of icons. It concluded thus:

Wherefore we define with all strictness and care that the venerable and holy icons be set up, just as is the image of the venerable and life-giving Cross, inasmuch as matter consisting of paints and pebbles and other materials is suitable to the holy Church of God, on sacred vessels and vestments, on walls and panels, in houses and streets: both the images of our Lord and God and Saviour Jesus Christ, and of our undefiled Lady the Holy Mother of God, and of the honourable angels, and of all the Saints.

For the more continuously these are seen by means of pictorial representation, the more their beholders are led to remember and to love the originals, and to give them respect and honourable obeisance: not that we should worship them with the true worship which is appropriate only to the Divine; yet still with offering of candles and incense, in the same way as we do to the form of the life-giving and venerable Cross and to the holy Gospel-Book, and to other sacred objects, even as was the pious custom in ancient days also.

That last sentence sounded a gentle note of warning: icons were to be objects of veneration (*proskynesis*) rather than adoration (*latreia*). The point may seem self-evident: anything else would be flagrant idolatry. But the delegates were well aware that it was the blurring of the distinction between the two that had been at least partially responsible for the rise of the iconoclast movement in the first place. It was as well to keep the faithful on their guard.

For its eighth and last session the entire Council moved to Constantinople where, on 23 October, it met in the palace of Magnaura under the joint presidency of Irene and her son. The definition of doctrine was read again, and was unanimously approved. It was then solemnly signed by the Empress and the Emperor, after which the delegates dispersed to their homes. Irene and Tarasius, having finally achieved their objective, had good cause to congratulate themselves.

Gibbon describes this second Council of Nicaea as 'a curious monument of superstition and ignorance, of falsehood and folly'. So in a way it was – particularly since, for all its outward unanimity, it heralded only a brief interruption in the iconoclast period: a quarter of a century later, its findings were to be repudiated in their turn and the holy images subjected once again to execration. The author of one of the most comprehensive works on iconoclasm, however, takes a radically different view.[1] For him, the Council ranks as 'one of those events, trivial in themselves, which are great crises in the history of Christianity', because 'it completed the process of identifying Christianity with the Graeco-Latin civilization'. The iconoclasts, he argues, like the monophysites before them, reflected the oriental, mystical side of the Christian religion towards which, thanks to the influence of the Eastern

1 E. J. Martin, *The History of the Iconoclastic Controversy.*

provinces – and, indeed, of Islam itself – the Byzantine Empire was constantly being drawn. But it never ceased to resist; and its resistance kept it rooted, theologically, in the Mediterranean world. If we accept this theory – and it seems difficult not to do so – the second Council of Nicaea can be seen as the sequel to that of Chalcedon, the Empire's 'last gesture of refusal to the claims of the Asiatic ideal'. Its tragedy was that, as the years went by, it increasingly lost political touch with the West, and consequently became 'a tragic monument of obstinate isolation' – a fact which will grow ever more apparent as our story continues.

The seventeen-year-old Emperor Constantine VI who signed the definitions reached by the second Council of Nicaea was still a figurehead; and despite his marriage to the beautiful Paphlagonian Mary of Amnia in the following year, a figurehead he was for the moment content to remain. How long he would have accepted this almost total exclusion from public affairs if his mother had been able to control her ambitions we cannot tell; but in 790 Irene overreached herself. Just when she should have been arranging to associate her son more closely with the imperial government, she resolved instead to inflict upon him a new and quite unnecessary humiliation – decreeing that henceforth she should take precedence over him as senior ruler, and that her name should always be mentioned before his. From that moment on Constantine found himself, whether he liked it or not, to be the rallying-point of all those who were opposed to his mother – and thus, inevitably, of many of the iconoclast old guard. Before long a group of them had formed a conspiracy with the object of seizing the Empress and banishing her to Sicily; but the ever-watchful Irene got wind of it in time, dealt firmly with those responsible, flung her son into prison and, to strengthen her position still further, demanded that the entire army swear an oath of allegiance to her personally.

Once again she had gone too far. In Constantinople and the European provinces, the soldiers swore their oath willingly enough; but in Asia Minor – where the iconoclast element remained strong – there was point-blank refusal. The mutiny, led by the troops of the Armeniakon Theme, spread rapidly: within a matter of days, Constantine was being acclaimed on all sides as the Empire's sole legitimate ruler. Hastily liberated from his prison, the young Emperor joined his adherents in Anatolia and returned with them in strength to the capital. Stauracius, Irene's Logothete and her chief lieutenant, was flogged, tonsured and banished to the Armeniakon; several lesser members of the Empress's court suffered similar fates. As for Irene herself, she was confined to her palace of Eleutherius, work on which had recently been completed. We should probably be mistaken in supposing that Constantine was personally responsible for such decisive measures; it is far likelier that the decisions were taken by his military supporters and that he remained his usual passive self. But his popularity was greater than it had ever been, his supremacy undisputed. The future was his.

And he threw it away. Weak, vacillating and easily led, he soon acquired the reputation of always believing the last thing he was told, and of following the most recent advice he was given. When in the autumn of 791 Harun al-Rashid's Saracens invaded his eastern provinces, he immediately concluded another shameful peace, involving the payment of a tribute which the Empire could ill afford; when at about the same time hostilities broke out along the Bulgarian frontier and he was obliged to go on campaign himself, he proved incapable of command and, at Marcellae in 792, ignominiously fled the field. That same year he actually allowed himself to be persuaded to recall his mother to the capital and restore her to her former power. For the secret iconoclasts in Constantinople, whose hopes he had thus betrayed, this was the last straw. A new plot was hatched, with the object of dethroning both mother and son in favour of the Caesar Nicephorus – one of the five brothers of Leo IV – despite the holy orders that had been forced on him a dozen years before; but it too was discovered, and for the first time in his life Constantine acted with decision. He had Nicephorus blinded; and, in the unlikely event that any of his other uncles should harbour similar ambitions, ordered that all four should have their tongues cut out.

The Emperor, it now appeared, was not only indecisive, disloyal and a coward; he was also capable of the most brutal cruelty. Few of his subjects could have retained any respect for so contemptible a ruler. Outside the iconoclast faction in the army of Asia Minor, one group only was prepared to accord him even a moderate degree of support: the representatives of the old monastic party, who had been gratified to find him apparently well disposed towards them – instead of openly favouring the iconoclasts as they had feared – and who had rejoiced still further when he had reinstated his mother on her former throne. But now they in their turn were to be alienated. In January 795 they learned to their horror that the Emperor had divorced his wife and was contemplating a second marriage. Mary of Amnia, for all her beauty, had not been a success. She had, admittedly, borne her husband a daughter, Euphrosyne, who thirty years later was to attain imperial rank as the wife of the

Emperor Michael II; but there had been no son to assure the succession, and Constantine was in any case bored with her, having long ago given his heart to Theodote, one of the court ladies. Mary was packed off to a nunnery; Patriarch Tarasius reluctantly condoned the divorce; and the following August, in the palace of St Mamas outside Constantinople, the Emperor and Theodote were married. Fourteen months later she presented him with a son.

The monks were scandalized. For an Emperor to remarry after his wife's death was one thing; but for him to put away his lawful Empress in favour of another woman – this was a sin against the Holy Ghost. Constantine's association with Theodote, they thundered, could in no circumstances be tolerated; nor could the bastard child be considered as a possible successor. The leaders of the protest, Abbot Plato of the monastery of Saccudion in Bithynia and his nephew Theodore – later to achieve celebrity as Abbot of the Studium in Constantinople – were exiled to Thessalonica, but their followers refused to be silenced. Nor was the adulterous Emperor the only object of these monkish fulminations; almost as much of their fury was directed against Tarasius, for having allowed the marriage to take place – even though he had been careful not to officiate himself.

Whether or not the worldly Patriarch ever revealed to his accusers that Constantine had threatened to ally himself openly with the iconoclasts if the necessary permission were refused, we do not know; it certainly did not prevent charges of heresy being prepared against him. As the months went by, moreover, the so-called Moechian controversy[1] was seen to have a significance which went far beyond the narrow issue of the Emperor's second marriage. Its long-term effect was further to deepen the split, not between iconoclasts and iconodules but between the two branches of the latter: the more or less fanatical monks on the one hand and, on the other, the moderates who understood that the Empire was something more than an outsize monastery, and that if the elements of Church and State were to work effectively in tandem there must be a degree of give and take on both sides. This split had already become apparent at the recent Council in Nicaea, during the discussion on the status of the recanting bishops; it was to continue for another century and more, dividing and weakening the Church on several occasions when unity was desperately needed and poisoning relations between churchmen who, working together, might have conferred lasting benefits on the Empire.

1 From the Greek *moicheia*, adultery.

Meanwhile, Constantine had forfeited his last remaining potential supporters in Constantinople and was now defenceless against his most formidable enemy – his mother, Irene. She had never forgiven him for her deposition, temporary as it had been; and she knew just how easily it could happen again. She was fully aware that her son's real sympathies lay with the iconoclasts, and vice versa; and she had no delusions about their strength among the army in Asia. While Constantine lived, another coup was always a possibility – and one which might well not only destroy her but undo all her work and reimpose iconoclastic doctrines throughout the Empire. For that reason, since her return to power, she had lost no opportunity of undermining his position in every way she could. It is more than probable that she had deliberately encouraged him in his plans for divorce and remarriage, the better to discredit him in the eyes of her own most fervent supporters, the monks. Almost certainly, when in an endeavour to redeem his military reputation he marched in the spring of 797 against the Saracens, it was her own agents who fed him false intelligence to the effect that the enemy had withdrawn across the frontier; only when he returned to Constantinople did he discover that Harun al-Rashid had done nothing of the kind and was still in occupation of large tracts of Byzantine territory. The murmurs of cowardice, never altogether silenced, grew louder again – just as Irene had intended that they should.

In June, she was ready to strike. One day, when Constantine was riding in procession from the Hippodrome to the Church of St Mamas in Blachernae, a party of soldiers leaped out from a side street and fell upon him. His own guards fought back, and during the ensuing mêlée he managed to escape and have himself rowed across the Bosphorus, where he hoped to find support. But Irene moved more quickly than her son. He was captured almost at once and brought back to the imperial palace; and there, on Tuesday 15 August at three o'clock in the afternoon, in the Porphyry Pavilion where he had been born twenty-seven years earlier, his eyes were put out. The act, we are told, was performed in a particularly brutal manner in order to ensure that he would not survive; and although some doubt remains as to how long he actually did so, there can be none that Irene was guilty of his murder. Theophanes tells us that, as a sign of divine disapprobation, the very sky was darkened; and that it remained so for the next seventeen days.

Since Constantine's young son by Theodote had died – probably of natural causes, though with our knowledge of his grandmother we can never be entirely sure – only a few months after his birth, Irene now found herself not only the sole occupant of the throne of Byzantium but the first woman ever to preside, not as a regent but in her own right, over the Empire. It was a position for which she had long striven but one which, in the event, she had little opportunity to enjoy. Over the past years her two chief advisers, the eunuchs Stauracius and Aetius, had developed an almost pathological jealousy of each other, to the point where their incessant intrigues made effective government impossible. Irene's popularity among her subjects – never great at the best of times – declined sharply after the murder of her son, and she now attempted to redeem it by granting enormous remissions of taxes, which the Empire could not begin to afford. Among the most favoured beneficiaries were the monastic institutions that had always been her chief source of support; in addition, the immensely profitable customs and excise duties levied at Abydos and in the Straits were cut by half, while the hated tax on receipts was abolished altogether, as was the municipal levy payable by all the free citizens of Constantinople.

But measures of this kind could only delay the inevitable. The Empress's more thoughtful subjects were disgusted at the sheer irresponsibility of her actions, and despised her for her assumption that their affections could be so easily bought. The largely iconoclast army of Asia, who had always detested her and had come near to mutiny after Constantine's murder, were horrified and humiliated by the new and increased tribute that she had promised to Harun al-Rashid, and must also have been asking themselves where their future pay was coming from. The civil service watched powerless while the imperial treasury grew emptier every day, and began to despair of ever setting the economy to rights. Meanwhile the reactionaries of every age and station throughout the Empire, who had always shaken their heads at the thought of a female Basileus, now saw their direst suspicions confirmed. It was clearly only a matter of time before one or another of these groups rose up – in the interests not of themselves but of Byzantium itself – and overthrew her.

When the coup finally occurred, which, of all the reasons suggested above, was the one that actually decided the conspirators to act as and when they did? Very probably, none of them: because by now there was another, which called still more urgently for swift and decisive action. On Christmas Day 800 at St Peter's in Rome, Charles, son of Pepin the Frank, had been crowned by Pope Leo III with the imperial crown and the title of Emperor of the Romans; and some time in the summer of 802 he sent ambassadors to Irene with a proposal of marriage.

*

Well before his coronation, Charles the Great – or, as he soon came to be called, Charlemagne – was an Emperor in all but name. He had become sole ruler of the Franks in 771, on the sudden death of his brother Carloman; two years later he had captured Pavia and proclaimed himself King of the Lombards. Returning to Germany, he had next subdued the heathen Saxons and converted them *en masse* to Christianity before going on to annex the already-Christian Bavarians. An invasion of Spain was less successful – though it provided the inspiration for the first great epic ballad of Western Europe, the *Chanson de Roland* – but Charles's subsequent campaign against the Avars in Hungary and Upper Austria had resulted in the destruction of their Kingdom as an independent state and its incorporation in turn within his own dominions. Thus, in little more than a generation, he had raised the Kingdom of the Franks from being just one of the many semi-tribal European states to a single political unit of vast extent, unparalleled since the days of imperial Rome.

And he had done so, for most of the time at least, with the enthusiastic approval of the Papacy. It was nearly half a century since Pope Stephen had struggled across the Alps to seek help against the Lombards from Charles's father Pepin – an appeal which might more properly have been addressed to the Byzantine Emperor, and indeed would have been if Constantine Copronymus could only have spared a few moments from his iconoclast obsession to turn his attention to the problem of Italy. Pepin and Charles had succeeded where Byzantium had failed; and although the rift between Rome and Constantinople had been theoretically healed at Nicaea, Pope Hadrian had in fact been far from satisfied by the report he had received from his representatives on their return to Rome. They had pointed out, for example, that when the Pope's message to Irene and Constantine had been read aloud to the assembled Council, all the controversial passages – including those in which he had protested against the uncanonical consecration of Patriarch Tarasius and the latter's use of the 'Ecumenical' title – had been suppressed. Neither had any indication been forthcoming that the disputed South Italian, Sicilian and Illyrian bishoprics might be returned to papal jurisdiction. Small wonder, then, that Hadrian and his successor Leo had remained loyal to their infinitely more reliable western champion, even if this did entail certain concessions where the cult of images was concerned – Charles rather inconveniently maintaining his own opinions on the subject which, while less extreme than those upheld by the Council of 754, approximated a good deal more closely to iconoclast doctrines than the Curia liked to admit.

The King of the Franks had been to Rome once before: on a state visit in 774 when, as a young man of thirty-two, he had been welcomed by Hadrian and, deeply impressed by all he saw, had confirmed his father's donation of that central Italian territory which formed the nucleus of the Papal State. In 800 he came on more serious business. Pope Leo, ever since his accession four years before, had been the victim of incessant intrigue on the part of a body of young Roman noblemen who were determined to remove him; and on 25 April he was actually set upon in the street and beaten unconscious. Only by the greatest good fortune was he rescued by friends and removed for safety to Charles's court at Paderborn. Under the protection of Frankish agents he returned to Rome a few months later, only to find himself facing a number of serious charges fabricated by his enemies, including simony, perjury and adultery.

By whom, however, could he be tried? Who, in other words, was qualified to pass judgement on the Vicar of Christ? In normal circumstances the only conceivable answer to that question would have been the Emperor at Constantinople; but the imperial throne was at this moment occupied by Irene. That the Empress was notorious for having blinded and murdered her own son was, in the minds of both Leo and Charles, almost immaterial: it was enough that she was a woman. The female sex was known to be incapable of governing, and by the old Salic tradition was debarred from doing so. As far as Western Europe was concerned, the Throne of the Emperors was vacant: Irene's claim to it was merely an additional proof, if any were needed, of the degradation into which the so-called Roman Empire had fallen.

Charles was fully aware, when he travelled to Rome towards the end of 800, that he had no more authority than Irene to sit in judgement at St Peter's; but he also knew that while the accusations remained unrefuted Christendom lacked not only an Emperor but a Pope as well, and he was determined to do all he could to clear Leo's name. As to the precise nature of his testimony, we can only guess; but on 23 December, at the high altar, the Pope swore a solemn oath on the Gospels that he was innocent of all the charges levelled against him – and the assembled synod accepted his word. Two days later, as Charles rose from his knees at the conclusion of the Christmas Mass, Leo laid the imperial crown upon his head, while the entire congregation cheered him to the echo. He had received, as his enemies were quick to point out, only a title: the crown brought with it not a single new subject or soldier, nor an acre of new territory. But that title was of more lasting significance than any number of conquests; for it meant that, after more than 400 years, there was once again an Emperor in Western Europe.

There remains the question of why the Pope acted as he did. Not, certainly, to engineer a deliberate split in the Roman Empire, still less to bring about two rival Empires where one had been before. There was, so far as he was concerned, no living Emperor at that time. Very well, he would create one; and because the Byzantines had proved so unsatisfactory from every point of view – political, military and doctrinal – he would select a westerner: the one man who by his wisdom and statesmanship and the vastness of his dominions, as well as by his prodigious physical stature, stood out head and shoulders above his contemporaries. But if Leo conferred a great honour on Charles that Christmas morning, he bestowed a still greater one on himself: the right to appoint, and to invest with crown and sceptre, the Emperor of the Romans. Here was something new, perhaps even revolutionary. No Pontiff had ever before claimed for himself such a privilege – not only establishing the imperial crown as his own personal gift but simultaneously granting himself implicit superiority over the Emperor whom he had created.

If, however, there was no precedent for this extraordinary step, by what authority was it taken? And so we come to what was arguably the most momentous – and the most successful – fraud of the Middle Ages: that known as the Donation of Constantine, according to which Constantine the Great, recognizing the primacy of his contemporary Pope Sylvester, had diplomatically retired to the 'province' of Byzantium, leaving his imperial crown for the Pope to bestow on whomsoever he might select as temporal Emperor of the Romans. This totally spurious document, fabricated around the turn of the century within the Curia, was to prove of inestimable value to papal claims for well over 600 years, its authenticity remaining unquestioned – even by the enemies of Rome – until it was finally exposed, in the middle of the fifteenth century, by the Renaissance humanist Lorenzo Valla.[1]

---

1 Dante, that staunch upholder of imperial claims, deplores it in a famous passage:

> *Ahi, Costantin, di quanto mal fu matre,*
> *Non la tua conversion, ma quella dote*
> *Che da te prese il primo ricco patre!*

> [Ah Constantine, how great an evil sprang
> Not from thine own conversion, but that gift
> That first rich Father did receive from thee!]

Inferno, xix, 115–17

Historians have long debated whether the imperial coronation had been jointly planned by Leo and Charles or whether, as appeared at the time, the King of the Franks was taken completely by surprise. Of the two possibilities, the latter seems a good deal more likely. Charles had never shown the faintest interest in claiming imperial status, and for the rest of his life continued to style himself *Rex Francorum et Langobardorum*. Nor, above all, did he wish to owe any obligation to the Pope; there is reason to believe that he was in fact extremely angry when he found such an obligation thrust upon him, and at any other time in his career he would almost certainly have refused with indignation. But now, at this one critical moment of history, he recognized an opportunity that might never be repeated. Irene, for all her faults, remained a marriageable widow – and, by all accounts, a remarkably beautiful one. If he could but persuade her to become his wife, all the imperial territories of East and West would be reunited under a single crown: his own.

The reaction in Constantinople to the news of Charles's coronation can easily be imagined. To any right-thinking Greek, it was an act not only of quite breath-taking arrogance, but also of sacrilege. The Byzantine Empire was built on a dual foundation: on the one hand, the Roman power; on the other, the Christian faith. The two had first come together in the person of Constantine the Great, Emperor of Rome and Equal of the Apostles, and this mystical union had continued through all his legitimate successors. It followed inevitably that, just as there was only one God in heaven, so there could be but one supreme ruler here on earth; all other claimants to such a title were impostors, and blasphemers as well.

Moreover, unlike the princes of the West, the Byzantines had no Salic Law. However much they might detest their Empress and even attempt to depose her, they never questioned her fundamental right to occupy the imperial throne. So much the greater, therefore, was their anxiety when they realized that Irene, far from being repelled by the very idea of marriage with an illiterate barbarian – for Charles, though he could read a little, made no secret of his inability to write – and insulted that he should even have presumed to advance such a proposal, appeared on the contrary to be intrigued, gratified and, in principle, disposed to accept.

In view of what we know of her character, her reasons are not hard to understand. Irene was a deeply selfish woman; she was also a pragmatist. By 802, when Charles's ambassadors arrived in Constantinople, she had reduced the Empire to degradation and penury. Her subjects loathed and despised her, her advisers were at each others' throats, her exchequer was exhausted. Sooner or later – more probably sooner – a coup was virtually inevitable, in which event her very life would be in danger. Now, suddenly and unexpectedly, there came a chance of salvation. It mattered little to her that her suitor was a rival Emperor, nor that he was in her eyes an adventurer and a heretic; if he were as uneducated as the reports suggested, she would probably be able to manipulate him as easily as she had manipulated her late husband and her son. Meanwhile by marrying him she would preserve the unity of the Empire and – far more important – save her own skin.

There were other attractions too. The proposal offered an opportunity to escape, at least for a while, from the stifling atmosphere of the imperial court. Irene, though twenty-two years a widow – during which time she had lived largely surrounded by women and eunuchs – was still, probably, only in her early fifties, and perhaps even younger: what could be more natural than that she should look favourably on the prospect of a new husband at last – particularly one rumoured to be tall and outstandingly handsome, a superb hunter with a fine singing voice and flashing blue eyes?

But it was not to be. Her subjects had no intention of allowing the throne to be taken over by this boorish Frank, in his outlandish linen tunic and his ridiculously cross-gartered scarlet leggings, speaking an incomprehensible language and unable even to sign his name except by stencilling it through a gold plate – as Theodoric the Ostrogoth had done three centuries before. On the last day of October 802, while Irene was recovering from some minor indisposition at Eleutherius, a group of high-ranking officials took over the Great Palace, summoned an assembly in the Hippodrome and declared her deposed. Arrested and brought to the capital, she made no protest, accepting the situation with quiet dignity and, we may suspect, something very like relief. She was sent into exile, first to the Princes' Islands in the Marmara and afterwards to Lesbos; and a year later she was dead.

With the overthrow of the Empress Irene, the first phase of Byzantine history is complete. Four hundred and seventy-two years had elapsed since that spring morning when Constantine the Great had inaugurated his New Rome at the mouth of the Bosphorus – a period of time approximately equal to that which separates us from the Reformation – during which both the Roman Empire and the city which lay at its heart had changed beyond recognition. The Empire itself was much diminished: Syria and Palestine, Egypt and North Africa and Spain had all been engulfed by the Muslim tide, while Central Italy had fallen first to the Lombards and then to the Franks, who had passed it on in their turn to the Pope. Constantinople itself, on the other hand, had grown dramatically, and was by now incontestably the largest city, as well as the richest and most sumptuous, in the world. Periodic visitations of the plague had taken their toll, but by the dawn of the ninth century the population can have numbered not less than a quarter of a million souls – and in all likelihood considerably more.

It remained, however, the beleaguered city that it had always been. To the East the Saracens, superbly trained and organized, were now a greater long-term danger than the Persians at their most menacing; to the West, though the Goths, Huns and Avars had all in turn been satisfactorily dealt with, the pressure now exerted by the Bulgars and the Slavs was as remorseless as ever. Had Constantine selected any less strategic site for his capital, had Theodosius and his successors expended a jot less time and energy on the Land and Sea Walls, one or the other of those enemies would surely have smashed their way through – and this book would have been a good deal shorter than it is.

But even at the worst of times – with the Persians encamped across the Bosphorus, the Avars at the gates, or the Saracen galleys thronging the Marmara – every Byzantine, from the Basileus down to the meanest of his subjects, had drawn strength and comfort from a single, unshakeable article of faith: that the Roman Empire was one and indivisible, its ruler chosen by God as His Vice-Gerent on earth. Other, lesser Princes of Christendom might not invariably show him the respect he deserved, might even on occasion take up arms against him; but never once had they laid claim to a similar title for themselves. Now, without warning, the unthinkable had occurred. A jumped-up barbarian chieftain was calling himself Emperor, and had been crowned as such by the Pope in Rome. Henceforth there would be two Empires, not one. The old order was gone. The Christian world would never be the same again.

Byzantine Monuments Surviving in Istanbul

[Dating from before A D 800]

This is a history, not a guide book. Readers visiting Istanbul may however like to know what monuments still survive from these early centuries of Byzantium. The following list is not absolutely complete, but it includes all monuments, or remains of them, that could conceivably be of interest to the non-specialist.

*** Buildings of world importance, worth going to Istanbul to see.
 ** Memorable.
  * Interesting, but too small or too ruined for the average short-term visitor.

Unstarred items are ruins or vestiges, listed more for their curiosity value than anything else.

NOTE

This list would have been nowhere near as comprehensive as it is but for the encyclopaedic knowledge of Mr John Freely, whose *Strolling through Istanbul* (London, 1987) has been of invaluable assistance.

** AQUEDUCT OF VALENS

Built by the Emperor Valens in 375 as part of his new system of water supply to the capital, bridging the valley between the Fourth and Third Hills. It was originally some 1,000 metres long, of which about 900 metres remain.

* CATACOMBS

Behind the mosque of Murat Pasha at the corner of Millet Caddesi and Vatan Caddesi, a number of vaulted chambers only recently discovered and thought to date from the sixth century.

CHURCHES

*** *St Sophia*   The seat of the Patriarch of Constantinople, the Church of the Holy Wisdom was first dedicated by Constantius, son of Constantine the Great, in 360. The present building is the third on the site, redesigned by Justinian after the Nika riots of 532 and dedicated by him on 26 December 537. There have been inevitable restorations, but the Great Church remains structurally much the same as in his day, the principal differences having been occasioned by its conversion into a mosque after the Turkish conquest of 1453.

*** *St Eirene*   Just inside the first courtyard of Topkapi Palace, the Church of the Holy Peace was one of the earliest Christian churches in Byzantium. Rebuilt by Constantine the Great or his son Constantius, it served as the patriarchal cathedral until the building of St Sophia nearby. Like the latter, it was destroyed by fire in the Nika riots but was rebuilt again by Justinian and rededicated in 537. Usually locked, but permission to visit can be sought from the Director of St Sophia. The rewards are great.

*** *SS Sergius and Bacchus*   Now a mosque known as Küçük Ayasofya, standing just at the point where the Hippodrome, if projected further along its present axis, would meet the Sea Walls. Begun by Justinian and Theodora in 527, it is therefore earlier than St Sophia or St Eirene.

* *St John of Studium*   Near the junction of the Land Walls and the Marmara, founded in 462 and thus the oldest church surviving in the city – insofar as it has survived, for it is now a ruin open to the sky. Of the famous monastery, perhaps the greatest spiritual and cultural centre of Byzantium, nothing remains.

* *Martyrium of SS Karpos and Papylos*   Just below the modern Greek church of St Menas, where it now serves as a carpenter's shop. A large circular domed chamber of brick, dating from the fourth or fifth century.

* *St Polyeuktos*   Beside the huge Sehzade Basi intersection just west of the Aqueduct of Valens, built between 524 and 527. A ruin, but an impressive one.

Theotokos in Chalcoprateia   Of the once great and splendid fifth-century church there remains only the aspe and a length of crenellated wall beside Alemdar Caddesi, some 100 yards west of St Sophia.

CISTERNS

** *The Basilica Cistern* (*Yerebatansaray*)   Built by Justinian after the Nika revolt in 532. The grandest and most beautiful of all the covered cisterns in the city, with 12 rows of 28 columns. Now magnificently restored, and not to be missed.

** *Binbirderek*   Off Divan Yolu to the left, about a quarter of a mile from St Sophia. The name means 'The 1,001 columns'; there are in fact 16 rows of 14, the full height being some 14.5 m. The cistern may have been begun in the reign of Constantine the Great, though it was probably enlarged in the fifth or sixth century. Open to the public, but pitch dark, dank and filthy.

Open Cistern of Aetios   On the Fevzi Pasha Caddesi, just short of the Mosque of Mihrimar. Built in 421 and measuring 224 m by 85 m, it has now been converted into a sports stadium.

Open Cistern of Aspar   Immediately south-west of the Mosque of Sultan Selim I. Built in about 470 by Aspar, and covering 152 square metres, it is now occupied by a sunken kitchen-garden and farm buildings.

Open Cistern of St Mocius   In the Altimermer district. Built during the reign of Arcadius (491–518) and extending over 25,000 square metres, it is the largest of the early Byzantine reservoirs in the city. Now vegetable gardens and orchards.

* *Covered Cistern of Pulcheria*   Opposite the south-east corner of the Cistern of Aspar. The attribution is uncertain, but the date is almost certainly fifth or sixth century. Four rows of Corinthian columns. Not open to the public.

* *Covered Cistern of the Studium*   At the south-east corner of the outer precincts. Now a junk store, but quite impressive with its 23 Corinthian columns in granite.

COLUMNS

* *Column of Arcadius*   On Cerrah Pasha Caddesi, in the second street on the right beyond the mosque. Only the plinth remains of the column erected in 402 by the Emperor, on the model of the Column of Constantine. Inside, a staircase leads to the top of the ruin, where a short length of the column (demolished in 1715) can still be seen.

* *Column of Constantine*   Erected by Constantine to mark the dedication of the city. Still standing, but in a sorry state.

* *Column of the Goths*   In Gulhane Park, behind and below the Palace of Topkapi. A granite monolith with a Corinthian capital, bearing the

inscription FORTUNAE REDUCI OB DEVICTOS GOTHOS, 'To Fortune, Returned owing to the Defeat of the Goths'. Erected probably by Constantine the Great, but possibly by Claudius II Gothicus (268–70).

* *Column of Marcian (Kiz Tasi)*   Some 200 yards south of the Fatih Mosque. Erected, according to the inscription, by the Prefect Tatianus in honour of the Emperor (450–57). It has since been credited by the Turks with the power of telling true virgins from false ones.

** THE HIPPODROME

Now known as At Meydani, this centre of popular life in Constantinople has preserved its essential outline, together with the central *spina* containing the Obelisk of Tutmose III (1549–1503 BC), the base of the Serpent Column from the Temple of Apollo at Delphi and the rough pillar of stone which the inscription on its plinth compares, somewhat optimistically, to the Colossus of Rhodes.

* HOSPICE OF SAMSON

All that remains of this charitable foundation described by Procopius is a jumble of ruins (with a few reconstructed columns) between St Eirene and the outer wall of Topkapi Palace.

PALACES

* *The Great Palace*   Built by Constantine the Great, it remained the principal residence of the Emperors until the Fourth Crusade in 1204. Little remains *in situ* except the ruins of the old marine gate of the Bucoleon, marked by three large windows framed in marble, now part of the Sea Walls. The fascinating **floor mosaics can be seen in the new Mosaic Museum.

Palace of Antiochus   Some 300 yards west of St Sophia on Divan Yolu, the ruins are all that is left of the palace of a great fifth-century nobleman. It was later converted into a martyrium for the body of St Euphemia of Chalcedon.

* *Palace of Romanus*   Some 200 yards south of the Tulip Mosque are the ruins of what was once the Bodrum (Subterranean) Mosque, previously a Byzantine church which formed part of the monastery of the Myrelaion. The huge rotunda below the terrace next to it was built in the fifth century as the reception hall of a palace, but never finished.

Later it was roofed over and used as a cistern, on which the palace of Romanus was built.

*** WALLS

The oldest part of the walls which surround the city to the west of the Golden Horn dates from the time of Constantine; but by far the greatest length – including almost all the present Land Walls – is essentially the work of Anthemius, Prefect of the East under Theodosius II, who completed them in 413. The Land Walls and those along the Marmara are continuous; those lining the Horn have largely disappeared.

List of Emperors

284–305	Diocletian	⎫ *Joint Emperors*
286–305	Maximian	⎬
305–306	Constantius I Chlorus	⎫
305–311	Galerius	⎬ *Joint Emperors*
306–312	Maxentius (replaced Constantius)	⎭
306–324	Constantine I the Great	⎫ *Joint Emperors*
312–324	Licinius	⎬
324–337	Constantine I *Sole Emperor*	
337–340	Constantine II	⎫
337–350	Constantius II	⎬ *Joint Emperors*
337–350	Constans	⎭
350–361	Constantius II *Sole Emperor*	
361–363	Julian	
363–364	Jovian	
364–375	Valentinian I	⎫ *Joint Emperors*
364–378	Valens	⎬
375–383	Gratian	⎫
379–392	Theodosius I	⎬ *Joint Emperors*
383–392	Valentinian II (replaced Gratian)	⎭
392–395	Theodosius I	

	EAST		WEST
395–408	Arcadius	395–423	Honorius
408–450	Theodosius II	423	Constantius III
		423–425	Johannes
450–457	Marcian	425–455	Valentinian III
		455	Petronius Maximus
		455–456	Avitus
457–474	Leo I	457–461	Marjorian
		461–465	Libius Severus
		467–472	Anthemius

	EAST		WEST
		472	Olybrius
		472–474	Glycerius
474	Leo II	474	Julius Nepos
474–491	Zeno	474–476	Romulus Augustulus
[475–476	Basiliscus]		
491–518	Anastasius I		
518–527	Justin I		
527–565	Justinian I		
565–578	Justin II		
578–582	Tiberius II Constantine		
582–602	Maurice		
602–610	Phocas		
610–641	Heraclius		
641	Constantine III Heraclonas } *Joint Emperors*		
641–668	Constans II 'Pogonatus'		
668–685	Constantine IV		
685–695	Justinian II 'Rhinotmetus'		
695–698	Leontius		
698–705	Tiberius III		
705–711	Justinian II 'Rhinotmetus'		
711–713	Philippicus Bardanes		
713–715	Anastasius II		
715–717	Theodosius III		
717–741	Leo III		
741	Constantine V 'Copronymus'		
742	Artabasdus		
743–775	Constantine V 'Copronymus'		
775–780	Leo IV		
780–797	Constantine VI		
797–802	Irene	800–814	Charlemagne

Bibliography

I. Original Sources

COLLECTIONS OF SOURCES

BLOCKLEY, R. C. The Fragmentary Classicising Historians of the Later Roman Empire. English translations. Vol. II, Liverpool 1983 (B.F.C.H.).

Corpus Scriptorum Ecclesiasticorum Latinorum. 57 vols. Vienna 1866– (incomplete) (C.S.E.L.).

Corpus Scriptorum Historiae Byzantinae. Bonn 1828–   (incomplete) (C.S.H.B.).

COUSIN, L. Histoire de Constantinople. French translations. 8 vols. Paris 1685 (C.H.C.).

HOARE, F. R. The Western Fathers. English translations. London 1954 (H.W.F.).

MIGNE, J. P. *Patrologia Graeca.* 161 vols. Paris 1857–66 (M.P.G.).

–– *Patrologia Latina.* 221 vols. Paris 1844–55 (M.P.L.).

Monumenta Germaniae Historica. Eds. G. H. Pertz, T. Mommsen *et al.* Hanover 1826–   (in progress) (M.G.H.).

MULLER, C. I. T. *Fragmenta Historicorum Graecorum.* 5 vols. Paris 1841–83 (M.F.H.G.).

MURATORI, L. A. *Rerum Italicarum Scriptores.* 25 vols. Milan 1723–51 (M.R.I.S.).

Nicene and Post-Nicene Fathers, Library of the. 2nd series. 14 vols. with trans. Oxford 1890–1900 (N.P.N.F.).

INDIVIDUAL SOURCES

AGATHIAS of Myrina. *The Histories.* Trans. J. D. Frendo. Berlin 1975.

AGNELLUS of Ravenna. *De Sancto Felice.* In *Liber Pontificalis Ecclesiae Ravennatis,* ed. O. Holder-Egger. In M.G.H., *Scriptores Rerum Lango-bardicarum et Italicarum, saec. VI–IX.* Hanover 1878.

AL-BALADHURI. *Kitab Futuh al-Buldan*. Trans. as *The Origins of the Islamic State* by Philip K. Hitti. New York 1916.

AMBROSE, Saint. *Opera*. In C.S.E.L., Vol. 73. 10 parts. Vienna 1955–64.

AMMIANUS MARCELLINUS. *Rerum Gestarum Libri*. Ed. V. Gardt-hausen. 2 vols. Leipzig 1874–5.

ANASTASIUS, Bibliothecarius. In M.P.L., Vol. 80; M.P.G., Vol. 108.

ANONYMUS VALESII. Usually included with Ammianus Marcellinus, *q.v.*

AURELIUS VICTOR. *De Caesaribus*. Eds. F. Pichlmayr and R. Gruendal. Leipzig 1966.

CANDIDUS the Isaurian. History. Trans. in B.F.C.H.

CEDRENUS, Georgius. In C.S.H.B.; also M.P.G., Vols. 121–2.

CLAUDIAN. *Carmina*. Ed. T. Birt. In M.G.H., Vol. 10 (Eng. verse trans. by A. Hawkins. 2 vols. London 1817).

CONSTANTINE VII PORPHYROGENITUS. *De Administrando Imperio*. Gk. text with Eng. trans. by R. J. H. Jenkins. Washington 1969.

— Commentary, by R. J. H. Jenkins. London 1962.

CORIPPUS. *De Laudibus Justini Augusti Minoris*. In M.G.H., *Auctores Antiquissimi*, III, ii.

EUNAPIUS. History. Trans. in B.F.C.H.

EUSEBIUS, Bishop of Caesarea. *A History of the Church from Christ to Constantine*. Trans. G. A. Williamson. London 1965.

— Life of Constantine. Trans. A. C. McGiffert in N.P.N.F., Vol. 2.

EUTROPIUS. *Breviarium ab Urbe Condita*. Ed. F. Ruehl. Leipzig 1887. Trans. J. S. Watson, London 1890.

EVAGRIUS. In M.F.H.G., Vol. 5.

GEORGE of Pisidia. The Heracliad, The Persian Expedition and the *Bellum Avaricum*. In C.S.H.B., Vol. 19; also M.P.H., Vol. 92.

GERMANUS, Patriarch. Letters. In M.P.G., Vol. 98, 156ff.

GREGORY of Nazianzus, St. Selected Orations and Letters. Trans. C. G. Browne and J. E. Swallow in N.P.N.F., Vol. 7.

JEROME, Saint. *Letters*. Fr. trans. by J. Labourt. 8 vols. Paris 1951–63.

JOANNES ANTIOCHENUS. In M.F.H.G., Vols. 4–5.

JOANNES LYDUS. *On Powers, or The Magistracies of the Roman State*. Ed. and trans. A. C. Bandy. Philadelphia 1983.

JOHN CHRYSOSTOM, Saint. *Oeuvres Complètes*. Fr. trans. Abbé Joly. 8 vols. Paris 1864–7.

JOHN of Damascus. Orations. In M.P.G., Vol. 94, 1232ff.

JOHN, Bishop of Ephesus. *Ecclesiastical History*, Pt. III. Ed. and trans. R. P. Smith. Oxford 1860.

JORDANES (JORNANDES). In M.R.I.S., Vol. 1.

JULIAN, Emperor. *Works*. Trans. W. C. Wright. 3 vols. London 1913.

LACTANTIUS. *On the Deaths of the Persecutors*. Trans. W. Fletcher. Ante-Nicene Library. Edinburgh 1871.

LEO, Grammaticus. Lives of the Emperors (813–948). In C.H.C., Vol. III.

LIBANIUS. *Selected Works*. Trans. A. F. Norman. 2 vols. London and Cambridge, Mass. 1969 and 1977.

Liber Pontificalis. De Gestis Romanorum Pontificum. Text, intr. and comm. by L. Duchesne. 2 vols. Paris 1886–92 (reprint, Paris 1955).

MALALAS, JOHN. In M.P.G., Vol. 97.

MARTIN I, Pope. Letters. In M.P.L., Vol. 87.

MENANDER, Protector. Embassies. In C.H.C., Vol. III.

NICEPHORUS, St, Patriarch. *Opuscula Historica* (602–770). Ed. C. de Boor. Leipzig 1880. Fr. trans. in C.H.C., Vol. III.

OLYMPIODORUS. History. In B.F.C.H.

Paschal Chronicle. In M.P.G., Vol. 92.

PAUL the Deacon. *Historia Langobardorum*. In M.G.H., *Scriptores*, Vols. ii, xiii. Eng. trans. by W. C. Foulke, Philadelphia 1905.

PAULINUS. Life of Ambrose. In H.W.F.

PHILOSTORGIUS. *Historia Ecclesiae*. In M.P.G., Vol. 65. Partial trans. E. Walford, London 1851.

PRISCUS. History. Trans. in B.F.C.H.

PROCOPIUS of Caesarea. Works. Trans. H. B. Dewing. 7 vols. London 1914–40.

RUFINUS, TYRANNIUS. Ecclesiastical History. Trans. in N.P.N.F., Vol. 3.

SEBEOS, Bishop. *Histoire d'Héraclius*. Trans. and ed. F. Macler. Paris 1904.

SIDONIUS, APOLLINARIS. *Poems and Letters*. Trans. W. C. Anderson. 2 vols. London 1936.

SOCRATES SCHOLASTICUS. Ecclesiastical History. Trans. in N.P.N.F., Vol. 2.

SOZOMEN. Ecclesiastical History. Trans. (anon.) in N.P.N.F., Vol. 2.

THEODORET. *History of the Church*. Trans. (anon.) London 1854.

THEOPHANES, St (called Isaacius). *Chronographia*. Ed. C. de Boor. 2 vols. Leipzig 1883 (reprinted Hildesheim 1963). Also in M.P.G., Vols. 108–9.

THEOPHYLACT, Simocatta. History of the Emperor Maurice. In C.S.H.B., 1924. Fr. trans. in C.H.C., Vol. III.

ZONARAS, Joannes. *Annales*. Ex rec. M. Pindari. In C.S.H.B. and M.P.G., 134–5.

ZOSIMUS (Panopolitanus). *Historia*. Ed. with Latin trans. J.F. Reitemeyer. Leipzig 1784.

II. Modern Works

ALFOLDI, A. *The Conversion of Constantine and Pagan Rome*. Oxford 1948.

ANDREOTTI, R. *Il Regno dell' Imperatore Giuliano*. Bologna 1936.

BAYNES, N. H. 'Constantine the Great and the Christian Church'. *Proceedings of the British Academy*. 1929.

BAYNES, N. H. *Byzantine Studies and Other Essays*. London 1955.

BAYNES, N. H. and MOSS, H. St L. B. (eds.) *Byzantium: an Introduction to East Roman Civilisation*. Oxford 1948.

BIDEZ, J. *La Vie de l'Empereur Julien*. Paris 1930.

BOWERSOCK, G. W. *Julian the Apostate*. London 1978.

BROWNING, R. *Justinian and Theodora*. London 1971.

—— *The Emperor Julian*. London 1975.

—— *The Byzantine Empire*. London 1980.

BURCKHARDT, J. *The Age of Constantine the Great*. Trans. M. Hadas. London 1849.

BURY, J. B. *A History of the Later Roman Empire (395–800 A.D.)*. 2 vols. London 1889.

BUTLER, A. J. *The Arab Conquest of Egypt and the Last Thirty Years of Roman Dominion*. Oxford 1902.

BYRON, R. *The Byzantine Achievement*. London 1929.

CAETANI, G. C. *Annali dell' Islam*. Vols. I–VIII. Milan 1905–18.

Cambridge Medieval History. Esp. Vol. IV, *The Byzantine Empire, 717–1453*. New edition, ed. J. M. Hussey. 2 vols. Cambridge 1966–7.

CHARLESWORTH, M. P. *The Roman Empire*. Oxford 1951.

COBHAM, C. D. *The Patriarchs of Constantinople*. Cambridge 1911.

DELEHAYE, H. *Les Saints Stylites*. Brussels and Paris 1923.

Dictionnaire d'Histoire et de Géographie Ecclésiastiques. Eds. A. Baudrillart, R. Aubert and others. Paris 1912–   (in progress).

Dictionnaire de Théologie Catholique. 15 vols in 30. Paris 1909–50 (with supplements).

DIEHL, C. *L'Afrique Byzantine*. 2 vols. Paris 1896.

—— *Figures Byzantines*. 2 ser. Paris 1906 and 1913.

—— *Histoire de l'Empire Byzantin*. Paris 1918.

—— *Choses et Gens de Byzance*. Paris 1926.

DOWNEY, G. *Constantinople in the Age of Justinian.* University of Oklahoma 1960.

DRAPEYRON, L. *L'Empereur Héraclius et l'Empire Byzantin.* Paris 1869.

DUDDEN, F. H. *The Life and Times of St Ambrose.* 2 vols. Oxford 1935.

DUNLOP, D. M. *The History of the Jewish Khazars.* Princeton 1954.

EBERSOLT, J. *Le Grand Palais de Constantinople et le Livre des Cérémonies.* Paris 1910.

Enciclopedia Italiana. 36 vols. 1929–39 (with later appendices).

Encyclopaedia Britannica. 11th ed. 29 vols. Cambridge 1910–11.

—— 15th ed. 30 vols. University of Chicago 1974.

FINLAY, G. *History of Greece, BC 146 to AD 1864.* New ed. Ed. H. F. Tozer, 1877. 8 vols.

FIRTH, J. B. *Constantine the Great.* New York 1905.

FISHER, H. A. L. *A History of Europe.* London 1935.

FLICHE, A. and MARTIN, V. *Histoire de l'Eglise, depuis les Origines jusqu'à nos Jours.* Paris 1934.

FRENCH, R. M. *The Eastern Orthodox Church.* London and New York 1951.

GARDNER, A. *Julian, Emperor and Philosopher, and the Last Struggle of Paganism against Christianity.* London 1895.

—— *Theodore of Studium.* London 1905.

GIBBON, E. *The History of the Decline and Fall of the Roman Empire.* 7 vols. Ed. J. B. Bury. London 1896.

GORDON, C. D. *The Age of Attila* (trans. of contemporary sources). University of Michigan 1966.

GRANT, M. *The History of Rome.* London 1978.

GROSVENOR, E. A. *Constantinople.* 2 vols. Boston 1895.

GWATKIN, H. M. *Eusebius of Caesarea.* London 1896.

HARNACK, T. G. *A History of Dogma.* Eng. trans. London 1899.

HEAD, C. *Justinian II of Byzantium.* University of Wisconsin Press 1972.

HEFELE, C. J. von. *Histoire des Conciles d'après les Documents Originaux* (Fr. trans. from German by H. Leclercq). 5 vols in 10. Paris 1907–13.

HILL, Sir George. *A History of Cyprus.* 3 vols. Cambridge 1913.

HITTI, P. K. *History of the Arabs.* 3rd ed. New York 1951.

HODGKIN, T. *Italy and her Invaders.* 8 vols. Oxford 1880–99.

HOLMES, W. G. *The Age of Justinian and Theodora.* 2 vols. London 1907.

HUSSEY, J. M. *The Byzantine World.* London and New York 1957.

JANIN, R. *Constantinople Byzantine.* Paris 1950.

JENKINS, R. *Byzantium: The Imperial Centuries, AD 610–1071.* London 1966.

JONES, A. H. M. *Constantine and the Conversion of Europe*. London 1948.

KRAUTHEIMER, R. *Early Christian and Byzantine Architecture* (Pelican History of Art). London 1965.

LETHABY, W. R. and SWAINSON, H. *The Church of Sancta Sophia, Constantinople: a Study of Byzantine Building*. London 1894.

MACLAGAN, M. *The City of Constantinople*. London 1968.

MACMULLEN, R. *Constantine*. London 1970.

MAINSTONE, R. J. *Hagia Sophia: Architecture, Structure and Liturgy of Justinian's Great Church*. London 1988.

MANN, H. K. *The Lives of the Popes in the Middle Ages*. 18 vols. London 1902–32.

MARIN, E. *Les Moines de Constantinople*. Paris 1897.

MARTIN, E. J. *A History of the Iconoclastic Controversy*. London 1930.

MILMAN, H. H. *The History of Christianity from the Birth of Christ to the Abolition of Paganism in the Roman Empire*. 3 vols. Rev. ed. 1867.

NEANDER, A. *General History of the Christian Religion and Church*. 9 vols. Eng. trans. London 1876.

New Catholic Encyclopaedia. Washington, DC 1967.

OCKLEY, S. *History of the Saracens*. 4th ed. London 1847.

OMAN, C. W. C. *The Byzantine Empire*. London 1897.

OSTROGORSKY, G. *History of the Byzantine State*. Trans. J. Hussey. 2nd ed. Oxford 1968.

PEROWNE, S. *The End of the Roman World*. London 1966.

RIDLEY, F. A. *Julian the Apostate and the Rise of Christianity*. London 1937.

RUNCIMAN, S. *A History of the First Bulgarian Empire*. London 1930.

SETTON, K. M. *The Byzantine Background to the Italian Renaissance*. Proceedings of the American Philosophical Society, Vol. 100, no. 1 (February 1956).

SMITH, J. H. *Constantine the Great*. London 1971.

SMITH, W. and WACE, H. *Dictionary of Christian Biography*. 4 vols. London 1877–87.

STEIN, E. *Histoire du Bas-Empire, II: de la Disparition de l'Empire de l'Occident à la Mort de Justinien (476–565)*. Paris and Brussels 1949.

SUMNER-BOYD, H. and FREELY, J. *Strolling through Istanbul*. Istanbul 1972.

SWIFT, E. A. *Hagia Sophia*. New York 1940.

SYKES, Sir Percy. *A History of Persia*. 2 vols. 3rd ed. London 1930.

THOMPSON, E. A. *A History of Attila and the Huns*. London 1948.

VAN DER MEER, F. *Atlas of Western Civilisation*. Trans. T. A. Birrell. Amsterdam 1954.

— and MOHRMANN, C. *Atlas of the Early Christian World*. Trans. M. F. Hedlund and H. H. Rowley. London 1958.

VASILIEV, A. A. *The Goths in the Crimea*. Cambridge, Mass. 1936.

— *Justin the First: an Introduction to the Epoch of Justinian the Great*. Cambridge, Mass. 1950.

— *History of the Byzantine Empire, 324–1453*. Madison, Wisconsin 1952.

VOGT, J. *The Decline of Rome: The Metamorphosis of Ancient Civilisation*. Trans. J. Sondheimer. London 1967.

Index

Lucian of Antioch, St, 52
Lüleburgaz (Arcadiopolis), 261
Lupicinus, Count of Thrace, 107
Lydia, 196 & n.

Macarius, Bishop of Jerusalem, 68
Macedonius, Patriarch of Constantinople, 79, 186, 191
Magnentius, Roman Emperor, 82, 96
Malalas, John, 149, 157
Malchus, 168
Manuel I Comnenus, Emperor, 66n
Marcellae, Battle of (792), 373
Marcellinus, Lord of Dalmatia, 166
Marcellinus, Ammianus, 88–9, 92, 95, 97–8, 101–2
Marcian, Emperor, 155, 159, 164–6, 327 & n.; death, 163
Marcian, son of Anthemius, 175
Marcus, deacon, 141n
Marcus Graecus, 323n
Marcus Martianus, 48–9
Mardaites, 324, 329
Maria, wife of Emperor Honorius, 129, 132
Marina, Princess, 140
Marjorian, Roman Emperor, 171
Martianus, Marcus, 48–9
Martin I, Pope, 318–20, 332, 335
Martina, wife of Emperor Heraclius: marriage, 288, 309; accompanies Heraclius on campaign, 290–1; children, 291, 300, 309; and decline of Heraclius, 309; succession and intrigues, 309, 312–13, 317; mutilation and exile, 313
Martyropolis, 273, 292
Marwan II, Caliph, 363
Mary, Virgin, 147
Mary of Amnia, wife of Constantine VI, 372–3
Maslana, Prince, 350–1, 353
Matasuntha, Queen of Vitiges, 217, 219, 226; Germanus marries, 250
Mauriac (Mauritian) Plain, Battle of (451), 158
Maurice, Emperor: reign, 272–5, 278–9; deposed by army mutiny, 276–7; killed, 278; and Avars, 289n; settles Armenian cavalrymen in Anatolia, 329
Maurus, Patrician, 344
Maxentius, son of Maximian, 36–9, 43
Maximian 'Augusti', joint Emperor, 33, 34n, 36, 42, 57–8
Maximianus, Archbishop of Ravenna, 263
Maximin, envoy to Attila, 154
Maximin, General, 238–9
Maximin Daia Caesar, 37, 44–6
Maximus, Magnus Clemens, 109–11, 114, 160
Maximus, Petronius, Roman Emperor, 160–1; killed, 162
Maximus the Confessor, 317, 319–20
Mecca, 302, 304

Mediolanum (now Milan), 222–3
Melchiades, Pope, 40
Meletian Church, 52, 71
Mennas, Patriarch of Constantinople, 247–8
Mercurius, St, 98n
Michael II, Emperor, 374
Michael Psellus, 261n
Michael Lachanodrakon, 362
Milan (Mediolanum): siege and sack of (538–9), 222–3
Milvian Bridge, Battle of the (312), 39–40, 42, 60
Minervina, first wife of Constantine, 36
Moechian controversy, 374 & n
Mohammed, 302–4
monophysitism, 155–6, 169, 181–2, 184–6, 246–8, 270–1, 305–6, 309, 327n, 347; and iconoclasm, 354
monothelitism, 309–10, 317–19, 326–7, 347, 349
Monte Cassino, 217n
Muawiya, Caliph, 315–16, 320, 323–4, 328
Mugello valley, Battle of (542), 238
Mundilas, General, 223
Mundus, General, 200, 215
Mustafa III, Sultan, 66n

Naples, 215–16, 235, 238
Narses, Great King of Persia, 64, 96
Narses, commander of imperial bodyguard, later chamberlain: and Nika revolt, 200; in Italy, 220–1, 223; relations with Belisarius, 221–2; withdrawn from Italy, 223; successes in Italy, 244, 251–3, 255, 268–9; forces sent to Spain, 254; wins Corsica, 254; and Lombards, 268n, 269
Narses, General, 280
Nepos, Julius, Roman Emperor, 171–2, 174
Nepotianus, Popilius, 80–1
Nero, Roman Emperor, 59n
Nestorius, Bishop of Constantinople, and Nestorian heresy, 147–8, 155–6, 247
Nicaea, Councils of, see Church Councils, Ecumenical
Nicephorus, 313, 342, 366
Nicephorus Caesar, 373
Nicetas, son of Gregorius, 282
Nicomedia (now Izmit), 33–5, 351
Nika revolt (532), 197–200
Nikopol (Securisca), 276
Nisibis, 102–3
Nocera, Battle of (552), 252

Odoacer (Odovacar), Patrician, 172–4, 176–7, 181
Olybrius, Roman Emperor, 163n, 171
Olympias, daughter of Ablavius, 80
Olympiodorus, 143n
Olympius, minister of Honorius, 132–3

Olympus, Exarch of Ravenna, 318
Omar, Caliph, 304, 307, 314–15
Omayyad Caliphate, 323, 363
Opsikion Theme, 287, 330–2, 348–9
Orestes, 171–2
Osimo (*formerly* Auximum), 220, 223, 240
Ostrogorsky, Georg, 331n
Ostrogoths, 63, 107; kingdom in Italy, 208, 212–15, 224, 237; *see also* Goths
Othman, Caliph, 314–16
Otranto (*formerly* Hydruntum), 239–40

Palermo (*formerly* Panormus), 215n
Pamphilus, 34
Pamprepius, 177
Pandects (of law), 197
Panormus (*now* Palermo, Sicily), 215n
Papacy: rise of, 174; and 484 schism, 182; reconciliation with Eastern Church, 189, 191; *see also individual popes*
Papal States: established, 365
Patricius Caesar, son of Aspar, 167, 175
Patricius, Master of the Offices, 169
Paul VI, Pope, 345n
Paul, Patriarch of Constantinople, 317, 319
Paul the Chain, 90
Paul the Deacon, 338
Paul the Silentiary, 202–3
Paulinus, Master of the Offices, 149–50
Pelagius, Deacon, 241
Pelagius, Patrician and silentiary, 182–3
Pelagius, Pope, 274
Pepin the Short, Frankish King, 364–5, 377
Persepolis, 299
Persia: as threat to Rome, 63; war with, 81–2; Julian's expedition against, 94, 96–8; treaty with Rome, 102; war with Empire, 187; 194–5; 'Everlasting Peace' (532), 195, 205, 229; Vandals fight against, 212; threat to Justinian, 224, 229; invade Empire, 227, 229; withdrawal, 233; annihilates imperial force in Armenia, 235; Justinian pays tribute to, 260; control of trade, 265–6; war resumes (572), 270; Maurice and, 272–3; war ends (591), 273; 603 invasion by, 280; Jews support, 281, 285; as threat to Heraclius, 284–6; Heraclius campaigns against, 289–93; and siege of Constantinople, 296; Heraclius defeats, 297–8; peace treaty (628), 300–1
Pesaro (Italy), 240
Peter, General, brother of Emperor Maurice, 276, 278–9
Peter the Patrician, 214
Peter the Stammerer, 182, 191
Petra (city in Lazica), 230
Petronius Maximus, Roman Emperor, 160–2
Pharas the Herulian, 210

Philippicus Bardanes (Vardan), Emperor, 343–4, 347–9
Philostorgus, 58
Phocas, Emperor: accession, 276–7; appearance and cruelty, 279, 338; and Persian war, 280; killed, 282–3
Phoenicus (*now* Finike), Battle of (655), 316
Pholoe, 123, 129
Photius, son of Antonina, 231–2
Pius IX, Pope, 39n
Placidia, wife of Olybrius, 163n
Placidia, Galla, *see* Galla Placidia
plague, bubonic (542), 233
Plato, Abbot of Saccudion, 374
Pollentia, Battle of (402), 128
Pompeianus, Euricus, 38
Pompeius, nephew of Emperor Anastasius, 187, 200
Popilius Nepotianus, brother-in-law of Constantine, 80–1
Porphyrius, Bishop of Gaza, 141
Praetextus, High Priest, 64
Prisca, widow of Diocletian, 46
Priscus, envoy to Attila, 154–5, 165
Priscus, son-in-law of Phocas, 282
Probus, nephew of Anastasius, 198
Procopius, friend of Julian, 103, 105
Procopius of Caesarea, historian: on murder of Valentinian, 161n; Gibbon criticizes, 161n, 166n, 243; describes campaign against Vandals, 166–7; on Zeno's agreement with Theodoric, 178; on Anastasius's economic success, 184n; on Justin, 188; vilifies Theodora and Justinian, 191–3; on Tribonian, 196–7; on rebuilding of St Sophia, 202–3; on Antonina, 206, 231–2; on Hilderic, 206; accompanies Belisarius on Carthage expedition, 207–10; on Triumph accorded to Belisarius, 211n; in Italy with Belisarius, 221; reports Totila's letter, 228n; describes Belisarius's reception of Chosroes' envoy, 232–3; on death of Hildebad, 236n; on fall of Rome, 243; on Narses' success in Italy, 252; on Justinian's poor Greek, 263; on Chalkē, 355
Propontis (*now* Sea of Marmara), 31
Psellus, Michael, 261n
Pulcheria, Princess, 140–2, 150, 155, 163

Quadi, 106
Quinisextum, Synod (691), 331–2, 338, 341

Ravenna: captured by Theodosius II (425), 144–5; Theodoric in, 179–80; Vitiges withdraws to, 217; Belisarius occupies, 224–6, 235; Church of S. Vitale, 263, 356; Exarchate created, 273, 278; Justinian sends expedition against, 340, 342; revolt against iconoclasm, 356; captured by Lombards, 364

READ MORE IN PENGUIN

In every corner of the world, on every subject under the sun, Penguin represents quality and variety – the very best in publishing today.

For complete information about books available from Penguin – including Puffins, Penguin Classics and Arkana – and how to order them, write to us at the appropriate address below. Please note that for copyright reasons the selection of books varies from country to country.

In the United Kingdom: Please write to *Dept. JC, Penguin Books Ltd, FREEPOST, West Drayton, Middlesex UB7 0BR.*

If you have any difficulty in obtaining a title, please send your order with the correct money, plus ten per cent for postage and packaging, to *PO Box No. 11, West Drayton, Middlesex UB7 0BR*

In the United States: Please write to *Consumer Sales, Penguin USA, P.O. Box 999, Dept. 17109, Bergenfield, New Jersey 07621-0120.* VISA and MasterCard holders call 1-800-253-6476 to order all Penguin titles

In Canada: Please write to *Penguin Books Canada Ltd, 10 Alcorn Avenue, Suite 300, Toronto, Ontario M4V 3B2*

In Australia: Please write to *Penguin Books Australia Ltd, P.O. Box 257, Ringwood, Victoria 3134*

In New Zealand: Please write to *Penguin Books (NZ) Ltd, Private Bag 102902, North Shore Mail Centre, Auckland 10*

In India: Please write to *Penguin Books India Pvt Ltd, 706 Eros Apartments, 56 Nehru Place, New Delhi 110 019*

In the Netherlands: Please write to *Penguin Books Netherlands bv, Postbus 3507, NL-1001 AH Amsterdam*

In Germany: Please write to *Penguin Books Deutschland GmbH, Metzlerstrasse 26, 60594 Frankfurt am Main*

In Spain: Please write to *Penguin Books S. A., Bravo Murillo 19, 1° B, 28015 Madrid*

In Italy: Please write to *Penguin Italia s.r.l., Via Felice Casati 20, I–20124 Milano*

In France: Please write to *Penguin France S. A., 17 rue Lejeune, F–31000 Toulouse*

In Japan: Please write to *Penguin Books Japan, Ishikiribashi Building, 2–5–4, Suido, Bunkyo-ku, Tokyo 112*

In Greece: Please write to *Penguin Hellas Ltd, Dimocritou 3, GR–106 71 Athens*

In South Africa: Please write to *Longman Penguin Southern Africa (Pty) Ltd, Private Bag X08, Bertsham 2013*

READ MORE IN PENGUIN

HISTORY

The Guillotine and the Terror   Daniel Arasse

'A brilliant and imaginative account of the punitive mentality of the revolution that restores to its cultural history its most forbidding and powerful symbol' – Simon Schama.

The Second World War   A J P Taylor

A brilliant and detailed illustrated history, enlivened by all Professor Taylor's customary iconoclasm and wit.

Daily Life in Ancient Rome   Jerome Carcopino

This classic study, which includes a bibliography and notes by Professor Rowell, describes the streets, houses and multi-storeyed apartments of the city of over a million inhabitants, the social classes from senators to slaves, and the Roman family and the position of women, causing *The Times Literary Supplement* to hail it as a 'thorough, lively and readable book'.

The Anglo-Saxons   Edited by James Campbell

For anyone who wishes to understand the broad sweep of English history, Anglo-Saxon society is an important and fascinating subject. And Campbell's is an important and fascinating book. It is also a finely produced and, at times, a very beautiful book' – *London Review of Books*

The Making of the English Working Class   E. P. Thompson

Probably the most imaginative – and the most famous – post-war work of English social history. 'A magnificent, lucid, angry historian ... E. P. Thompson has performed a revolution of historical perspective' – *The Times*

The Habsburg Monarchy 1809–1918   A J P Taylor

Dissolved in 1918, the Habsburg Empire 'had a unique character, out of time and out of place'. Scholarly and vividly accessible, this 'very good book indeed' (*Spectator*) elucidates the problems always inherent in the attempt to give peace, stability and a common loyalty to a heterogeneous population.

READ MORE IN PENGUIN

HISTORY

Citizens Simon Schama

The award-winning chronicle of the French Revolution. 'The most marvellous book I have read about the French Revolution in the last fifty years' – Richard Cobb in *The Times*

To the Finland Station Edmund Wilson

In this authoritative work Edmund Wilson, considered by many to be America's greatest twentieth-century critic, turns his attention to Europe's revolutionary traditions, tracing the roots of nationalism, socialism and Marxism as these movements spread across the Continent creating unrest, revolt and widespread social change.

Jasmin's Witch Emmanuel Le Roy Ladurie

An investigation into witchcraft and magic in south-west France during the seventeenth century – a masterpiece of historical detective work by the bestselling author of Montaillou.

Stalin Isaac Deutscher

'The Greatest Genius in History' and the 'Life-Giving Force of socialism'? Or a despot more ruthless than Ivan the Terrrible and a revolutionary whose policies facilitated the rise of Nazism? An outstanding biographical study of a revolutionary despot by a great historian.

Aspects of Antiquity M. I. Finley

Profesor M. I. Finley was one of the century's greatest ancient historians; he was also a master of the brief, provocative essay on classical themes. 'He writes with the unmistakable enthusiasm of a man who genuinely wants to communicate his own excitement' – Philip Toynbee in the *Observer*

British Society 1914–1945 John Stevenson

'A major contribution to the *Penguin Social History of Britain*, which will undoubtedly be the standard work for students of modern Britain for many years to come' – *The Times Educational Supplement*

BY THE SAME AUTHOR

Christmas Crackers

A delightful and amusing harvest of wit and wisdom, reaped with care and laid up with affection.

Over the past ten years John Julius Norwich has sent out commonplace selections of prose and poetry to his friends at Christmas. Collected here in one volume are these Crackers; from contributors as diverse as Confucius and W. S. Gilbert, Samuel Pepys and Dorothy Parker, on subjects as varied as love, the longest palindrome, death, the Prince of Orange's woollen drawers and the French, German and Russian versions of *Jabberwocky*.

'A bouquet of individually picked flowers culled by a master gardener, and arranged in a manner that would get him first prize in any literary flower show' – Bernard Levin in *The Times*

More Christmas Crackers

Along with superb poetry from Dante to Dylan Thomas, and little-known gems from wits like Noël Coward and Oscar Wilde, Lord Norwich has brought together French puns, unusual epitaphs, unfortunately worded hymns, extracts from the worst-ever English novel, and verse inspired by a mysterious inscription on a Venetian lamppost. Lyrical and cynical, exuberant and world-weary, pithy and gloriously wordy, this magnificent anthology contains riches guaranteed to appeal to every taste.

BY THE SAME AUTHOR

Byzantium: The Apogee

In *Byzantium: The Early Centuries* John Julius Norwich told the epic tale of the Roman Empire's second capital up to Christmas Day 800 AD – when Pope Leo III crowned Charlemagne as a rival emperor. This second volume covers the following three centuries.

The Byzantine Empire, although being surrounded by hostile Turks, Bulgars, Russians and various barbarian tribes, and despite being controlled by an extraordinary sequence of adventurers, drunkards, lustful emperors, sinister eunuchs and unworldly scholars, somehow managed to survive. Here, Lord Norwich continues his compelling chronicle up to the coronation of the heroic Alexius Comnenus in 1081. For sheer vividness and pace his account could hardly be bettered.

'Eminently readable' – Frederick Raphael in the *Spectator*

A History of Venice

John Julius Norwich's loving and scholarly portrayal of 'the most beautiful and magical of cities'.

'The standard Venetian history in English, indispensable not only to academic students but to any one of us who take our Venetian involvements with a proper seriousness' – Jan Morris in *The Times*

'As a historian Lord Norwich knows what matters. As a writer he has a taste for beauty, a love of language and an enlivening wit ... He contrives, as no English writer has done before, to sustain a continuous interest in that crowded history' – Hugh Trevor-Roper

'Lord Norwich has the gift of historical perspective, as well as clarity and wit. Few can tell a good story better than he' – J. G. Links in the *Spectator*

BY THE SAME AUTHOR

The Normans in Sicily

When *The Normans in the South* was first published, it was acclaimed for its 'diligence, narrative skill, and a scholarship fired by enthusiasm' (*Sunday Telegraph*) which made it 'instructive throughout, as well as consistently entertaining' (*The New York Times Book Review*). In this volume it is published together with its sequel, *The Kingdom in the Sun*.

In 1016, a rebel Lombard lord at the shrine of Monte Sant' Angelo appealed for help to a group of pilgrims – and unwittingly set in motion 'the other Norman Conquest'. Here is the epic story of the House of Hauteville; of Robert Guiscard, perhaps the most extraordinary European adventurer between Caesar and Napoleon, who briefly held at bay the Pope, the Eastern and the Western Emperors; of his brother Roger, who helped him win Sicily from the Saracens; and of his nephew Roger II, crowned at Palermo in 1130. *The Kingdom in the Sun* vividly evokes his and his successors' 'sad, superb, half-forgotten Kingdom', cultivated, cosmopolitan and tolerant, which lasted a mere sixty-four years. It concludes with the poignant defeat of the bastard King Tancred in 1194, putting a close to 'the happiest and most glorious chapter of the island's history'. With a comprehensive Appendix listing all Sicily's surviving Norman monuments, the result is both a superb traveller's companion and a masterpiece of the historian's art.